Sociology

The Classic Statements

SOCIOLOGY

The Classic Statements

Edited by

MARCELLO TRUZZI

University of Michigan

RANDOM HOUSE New York

Published in the United States by Random House, Inc., New York, and simultaneously in Canada by Random House of Canada Limited, Toronto.

ISBN: 0–394–31280–5

Library of Congress Catalog Card Number: 73–131951

Manufactured in the United States of America by H. Wolff Book Mfg. Co., Inc., New York, N.Y.

First Edition

9 8 7 6 5 4 3 2 1

CONTENTS

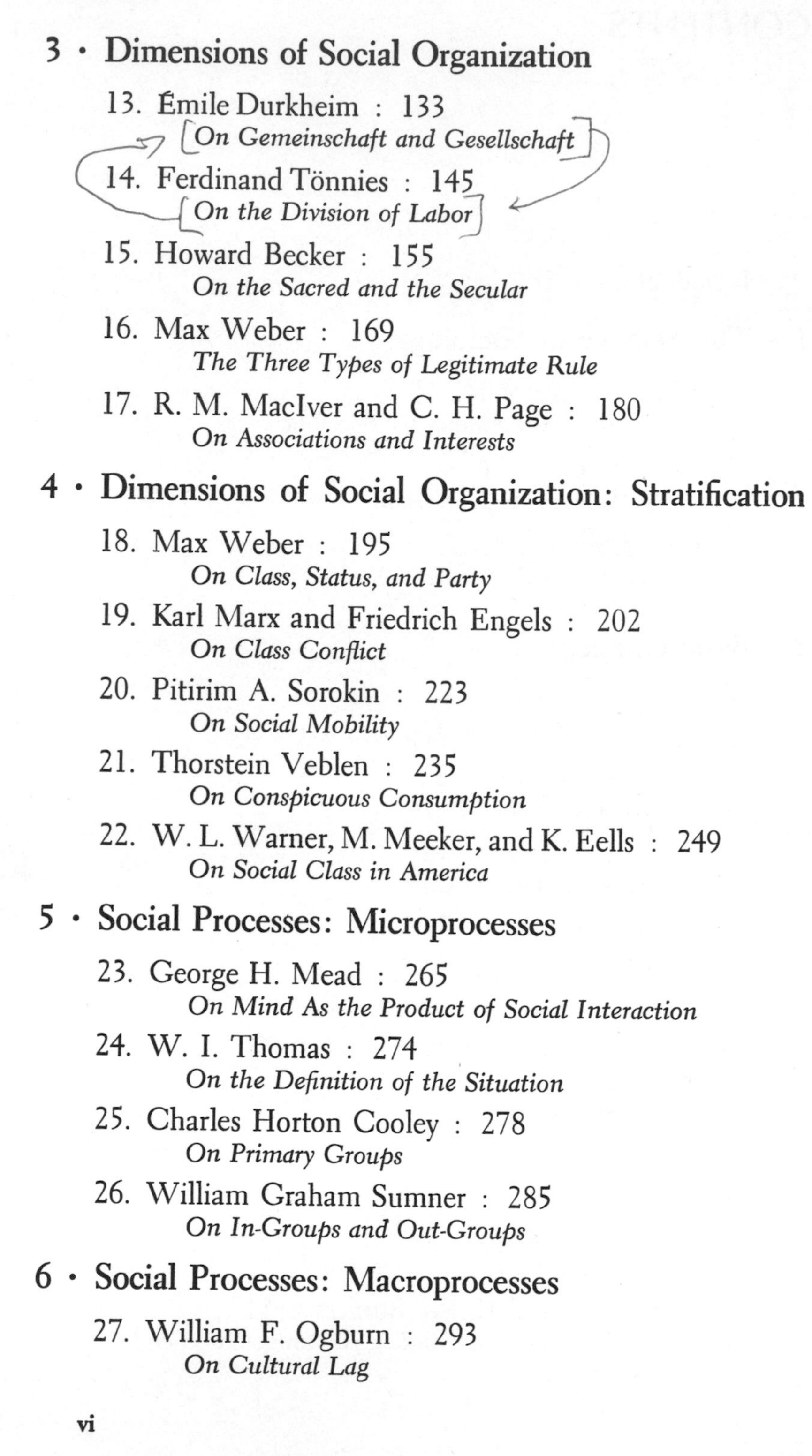

INTRODUCTION

In light of the fact that so many collections are currently available for supplementary use in introductory sociology courses, any new anthology of sociological writings needs justification. Instructors of beginning courses in sociology have often stated that a primary function of the first course in sociology, as in any science, is to familiarize the student with the basic concepts and technical language of the discipline. The later courses have the primary responsibility of engaging the student in the theoretical, methodological, and conceptual issues involved in the various substantive areas. It is this assumption that has guided me in the planning of this book.

Examination of the numerous anthologies available for use in the first course in sociology quickly reveals that they consist largely of compilations of contemporary professional research articles written for other professional researchers. Such articles presume a familiarity with the basic concepts and technical language of the field, and were never intended by their authors to be read by the beginning undergraduate. Deviating from this pattern, this anthology presents the student with the seminal statements that introduced many of the elemental constructs still used in the sociological enterprise. Thus, not only is the student presented with a preliminary statement of these essential ideas—largely preliminary because they were often the *first* important statements of such ideas and therefore could not presume much necessary prior knowledge on the part of the reader—but he also has an opportunity to encounter many of the greatest thinkers in sociology at first hand rather than through some second-hand and often distorted presentation.

This emphasis upon these largely early sociological writings is not meant to imply that there has been a lack of progress in the conceptual development within sociology. As Alfred North Whitehead stated: "A science which hesitates to forget its founders is lost." [1] A good case can be made for emphasizing the contemporary developments in sociology and for avoiding preoccupations with the past. However, it is in no sense a denial of the newer developments in sociology to extract from its greatest early figures those important nuggets of analysis and conceptualization that have demonstrated enduring value.[2] And acquainting the beginning student with the important early figures in our discipline may deter him from later neglecting to examine the abundance of these intense and scholarly early treatments of many current problems. Quite apart from the normative importance of properly crediting priorities in science,[3] it has been convincingly argued, most notably by Pitirim A. Sorokin,[4] that there have already been far too many cases in which contemporary sociologists have neglected to examine the past. In the process, they have deluded themselves and their followers with false discoveries and pseudoinitiations that were long since more deeply examined and logically, if not always empirically, found to be seriously wanting.[5] This contemporary neglect of the past is further reflected in a recent content analysis of articles in the major sociology journals. One major finding was that there was a "tendency of sociologists to confine their attention almost entirely to the work of colleagues who have published in the two principal journals within a five year time span while ignoring earlier works . . ."[6] The science of sociology can afford to forget its founders only when it has truly and firmly built upon their works.[7]

The unfortunate lack of current concern with many of the seminal works in sociology is reflected in the parochial image many students now obtain about sociology after having taken several courses in the discipline. Informal interviews with sociology majors in several schools revealed to me that many of them believed the major figures in sociology to be the authors of their elementary textbooks. Similar conversations with graduate students often reveal a remarkable lack of familiarity with the seminal figures and their works; all too often, the student is only aware of the works of a very few and select number of contemporary theorists, sometimes only those at his own university. In addition, many of the best sociology departments in this country do not consistently offer a course in the history of sociology or general social thought. This emphasis on the contemporary, coupled with the publication explosion, makes it likely that the problem will grow worse. It is hoped that this volume might help impede the erosion of so much of our still valuable intellectual past.[8]

Despite the "preservative" emphasis of this volume, it is fully recognized that the introductory sociology course must deal with current empirical research. This volume is intended as merely one of numerous supplementary adjuncts available for the introductory course. Many collections that might be used in conjunction with this one are available to those who would emphasize current empirical research. In addition to such outside sources, however, each of the readings in this book is introduced by a short statement that concentrates on (1) placing the article within a meaningful context, (2) citing the basic works of the theorist being read should the student wish to pursue his thoughts in greater detail, and (3) citing bibliographic examples of contemporary works (both critical and empirical) that have built upon and extended the basic concepts introduced by the pioneer theorists.[9] The instructor and students can thus turn to these cited works for contemporary elaborations of the basic ideas being presented.

NOTES

1. A. N. Whitehead, *The Aims of Education* (New York: Macmillan, 1929), p. 162.
2. The instructor and student are directed to some of these newer conceptual and research directions in the introductions preceding each reading.
3. Cf., Robert K. Merton, "Priorities in Scientific Discovery: A Chapter in the Sociology of Science," *American Sociological Review,* 22 (1957), 635–659; and his "Resistance to Systematic Study of Multiple Discoveries in Science," *Archives Europeenes de Sociologie,* 4 (1963), 237–283.
4. Pitirim A. Sorokin, *Fads and Foibles in Modern Sociology and Related Sciences* (Chicago: Henry Regnery, 1956), pp. 3–20.
5. For a related example, see: Marcello Truzzi, "Adam Smith and Contemporary Issues in Social Psychology," *Journal of the History of Behavioral Sciences,* 2 (1966), 221–224.
6. Julia S. Brown and Brian G. Gilmartin, "Sociology Today: Lacunae, Emphases and Surfeits," *The American Sociologist,* 4 (1969), 289.
7. An important factor leading to the sociologist's neglect of his predecessors' work is the relatively poor retrieval system available to the discipline which sorely needs better indexing and abstracting sources than are now present. This problem is growing in severity with little sign of relief.
8. An important evidence for the relevance of many of these old formulations is the periodic re-discovery of one of our pioneers. For example, the work of Herbert Spencer is becoming influential again after some thirty years of neglect; see: Robert L. Carneiro (ed.), *The Evolution of Society: Selections from Herbert Spencer* (Chicago: University of Chicago Press, 1967).
9. Since this volume is intended for the beginning student, emphasis is placed upon books and articles in English which are available in most university libraries. Works in foreign languages are largely ignored.

1

The Science of Sociology

1

PITIRIM A. SOROKIN

On Sociology Among the Social Sciences

Pitirim A. Sorokin (1889–1968), the great Russian sociologist, probably left contemporary sociology more classic or seminal statements than any other scholar in the second quarter of the twentieth century. His works encompassed the entire range of sociological endeavor, including, among others, such diverse areas as macrosociological and cultural theory, small-group experimentation, social stratification, rural sociology, the philosophy of history, and the sociology of altruistic love.[1] *There are very few areas in sociology upon which he did not leave a lasting imprint.*[2] *An immensely productive scholar, Sorokin was also a man of political action and a major critic of contemporary social trends.*[3]

In the selection that follows, Sorokin delineates his answer to the primary questions: What is sociology? What is sociology's relation to the other social sciences?

Bibliographical Notes

1. Sorokin wrote some 36 books and approximately 300 articles. In examining his works, the reader must be careful to separate his professional or scholarly writings from his "popular" and usually highly polemical pieces. Sorokin's major scholarly works include: Sistema sociologii *(Russian, 1920);* Sociology of Revolution *(1925);* Social Mobility *(1927);* Contemporary Sociological Theories *(1928);* A Systematic Source Book in Rural Sociology, *3 vols. (with C. C. Zimmerman and C. J. Galpin, 1930–1932);* Social and Cultural Dynamics, *4 vols. (1937–1941);* Time-Budgets and Human Behavior *(with C. Q. Berger,*

1939); Sociocultural Causality, Space, Time (1943); Society, Culture and Personality (1947); Social Philosophies of an Age of Crisis (1953); The Ways and Power of Love (1945); *and* Power and Morality (*with W. A. Lunden,* 1959). *To this list should be added his last book (he averaged almost one volume per year),* Sociological Theories of Today (*New York: Harper & Row, 1966), produced when Sorokin was already seventy-five years old but still more intellectually vigorous than many of his youthful colleagues.*

Extensive but selective bibliographies of Sorokin's work can be found in: Charles P. Loomis and Zona K. Loomis, Modern Social Theories (*New York: Van Nostrand, 1965), pp. 769–776; and Philip J. Allen (ed.),* Pitirim A. Sorokin in Review (*Durham, N.C.: Duke University Press, 1963), pp. 497–506.*

2. *Appraisals of Sorokin's contributions can be found in: Philip J. Allen (ed.),* Pitirim A. Sorokin in Review (*Durham, N.C.: Duke University Press, 1963); and Edward A. Tiryakian (ed.),* Sociological Theory, Values, and Sociocultural Change: Essays in Honor of Pitirim A. Sorokin (*New York: Free Press of Glencoe, 1963).*

3. *Sorokin's most polemical works include:* Crisis of Our Age (1941); Man and Society in Calamity (1942); S.O.S.: The Meaning of Our Crisis (1951); *and* The American Sex Revolution (1957). *Sorokin also aimed his barbs against sociology itself in his* Fads and Foibles in Modern Sociology and Related Sciences (1956).

---

1. *Generalizing and Individualizing Sciences*

The superorganic or sociocultural universe is studied by all the social and humanistic disciplines. The question arises, therefore, how sociology differs from economics, politics, history, psychology, and other social sciences. Though in a deeper sense all scientific disciplines make one indivisible science, for practical purposes a division of labor requires specialization in each discipline. Physics differs from chemistry and both from biology, though the boundary lines between them are relative and overlapping. Physical mechanics overlaps with geometry and mathematics; both overlap with chemistry, and all three with biology, giving us organic chemistry and mathematical physics. The difference between sociology and the other social disciplines is also relative; nevertheless, they are as distinct as physics, chemistry, and biology.

Within the great team of social and humanistic disciplines that deal with the superorganic world, sociology has its own distinctive task and performs its functions in a manner tangibly different from that of other members of the team. First, in contradistinction to history and other *individualizing* sciences, sociology is a *generalizing* science. Whereas history concentrates its attention upon the study of the sociocultural phenomena that are unique and unrepeated in time and space (the United States as a distinctive nation; Christianity as a unique religion; Abraham Lincoln as a particular man; the Thirty Years' War as dissimilar from all other wars), sociology studies the properties of the superorganic that are repeated in time and space, that is to say, those common to all sociocultural phenomena (general sociology) or else to all varieties of a given class of sociocultural phenomena—to all wars, all nations, all revolutions, all religions, etc. (special sociologies). By virtue of this generalizing quality sociology differs profoundly from history and other individualizing humanistic disciplines.[1]

2. *Contrast with Other Social Sciences*

In no less degree does the task of sociology differ from that of such generalizing social sciences as economics, political science, and the science of law. Economics too is a generalizing science, in that it seeks to discover and formulate the properties, relationships, and uniformities that are repeated in time and space and are common either to all economic phenomena (such as the laws of demand and supply or of marginal utility, in general economics), or to all economic phenomena of a certain class (like Gresham's law in the special economics of money, the law of diminishing returns in the special economics of agriculture, and so on). The same can be said, with proper modifications, of any other generalizing social science.

Sociology differs from such disciplines in several ways. In the first place, each of these sciences deals with only one compartment of the sociocultural universe, economics with the economic compartment, politics with the political compartment. Sociology deals, along its special lines, with all compartments of that universe. For instance, economics studies business organizations as a variety of society; political science analyzes the state as a specific kind of society; the science of religion investigates the church as a special form of society. General sociology, on the other hand, is concerned with society as a genus, with the properties and relationships that are found in any society, be it a business firm, a church, a state, a club, the family, or anything else. To take another example: Economics deals with business cycles and fluctuations; political science studies cycles and fluctuations in political life. Sociology sees cycles and fluctuations as generic social phenomena appearing in practically all social processes: economic, political, artistic, religious, philosophical, and their interconnections with one another. The same is true of such social processes as competition and exploitation, domination and subordination, stratification and differentiation, solidarity and antagonism, and so forth. Each of these processes appears not only in single compartments of the superorganic but in practically all compartments of sociocultural life, and as such requires a study of its generic form and of the connections which each special form bears to the other special forms of the same process. Such a study transcends the boundary lines of any compartmentalized discipline. It demands a special science that deals with the generic form of all these phenomena and with the interrelations of all the main varieties with one another. This task has been performed by sociology. Schematically this may be expressed as follows. Let the designated classes of social phenomena consist of the following elements and relationships:

economic: *a, b, c, n, m, f*
political: *a, b, c, h, d, j*
religious: *a, b, c, g, i, q*
and so on.

Granting that all the other varieties of sociocultural phenomena have the same common elements and relationships, *a, b, c*—and since they all belong to the same genus of sociocultural phenomena they cannot help having them—a study of these common elements *a, b, c,* would comprise the first task of sociology. On the other hand, an investigation of how the noncommon elements, for instance, *n, h, g,* are connected with one another—how, for instance, business cycles are related to cycles in the movement of criminality, scientific theories, suicide, artistic tastes, revolutions, etc.—this constitutes its second main task. Neither of these tasks is discharged by any of the compartmentalized social sciences, nor do either of them logically belong to such a science. They comprise the specific domain of sociology.

Along with this deep difference between the tasks of sociology and those of the other generalizing social sciences stands the important difference in their fundamental presuppositions concerning the *nature of man and the interrelations of social phenomena.* The compartmentalized character of economics forces it to postulate *homo economicus*

—the purely economic creature controlled by economic self-interest and utilitarian rationality, to the utter exclusion of noneconomic religious beliefs and nonutilitarian moral convictions, of antiegotistic altruism and profitless artistic values, of nonrational mores and irrational passions. In conformity with this, economic phenomena are assumed to be entirely isolated from other sociocultural phenomena and undisturbed by religious, legal, political, artistic, or moral forces. In a similar one-sided manner have been conceived *homo politicus* in the political realm, *homo religiosus* in the religious sphere, and so on.

In contradistinction to these presuppositions, *homo socius* of sociology is viewed as a generic and manifold *homo*, simultaneously and inseparably economic, political, religious, ethical, and artistic, partly rational and utilitarian, partly nonrational and even irrational, with all these aspects incessantly influencing one another. Consequently each class of sociocultural phenomena is viewed by sociology as connected with all the other classes (with varying degrees of interdependence), as influenced by and affecting the rest of the sociocultural universe. In this sense sociology studies man and the sociocultural universe as they really are, in all their manifoldness—as genuine wholes, in distinct contrast to the other sciences, which, for analytical purposes, view them artificially in merely one aspect, entirely isolated from the whole.

From these two fundamental differences follow several others that distinguish the essential principles and methods of sociology from those of other social sciences.

. . .

3. *Limitations of the Compartmentalized Disciplines*

What has been said of the causation of suicide applies still more pertinently to the causation of crime, revolution, war, and practically all other sociocultural phenomena. Unless they are studied as *repeated* phenomena, viewed at the same time in the matrix of the *whole* of the respective society and culture, none of them can be adequately understood or their real causes discovered. For instance, if one asks why criminality in the United States shows a higher rate than in certain other nations, what are the causes of the fluctuations of a specific crime or of all crimes, or why the severity of punishment for various crimes now increases and now decreases, none of these questions can be properly answered without a study of crime as a recurrent factor in the general structure of the society and culture in question. It can be confidently asserted that no specialized causal theory of crime—biological, psychiatric, economic, geographic, ecological, educational—can adequately account for its frequency in various societies and groups, for its fluctuation in the course of time, for its prevalent types, or even explain why certain actions are regarded as criminal while others are not. The inadequacy of such one-sided theories is due precisely to their "atomistic," singularistic, and compartmentalized approach, their neglect of the generalizing approach that views society and culture as a whole. This is even more true of large-scale sociocultural phenomena, such as wars and revolutions. Even compartmentalized phenomena, as studied from the standpoint of economics or political science, law or ethics, the fine arts, or history, cannot be fully understood without a consideration of the sociocultural constellation in which they recur. K. Mannheim correctly observes that—for instance, in political science—"sooner or later one is confronted with the question *why* do the countries at the same period and on the same plane of development have wholly different types of constitutions and forms of government, and *why* when the technique and constitution belonging to one country are taken over by another do they change their form in the adopting country? . . . Thus the political scientist is thrown back on certain unknown entities which he labels 'the national spirit' or 'the cultural heritage of a people.'" This means that it is necessary to consider society and culture as a whole. The same is true when he considers the problem of power and domination or many economic problems. ". . . It is for instance becoming increasingly evident that the choices made by individuals in their capacity as consumers are not fortuitous, but conform to certain collective standards which . . . are determined by non-economic 'social' factors. *What* social factors? To be able to answer this and similar questions, the economist, like the political scientist, seeks as it were a theory of the constants and variables in the formation of human wants." [2] Again it is necessary to go beyond the confines of a special field.

In medicine it is routine procedure for every competent physician, before diagnosing the disease of the patient, to investigate his whole organism and its life history. In the social sciences this routine unfortunately is neither established nor its necessity well understood. As in medicine the specialized approach here is fruitful and reasonable only when the whole of the sociocultural universe is recognized by this or that science. Otherwise it is bound to be inadequate and often misleading. In the great team of the social sciences sociology has been performing exactly this role.[3]

The above gives a sufficient idea of the specific functions of sociology in the team of the social and humanistic sciences; what these functions are in concrete forms; and why such a science is necessary whether it is called sociology or abracadabra.

4. *Sociology as a Special Science*

Though sociology is a generalizing science dealing with the sociocultural universe as a whole, this does not mean that it is an encyclopedic survey of all the social sciences or that it is a vague philosophical synthesis. The study of the common and current properties, relationships, and uniformities of sociocultural phenomena involves as much specialization as does a study of the unique or segmentary traits and relationships. *In spite of its generalizing nature sociology remains a strictly special science.* Though the president or treasurer of a firm deals with the company as a whole it does not follow that his work is not specialized or that he does the work of all the firm's employees; for the same reason sociology, studying the sociocultural universe as a whole, does not attempt to do the work of the other social sciences. Just as the task of a treasurer or president is not impossible, so the tasks of generalizing sciences—like physics and chemistry, which deal with the repeated properties and relationships of the whole material universe; or general biology, which studies the properties and repeated relationships of the living world, and sociology, which does the same in regard to the superorganic world—these tasks do not necessarily surpass the capacity of a single science. Perhaps they are more difficult than the tasks of a very narrow specialty, but that they are in no way impossible is evidenced by the very existence of such disciplines.

5. *Interdependence Between Sociology and Other Sciences*

In its generalizing functions sociology depends upon the findings of other special sciences; but every science depends upon several others and the special sciences depend upon the generalizing sciences no less, rather more in fact. Physics uses mathematics, mechanics, geometry, and chemistry; and each of these disciplines employs the others. It is impossible for a scholar to work upon any important problem without making use of the findings of other disciplines and scholars. No special problem in physics or chemistry can be solved without a knowledge of the body of these generalizing disciplines. The same is true of special problems in biology and of the main principles of general biology. The specialized science of geology depends much more upon general physics, chemistry, and biology than these depend upon geology.

Similarly, if sociology depends upon history, economics, political science and other compartmentalized social disciplines, these depend no less upon the generalizing science of sociology. Generalizing sociological theories of Plato and Aristotle have exerted a great influence upon the political, economic, legal, historical and other special sciences right up to the present moment. The same is true, in various degrees, of the generalizing conclusions of the works of Augustine and Thomas Aquinas, Hobbes and Machiavelli, Ibn Khaldun and Vico, Montesquieu and Locke, Rousseau and Bossuet, Auguste Comte and Herbert Spencer, Hegel and Marx, Spengler, Durkheim, Tarde, Max Weber, and Pareto. One can cite hundreds of historical, economic, political, anthropological, psychological . . . linguistic and even synological works written along the lines of either Augustinian (Orosius's *History*), or Thomistic, Machiavellian, Hobbesian, Hegelian, Spencerian, Comtean, or Marxian sociological principles.

Emergence of any important sociological system has invariably influenced a series of compartmentalized disciplines, in their leading principles, interpretations, problems studied, methods and techniques of investigation. Almost all the special social and humanistic disciplines in the second half of the nineteenth century were built up along either Hegelian or Comtian-Spencerian principles. Those of more recent times have been enormously affected by Marxian sociology in economic interpretations of data; by Tardian-Durkheimian, Weberian, Paretian and Spenglerian sociological principles and methods.

Even more, the emergence of sociology as a systematic science has been followed by "sociologization" of all the special disciplines in the last few decades. Their content, methods, interpretations, including even those whose authors have been inimical to sociology, have become increasingly sociological and have led to the appearance in all these disciplines of the sociological or institutional schools in jurisprudence and history (so called social histories), in economics and political science, in anthropology and psychology (social psychology), in sciences that examine fine arts and ethics, religion and even logic. Such a "sociologization" of these disciplines is eloquent evidence of the influence of sociology upon them. The dependence between sociology and the other social sciences is mutual; it is interdependence, not a one-sided dependence of sociology upon the other sciences.[4]

As a generalizing discipline general sociology has to be somewhat abstract and theoretical, and for this reason may appear to many a "practical man" as an impractical academic preoccupation, divorced from concrete actuality and devoid of practical utilitarian value. Here as well as in all such reasonings of too practical men (who, according to Lao-tzu are the most impractical), the fallacy of their conclusion is evident. Mathematics is possibly the most abstract and theoretical of all the sciences. And yet its practical importance is unquestionable. Algebra and calculus are more abstract than arithmetic. And yet who would conclude they are less important practically than arithmetic? General theoretical physics, chemistry, and biology are much more abstract and "impractical" than a cookbook or instruction book for a Chevrolet or other automobile. And yet without theoretical physics, chemistry, and biology neither an automobile nor a good cookbook could be produced. The same is true of sociology as a generalizing, theoretical, and somewhat abstract discipline. Its practical influence—whether good or bad does not concern us here—has been rather startling. In most of the great social revolutions, reforms, and reconstructions it is sociology of this or that kind which has been the leading ideology and guide. Thus Lockean sociology played this part in the Revolution of 1688 and the establishment of the liberal democratic regime in England; the thinking of Voltaire, Rousseau, and other Encyclopedists had a similar role in the French Revolution of 1789 and subsequent years. In our own time Marxian sociology has been the driving intellectual scheme and "the gospel" of the Communist revolution in Russia; the racial sociologies of A. Gobineau, H. S. Chamberlain, and others became the credo of the Nazi revolution and the Third Reich. From the sociology of Confucius to that of the present the practical effects of this study have been influential (although often fallacious sociologies, unhappily, instead of the valid ones). This fact is sufficient to dispel the illusions of the too practical men in this field.

To summarize: sociology is a generalizing science of sociocultural phenomena viewed in their generic forms, types, and manifold interconnections.

6. *General and Special Sociologies*

Like biology, which is divided into general and special biologies (botany, zoology, and their further subdivisions), and like economics, which is divided into general and special economics (banking and money, transportation and agriculture), sociology can also be divided into general and special sociologies. *General sociology* studies (a) the properties and uniformities common to all sociocultural phenomena in their structural and dynamic aspects as well as (b) the recurring interrelationships between the sociocultural and the cosmic phenomena; the sociocultural and the biological phenomena; the various classes of sociocultural phenomena.

Structural general sociology studies (a) the structure and composition of the generic sociocultural phenomenon (corresponding to the study of the structure of a cell as a phenomenon of life or that of an atom in physics); (b) the main structural types of the groups or institutions into which human population is differentiated and stratified and their relationship to one another; (c) the main structural types of the cultural systems and their relationships with one another; (d) the structure and types of personality embedded in social groups and cultural systems.

Dynamic general sociology investigates (a) recurring social processes, such as social contact, interaction, socialization, conflict, domination, subordination, adaptation, amalgamation, migration, mobility; how social systems are born, how they acquire and lose members; how they distribute these within the system, how they become organized and disorganized, and how all these processes affect the personality of the individuals involved; (b) recurring cultural processes—invention, diffusion, integration and disintegration, conversion and the accumulation of cultural traits and systems—and how they affect the personality of the individuals involved; (c) rhythms, tempos, periodicities, trends and fluctuations in social and cultural processes, together with the general problem of sociocultural change and evolution; (d) recurring sociocultural processes in persons, and how and why persons change.

Special sociologies each do the same in regard to a special class of sociocultural phenomena chosen for intensive study. The most developed special sociologies are at present: sociology of population, rural sociology, urban sociology; sociology of the family, of law, of religion, of knowledge; sociology of war, of revolution, of social disorganization;

sociology of crime and punishment (criminology); sociology of the fine arts; sociology of economic phenomena; and several others.

GENERAL		SPECIAL
Structural [5]	*Dynamic*	
Theory of: a. social systems and congeries; b. cultural systems and congeries; c. personalities in their structural aspect, main types, and interrelations.	Theory of the recurring: a. social processes and change; b. cultural processes and change; c. personality processes and change in their types, interrelationships, rhythms, trends, and causal factors.	Theory of structure and dynamics of the respective class of sociocultural phenomena studied in their generic and repeated aspects and relationship.

In a schematic form the main divisions of sociology can be represented as above.

This delineation of sociology is logically more adequate[6] and better corresponds to what sociology has actually been than other definitions, such as the science "of culture," "of society," "of human relations," "of social interaction," "of forms of social relationships," and the like. These definitions are far too loose. They do not point out the specific characteristics of sociology or differentiate it from other social sciences. On the other hand, the sound part of these definitions is well incorporated into the above delineation.

This tabular definition presents the logical structure of sociology as a scientific discipline regardless of who carries on the studies; whether a sociologist ex-officio or historian, economist, or engineer. From the fact that Sir Isaac Newton wrote his *Principia* and his *Observations upon the Prophecies of Daniel* it does not follow that both works belong to the same science; one is a great treatise in mechanics, the other in theology, though both were written by the same man. Likewise, many important sociological works were written by historians like F. de Coulanges, by engineers like Le Play and Herbert Spencer, or mathematicians like August Comte. Many sociological generalizations are found in treatises on history, philosophy, economics, and other sciences. And conversely, some ex-officio sociologists have written books that do not belong to sociology but fall into the domain of some other science. Even in textbooks of sociology one can find large portions that belong to presociology or other disciplines. This difference between the logical nature of sociology and the ex-officio authorship of a sociological study must be kept clearly in mind.[7]

NOTES

1. On the profound difference between the generalizing and the individualizing sciences see H. Rickert, *Die Grenzen der Naturwissenschaftlichen Begriffsbildung* (Tübingen, 1902); A. Xénopol, *La théorie de l'histoire* (Paris, 1908); A. Tschuproff, *Essays in the Theory of Statistics* (St. Petersburg, 1909).
2. K. Mannheim, "The Place of Sociology," *Conference on the Social Sciences: Their Relations in Theory and in Teaching* (London, 1935), pp. 3 ff. See also M. Weber, "Wirtschaftssoziologie," in *Wirtschaft und Gesellschaft* (Tübingen, 1922); A. Löwe, *Economics and Sociology* (London, 1935).
3. The urgency of the standpoint of the whole is increasingly recognized by biology, psychology, and other disciplines. See, for instance, W. Köhler, *Gestalt Psychology* (New York, 1929); R. H. Wheeler, "Organismic Vs. Mechanistic Logic," *Psychological Review* (July, 1935).
4. If sociology has been enormously influenced by biology, then biology has also been affected by sociology in many ways. Darwin's theory of evolution and of the struggle for existence was suggested by Malthus' work; Spencer's formula of evolution or progress is still the most generally used formula of biological evolution, while several biological concepts like the division of labor and differentiation were taken from sociology. See G. Tarde, "La théorie organique des sociétés" in *Annales de l'Institut International de sociologie,* Vol. IV. In the last few decades biology has increasingly emphasized the social factors in causation of many biological phenomena, especially in the aetiology of various diseases and of transformation and modification of organisms, not to mention the emergence of various offshoots of biology—"ecology," "animal sociology," "plant sociology," and the like. In all these respects the impact of sociology has been so considerable that several prominent biologists entitle their studies "Soziologie innerer Krankheiten," "Soziologie Geschlechtskrankheiten," "Ueber den Einfluss der Berufe auf das Herz," "Krankheit und soziale Lage," and the like. Several corresponding studies with sociological titles are to be found in the *Handbuch der soziale Hygiene* (Berlin, 1926–29), all volumes; or M. Mosse and G. Tugendreich (ed.), *Krankheit und soziale Lage* (Munich, 1913). Some branches of medical science, psychiatry, for example, are becoming increasingly sociological. These and many other facts unmistakably show that biology and sociology influence one another. Later on in this work [*Society, Culture and Personality*] it will be shown that even mathematics, physics, and chemistry are socially conditioned in their nature and development. The sociology of knowledge has contributed to the demonstration of this condition, making these sciences aware of the psychosocial implications of many of their propositions.
5. One can easily see that in this division of sociology into structural and dynamic I follow Comte's division of sociology into social statics and dynamics. So far it has been the most fruitful of all the divisions.
6. Theoretical sociology studies the sociocultural universe as it is, in contradistinction from *normative* sociology, that sets forth the ideal sociocultural world as it ought to be; and from *practical* or *applied* sociology which, like medicine or agronomy, consists in a scientific arrangement of a certain objective—elimination of poverty, war, etc. Like many applied disciplines, applied sociology or the art of social engineering, must use not only the data of sociology but of several other sciences. And as

with any applied discipline its validity depends upon the level of knowledge attained by theoretical sociology; as long as this is low, no successful and efficient applied social engineering is possible. In this work we are concerned only with theoretical sociology. On the difference between the theoretical, normative, and applied disciplines see my "Sociology and Ethics" in W. F. Ogburn and A. Goldenweiser, *The Social Sciences and Their Interpretations* (Boston, 1927); and H. Poincaré, *Dernières pensées,* Ch. on "Sciences and Ethics" (Paris, 1913).

7. On sociology as a science see P. A. Sorokin, "Sociology as a Science," and S. Rice, "What is Sociology," both in *SF*, Vol. X (1931); see there other articles on this topic in subsequent numbers. K. Mannheim, "The Place of Sociology,' in *Conference on the Social Sciences: Their Relations in Theory and Teaching* (London, 1935); R. Thurnwald (ed.), *Soziologie von Heute,* (Leipzig, 1932); articles by A. Walther, H. Freyer, F. Plenge, P. A. Sorokin, M. Ginsberg, W. Ogburn, R. MacIver, S. R. Steinmetz, F. Tönnies, R. Thurnwald; in W. Ogburn and A. Goldenweiser (eds.), *The Social Sciences and Their Interrelations* (Boston, 1927); L. von Weise, *Sociology* (New York, 1941).

2

MAX WEBER

On Science As a Vocation

Ever since the introduction of his ideas into American sociology by P. A. Sorokin[1] *and T. Parsons,*[2] *the great German sociologist Max Weber (1864–1920) has been recognized as one of the intellectual giants of the discipline and one of the great influences upon American sociology.*[3] *Weber introduced important substantive and theoretical analyses. In addition, he is generally regarded as the outstanding spokesman for what is usually labeled the* value-free *approach in sociology. Essentially, this posture states that it is inappropriate for the sociologist to take normative positions as part of his role as a scientist. According to Weber, science simply states facts and their relations and makes no moral judgements of those facts. Weber was himself a man of political action and was not opposed to the use of scientific knowledge for moral ends. He felt the problem concerns the separation of roles: the man who is a sociologist can take and probably must take evaluative positions about social facts, but he can not do this in his role as sociologist. Weber believed that, to the degree that sociology is a science, it must limit itself to factual statements about the empirical social world. Though the* man *may take a moral position, the* sociologist *must not. To the degree that a man who is a sociologist makes value statements, he makes these outside his scientific role as sociologist.*[4]

Bibliographical Notes

1. Pitirim A. Sorokin, Contemporary Sociological Theories Through the First Quarter of the Twentieth Century *(New York: Harper and Row, 1928).*

Reprinted from H. H. Gerth and C. Wright Mills, translators and editors, *From Max Weber: Essays in Sociology* (New York: Oxford University Press, 1958 Galaxy edition), pp. 142–151. Copyright 1946 by Oxford University Press, Inc. Reprinted by permission of the publisher.

2. *Talcott Parsons,* The Structure of Social Action (*New York: McGraw-Hill,* 1937).

3. *In their English translations, most of Weber's work has appeared under the following titles in volumes mostly edited by the translators from his massive works* Wirtschaft und Gesellschaft *and* Gesammelte Aufsatze zur Sozial-und Wirtschaftgeschichte: The Protestant Ethic and the Spirit of Capitalism, From Max Weber, Max Weber on the Methodology of the Social Sciences, The Theory of Social and Economic Organization, The Religion of China, The Religion of India, Ancient Judaism, Max Weber on Law in Economy and Society, *and* General Economic History. *An excellent bibliographical and critical survey of his work is available in: Reinhard Bendix,* Max Weber: An Intellectual Portrait (*New York: Doubleday and Co., Anchor Books,* 1962).

4. *In recent years, the value-free approach has come under significant attack, see, for example, Alvin W. Gouldner, "Anti-Minotaur: The Myth of a Value-Free Sociology,"* Social Problems, 9 (*1962*), *199–213.*

What did science mean to these men who stood at the threshold of modern times? To artistic experimenters of the type of Leonardo and the musical innovators, science meant the path to *true* art, and that meant for them the path to true *nature.* Art was to be raised to the rank of a science, and this meant at the same time and above all to raise the artist to the rank of the doctor, socially and with reference to the meaning of his life. This is the ambition on which, for instance, Leonardo's sketch book was based. And today? 'Science as the way to nature' would sound like blasphemy to youth. Today, youth proclaims the opposite: redemption from the intellectualism of science in order to return to one's own nature and therewith to nature in general. Science as a way to art? Here no criticism is even needed.

But during the period of the rise of the exact sciences one expected a great deal more. If you recall Swammerdam's statement, 'Here I bring you the proof of God's providence in the anatomy of a louse,' you will see what the scientific worker, influenced (indirectly) by Protestantism and Puritanism, conceived to be his task: to show the path to God. People no longer found this path among the philosophers, with their concepts and deductions. All pietist theology of the time, above all Spener, knew that God was not to be found along the road by which the Middle Ages had sought him. God is hidden, His ways are not our ways, His thoughts are not our thoughts. In the exact sciences, however, where one could physically grasp His works, one hoped to come upon the traces of what He planned for the world. And today? Who—aside from certain big children who are indeed found in the natural sciences—still believes that the findings of astronomy, biology, physics, or chemistry could teach us anything about the *meaning* of the world? If there is any such 'meaning,' along what road could one come upon its tracks? If these natural sciences lead to anything in this way, they are apt to make the belief that there is such a thing as the 'meaning' of the universe die out at its very roots.

And finally, science as a way 'to God'? Science, this specifically irreligious power? That science today is irreligious no one will doubt in his innermost being, even if he will not admit it to himself. Redemption from the rationalism and intellectualism of science is the fundamental presupposition of living in union with the divine. This, or something similar in meaning, is one of the fundamental watchwords one hears among German youth, whose feelings are attuned to religion or who crave religious experiences. They crave not only religious experience but experience as such. The only thing that is strange is the method that is now followed: the spheres of the irrational, the only spheres that intellectualism has not yet touched, are now raised into consciousness and put under its lens. For in practice this is where the modern intellectualist form of romantic irrationalism leads. This method of emancipation from intellectualism may well bring about the very opposite of what those who take to it conceive as its goal.

After Nietzsche's devastating criticism of those 'last men' who 'invented happiness,' I may leave aside altogether the naive optimism in which science—that is, the technique of mastering life which rests upon science—has been celebrated as the way to happiness. Who believes in this?—aside from a few big children in university chairs or editorial offices. Let us resume our argument.

Under these internal presuppositions, what is the meaning of science as a vocation, now after all these former illusions, the 'way to true being,' the 'way to true art,' the 'way to true nature,' the 'way to true God,' the 'way to true happiness,' have been dispelled? Tolstoi has given the simplest answer, with the words: 'Science is meaningless because it gives no answer to our question, the only question important for us: "What shall we do and how shall we live?"' That science does not give an answer to this is indisputable. The only question that remains is the sense in which science gives 'no' answer, and whether or not science might yet be of some use to the one who puts the question correctly.

Today one usually speaks of science as 'free from presuppositions.' Is there such a thing? It depends upon what one understands thereby. All scientific work presupposes that the rules of logic and method are valid; these are the general foundations of our orientation in the world; and, at least for our special question, these presuppositions are the least problematic aspect of science. Science further presupposes that what is yielded by scientific work is important in the sense that it is 'worth being known.' In this, obviously, are contained all our problems. For this presupposition cannot be proved by scientific means. It can only be *interpreted* with reference to its ultimate meaning, which we must reject or accept according to our ultimate position towards life.

Furthermore, the nature of the relationship of scientific work and its presuppositions varies widely according to their structure. The natural sciences, for instance, physics, chemistry, and astronomy, presuppose as self-evident that it is worth while to know the ultimate law of cosmic events as far as science can construe them. This is the case not only because with such knowledge one can attain technical results but for its own sake, if the quest for such knowledge is to be a 'vocation.' Yet this presupposition can by no means be proved. And still less can it be proved that the existence of the world which these sciences describe is worth while, that it has any "meaning,' or that it makes sense to live in such a world. Science does not ask for the answers to such questions.

Consider modern medicine, a practical technology which is highly developed scientifically. The general 'presupposition' of the medical enterprise is stated trivially in the assertion that medical science has the task of maintaining life as such and of diminishing suffering as such to the greatest possible degree. Yet this is problematical. By his means the medical man preserves the life of the mortally ill man, even if the patient implores us to relieve him of life, even if his relatives, to whom his life is worthless and to whom the costs of maintaining his worthless life grow unbearable, grant his redemption from suffering. Perhaps a poor lunatic is involved, whose relatives, whether they admit it or not, wish and must wish for his death. Yet the presuppositions of medicine, and the penal code, prevent the physician from relinquishing his therapeutic efforts. Whether life is worth while living and when—this question is not asked by medicine. Natural science gives us an answer to the question of what we must do if we wish to master life technically. It leaves quite aside, or assumes for its purposes, whether we should and do wish to master life technically and whether it ultimately makes sense to do so.

Consider a discipline such as aesthetics. The fact that there are works of art is given for aesthetics. It seeks to find out under what conditions this fact exists, but it does not raise the question whether or not the realm of art is perhaps a realm of diabolical grandeur, a realm of this world, and therefore, in its core, hostile to God and, in its innermost and aristocratic spirit, hostile to the brotherhood of man. Hence, aesthetics does not ask whether there *should* be works of art.

Consider jurisprudence. It establishes what is valid according to the rules of juristic thought, which is partly bound by logically compelling and partly by conventionally given schemata. Juridical thought holds when certain legal rules and certain methods of interpretations are recognized as binding. Whether there should be law and whether one should establish just these rules—such questions jurisprudence does not answer. It can only state: If one wishes this result, according to the norms of our legal thought, this legal rule is the appropriate means of attaining it.

Consider the historical and cultural sciences. They teach us how to understand and interpret political, artistic, literary, and social phenomena in terms of their origins. But they give us no answer to the question, whether the existence of these cultural phenomena have been and are *worth while*. And they do not answer the further question, whether it is worth the effort required to know them. They presuppose that there is an interest in partaking, through this procedure, of the community of 'civilized men.' But they cannot prove 'scientifically' that this is the case; and that they presuppose this interest by no means proves that it goes without saying. In fact it is not at all self-evident.

Finally, let us consider the disciplines close to me: sociology, history, economics, political science, and those types of cultural philosophy that make it their task to interpret these sciences. It is said, and I agree, that politics is out of place in the lecture-room. It does not belong there on the part of the students. If, for instance, in the lecture-room of my former colleague Dietrich Schäfer in Berlin, pacifist students were to surround his desk and make an uproar, I should deplore it just as much as I should deplore the uproar which anti-pacifist students are said to have made against Professor Förster, whose views in many ways are as remote as could be from mine. Neither does politics, however, belong in the lecture-room on the part of the docents, and when the docent is scientifically concerned with politics, it belongs there least of all.

To take a practical political stand is one thing, and to analyze political structures and party positions is another. When speaking in a political meeting about democracy, one does not hide one's personal standpoint; indeed, to come out clearly and take a stand is one's damned duty. The words one uses in such a meeting are not means of scientific analysis but means of canvassing votes and winning over others. They are not plowshares to loosen the soil of contemplative thought; they are swords against the enemies: such words are weapons. It would be an outrage, however, to use words in this fashion in a lecture or in the lecture-room. If, for instance, 'democracy' is under discussion, one considers its various forms, analyzes them in the way they function, determines what results for the conditions of life the one form has as compared with the other. Then one confronts the forms of democracy with non-democratic forms of political order and endeavors to come to a position where the student may find the point from which, in terms of his ultimate ideals, he can take a stand. But the true teacher will beware of imposing from the platform any political position upon the student, whether it is expressed or suggested. 'To let the facts speak for themselves' is the most unfair way of putting over a political position to the student.

Why should we abstain from doing this? I state in advance that some highly esteemed colleagues are of the opinion that it is not possible to carry through this self-restraint and that, even if it were possible, it would be a whim to avoid declaring oneself. Now one cannot demonstrate scientifically what the duty of an academic teacher is. One can only demand of the teacher that he have the intellectual integrity to see that it is one thing to state facts, to determine mathematical or logical relations or the internal structure of cultural values, while it is another thing to answer questions of the *value* of culture and its individual contents and the question of how one should act in the cultural community and in political associations. These are quite heterogeneous problems. If he asks further why he should not deal with both types of problems in the lecture-room, the answer is: because the prophet and the demagogue do not belong on the academic platform.

To the prophet and the demagogue, it is said: 'Go your ways out into the streets and speak openly to the world,' that is, speak where criticism is possible. In the lecture-room we stand opposite our audience, and it has to remain silent. I deem it irresponsible to exploit the circumstance that for the sake of their career the students have to attend a teacher's course while there is nobody present to oppose him with criticism. The task of the teacher is to serve the students with his knowledge and scientific experience and not to imprint upon them his personal political views. It is certainly possible that the individual teacher will not entirely succeed in eliminating his personal sympathies. He is then exposed to the sharpest criticism in the forum of his own conscience. And this deficiency does not prove anything; other errors are also possible, for instance, erroneous statements of fact, and yet they prove nothing against the duty of searching for the truth. I also reject this in the very interest of science. I am ready to prove from the works of our historians that whenever the man of science introduces his personal value judgment, a full understanding of the facts *ceases*. But this goes beyond tonight's topic and would require lengthy elucidation.

I ask only: How should a devout Catholic, on the one hand, and a Freemason, on the other, in a course on the forms of church and state or on religious history ever be brought to evaluate these subjects alike? This is out of the question. And yet the academic teacher must desire and must demand of himself to serve the one as well as the other by his knowledge and methods. Now you will rightly say that the devout Catholic will never accept the view of the factors operative in bringing about Christianity which a teacher who is free of his dogmatic presuppositions presents to him. Certainly! The difference, however, lies in the following: Science 'free from presuppositions,' in the sense of a rejection of religious bonds, does not know of the 'miracle' and the 'revelation.' If it did, science would be unfaithful to its own 'presuppositions.' The believer knows both, miracle and revelation. And science 'free from presuppositions' expects from him no less—and no more—than acknowledgment that *if* the process can be explained without those supernatural interventions, which an empirical explanation has to eliminate as causal factors, the process has to be explained the way science attempts to do. And the believer can do this without being disloyal to his faith.

But has the contribution of science no meaning at all for a man who does not care to know facts as such and to whom only the practical standpoint matters? Perhaps science nevertheless contributes something.

The primary task of a useful teacher is to teach his students to recognize 'inconvenient' facts—I mean facts that are inconvenient for their party opinions. And for every party opinion there are facts that are extremely inconvenient, for my own opinion no less than for others. I believe the teacher accomplishes more than a mere intellectual task if he compels his audience to accustom itself to the existence of such facts. I would be so immodest as even to apply the expression 'moral achievement,' though perhaps this may sound too grandiose for something that should go without saying.

Thus far I have spoken only of practical reasons for avoiding the imposition of a personal point of view. But these are not the only reasons. The impossibility of 'scientifically' pleading for practical and interested stands—except in discussing the means for a firmly given and presupposed end—rests upon reasons that lie far deeper.

'Scientific' pleading is meaningless in principle because the various value spheres of the world stand in irreconcilable conflict with each other. The elder Mill, whose philosophy I will not praise otherwise, was on this point right when he said: If one proceeds from pure experience, one arrives at polytheism. This is shallow in formulation and sounds paradoxical, and yet there is truth in it. If anything, we realize again today that something can be sacred not only in spite of its not being beautiful, but rather because and in so far as it is not beautiful. You will find this documented in the fifty-third chapter of the book of Isaiah and in the twenty-first Psalm. And, since Nietzsche, we realize that something can be beautiful, not only in spite of the aspect in which it is not good, but rather in that very aspect. You will find this expressed earlier in the *Fleurs du mal,* as Baudelaire named his volume of poems. It is commonplace to observe that something may be true although it is not beautiful and not holy and not good. Indeed it may be true in precisely those aspects. But all these are only the most elementary cases of the struggle that the gods of the various orders and values are engaged in. I do not know how one might wish to decide 'scientifically' the value of French and German culture; for here, too, different gods struggle with one another, now and for all times to come.

We live as did the ancients when their world was not yet disenchanted of its gods and demons, only we live in a different sense. As Hellenic man at times sacrificed to Aphrodite and at other times to Apollo, and, above all, as everybody sacrificed to the gods of his city, so do we still nowadays, only the bearing of man has been disenchanted and denuded of its mystical but inwardly genuine plasticity. Fate, and certainly not 'science,' holds sway over these gods and their struggles. One can only understand what the godhead is for the one order or for the other, or better, what godhead is in the one or in the other order. With this understanding, however, the matter has reached its limit so far as it can be discussed in a lecture-room and by a professor. Yet the great and vital problem that is contained therein is, of course, very far from being concluded. But forces other than university chairs have their say in this matter.

What man will take upon himself the attempt to 'refute scientifically' the ethic of the Sermon on the Mount? For instance, the sentence, 'resist no evil,' or the image of turning the other cheek? And yet it is clear, in mundane perspective, that this is an ethic of undignified conduct; one has to choose between the religious dignity which this ethic confers and the dignity of manly conduct which preaches something quite different; 'resist evil—lest you be co-responsible for an overpowering evil.' According to our ultimate standpoint, the one is the devil and the other the God, and the individual has to decide which is God for him and which is the devil. And so it goes throughout all the orders of life.

The grandiose rationalism of an ethical and methodical conduct of life which flows from every religious prophecy has dethroned this polytheism in favor of the 'one thing that is needful.' Faced with the realities of outer and inner life, Christianity has deemed it necessary to make those compromises and relative judgments, which we all know from its history. Today the routines of everyday life challenge religion. Many old gods ascend from their graves; they are disenchanted and hence take the form of impersonal forces. They strive to gain power over our lives and again they resume their eternal struggle with one another. What is hard for modern man, and especially for the younger generation, is to measure up to *workaday* existence. The ubiquitous chase for 'experience' stems from this weakness; for it is weakness not to be able to countenance the stern seriousness of our fateful times.

Our civilization destines us to realize more clearly these struggles again, after our eyes have been blinded for a thousand years—blinded by the allegedly or presumably exclusive orientation towards the grandiose moral fervor of Christian ethics.

But enough of these questions which lead far away. Those of our youth are in error who react to all this by saying, 'Yes, but we happen to come to lectures in order to experience something more than mere analyses and statements of fact.' The error is that they seek in the professor something different from what stands before them. They crave a leader and not a teacher. But we are placed upon the platform solely as teachers. And these are two different things, as one can readily see. Permit me to take you once more to America, because there one can often observe such matters in their most massive and original shape.

The American boy learns unspeakably less than the German boy. In spite of an incredible number of examinations, his school life has not had the significance of turning him into an absolute creature of examinations, such as the German. For in America, bureaucracy, which presupposes the examination diploma as a ticket of admission to the realm of office prebends, is only in its beginnings. The young American has no respect for anything or anybody, for tradition or for public office—unless it is for the personal achievement of individual men. This is what the American calls 'democracy.' This is the meaning of democracy, however distorted its intent may in reality be, and this intent is what matters here. The American's conception of the teacher who faces him is: he sells me his knowledge and his methods for my father's money, just as the greengrocer sells my mother cabbage. And that is all. To be sure, if the teacher happens to be a football coach, then, in this field, he is a leader. But if he is not this (or something similar in a different field of sports), he is simply a teacher and nothing more. And no young American would think of having the teacher sell him a *Weltanschauung* or a code of conduct. Now, when formulated in this manner, we should reject this. But the question is whether there is not a grain of salt contained in this feeling, which I have deliberately stated in extreme with some exaggeration.

Fellow students! You come to our lectures and demand from us the qualities of leadership, and you fail to realize in advance that of a hundred professors at least ninety-nine do not and must not claim to be football masters in the vital problems of life, or even to be 'leaders' in matters of conduct. Please, consider that a man's value does not depend on whether or not he has leadership qualities. And in any case, the qualities that make a man an excellent scholar and academic teacher are not the qualities that make him a leader to give directions in practical life or, more specifically, in politics. It is pure accident if a teacher also possesses this quality, and it is a critical situation if every teacher on the platform feels himself confronted with the students' expectation that the teacher should claim this quality. It is still more critical if it is left to every academic teacher to set himself up as a leader in the lecture-room. For those who most frequently think of themselves as leaders often qualify least as leaders. But irrespective of whether they are or are not, the platform situation simply offers no possibility of *proving* themselves to be leaders. The professor who feels called upon to act as a counselor of youth and enjoys their trust may prove himself a man in personal human relations with them. And if he feels called upon to intervene in the struggles of world views and party opinions, he may do so outside, in the market place, in the press, in meetings, in associations, wherever he wishes. But after all, it is somewhat too convenient to demonstrate one's courage in taking a stand where the audience and possible opponents are condemned to silence.

Finally, you will put the question: 'If this is so, what then does science actually and positively contribute to practical and personal "life"?' Therewith we are back again at the problem of science as a 'vocation.'

First, of course, science contributes to the technology of controlling life by calculating external objects as well as man's activities. Well, you will say, that, after all, amounts to no more than the greengrocer of the American boy. I fully agree.

Second, science can contribute something that the greengrocer cannot: methods of thinking, the tools and the training for thought. Perhaps you will say: well, that is no vegetable, but it amounts to no more than the means for procuring vegetables. Well and good, let us leave it at that for today.

Fortunately, however, the contribution of science does not reach its limit with this. We are in a position to help you to a third objective: to gain *clarity*. Of course, it is presupposed that we ourselves possess clarity. As far as this is the case, we can make clear to you the following:

In practice, you can take this or that position when concerned with a problem of value—for simplicity's sake, please think of social phenomena as examples. *If* you take such and such a stand, then, according to scientific experience, you have to use such and such a *means* in order to carry out your conviction practically. Now, these means are perhaps such that you believe you must reject them. Then you simply must choose between the end and the inevitable means. Does the end 'justify' the means? Or does it not? The teacher can confront you with the necessity of this choice. He cannot do more, so long as he wishes to remain a teacher and not to become a demagogue. He can, of course, also tell you that if you want such and such an end, then you must take into the bargain the subsidiary consequences which according to all experience will occur. Again we find ourselves in the same situation as before. These are still problems that can also emerge for the technician, who in numerous instances has to make decisions according to the principle of the lesser evil or of the relatively best. Only to him one thing, the main thing, is usually given, namely, the end. But as soon as truly 'ultimate' problems are at stake for us this is not the case. With this, at long last, we come to the final service that science as such can render to the aim of clarity, and at the same time we come to the limits of science.

3

GEORG SIMMEL

On the Field of Sociology

Georg Simmel (1858–1918),[1] *a brilliant German sociologist of what P. A. Sorokin termed the* formal *school,*[2] *was deeply concerned with the basic question: What is society? Whereas Sorokin saw sociology as the "generalizing science of sociocultural phenomena viewed in their generic forms, types, and manifold interconnections," Simmel took a narrower view. Arguing that the* content *of all fields of social phenomenon was already studied by the various social science disciplines (economics, political science, history, linguistics, etc.), Simmel contended that the appropriate sphere of sociology, if it were to represent a truly separate discipline, was the study of the* forms *of socialization and human relationship. Thus, sociology, as envisioned by Simmel, was a highly abstract science, like geometry.*[3]

Although Simmel was a fountain of insights and seminal ideas, he failed to develop a consistent sociological system. In recent years, however, American sociologists have shown renewed interest in his works. Particular attention has been paid to Simmel's insightful analyses of social relationships in everyday life,[4] *his concern for conflict in groups,*[5] *and his attempt to systematize human relations and social processes.*[6]

Bibliographical Notes

1. A full bibliography of Simmel's writings and an excellent introduction to his work may be found in: Kurt H. Wolf (ed. and trans.), The Sociology of Georg Simmel *(New York: Free Press, 1950). Overviews of his work may be found in: Nicholas J. Spykman,* The Social Theory of Georg Simmel *(New York: Atherton Press, 1966 Atheling*

Reprinted from Georg Simmel, "The Problem of Sociology," translated by Albion W. Small, *The American Journal of Sociology,* 15, 3 (1909), 290–303, 315–316.

edition, originally published in 1925); Kurt H. Wolf (ed.), Georg Simmel, 1858–1918 *(Columbus: Ohio State University Press, 1959); and Lewis A. Coser (ed.),* Georg Simmel *(Englewood Cliffs, N.J.: Prentice-Hall, 1965).*

2. *Cf., P. A. Sorokin,* Contemporary Sociological Theories *(New York: Harper & Row, 1964 Harper Torchbook edition, originally published in 1928), pp. 488–513.*

3. *The reader is referred to P. A. Sorokin,* Contemporary Sociological Theories *(New York: Harper & Row, 1964), pp. 495–507, for a scathing criticism of Simmel's approach to sociology as a highly abstract science. This and other criticisms may be found in Lewis Coser,* Georg Simmel *(Englewood Cliffs, N.J.: Prentice-Hall, 1965).*

4. *Concern for Simmel's work is well documented in the writings of those engaged in some of the current phenomenological and ethnographic approaches present in sociology (e.g., the works of Erving Goffman, Harold Garfinkel, Marvin Scott, Stanford Lyman, Alfred Schutz).*

5. *Such influence is especially visible in: Lewis A. Coser,* The Functions of Social Conflict *(New York: Free Press, 1956); and Theodore M. Mills, "Some Hypotheses on Small Groups from Simmel,"* American Journal of Sociology, *63 (1958), 642–650.*

6. *Little attempt has been made to develop a taxonomy of social relationships since that of Leopold von Weise (in his* Allgemeine Soziologie *in 1924), although a modern approach to this problem can be found in: Samuel F. Sampson,* A Novitiate in a Period of Change: An Experimental and Case Study of Social Relationships *(Unpublished doctoral dissertation, Cornell University, 1968).*

New tendencies of thought often appear with the purely abstract character of which, nevertheless, only the interests of a new feeling and willing mingle in the proposing of questions and the forms of intellectuality. Accordingly, the claims which sociology is wont to make are the theoretical continuation and reflection of the practical power which, in the nineteenth century, the masses had gained, in contrast with the interests of the individual. . . . Along with this reciprocal class-consciousness, . . . thought all at once became aware that, as a general proposition, every individual is determined by innumerable influences from its human environment. . . . Inasmuch as we brought ourselves to the consciousness that all human activity ran its course within society, and that nothing can withdraw itself from the influence of society, it followed that everything which was not science of external nature must be science of society. Society appeared as the inclusive territory, in which ethics and history of civilization, aesthetics and demography, politics and ethnology, congregated; since the subject-matter of these sciences occurred within the framework of society. That is, the science of man was science of society. This conception of sociology as science of everything human was supported by the fact that it was a *new* science, and in consequence all possible problems, which could not find a place elsewhere, crowded to it—as a newly opened territory is always at first the *Dorado* of the homeless and the unattached. The at first unavoidable indefiniteness and indefensibility of boundaries afford right of asylum to everybody. More closely examined, meanwhile, this throwing together of all previous fields of knowledge begets nothing new; it merely signifies that all historical, psychological, normative sciences are dumped into one great pot, on which we paste the label "Sociology." That would amount merely to the gaining of a new *name*, while everything which it signifies is already secure in its content and its relationships, or is produced within the previous provinces of investigation. The fact that human thought and action occur in society, and are determined by it, as little makes sociology the all-embracing science of the same, as chemistry, botany, and astronomy can be made contents of psychology because their phenomena in the last analysis are actual only in human consciousness, and are subject to the presuppositions of the same.

At the basis of this error is a misunderstood but nevertheless very significant fact. The perception that in his whole nature, and in all its expressions, man is determined by the fact that he lives in reciprocal relationship with other men, must inevitably lead to a new way of thinking in all so-called psychical sciences. It is no longer possible to explain the historical facts in the broadest sense of the word, the contents of culture, the types of industry, the norms of morality, by reference solely to the individual, his understanding, and his interests. Still less is it possible, if this sort of explanation fails, to find recourse in metaphysical or magical causes. With reference to *speech*, for example, we no longer confront the alternative that it was either invented by individuals of genius, or that it was a gift of God to men. In *religious systems* the inventions of sly priests, and immediate revelation no longer divide the credit, etc. Instead of these things we now believe that historical phenomena are to be explained by the reactions and co-operations between the individuals, by the aggregation and sublimation of countless separate contributions, by the incorporation of the social energies in structures which exist and develop over and above the individuals. Sociology accordingly, in its relationships to the existing sciences, is a new *method*, an auxiliary to investigation, a means of approaching the phenomena of all these areas in a new way. This being the case, sociology is related to the older disciplines not otherwise than, in its time, *induction*, which, as a new principle of investigation, invaded all possible sciences, acclimated itself in each, and helped each to new solutions of the tasks within its field. Induction was not for that reason a special science, not to say an all-comprehending science. No more can these claims be urged upon like grounds for sociology. In so far as sociology rests its claims on the ground that man must be understood as a social being, and that society is the vehicle of all historical experience, it contains no *object* which is not already treated in one of the existing sciences. The actual situation is that sociology proposes only a *new way* for all these sciences, a method of science, which, for the very reason that it is applicable to the totality of the problems, is not a peculiar science in and of itself.

What then can the peculiar and new subject-matter (*Object*) be, the investigation of which constitutes sociology an independent and precisely delimited science? It is obvious that for such legitimation as a new science, it is not necessary that sociology should have discovered an object (*Gegenstand*) the existence of which had previously been unknown. Everything which we characterize as *object* in the most general sense, is a complex of definitions and relationships, each of which, impressed upon a plurality of objects, may become the subject-matter of a special science. Each science rests upon an abstraction, since it regards the totality of any given thing, which totality we can grasp as a unity through no one science—it regards this totality from one of its aspects, from the viewpoint of some particular concept. In antithesis with the totality of the thing and with things in general, each science grows through a decomposition of the unity and a corresponding division of labor, by virtue of which each thing is resolved into specific qualities and functions, after a concept is reached which is competent thus to resolve the thing into these factors and to grasp the latter according to methodological correlations, whenever they occur in the real things. Thus, for example, the linguistic facts, which we now combine as the material of comparative linguistic science, have for a long time occurred incidentally to phenomena which have been scientifically treated. That particular science had its origin with the discovery of the concept under which these facts, hitherto scattered in examples occurring in various languages, belong together in a unity and are governed by special laws. In similar fashion sociology, as a special science, might find its special object in the fact that it merely draws a new line through facts, which, as such, are quite well known. The only thing lacking might be the concept which now for the first time might be brought into action to make known the side of these facts lying along this line, and to display them as constituting, from the viewpoint of scientific method a unity, because of these newly systematized common relations. In presence of the highly complex facts of historical society, which cannot be interpreted from a single scientific viewpoint, the concepts *politics, economy, culture,* etc., beget such categories of cognition. It may be that these concepts combine certain parts of these facts, with elimination or merely accidental cooperation of the other parts, into a unique historical sequence. It may be that these concepts make intelligible the groupings of elements which, irrespective of the specific here and now, contain a timelessly necessary correlation. If now there is to be a sociology as a special science, the concept of *society,* as such, apart from the external aggregation of the phenomena, must subject the socio-historical data to a new abstraction and co-ordination. This must go to such an extent that certain peculiarities of the data already observed in other relations should be recognized as belonging together and consequently as constituting the subject-matter (*Objekte*) of a science.

Such a point of view results from an analysis of the idea of society, which may be characterized as a *discrimination between form and content of society.* We must accentuate the fact, however, that this is here properly only an analogy, for the sake of approximately designating the elements to be distinguished. This antithesis should be understood immediately in its peculiar sense, without prejudice to these provisional names from remoter meanings of the terms. I start then from the broadest conception of society, the conception which so far as possible disregards the conflicts about definitions; that is, I think of society as existing wherever several individuals are in reciprocal relationship. This reciprocity arises always from specific impulses, or by virtue of specific purposes. Erotic, religious, or merely associative impulses, purposes of defense or of attack, of play as well as of gain, of aid and instruction, and countless others bring it to pass that men enter into ways of being-together—relationships of acting for, with, against one another, in a correlation of conditions; that is, men exercise an influence upon these conditions of association and are influenced by them. These reactions signify that out of the individual bearers of those occasioning impulses and purposes a unity, that is, a "society," comes into being. For unity in the empirical sense is nothing other than reciprocity of elements. An organic body is a unity because its organs are in a relationship of more intimate intercharge of their energies than with any external being. A *state* is *one* because between its citizens the corresponding relationship of reciprocal influences exists. We could indeed not call the world *one* if each of its parts did not somehow influence every other, if anywhere the reciprocity of the influences, however mediated, were cut off. That unity, or socialization, may, according to the kind and degree of reciprocity, have very different gradations, from the ephemeral combination for a promenade to the family; from all relationships "at will," to membership in a state; from the temporary aggregation of the guests in a hotel to the intimate bond of a mediaeval guild. Everything now which is present in the individuals—the immediate concrete locations of all historical actuality—in the nature of impulse, interest, purpose, inclination, psychical adaptability, and movement of such sort that thereupon or therefrom occurs influence upon others, or the reception of influence from them—all this I designate as the content or the material, so to speak, of socialization. In and of themselves, these materials with which life is filled, these motivations which impel it, are not social in their nature. Neither hunger nor love, neither labor nor religiosity, neither the technique nor the functions and results of intelligence, as they are given immediately and in their strict sense, signify socialization. On the contrary, they constitute it only when they shape the isolated side-by-sideness of the individuals into definite forms of with-and-for-one-another, which belong under the general concept reciprocity. Socialization is thus the *form*, actualizing itself in countless various types, in which the individuals, on the basis of those interests—sensuous or ideal, momentary or permanent, conscious or unconscious, casually driving or purposefully leading—grow together into a unity, and within which these interests come to realization.

In every given social situation, content and societary form constitute a unified reality. A social form can no more attain existence detached from all content, than a spatial form can exist without a material of which it is the form. These are rather the actually inseparable elements of every social being and occurence—an interest, purpose, motive, and a form or manner of the reciprocity between the individuals through which, or in the shape of which, that content attains social reality.

That which constitutes "society" in every hitherto current sense of the term is evidently the thus indicated types of reciprocal influencing. Any collection of human beings whatsoever becomes "society," not by virtue of the fact that in each of the number there is a life-content which actuates the individual as such, but only when the vitality of these contents attains the form of reciprocal influencing. Only when an influence is exerted, whether immediately or through a third party, from one upon another, has a society come into existence in place of a mere spatial juxtaposition, or temporal contemporaneousness or succession of individuals. If, therefore, there is to be a science, the object of which is to be "society" and nothing else, it can investigate only these reciprocal influences, these kinds and forms of socialization. For everything else found within "society" and realized by means of it, and within its framework (*Rahmen*), is not "society" itself, but merely a content which builds or is built by this form of coexistence, and which indeed only together with "society" brings into existence the real structure, "society" in the wider and usual sense. That these two factors, inseparably united in reality, shall be separated in scientific abstraction, that the forms of reciprocity or socialization shall be brought methodologically under a unifying scientific viewpoint, in mental detachment from the contents through which alone they become socially actual—this seems to me the sole and the whole possibility of founding a special science of society as such. Only with such a science would the facts which we characterize as the socio-historical reality be actually projected upon the plane of the purely social.

. . . In the case of human associations which are the most unlike imaginable in purposes and in total meaning, we find nevertheless similar formal relationships between the individuals. Superiority and subordination, competition, imitation, division of labor, party structure, representation, inclusiveness toward the members and at the same time exclusiveness toward non-members, and countless similar variations are found, whether in a civic group or in a religious community, in a band of conspirators or an industrial organization, in an art school or in a family. However diverse, moreover, the interests may be from which the socializations arise, the *forms* in which they maintain their existence may nevertheless be similar. Then, second, that interest which is one and the same in *content*, may display itself in very diversely formed associatings. E. g., the economic interest realizes itself both through competition and through deliberate organization of the producer, now through detachment from other economic groups, now through attachment to them; the religious contents of life, while remaining identical in substance, demand now a free, now a centralized community form;

the interests which lie at the foundation of the relations of the sexes get their satisfaction in more varieties of family formations than can be enumerated; the pedagogical interest leads now to a despotic relation of teacher to pupil, now to individualistic reactions between teacher and each pupil, now to more collectivistic relations between the former and the totality of the latter. Just as the form in which the most diverse attempts occur may be identical, so the stuff may persist, while the associating of the individual which is the vehicle of this stuff may move in a variety of forms. Thereby, although in their objective concreteness stuff and form constitute an indissoluble unity of the social life, the facts furnish precisely that legitimation of the sociological problem which demands the identification, systematic arrangement, psychological explanation, and historical development of the pure forms of association.

This problem is in direct contrast with that in accordance with which the special social sciences have been hitherto created. The division of labor between them was determined entirely by the variety of the contents. National economy and church polity, the history of pedagogy or of morals, politics or theories of sexual relations, have divided the realm of the social phenomena among themselves so that a sociology which would comprehend the aggregate of these phenomena, with their interpenetrations of form and content, could prove itself to be nothing else than a correlation (*Zusammenfassung*) of these sciences. So long as the lines which we draw through historical reality, in order to divide it into separate regions of research, connect only those points which mark similar interest-contents—so long will this reality fail to afford any room for a special sociology. There is needed rather a line which, intersecting all those already drawn, detaches the pure fact of associating, in all its manifold forms, from its connection with the most various contents, and constitutes this fact its peculiar sphere. Sociology will thereby become a special science in the same sense, in spite of the differences of methods and results, in which epistemology is a special science. The latter has abstracted the categories or functions of cognition as such from the multitude of cognitions of specific things. Sociology belongs in the type of sciences whose special character consists not in the fact that their object belongs with others under a higher order of generalization (like classical philology and Germanistics, or optics and acoustics), but rather in that it brings a whole realm of objects under a particular point of view. Not its object but its manner of contemplation, the peculiar abstraction which it performs, differentiates it from the other historico-social sciences.

The concept "society" covers two meanings which, for scientific treatment, must be kept strictly distinct. "Society" is, first, the complex of associated individuals, the socially formed human material, as the full historical reality has shaped it. "Society" is, second, the sum of those forms of relationship by virtue of which individuals are changed into "society" in the former sense. . . . If we speak of social sciences according to the former sense, their object is everything which occurs in and with society. Social science in the latter sense has as its matter the forces (*sic*), relationships, and forms, through which human beings arrange themselves in association, which thus in independent exhibition (*in selbstständiger Darstellung*) constitute "society" *sensu strictissimo*. . . . [Though] history and the laws of the so-occurring aggregated structure are the affair of social science (*Gesellschaftswissenschaft*) in the wider sense, yet since social science has already split up into special social sciences, there remains for a sociology in the more restricted sense, i.e., in the sense which proposes a special task, nothing (*sic!*) but consideration of the abstracted forms, which do not so much bring socialization to pass as more strictly speaking *are* socialization (*Vergesellschaftung*); "society," in the sense which sociology can apply, is consequently either the abstract general concept for these forms, the genus of which they are the species, or the sum of the same in operation at a given time. It follows further from this concept that a given assortment of individuals may be a society in a greater or a lesser degree. With each new growth of synthetic formations, which each construction of party groups, with each combination for common work, or in common feeling and thinking, with each more decisive assignment of serving and ruling, with each convivial meal, with each self-adornment to impress others, the same group becomes more "society" than it was before. There is never in existence "society" in an absolute sense, i.e., of such a sort that all these particular phenomena would occur in accordance with "society" as a presupposition; for there is no such thing as reciprocal influencing in an absolute sense, but merely particular species of the same. With the occurence of these species society also puts in an appearance. They are, however, neither the cause nor the consequence of society. *They are themselves immediately society.*

. . . The like is the case with the facts of socialization. That people influence one another, that the one does or suffers something, manifests a being or a becoming, because others are there and express themselves, act, or feel—all that is of course psychical phenomena, and the historical occurrence of each several case of it is to be understood only through psychological repetition, through the plausibility of psychological series, through the interpretation of the externally observable by means of psychological categories. But a peculiar scientific purpose may leave this psychic occurrence as such quite out of sight, and it may give its attention to the contents of the same as they set themselves in order under the concept of socialization. Suppose, for example, it is made out that the relation of a stronger to a weaker person, which has the form of *primus inter pares*, tends to become a possession of absolute power and gradually to eliminate the elements of equality. Although in historical reality this is a psychical occurrence, from the sociological viewpoint we are now interested only in the questions, How do the various stadia of the super- and sub-ordination in this case follow one another? To what degree is a super-ordination in a given relationship compatible with equality in other particulars? Beginning with what degree of superiority does the super-ordination wholly destroy the equality? Does the question of combination, the possibility of co-operation, press more urgently in the earlier or the later stages of such development? Or, it is discovered that enmities are most bitter when they arise on the basis of a previous or still somehow appreciable community and coherence, as feuds between blood relatives have been called the hottest hatreds. As an occurrence, this can be made intelligible or even discribed only psychologically; but considered as a sociological formation, the course of events in the consciousness of each of two individuals is not of interest in itself, but rather the synopsis of the two under the category of union and disunion—how far the relation between two individuals or parties may include hostility and attachment, and still give to the whole relation the shading of the latter, and when will it take on the coloring of the former; what sorts of attachment, as recollection or as ineffaceable instinct, furnish the means for more cruel, deeper wounding injury than is possible in the case of alienation from the beginning; in brief, how is that observation to be represented as realization of forms of relationship between people; what peculiar combination of the social categories does it present? That is the present point, although the singular or typical description of the occurrence itself must always be solely psychological.

2

Basic Concepts

4

AUGUSTE COMTE

On the Positivistic Approach to Society

Isidore Auguste Marie Francois Xavier Comte (1798–1857) is generally spoken of as the Father of Sociology.[1] *Beginning with a conception of the possibility of a* social physics *(a name he found had already been used by the Belgian scientist Quetelet to describe a statistical work), Comte christened his new positivistic approach to the social world* sociology. *Comte conceived of philosophy as going through three stages, beginning with a* theological *state in which things were interpreted supernaturally, followed by a* metaphysical *state in which barren abstractions were used to explain phenomena, culminating in a* positivistic *state in which reasoning and observation were combined as the means towards knowledge. All aspects of the search for knowledge went through these progressive stages. Comte believed that mankind was on the threshold of the Positive Age, an era in which all human understanding would be based on the positivistic approach to reality. Comte argued that this approach, which had already proved so useful in dealing with the natural (that is, the physical) world, should now be applied to investigation of society and its laws.*[2]

Bibliographical Notes

1. *Comte's principal works include:* The Positive Philosophy *in six volumes (1830–1842);* A Discourse on the Positive Spirit *(1844);* A General View of Positivism *(1848);* System of Positive Polity, *in four volumes (1851–1854);* The Catechism of Positive Religion *(1852);* Appeal to Conservatives *(1855); and* Religion of Humanity: Subjective Synthesis or Universal System of the Conceptions Adapted to the

Reprinted from Auguste Comte, *The Positive Philosophy* (translated and condensed by Harriet Martineau), Vol. 2 (New York: D. Appleton & Co., 1854), 68–74 and 95–110.

Normal State of Humanity (1856). *Comte's most relevant writings for today have recently been edited in: George Simpson (ed.),* Auguste Comte: Sire of Sociology *(New York: Thomas Y. Crowell, 1969).*

2. *For an exceptionally good brief but well-integrated sketch of Comte's life and work, see Rene König, "Comte, Auguste," in* International Encyclopedia of the Social Sciences, *Vol. 3 (New York: Macmillan and Free Press, 1968), pp. 201–206. See also: George Simpson, "Introduction," in George Simpson (ed.),* Auguste Comte: Sire of Sociology *(New York: Thomas Y. Crowell, 1969), pp. 1–23; and Harry Elmer Barnes, "The Social and Political Philosophy of Auguste Comte: Positivist Utopia and the Religion of Humanity," in his* An Introduction to the History of Sociology *(Chicago: University of Chicago Press, 1948), pp. 81–109.*

If we look with a philosophical eye upon the present state of social science, we cannot but recognize in it the combination of all the features of that theologico-metaphysical infancy which all the other sciences have had to pass through. . . .

If we contemplate the positive spirit in its relation to scientific conception . . . we shall find that this philosophy is distinguished from the theologico-metaphysical by its tendency to render relative the ideas which were at first absolute. This inevitable passage from the absolute to the relative is one of the most important philosophical results of each of the intellectual revolutions which has carried on every kind of speculation from the theological or metaphysical to the scientific state. In a scientific view, this contrast between the relative and the absolute may be regarded as the most decisive manifestation of the antipathy between the modern philosophy and the ancient.

Men were long in learning that Man's power of modifying phenomena can result only from his knowledge of their natural laws; and in the infancy of each science, they believed themselves able to exert unbounded influence over the phenomena of that science . . . We see the metaphysical school . . . attributing observed events to chance, and sometimes, when that method is too obviously absurd, exaggerating ridiculously the influence of the individual mind upon the course of human affairs . . . It represents the social action of Man to be indefinite and arbitrary, as was once thought in regard to biological, chemical, physical, and even astronomical phenomenona, in the earlier stages of their respective sciences . . . There is no chance of order and agreement but in subjecting social phenomena, like all others, to invariable natural laws, which shall, as a whole, prescribe for each period, with entire certainty, the limits and character of political action—in other words, introducing into the study of social phenomena the same positive spirit which has regenerated every other branch of human speculation. Such a procedure is the true scientific basis of human dignity; as the chief tendencies of man's nature thus acquire a solemn character of authority which must be always respected by rational legislation; whereas the existing belief in the indefinite power of political combinations, which seems at first to exalt the importance of Man, issues in attributing to him a sort of social automatism passively directed by some supremacy of either Providence or the human ruler . . .

The last of the preliminary considerations that we have to review is that of the scientific prevision of phenomena, which, as the test of true science, includes all the rest. We have to contemplate social phenomena as susceptible of prevision, like all other classes, within the limits of exactness compatible with their higher complexity. Comprehending the three characteristics . . . we have been examining, prevision of social phenomena supposes first, that we have abandoned the region of metaphysical idealities, to assume the ground of observed realities by a systematic subordination of imagination to observation; secondly, that political conceptions have ceased to be absolute, and have become relative to the variable state of civilization, so that theories, following the natural course of facts, may admit of our foreseeing them; and, thirdly, that permanent political action is limited by determinate laws, since if social events were always exposed to disturbance by the accidental intervention of the legislator, human or divine, no scientific prevision of them would be possible. Thus, we may concentrate the conditions of the spirit of positive social philosophy on this one great attribute of scientific prevision . . .

The next step . . . is to examine . . . the means of investigation proper to Social Science . . . We may expect to find in Sociology a more varied and developed system of resources than in any other, in proportion to the complexity of the phenomena, while yet this extension of means does not compensate for the increased imperfection arising from the intricacy. The extension of the means is also more difficult to verify than in any prior case from the novelty of the subject; and I can scarcely hope that such a sketch as I must present here will command such confidence as will arise when a complete survey of the science shall have confirmed what I now offer.

As Social Physics assumes a place in the hierarchy of sciences after all the rest and therefore dependent on them, its means of investigation must be of two kinds: those which arise from the connection of sociology with the other sciences; and these last, though indirect, are as indispensable as the first. I shall review . . . the direct resources of the science.

Very imperfect and even vicious notions prevail at present as to what Observation can be and can effect in Social Science. The chaotic state of doctrine of the last century has extended to Method; and amidst our intellectual disorganization, difficulties have been magnified; precautionary methods, experimental and rational, have been broken up; and even the possibility of obtaining social knowledge by observation has been dogmatically denied; but if the sophisms put forth on this subject were true, they would destroy the certainty, not only of social science, but of all the simpler and more perfect ones that have gone before. The ground of doubt assigned is the uncertainty of human testimony; but all the sciences, up to the most simple, require proofs of testimony: that is, in the elaboration of the most positive theories, we have to admit observations which could not be directly made, nor even repeated, by those who use them, and the reality of which rests only on the faithful testimony of the original investigators; there being nothing in this to prevent the use of such proofs, in concurrence with immediate observations. In Astronomy, such a method is obviously necessary; it is equally, though less obviously, necessary even in mathematics; and, of course, much more evidently in the case of the more complex sciences. How could any science emerge from the nascent state—how could there be any organization of intellectual labor, even if research were restricted to the utmost, if every one rejected all observations but his own? The stoutest advocates of historical skepticism do not go so far as to advocate this. It is only in the case of social phenomena that the paradox is proposed; and it is made use of there because it is one of the weapons of the philosophical arsenal which the revolutionary metaphysical doctrine constructed for the intellectual overthrow of the ancient political system. The next great hindrance to the use of observation is the empiricism which is introduced into it by those who, in the name of impartiality, would interdict the use of any theory whatever. No logical dogma could be more thoroughly irreconcilable with the spirit of the positive philosophy, or with its special character in regard to the study of social phenomena, than this. No real observation of any kind of phenomena is possible, except in as far as it is first directed, and finally interpreted, by some theory: and it was this logical need which, in the infancy of human reason, occasioned the rise of theological philosophy, as we shall see in the course of our historical survey. The positive philosophy does not dissolve this obligation, but, on the contrary, extends and fulfils it more and more, the further the relations of phenomena are multiplied and perfected by it. Hence it is clear that, scientifically speaking, all isolated, empirical observation is idle, and even radically uncertain; that science can use only those observations which are connected, at least hypothetically, with some law; that it is such a connection which makes the chief difference between scientific and popular observation, embracing the same facts, but contemplating them from different points of view: and that observations empirically conducted can at most supply provisional materials, which must usually undergo an ulterior revision. The rational method of observation becomes more necessary in proportion to the complexity of the phenomena, amid which the observer would not know what he ought to look at in the facts before his eyes, but for the guidance of a preparatory theory; and thus it is that by the connection of foregoing facts we learn to see the facts that follow. This is undisputed with regard to astronomical, physical, and chemical research, and in every branch of biological study, in which good observation of its highly complex phenomena is still very rare, precisely because its positive theories are very imperfect. Carrying on the analogy, it is evident that in the corresponding divisions, statical and dynamical, of social science, there is more need than anywhere else of theories which shall scientifically connect the facts that are happening with those that have happened: and the more we reflect, the more distinctly we shall see that in proportion as known facts are mutually connected we shall be better able not only to estimate, but to perceive those which are yet unexplored. I am not blind to the vast difficulty which this requisition imposes on the institution of positive sociology—obliging us to create at once, so to speak, observations and laws, on account of their indispensable connection, placing us in a sort of vicious circle, from which we can issue only by employing in the first instance materials which are badly elaborated, and doctrines which are ill-conceived. How I may succeed in a task so difficult and delicate, we shall see . . . ; but, however that may be, it is clear that it is the absence of any positive theory which at present renders social observations so vague and incoherent. There can never be any lack of facts; for in this case even more than in others, it is the commonest sort of facts that are most important, whatever the collectors of secret anecdotes may think; but, though we are steeped to the lips in them, we can make no use of them, nor even be aware of them, for want of speculative guidance in examining them. The statical observation of a crowd of phenomena can not take place without some notion, however elementary, of the laws of social interconnection: and dynamical facts could have no fixed direction if they were not attached, at least by a provisional hypothesis, to the laws of social development. The positive philosophy is very far from discouraging historical or any other erudition; but the precious night-watchings, now so lost in the laborious acquisition of a conscientious but barren learning, may be made available by it for the constitution of true social science, and the increased honor of the earnest minds that are devoted to it. The new philosophy will supply fresh and nobler subjects, unhoped-for insight, a loftier aim, and therefore a higher scientific dignity. It will discard none but aimless labors, without principle and without character; as in Physics, there is no room for compilations of empirical observations; and at the same time, philosophy will render justice to the zeal of students of a past generation, who, destitute of the favorable guidance which we, of this day, enjoy, followed up their laborious historical researches with an instinctive perseverance, and in spite of the superficial disdain of the philosophers of the time. No doubt, the same danger attends research here as elsewhere: the danger that, from the continuous use of scientific theories, the observer may sometimes pervert facts, by erroneously supposing them to verify some ill-grounded speculative prejudices of his own. But we have the same guard here as elsewhere—in the further extension of the science: and the case would not be improved by a recurrence to empirical methods, which would be merely leaving theories that may be misapplied but can always be rectified, for imaginary notions which can not be substantiated at all. Our feeble reason may often fail in the application of positive theories; but at least they transfer us from the domain of imagination to that of reality, and expose us infinitely less than any other kind of doctrine to the danger of seeing in facts that which is not.

It is now clear that Social Science requires, more than any other, the subordination of Observation to the statical and dynamical laws of phenomena. No social fact can have any scientific meaning till it is connected with some other social fact; without which connection it remains a mere anecdote, involving no rational utility. This condition so far increases the immediate difficulty that good observers will be rare at first, though more abundant than ever as the science expands; and here we meet with another confirmation of what I said at the outset . . . —that the formation of social theories should be confided only to the best organized minds, prepared by the most rational training. Explored by such minds, according to rational views of co-existence and succession, social phenomena no doubt admit of much more varied and extensive means of investigation than phenomena of less complexity. In this view, it is not only the immediate inspection or direct description of events that affords useful means of positive exploration; but the consideration of apparently insignificant customs, the appreciation of various kinds of monuments, the analysis and comparison of languages, and a multitude of other resources. In short, a mind suitably trained becomes able by exercise to convert almost all impressions from the events of life into sociological indications, when once the connection of all indications with the leading ideas of the science is understood. This is a facility afforded by the mutual relation of the various aspects of society, which may partly compensate for the difficulty caused by that mutual connection: if it renders observation more difficult, it affords more means for its prosecution.

It might be supposed beforehand that the second method of investigation, Experiment, must be wholly inapplicable in Social Science; but we shall find that the science is not entirely deprived of this resource, though it must be one of inferior value. We must remember . . . that there are two kinds of experimentation—the direct and the indirect: and that it is not necessary to the philosophical character of this method that the circumstances of the phenomenon in question should be, as is vulgarly supposed in the learned world, artificially instituted. Whether the case be natural or factitious, experimentation takes place whenever the regular course of the phenomenon is interfered with in any determinate manner. The spontaneous nature of the alteration has no effect on the scientific value of the case, if the elements are known. It is in this sense that experimentation is possible in Sociology. If direct experimentation had become too difficult amidst the complexities of biology, it may well be considered impossible in Social Science. Any artificial disturbance of any social element must affect all the rest, according to the laws both of co-existence and succession; and the experiment would therefore, if it could be instituted at all, be deprived of all scientific value, through the impossibility of isolating either the conditions or the results of the phenomenon. But we saw . . . that pathological cases are the true scientific equivalent of pure experimentation, and why. The same reasons apply, with even more force, to sociological researches. In them, pathological analysis consists in the examination of cases, unhappily too common, in which the natural laws, either of harmony or of succession, are disturbed by any causes, special or general, accidental or transient; as in revolutionary times especially; and above all, in our own. These disturbances are, in the social body, exactly analogous to diseases in the individual organism: and I have no doubt whatever that the analogy will be more evident (allowance being made for the unequal complexity of the organisms) the deeper the investigation goes. In both cases it is . . . a noble use to make of our reason, to disclose the real laws of our nature, individual or social, by the analysis of its sufferings. But if the method is imperfectly instituted in regard to biological questions, much more faulty must it be in regard to the phenomena of Social Science, for want even of the rational conceptions to which they are to be referred. We see the most disastrous political experiments for ever renewed, with only some insignificant and irrational modifications, though their first operation should have fully satisfied us of the uselessness and danger of the expedients proposed. Without forgetting how much is ascribable to the influence of human passions, we must remember that the deficiency of an authoritative rational analysis is one of the main causes of the barrenness imputed to social experiments, the course of which would become much more instructive if it were better observed. The great natural laws exist and act in all conditions of the organism; for as . . . in the case of biology, it is an error to suppose that they are violated or suspended in the case of disease: and we are therefore justified in drawing our conclusions, with due caution, from the scientific analysis of disturbance to the positive theory of normal existence. This is the nature and character of the indirect experimentaion which discloses the real economy of the social body in a more marked manner than simple observation could do. It is applicable to all orders of sociological research, whether relating to existence or to movement, and regarded under any aspect whatever, physical, intellectual, moral or political; and to all degrees of the social evolution, from which, unhappily, disturbances have never been absent. As for its present extension, no one can venture to offer any statement of it, because it has never been duly applied in any investigation in political philosophy; and it can become customary only by the institution of the new science which I am endeavoring to establish. But I could not omit this notice of it, as one of the means of investigation proper to social science.

As for the third of those methods, Camparison, the reader must bear in mind the explanations offered, in our survey of biological philosophy, of the reasons why the comparative method must prevail in all studies of which the living organism is the subject; and the more remarkably, in proportion to the rank of the organism. The same considerations apply in the present case, in a more conspicuous degree; and I may leave it to the reader to make the application, merely pointing out the chief differences which distinguish the use of the comparative method in sociological inquiries.

It is a very irrational disdain which makes us object to all comparison between human society and the social state of the lower animals. This unphilosophical pride arose out of the protracted influence of the theologico-metaphysical philosophy; and it will be corrected by the positive philosophy, when we better understand and can estimate the social state of the higher orders of mammifers, for instance. We have seen how important is the study of individual life, in regard to intellectual and moral phenomena—of which social phenomena are the natural result and complement. There was once the same blindness to the importance of the procedure in this case as now in the other; and as it has given way in the one case, so it will in the other. The chief defect in the kind of sociological comparison that we want is that it is limited to statical considerations; whereas the dynamical are, at the present time, the preponderant and direct subject of science. The restriction results from the social state of animals being, though not so stationary as we are apt to suppose, yet suceptible only of extremely small variations, in no way comparable to the continued progression of humanity in its feeblest days. But there is no doubt of the scientific utility of such a comparison, in the statical province, where it characterizes the elementary laws of social interconnection, by exhibiting their action in the most imperfect state of society, so as even to suggest useful inductions in regard to human society. There can not be a stronger evidence of the natural character of the chief social relations, which some people fancy that they can transform at pleasure. Such sophists will cease to regard the great ties of the human family as factitious and arbitrary when they find them existing, with the same essential characteristics, among the animals, and more conspicuously, the nearer the organisms approach to the human type. In brief, in all that part of sociology which is almost one with intellectual and moral biology, or with the natural history of Man; in all that relates to the first germs of the social relations, and the first institutions which were founded by the unity of the family or the tribe, there is not only great scientific advantage, but real philosophical necessity for employing the rational comparison of human with other animal societies. Perhaps it might even be desirable not to confine the comparison to societies which present a character of voluntary cooperation, in analogy to the human. They must always rank first in importance: but the scientific spirit, extending the process to its final logical term, might find some advantage in examining those strange associations, proper to the inferior animals, in which an involuntary cooperation results from an indissoluble organic union, either by simple adhesion or real continuity. If the science gained nothing by this extension, the method would. And there is nothing that can compare with such an habitual scientific comparison for the great service of casting out the absolute spirit which is the chief vice of political philosophy. It appears to me, moreover, that, in a practical view, the insolent pride which induces some ranks of society to suppose themselves as, in a manner, of another species than the rest of mankind, is in close affinity with the irrational disdain that repudiates all comparison between human and other animal nature. However all this may be, these considerations apply only to a methodical and special treatment of social philosophy. Here, where I can offer only the first conception of the science, in which dynamical considerations must prevail, it is evident that I can make little use of the kind of comparison; and this makes it all the more necessary to point it out, lest its omission should occasion such scientific inconveniences as I have just indicated. The commonest logical procedures are generally so characterized by their very application, that nothing more of a preliminary nature is needed than the simplest examination of their fundamental properties.

To indicate the order of importance of the forms of society which are to be studied by the Comparative Method, I begin with the chief method, which consists in a comparison of the different coexisting states of human society on the various parts of the earth's surface—those states being completely independent of each other. By this method, the different stages of evolution may all be observed at once. Though the progression is single and uniform, in regard to the whole race, some very considerable and very various populations have, from causes which are little understood, attained extremely unequal degrees of development, so that the former states of the most civilized nations are now to be seen, amid some partial differences, among contemporary populations inhabiting different parts of the globe. In its relation to Observation, this kind of comparison offers the advantage of being applicable both to statical and dynamical inquiries, verifying the laws of both, and even furnishing occasionally valuable direct inductions in regard to both. In the second place, it exhibits all possible degrees of social evolution to our immediate observation. From the wretched inhabitants of Tierra del Fuego to the most advanced nations of western

Europe, there is no social grade which is not extant in some points of the globe, and usually in localities which are clearly apart. We shall find that some interesting secondary phases of social development, of which the history of civilization leaves no perceptible traces, can be known only by this comparative method of study; and these are not, as might be supposed, the lowest degrees of evolution, which every one admits can be investigated in no other way. And between the great historical aspects, there are numerous intermediate states which must be observed thus, if at all. This second part of the comparative method verifies the indications afforded by historical analysis, and fills up the gaps it leaves: and nothing can be more rational than the method, as it rests upon the established principle that the development of the human mind is uniform in the midst of all diversities of climate, and even of race; such diversities having no effect upon anything more than the rate of progress. But we must beware of the scientific dangers attending the process of comparison by this method. For instance, it can give us no idea of the order of succession, as it presents all the states of development as coexisting: so that, if the order of development were not established by other methods, this one would infallibly mislead us. And again, if we were not misled as to the order, there is nothing in this method which discloses the filiation of the different systems of society; a matter in which the most distinguished philosophers have been mistaken in various ways and degrees. Again, there is the danger of mistaking modifications for primary phases; as when social differences have been ascribed to the political influence of climate, instead of that inequality of evolution which is the real cause. Sometimes, but more rarely, the mistake is the other way. Indeed, there is nothing in the matter that can show which of two cases presents the diversity that is observed. We are in danger of the same mistake in regard to races; for, as the sociological comparison is instituted between peoples of different races, we are liable to confound the effects of race and of the social period. Again, climate comes in to offer a third source of interpretation of comparative phenomena, sometimes agreeing with, and sometimes contradicting the two others; thus multiplying the chances of error, and rendering the analysis which looked so promising almost impracticable. Here, again, we see the indispensable necessity of keeping in view the positive conception of human development as a whole. By this alone can we be preserved from such errors as I have referred to, and enriched by any genuine results of analysis. We see how absurd in theory and dangerous in practice are the notions and declamations of the empirical school, and of the enemies of all social speculation: for it is precisely in proportion to their elevation and generality that the ideas of positive social philosophy become real and effective—an illusion and uselessness belonging to conceptions which are too narrow and too special, in the departments either of science or of reasoning. But it is a consequence from these last considerations that this first sketch of sociological science, with the means of investigation that belong to it, rests immediately upon the primary use of a new method of observation, which is so appropriate to the nature of the phenomena as to be exempt from the dangers inherent in the others. This last portion of the comparative method is the Historical Method, properly so called; and it is the only basis on which the system of political logic can rest.

The historical comparison of the consecutive states of humanity is not only the chief scientific device of the new political philosophy. Its rational development constitutes the substratum of the science, in whatever is essential to it. It is this which distinguishes it thoroughly from biological science . . . The positive principle of this separation results from the necessary influence of human generations upon the generations that follow, accumulating continuously till it constitutes the preponderating consideration in the direct study of social development. As long as this preponderance is not directly recognised, the positive study of humanity must appear a simple prolongation of the natural history of Man: but this scientific character, suitable enough to the earlier generations, disappears in the course of the social evolution, and assumes at length a wholly new aspect, proper to sociological science, in which historical considerations are of immediate importance. And this preponderant use of the historical method gives its philosophical character to sociology in a logical as well as a scientific sense. By the creation of this new department of the comparative method, sociology confers a benefit on the whole of natural philosophy; because the positive method is thus completed and perfected, in a manner which, for scientific importance, is almost beyond our estimate. What we can now comprehend is that the historical method verifies and applies, in the largest way, that chief quality of sociological science—its proceeding from the whole to the parts. Without this permanent condition of social study, all historical labor would degenerate into being a mere compilation of provisional materials. As it is in their development, especially, that the various social elements are interconnected and inseparable, it is clear that any partial filiation must be essentially untrue. Where, for instance, is the use of any exclusive history of any one science or art, unless meaning is given to it by first connecting it with the study of human progress generally? It is the same in every direction, and especially with regard to political history, as it is called; as if any history could be other than political, more or less! The prevailing tendency to speciality in study would reduce history to a mere accumulation of unconnected delineations, in which all idea of the true filiation of events would be lost amid the mass of confused descriptions. If the historical comparisons of the different periods of civilization are to have any scientific character, they must be referred to the general social evolution: and it is only thus that we can obtain the guiding ideas by which the special studies themselves must be directed.

In a practical view, it is evident that the preponderance of the historical method tends to develop the social sentiment, by giving us an immediate interest in even the earliest experiences of our race, through the influence that they exercised over the evolution of our own civilization. As Condorcet observed, no enlightened man can think of the battles of Marathon and Salamis without perceiving the importance of their consequences to the race at large. This kind of feeling should, when we are treating of science, be carefully distinguished from the sympathetic interest which is awakened by all delineations of human life—in fiction as well as in history. The sentiment I refer to is deeper, because in some sort personal; and more reflective, because it results from scientific conviction. It can not be excited by popular history in a descriptive form; but only by positive history, regarded as a true science, and exhibiting the events of human experience in co-ordinated series which manifest their own graduated connection. This new form of the social sentiment must at first be the privilege of the choice few; but it will be extended, somewhat weakened in force, to the whole of society, in proportion as the general results of social physics become sufficiently popular. It will fulfill the most obvious and elementary idea of the habitual connection between individuals and contemporary nations, by showing that the successive generations of men concur in a final end, which requires the determinate participation of each and all. This rational disposition to regard men of all times as fellow-workers is as yet visible in the case of only the most advanced sciences. By the philosophical preponderance of the historical method, it will be extended to all the aspects of human life, so as to sustain, in a reflective temper, that respect for our ancestors which is indispensable to a sound state of society, and so deeply disturbed at present by the metaphysical philosophy.

As for the course to be pursued by this method—it appears to me that its spirit consists in the rational use of social series; that is, in a successive estimate of the different states of humanity which shall show the growth of each disposition, physical, intellectual, moral, or political, combined with the decline of the opposite disposition, whence we may obtain a scientific prevision of the final ascendency of the one and extinction of the other—care being taken to frame our conclusions according to the laws of human development. A considerable accuracy of prevision may thus be obtained, for any determinate period, and with any particular view; as historical analysis will indicate the direction of modifications, even in the most disturbed times. And it is worth noticing that the prevision will be nearest the truth in proportion as the phenomena in question are more important and more general; because then continuous causes are predominant in the social movement; and disturbances have less power. From these first general aspects, the same rational certainty may extend to secondary and special aspects, through their statical relations with the first; and thus we may obtain conclusions sufficiently accurate for the application of principles.

If we desire to familiarize ourselves with this historical method, we must employ it first upon the past, by endeavoring to deduce every well-known historical situation from the whole series of its antecedents. In every science we must have learned to predict the past, so to speak, before we can predict the future; because the first use of the observed relations among fulfilled facts is to teach us by the anterior succession what the future succession will be. No examination of facts can explain our existing state to us, if we have not ascertained, by historical study, the value of the elements at work; and thus it is in vain that statesmen insist on the necessity of political observation, while they look no further than the present, or a very recent past. The present is, by itself, purely misleading, because it is impossible to avoid confounding principal with secondary facts, exalting conspicuous transient manifestations over fundamental tendencies, which are generally very quiet; and above all, supposing those powers, institutions, and doctrines, to be in the ascendant, which are, in fact, in their decline. It is clear that the only adequate corrective of all this is a philosophical understanding of the past; that the comparison can not be decisive unless it embraces the whole of the past; and that the sooner we stop, in travelling up the vista of time, the more serious will be the mistakes we fall into. Before our very eyes, we see statesmen going no farther back than the last century, to obtain an explanation of the confusion in which we are living; the most abstract of politicians may take in the preceding century, but the philosophers themselves hardly venture beyond the sixteenth; so that those who are striving to find the issue of the revolutionary period have actually no conception of it as a whole, though that whole is itself only a transient phase of the general social movement.

The most perfect methods may, however, be rendered deceptive by misuse: and this we must bear in mind. We have seen that mathematical analysis itself may betray us into substituting signs for idea, and that it conceals inanity of conception under an imposing verbiage. The difficulty in the case of the historical method in sociology is in applying it, on account of the extreme complexity of the materials we have to deal with. But for this, the method would be entirely safe. The chief danger is of our supposing a continuous decrease to indicate a final extinction, or the reverse; as in mathematics it is a common sophism to confound continuous variations, more or less, with unlimited variations. To take a strange and very marked example: if we consider that part of social development which relates to human food, we can not but observe that men take less food as they advance in civilization. If we compare savage with more civilized peoples, in the Homeric poems or in the narratives of travellers, or compare country with town life, or any generation with the one that went before, we shall find this curious result. . . . The laws of individual human nature aid in the result by making intellectual and moral action more preponderant as Man becomes more civilized. The fact is thus established, both by the experimental and the logical way. Yet nobody supposes that men will ultimately cease to eat. In this case, the absurdity saves us from a false conclusion; but in other cases, the complexity disguises much error in the experiment and the reasoning. In the above instance, we must resort to the laws of our nature for that verification which, taken all together, they afford to our sociological analysis. As the social phenomenon, taken as a whole, is simply a development of humanity, without any real creation of faculties, all social manifestations must be found, if only in their germ, in the primitive type which biology constructed by anticipation for sociology. Thus every law of social succession disclosed by the historical method must be unquestionably connected, directly or indirectly, with the positive theory of human nature; and all inductions which can not stand this test will prove to be illusory, through some sort of insufficiency in the observations on which they are grounded. The main scientific strength of sociological demonstrations must ever lie in the accordance between the conclusions of historical analysis and the preparatory conceptions of the biological theory. And thus we find, look where we will a confirmation of that chief intellectual character of the new science—the philosophical preponderance of the spirit of the whole over the spirit of detail.

This method ranks, in sociological science, with that of zoological comparison in the study of individual life; . . . the succession of social states exactly corresponds, in a scientific sense, with the gradation of organisms in biology; and the social series, once clearly established, must be as real and as useful as the animal series. When the method has been used long enough to disclose its properties, I am disposed to think that it will be regarded as so very marked a modification of positive research as to deserve a separate place; so that, in addition to Observation, properly so called, Experiment, and Comparison, we shall have the Historical Method, as a fourth and final mode of the art of observing. It will be derived, according to the usual course, from the mode which immediately precedes it: and it will be applied to the analysis of the most complex phenomena.

I must be allowed to point out that the new political philosophy, sanctioning the old leadings of popular reason, restores to History all its scientific rights as a basis of wise social speculation, after the metaphysical philosophy had striven to induce us to discard all large consideration of the past. In the foregoing departments of natural philosophy we have seen that the positive spirit, instead of being disturbing in its tendencies, is remarkable for confirming, in the essential parts of every science, the inestimable intuitions of popular good sense; of which indeed science is merely a systematic prolongation, and which a barren metaphysical philosophy alone could despise. In this case, so far from restricting the influence which human reason has ever attributed to history in political combinations, the new social philosophy increases it, radically and eminently. It asks from history something more than counsel and instruction to perfect conceptions which are derived from another source: it seeks its own general direction, through the whole system of historical conclusions.

5

ÉMILE DURKHEIM

On Social Facts

Émile Durkheim (1858–1917), the great French sociologist, has, along with Weber, been one of the few European sociologists whose influence has permeated nearly all of contemporary American sociological thought.[1] *Durkheim followed Auguste Comte in his positivistic emphasis on empiricism and the importance of the group as a determining force in human activities. The cornerstone of Durkheim's thought was his sociological realism, the belief in the ultimate social reality of the group rather than the individual. In contrast to the individualistic nominalism found in the formulations of other theorists (e.g., Herbert Spencer), Durkheim argued for the methodological equation of social with physical "facts" (the modern equivalent of "facts" is "variables"). Further, Durkheim argued that social facts were not reducible to individual facts; thus social facts could not be explained by individual facts. Sociology was the study of such irreducible social facts and therefore could not be considered simply a different form of psychology.*

Today, few sociologists would completely agree with Durkheim. However, many would concur that social variables *can be regarded as* real *in the same sense as physical variables are real; thus, a social group is just as valid a scientific variable as an atom (neither one of which anyone has ever actually "seen").*[2] *It also seems clear that many social variables are not reducible to psychological ones. For example, a social* role *is not the property of a single actor, it is essentially defined as a characteristic within a system of social actors. Most contemporary sociologists, however, are far from wholeheartedly accepting Durkheim's argument that* all *social facts can be explained only by other social*

---

facts.[3] *Witness the great increase in the number of social psychologists within sociology, all of whom argue that explanations of social events can be derived from an examination of the interaction of social and psychological variables.*

Even the minimum Durkheimian belief that social and physical facts can be methodologically equated is not universally accepted within the field of sociology. Though today his position appears to be dominant in the discipline, many sociologists have argued that social facts are qualitatively different from physical facts owing to what Florian Znaniecki called the "humanistic coefficient." Therefore, they contend, there are radical differences between the social and physical sciences.[4] *These dissenting thinkers emphasize the importance of* understanding *the psychological motives and views of the social actors involved; their concern is centered upon the mediating processes of* meanings *of social action for the actors rather than upon the social actions themselves. In effect, however, their arguments are largely philosophical. They deal with what the goals of science* should *be (in this case, whether it ought to aim for a formal scientific explanation of a deductive variety or for a subjective understanding of the phenomena in question). In actual practice, most sociologists have followed Durkheim in treating social phenomena in a manner patterned after that of the natural sciences, using behavioristic and experimental methods, with frequent explanatory success. The method may be limited, as the critics have argued, but it has thus far proven fruitful. The exact limitations of the Durkheimian approach to social facts, therefore, will have to be discovered in the course of future investigations.*

Bibliographical Notes

1. Durkheim's major works (the titles are given in their English translations) include: The Division of Labor in Society *(1893),* The Rules of Sociological Method *(1895),* Suicide *(1897),* The Elementary Forms of Religious Life *(1915),* Education and Sociology *(1922),* Sociology and Philosophy *(1924), and* Professional Ethics and Civic Morals *(1950). Excellent critical secondary works on Durkheim include: Harry Alpert,* Émile Durkheim and His Sociology *(New York: Columbia University Press, 1939); Robert A. Nisbet (including selected essays by Durkheim),* Émile Durkheim *(Englewood Cliffs, N.J.: Prentice-Hall, 1965); Kurt H. Wolff (ed.),* Essays on Sociology and

Philosophy (*New York: Harper Torchbook, 1964*); *and Robert Bierstedt,* Émile Durkheim (*New York: Dell, 1966*).

2. *For an excellent modern discussion promulgating sociological realism, see: Charles K. Warriner, "Groups Are Real: A Reaffirmation,"* American Sociological Review, 21 (*1956*), *549–554.*

3. *A parallel argument to that of Durkheim's can be found in the culturological position in anthropology; see: Leslie White, "Culturological vs. Psychological Interpretations of Human Behavior,"* American Sociological Review, 12 (*1947*), *686–698.*

4. *An excellent short discussion of the Durkheimian position versus that of the sociological "humanists" can be found in Severyn T. Bruyn,* The Humanistic Perspective in Sociology (*Englewood Cliffs, N.J.: Prentice-Hall, 1966*), *pp.* 2–9.

Before inquiring into the method suited to the study of social facts, it is important to know which facts are commonly called "social." This information is all the more necessary since the designation "social" is used with little precision. It is currently employed for practically all phenomena generally diffused within society, however small their social interest. But on that basis, there are, as it were, no human events that may not be called social. Each individual drinks, sleeps, eats, reasons; and it is to society's interest that these functions be exercised in an orderly manner. If, then, all these facts are counted as "social" facts, sociology would have no subject matter exclusively its own, and its domain would be confused with that of biology and psychology.

But in reality there is in every society a certain group of phenomena which may be differentiated from those studied by the other natural sciences. When I fulfil my obligations as brother, husband, or citizen, when I execute my contracts, I perform duties which are defined, externally to myself and my acts, in law and in custom. Even if they conform to my own sentiments and I feel their reality subjectively, such reality is still objective, for I did not create them; I merely inherited them through my education. How many times it happens, moreover, that we are ignorant of the details of the obligations incumbent upon us, and that in order to acquaint ourselves with them we must consult the law and its authorized interpreters! Similarly, the church-member finds the beliefs and practices of his religious life ready-made at birth; their existence prior to his own implies their existence outside of himself. The system of signs I use to express my thought, the system of currency I employ to pay my debts, the instruments of credit I utilize in my commercial relations, the practices followed in my profession, etc., function independently of my own use of them. And these statements can be repeated for each member of society. Here, then, are ways of acting, thinking, and feeling that present the noteworthy property of existing outside the individual consciousness.

These types of conduct or thought are not only external to the individual but are, moreover, endowed with coercive power, by virtue of which they impose themselves upon him, independent of his individual will. Of course, when I fully consent and conform to them, this constraint is felt only slightly, if at all, and is therefore unnecessary. But it is, nonetheless, an intrinsic characteristic of these facts, the proof thereof being that it asserts itself as soon as I attempt to resist it. If I attempt to violate the law, it reacts against me so as to prevent my act before its accomplishment, or to nullify my violation by restoring the damage, if it is accomplished and reparable, or to make me expiate it if it cannot be compensated for otherwise.

In the case of purely moral maxims, the public conscience exercises a check on every act which offends it by means of the surveillance it exercises over the conduct of citizens, and the appropriate penalties at its disposal. In many cases the constraint is less violent, but nevertheless it always exists. If I do not submit to the conventions of society, if in my dress I do not conform to the customs observed in my country and in my class, the ridicule I provoke, the social isolation in which I am kept, produce, although in an attenuated form, the same effects as a punishment in the strict sense of the word. The constraint is nonetheless efficacious for being indirect. I am not obliged to speak French with my fellow-countrymen nor to use the legal currency, but I cannot possibly do otherwise. If I tried to escape this necessity, my attempt would fail miserably. As an industrialist, I am free to apply the technical methods of former centuries; but by doing so, I should invite certain ruin. Even when I free myself from these rules and violate them successfully, I am always compelled to struggle with them. When finally overcome, they make their constraining power sufficiently felt by the resistance they offer. The enterprises of all innovators, including successful ones, come up against resistance of this kind.

Here, then, is a category of facts with very distinctive characteristics: it consists of ways of acting, thinking, and feeling, external to the individual, and endowed with a power of coercion, by reason of which they control him. These ways of thinking could not be confused with biological phenomena, since they consist of representations and of actions; nor with psychological phenomena, which exist only in the individual consciousness and through it. They constitute, thus, a new variety of phenomena; and it is to them exclusively that the term "social" ought to be applied. And this term fits them quite well, for it is clear that, since their source is not in the individual, their substratum can be no other than society, either the political society as a whole or some one of the partial groups it includes, such as religious denominations, political, literary, and occupational associations, etc. On the other hand, this term "social" applies to them exclusively, for it has a distinct meaning only if it designates exclusively the phenomena which are not included in any of the categories of facts that have already been established and classified. These ways of thinking and acting therefore constitute the proper domain of sociology. It is true that, when we define them with this word "constraint," we risk shocking the zealous partisans of absolute individualism. For those who profess the complete autonomy of the individual, man's dignity is diminished whenever he is made to feel that he is not completely self-determinant. It is generally accepted today, however, that most of our ideas and our tendencies are not developed by ourselves but come to us from without. How can they become a part of us except by imposing themselves upon us? This is the whole meaning of our definition. And it is generally accepted, moreover, that social constraint is not necessarily incompatible with the individual personality.[1]

Since the examples that we have just cited (legal and moral regulations, religious faiths, financial systems, etc.) all consist of established beliefs and practices, one might be led to believe that social facts exist only where there is some social organization. But there are other facts without such crystallized form which have the same objectivity and the same ascendency over the individual. These are called "social currents." Thus the great movements of enthusiasm, indignation, and pity in a crowd do not originate in any one of the particular individual consciousnesses. They come to each one of us from without and can carry us away in spite of ourselves. Of course, it may happen that, in abandoning myself to them unreservedly, I do not feel the pressure they exert upon me. But it is revealed as soon as I try to resist them. Let an individual attempt to oppose one of these collective manifestations, and the emotions that he denies will turn against him. Now, if this power of external coercion asserts itself so clearly in cases of resistance, it must exist also in the first-mentioned cases, although we are unconscious of it. We are then victims of the illusion of having ourselves created that which actually forced itself from without. If the complacency with which we permit ourselves to be carried along conceals the pressure undergone, nevertheless it does not abolish it. Thus, air is no less heavy because we do not detect its weight. So, even if we ourselves have spontaneously contributed to the production of the common emotion, the impression we have received differs markedly from that which we would have experienced if we had been alone. Also, once the crowd has dispersed, that is, once these social influences have ceased to act upon us and we are alone again, the emotions which have passed through the mind appear strange to us, and we no longer recognize them as ours. We realize that these feelings have been impressed upon us to a much greater extent than they were created by us. It may even happen that they horrify us, so much were they contrary to our nature. Thus, a group of individuals, most of whom are perfectly inoffensive, may, when gathered in a crowd, be drawn into acts of atrocity. And what we say of these transitory outbursts applies similarly to those more permanent currents of opinion on religious, political, literary, or artistic matters which are constantly being formed around us, whether in society as a whole or in more limited circles.

To confirm this definition of the social fact by a characteristic illustration from common experience, one need only observe the manner in which children are brought up. Considering the facts as they are and as they have always been, it becomes immediately evident that all education is a continuous effort to impose on the child ways of seeing, feeling, and acting which he could not have arrived at spontaneously. From the very first hours of his life, we compel him to eat, drink, and sleep at regular hours; we constrain him to cleanliness, calmness, and obedience; later we exert pressure upon him in order that he may learn proper consideration for others, respect for customs and conventions, the need for work, etc. If, in time, this constraint ceases to be felt, it is because it gradually gives rise to habits and to internal tendencies that render constraint unnecessary; but nevertheless it is not abolished, for it is still the source from which these habits were derived. It is true that, according to Spencer, a rational education ought to reject such methods, allowing the child to act in complete liberty; but as this pedagogic theory has never been applied by any known people, it must be accepted only as an expression of personal opinion, not as a fact which can contradict the aforementioned observations. What makes these facts particularly instructive is that the aim of education is, precisely, the socialization of the human being; the process of education, therefore, gives us in a nutshell the historical fashion in which the social being is constituted. This unremitting pressure to which the child is subjected is the very pressure of the social milieu which tends to fashion him in its own image, and of which parents and teachers are merely the representatives and intermediaries.

It follows that sociological phenomena cannot be defined by their universality. A thought which we find in every individual consciousness, a movement repeated by all individuals, is not thereby a social fact. If sociologists have been satisfied with defining them by this characteristic, it is because they confused them with what one might call their reincarnation in the individual. It is, however, the collective aspects of the beliefs, tendencies, and practices of a group that characterize truly social phenomena. As for the forms that the collective states assume when refracted in the individual, these are things of another sort. This duality is clearly demonstrated by the fact that these two orders of phenomena are frequently found dissociated from one another. Indeed, certain of these social manners of acting and thinking acquire, by reason of their repetition, a certain rigidity which on its own account crystallizes them, so to speak, and isolates them from the particular events which reflect them. They thus acquire a body, a tangible form, and constitute a reality in their own right, quite distinct from the individual facts which produce it. Collective habits are inherent not only in the successive acts which they determine but, by a privilege of which we find no example in the biological realm, they are given permanent expression in a formula which is repeated from mouth to mouth, transmitted by education, and fixed even in writing. Such is the origin and nature of legal and moral rules, popular aphorisms and proverbs, articles of faith wherein religious or political groups condense their beliefs, standards of taste established by literary schools, etc. None of these can be found entirely reproduced in the applications made of them by individuals, since they can exist even without being actually applied.

No doubt, this dissociation does not always manifest itself with equal distinctness, but its obvious existence in the important and numerous cases just cited is sufficient to prove that the social fact is a thing distinct from its individual manifestations. Moreover, even when this dissociation is not immediately apparent, it may often be disclosed by certain devices of method. Such dissociation is indispensable if one wishes to separate social facts from their alloys in order to observe them in a state of purity. Currents of opinion, with an intensity varying according to the time and place, impel certain groups either to more marriages, for example, or to more suicides, or to a higher or lower birthrate, etc. These currents are plainly social facts. At first sight they seem inseparable from the forms they take in individual cases. But statistics furnish us with the means of isolating them. They are, in fact, represented with considerable exactness by the rates of births, marriages, and suicides, that is, by the number obtained by dividing the average annual total of marriages, births, suicides, by the number of persons whose ages lie within the range in which marriages, births, and suicides occur.[2] Since each of these figures contains all the individual cases indiscriminately, the individual circumstances which may have had a share in the production of the phenomenon are neutralized and, consequently, do not contribute to its determination. The average, then, expresses a certain state of the group mind (*l'âme collective*).

Such are social phenomena, when disentangled from all foreign matter. As for their individual manifestations, these are indeed, to a certain extent, social, since they partly reproduce a social model. Each of them also depends, and to a large extent, on the organopsychological constitution of the individual and on the particular circumstances in which he is placed. Thus they are not sociological phenomena in the strict sense of the word. They belong to two realms at once; one could call them sociopsychological. They interest the sociologist without constituting the immediate subject matter of sociology. There exist in the interior of organisms similar phenomena, compound in their nature, which form in their turn the subject matter of the "hybrid sciences," such as physiological chemistry, for example.

The objection may be raised that a phenomenon is collective only if it is common to all members of society, or at least to most of them—in other words, if it is truly general. This may be true; but it is general because it is collective (that is, more or less obligatory), and certainly not collective because general. It is a group condition repeated in the individual because imposed on him. It is to be found in each part because it exists in the whole, rather than in the whole because it exists in the parts. This becomes conspicuously evident in those beliefs and practices which are transmitted to us ready-made by previous generations; we receive and adopt them because, being both collective and ancient, they are invested with a particular authority that education has taught us to recognize and respect. It is, of course, true that a vast portion of our social culture is transmitted to us in this way; but even when the social fact is due in part to our direct collaboration, its nature is not different. A collective emotion which bursts forth suddenly and violently in a crowd does not express merely what all the individual sentiments had in common; it is something entirely different, as we have shown. It results from their being together, a product of the actions and reactions which take place between individual consciousnesses; and if each individual consciousness echoes the collective sentiment, it is by virtue of the special energy resident in its collective origin. If all hearts beat in unison, this is not the result of a spontaneous and pre-established harmony but rather because an identical force propels them in the same direction. Each is carried along by all.

We thus arrive at the point where we can formulate and delimit in a precise way the domain of sociology. It comprises only a limited group of phenomena. A social fact is to be recognized by the power of external coercion which it exercises or is capable of exercising over individuals, and the presence of this power may be recognized in its turn either by the existence of some specific sanction or by the resistance offered against every individual effort that tends to violate it. One can, however, define it also by its diffusion within the group, provided that, in conformity with our previous remarks, one takes care to add as a second and essential characteristic that its own existence is independent of the individual forms it assumes in its diffusion. This last criterion is perhaps, in certain cases, easier to apply than the preceding one. In fact, the constraint is easy to ascertain when it expresses itself externally by some direct reaction of society, as is the case in law, morals, beliefs, customs, and even fashions. But when it is only indirect, like the constraint which an economic organization exercises, it cannot always be so easily detected. Generality combined with externality may, then, be easier to establish. Moreover, this second definition is but another form of the first; for if a mode of behavior whose existence is external to individual consciousnesses becomes general, this can only be brought about by its being imposed upon them.[3]

But these several phenomena present the same characteristic by which we defined the others. These "ways of existing" are imposed on the individual precisely in the same fashion as the "ways of acting" of which we have spoken. Indeed, when we wish to know how a society is divided politically, of what these divisions themselves are composed, and how complete is the fusion existing between them, we shall not achieve our purpose by physical inspection and by geographical observations; for these phenomena are social, even when they have some basis in physical nature. It is only by a study of public law that a comprehension of this organization is possible, for it is this law that determines the organization, as it equally determines our domestic and civil relations. This political organization is, then, no less obligatory than the social facts mentioned above. If the population crowds into our cities instead of scattering into the country, this is due to a trend of public opinion, a collective drive that imposes this concentration upon the individuals. We can no more choose the style of our houses than of our clothing—at least, both are equally obligatory. The channels of communication prescribe the direction of internal migrations and commerce, etc., and even their extent. Consequently, at the very most, it should be necessary to add to the list of phenomena which we have enumerated as presenting the distinctive criterion of a social fact only one additional category, "ways of existing"; and, as this enumeration was not meant to be rigorously exhaustive, the addition would not be absolutely necessary.

Such an addition is perhaps not necessary, for these "ways of existing" are only crystallized "ways of acting." The political structure of a society is merely the way in which its component segments have become accustomed to live with one another. If their relations are traditionally intimate, the segments tend to fuse with one another, or, in the contrary case, to retain their identity. The type of habitation imposed upon us is merely the way in which our contemporaries and our ancestors have been accustomed to construct their houses. The methods of communication are merely the channels which the regular currents of commerce and migrations have dug, by flowing in the same direction. To be sure, if the phenomena of a structural character alone presented this permanence, one might believe that they constituted a distinct species. A legal regulation is an arrangement no less permanent than a type of architecture, and yet the regulation is a "physiological" fact. A simple moral maxim is assuredly somewhat more malleable, but it is much more rigid than a simple professional custom or a fashion. There is thus a whole series of degrees without a break in continuity between the facts of the most articulated structure and those free currents of social life which are not yet definitely molded. The differences between them are, therefore, only differences in the degree of consolidation they present. Both are simply life, more or less crystallized. No doubt, it may be of some advantage to reserve the term "morphological" for those social facts which concern the social substratum, but only on condition of not overlooking the fact that they are of the same nature as the others. Our definition will then include the whole relevant range of facts if we say: *A social fact is every way of acting, fixed or not, capable of exercising on the individual an external constraint;* or again, *every way of acting which is general throughout a given society, while at the same time existing in its own right independent of its individual manifestations.*[4]

NOTES

1. We do not intend to imply, however, that all constraint is normal. We shall return to this point later. [Durkheim's note.]
2. Suicides do not occur at every age, and they take place with varying intensity at the different ages in which they occur.
3. It will be seen how this definition of the social fact diverges from that which forms the basis of the ingenious system of M. Tarde. First of all, we wish to state that our researches have nowhere led us to observe that preponderant influence in the genesis of collective facts which M. Tarde attributes to imitation. Moreover, from the preceding definition, which is not a theory but simply a resume of the immediate data of observation, it seems indeed to follow, not only that imitation does not always express the essential and characteristic features of the social fact, but even that it never expresses them. No doubt, every social fact is imitated; it has, as we have just shown, a tendency to become general, but that is because it is social, i.e., obligatory. Its power of expansion is not the cause but the consequence of its sociological character. If, further, only social facts produced this consequence, imitation could perhaps serve, if not to explain them, at least to define them. But an individual condition which produces a whole series of effects remains individual nevertheless. Moreover, one may ask whether the word "imitation" is indeed fitted to designate an effect due to a coercive influence. Thus, by this single expression, very different phenomena, which ought to be distinguished, are confused.
4. This close connection between life and structure, organ and function, may be easily proved in sociology because between these two extreme terms there exists a whole series of immediately observable intermediate stages which show the bond between them. Biology is not in the same favorable position. But we may well believe that the inductions on this subject made by sociology are applicable to biology and that, in organisms as well as in societies, only differences in degree exist between these two orders of facts.

6

EDWARD B. TYLOR

On the Science of Culture

Edward Burnett Tylor (1832–1917) was one of the founders of cultural anthropology.[1] *Tylor's primary concern was the attempt to establish an evolutionary or progressive theory of cultural development. In his* Researches into the Early History of Mankind, *he attempted to establish the basic similarity of all human minds, a concept that has been called the "psychic unity of mankind." His* Primitive Culture *attempted to demonstrate the priority of Primitive Man in the chronological pattern of progress; that is, that Primitive Man represents an earlier stage in evolutionary change.*

Though many definitions of culture have been presented, some of them quite at variance with one another,[2] *Tylor's is still among the best and most quoted. As Leslie White has noted, Tylor appears to have been the first to have clearly grasped the idea of culture as a self-contained, self-determined process and the first to have "formulated in succinct fashion the culturological point of view and outlined the scope of the science of culture."* [3]

Bibliographical Notes

1. *Tylor's main works include:* Anahuac *(1861),* Researches into the Early History of Mankind *(1865), and* Primitive Culture *(1871). The reader interested in a survey of Tylor's life and work is referred to: Abram Kardiner and Edward Preble,* They Studied Man *(New York: New American Library of World Literature, Mentor Books, 1963), pp. 50–68; and Robert H. Lowie,* A History of Ethnological Theory *(New York: Rinehart, 1937), pp. 68–85.*

This excerpt is taken from E. B. Tylor, *Primitive Culture*, I (New York: Holt, Rinehart and Winston, 1877), pp. 1–6.

2. *See: A. L. Kroeber and C. Kluckhohn,* Culture: A Critical Review of Concepts and Definitions *(New York: Vintage Books, 1963); and William R. Catton, Jr., "The Development of Sociological Thought," in Robert E. L. Faris (ed.),* Handbook of Modern Sociology *(Chicago: Rand McNally, 1964), pp. 943–947. Some critics of the culture concept's multiple and varied usages question its very utility, for example: Glenn M. Vernon, "Has the Culture Concept Outlived Its Usefulness?" (paper presented at the Annual Meetings of the Eastern Sociological Society in Philadelphia, Pa., April 1966).*

3. *Leslie A. White,* The Science of Culture: A Study of Man and Civilization *(New York: Grove Press, 1949), pp. xviii–xix.*

Culture or Civilization, taken in its wide ethnographic sense, is that complex whole which includes knowledge, belief, art, morals, law, custom, and any other capabilities and habits acquired by man as a member of society. The condition of culture among the various societies of mankind, in so far as it is capable of being investigated on general principles, is a subject apt for the study of laws of human thought and action. On the one hand, the uniformity which so largely pervades civilization may be ascribed, in great measure, to the uniform action of uniform causes; while on the other hand its various grades may be regarded as stages of development or evolution, each the outcome of previous history, and about to do its proper part in shaping the history of the future . . .

Our modern investigators in the sciences of inorganic nature are foremost to recognize, both within and without their special fields of work, the unity of nature, the fixity of its laws, the definite sequence of cause and effect through which every fact depends on what has gone before it, and acts upon what is to come after it. They grasp firmly the Pythagorean doctrine of pervading order in the universal Kosmos. They affirm, with Aristotle, that nature is not full of incoherent episodes, like a bad tragedy. They agree with Leibnitz in what he calls "my axiom, that nature never acts by leaps (la nature n'agit jamais par saut)," as well as in his "great principle, commonly little employed, that nothing happens without its sufficient reason." Nor, again, in studying the structure and habits of plants and animals, or in investigating the lower functions even of man, are these leading ideas unacknowledged. But when we come to talk of the higher processes of human feeling and action, of thought and language, knowledge and art, a change appears in the prevalent tone of opinion. The world at large is scarcely prepared to accept the general study of human life as a branch of natural science, and to carry out, in a large sense, the poet's injunction to "Account for moral as for natural things." To many educated minds there seems something presumptuous and repulsive in the view that the history of mankind is part and parcel of the history of nature, that our thoughts, wills, and actions accord with laws as definite as those which govern the motion of waves, the combination of acids and bases, and the growth of plants and animals.

The main reasons of this state of the popular judgment are not far to seek. There are many who would willingly accept a science of history if placed before them with substantial definiteness of principle and evidence, but who not unreasonably reject the systems offered to them, as falling too far short of a scientific standard. Through resistance such as this, real knowledge always sooner or later makes its way, while the habit of opposition to novelty does such excellent service against the invasions of speculative dogmatism, that we may sometimes even wish it were stronger than it is. But other obstacles to the investigation of laws of human nature arise from considerations of metaphysics and theology. The popular notion of free human will involves not only freedom to act in accordance with motive, but also a power of breaking loose from continuity and acting without cause,—a combination which may be roughly illustrated by the simile of a balance sometimes acting in the usual way, but also possessed of the faculty of turning by itself without or against its weights. This view of an anomalous action of the will, which it need hardly be said is incompatible with scientific argument, subsists as an opinion patent or latent in men's minds, and strongly affecting their theoretic views of history, though it is not, as a rule, brought prominently forward in systematic reasoning. Indeed the definition of human will, as strictly according with motive, is the only possible scientific basis in such enquiries. Happily, it is not needful to add here yet another to the list of dissertations on supernatural intervention and natural causation, on liberty, predestination, and accountability. We may hasten to escape from the regions of transcendental philosophy and theology, to start on a more hopeful journey over more practicable ground. None will deny that, as each man knows by the evidence of his own consciousness, definite and natural cause does, to a great extent, determine human action. Then, keeping aside from considerations of extra-natural interference and causeless spontaneity, let us take this admitted existence of natural cause and effect as our standing-ground, and travel on it so far as it will bear us. It is on this same basis that physical science pursues, with ever-increasing success, its quest of laws of nature. Nor need this restriction hamper the scientific study of human-life, in which the real difficulties are the practical ones of enormous complexity of evidence, and imperfection of methods of observation.

Now it appears that this view of human will and conduct, as subject to definite law, is indeed recognized and acted upon by the very people who oppose it when stated in the abstract as a general principle, and who then complain that it annihilates man's free will, destroys his sense of personal responsibility, and degrades him to a soulless machine. He who will say these things will nevertheless pass much of his own life in studying the motives which lead to human action, seeking to attain his wishes through them, framing in his mind theories of personal character, reckoning what are likely to be the effects of new combinations, and giving to his reasoning the crowning character of true scientific enquiry, by taking it for granted that in so far as his calculation turns out wrong, either his evidence must have been false or incomplete, or his judgment upon it unsound. Such a one will sum up the experience of years spent in complex relations with society, by declaring his persuasion that there is a reason for everything in life, and that where events look unaccountable, the rule is to wait and watch in hope that the key to the problem may some day be found. This man's observation may have been as narrow as his inferences are crude and prejudiced, but nevertheless he has been an inductive philosopher "more than forty years without knowing it." He has practically acknowledged definite laws of human thought and action, and has simply thrown out of account in his own studies of life the whole fabric of motiveless will and uncaused spontaneity. It is assumed here that they should be just so thrown out of account in wider studies, and that the true philosophy of history lies in extending and improving the methods of the plain people who form their judgments upon facts, and check them upon new facts. Whether the doctrine be wholly or but partly true, it accepts the very condition under which we search for new knowledge in the lessons of experience, and in a word the whole course of our rational life is based upon it.

"One event is always the son of another, and we must never forget the parentage," was a remark made by a Bechuana chief to Casalis the African missionary. Thus at all times historians, so far as they have aimed at being more than mere chroniclers, have done their best to show not merely succession, but connexion, among the events upon their record. Moreover, they have striven to elicit general principles of human action, and by these to explain particular events, stating expressly or taking tacitly for granted the existence of a philosophy of history. Should any one deny the possibility of thus establishing historical laws, the answer is ready with which Boswell in such a case turned on Johnson: "Then, sir, you would reduce all history to no better than an almanack." That nevertheless the labours of so many eminent thinkers should have as yet brought history only to the threshold of science, need cause no wonder to those who consider the bewildering complexity of the problems which come before the general historian. The evidence from which he is to draw his conclusions is at once so multifarious and so doubtful, that a full and distinct view of its bearing on a particular question is hardly to be attained, and thus the temptation becomes all but irresistible to garble it in support of some rough and ready theory of the course of events. The philosophy of history at large, explaining the past and predicting the future phenomena of man's life in the world by reference to general laws, is in fact a subject with which, in the present state of knowledge, even genius aided by wide research seems but hardly able to cope. Yet there are departments of it which, though difficult enough, seem comparatively accessible. If the field of inquiry be narrowed from History as a whole to that branch of it which is here called Culture, the history, not of tribes or nations, but of the condition of knowledge, religion, art, custom, and the like among them, the task of investigation proves to lie within far more moderate compass. We suffer still from the same kind of difficulties which beset the wider argument, but they are much diminished. The evidence is no longer so wildly heterogeneous, but may be more simply classified and compared, while the power of getting rid of extraneous matter, and treating each issue on its own proper set of facts, makes close reasoning on the whole more available than in general history.

7

HERBERT SPENCER

On Society As a System

The Englishman Herbert Spencer (1820–1903) was one of the major figures in the intellectual revolution of the nineteenth century. He contributed to many fields, including philosophy, biology, psychology, anthropology, as well as sociology.[1] *Spencer centered his massive systematic philosophy around the concept of evolution, which he saw as "a change from a state of relatively indefinite, incoherent, homogeneity to a state of relatively definite, coherent, heterogeneity." Because of his emphasis on evolution and progress plus his use of a biological, organismic analogy in his examination of society, Spencer's sociological writing had fallen into disfavor in recent years (though it was initially immensely influential). However, scholars have begun to recognize that Spencer only meant his comparison of society to an organism analogically, which makes his view very similar to several modern system approaches found among contemporary structural-functionalist sociologies. This and renewed interest in evolutionary models of social change has resulted in a revival of interest in Spencer's work as a pioneer functionalist.*[2]

Bibliographical Notes

1. *Spencer's principal sociological works include:* Social Statics: The Conditions Essential to Human Happiness Specified and the First of Them Developed (*1850*); First Principles (*1862*); The Study of Sociology (*1873*); Descriptive Sociology: Or Groups of Sociological Facts, Classified and Arranged by Herbert Spencer, *compiled and abstracted by D. Duncan, R. Scheppig, and J. Collier, in 17 volumes*

Reprinted from Herbert Spencer, *The Principles of Sociology*, Vol. 1 (New York: D. Appleton and Co., 1923 edition), pp. 447–453, 455–357, 459–460, and 462.

(*1873–1934*); Principles of Sociology, *in 3 volumes* (*1876–1896*); The Man Versus the State (*1884*); *and* Facts and Comments (*1902*). *For the modern reader, a superb editing of Spencer's massive output can be found in: Robert L. Carneiro (ed.),* The Evolution of Society: Selections From Herbert Spencer (*Chicago: University of Chicago Press, 1967*).

2. *An excellent statement of the decline and revival of interest in Spencer can be found in: R. L. Carneiro,* "Editor's Introduction," *in R. L. Carneiro (ed.),* The Evolution of Society: Selections From Herbert Spencer (*Chicago: University of Chicago Press, 1967*) *pp. ix–lvii. An excellent contemporary work on Spencer (originally published in 1934) is: Jay Rumney,* Herbert Spencer's Sociology: A Study in the History of Social Theory (*New York: Atherton, 1966*). *A good short treatment of Spencer's views and their relevance today can be found in: Nicholas S. Timasheff,* Sociological Theory: Its Nature and Growth, *3rd ed.* (*New York: Random House, 1967*), *pp. 32–44.*

What Is a Society?

This question has to be asked and answered at the outset. Until we have decided whether or not to regard a society as an entity, and until we have decided whether, if regarded as an entity, a society is to be classed as absolutely unlike all other entities or as like some others, our conception of the subject matter before us remains vague.

It may be said that a society is but a collective name for a number of individuals. Carrying the controversy between nominalism and realism into another sphere, a nominalist might affirm that just as there exist only the members of a species while the species considered apart from them has no existence, so the units of a society alone exist, while the existence of the society is but verbal. Instancing a lecturer's audience as an aggregate which by disappearing at the close of the lecture proves itself to be not a thing but only a certain arrangement of persons, he might argue that the like holds of the citizens forming a nation.

But without disputing the other steps of his argument, the last step may be denied. The arrangement, temporary in the one case, is permanent in the other; and it is the permanence of the relations among component parts which constitutes the individuality of a whole as distinguished from the individualities of its parts. A mass broken into fragments ceases to be a thing, while conversely, the stones, bricks, and wood, previously separate, become the thing called a house if connected in fixed ways.

Thus we consistently regard a society as an entity because, though formed of discrete units, a certain concreteness in the aggregate of them is implied by the general persistence of the arrangements among them throughout the area occupied. And it is this trait which yields our idea of a society. . . .

But now, regarding a society as a thing, what kind of thing must we call it? It seems totally unlike every object with which our senses acquaint us. Any likeness it may possibly have to other objects cannot be manifest to perception, but can be discerned only by reason. If the constant relations among its parts make it an entity, the question arises whether these constant relations among its parts are akin to the constant relations among the parts of other entities. Between a society and anything else, the only conceivable resemblance must be one due to *parallelism of principle in the arrangement of components.*

There are two great classes of aggregates with which the social aggregate may be compared—the inorganic and the organic. Are the attributes of a society in any way like those of a non-living body—or are they in any way like those of a living body? or are they entirely unlike those of both?

The first of these questions needs only to be asked to be answered in the negative. A whole of which the parts are alive, cannot, in its general characters, be like lifeless wholes. The second question, not to be thus promptly answered, is to be answered in the affirmative. The reasons for asserting that the permanent relations among the parts of a society are analogous to the permanent relations among the parts of a living body we have now to consider.

A Society Is an Organism

When we say that growth is common to social aggregates and organic aggregates we do not thus entirely exclude community with inorganic aggregates. Some of these, as crystals, grow in a visible manner, and all of them, on the hypothesis of evolution, have arisen by integration at some time or other. Nevertheless, compared with things we call inanimate, living bodies and societies so conspicuously exhibit augmentation of mass that we may fairly regard this as characterizing them both. Many organisms grow throughout their lives and the rest grow throughout considerable parts of their lives. Social growth usually continues either up to times when the societies divide or up to times when they are overwhelmed.

Here, then, is the first trait by which societies ally themselves with the organic world and substantially distinguish themselves from the inorganic world.

It is also a character of social bodies, as of living bodies, that while they increase in size they increase in structure. Like a low animal, the embryo of a high one has few distinguishable parts, but while it is acquiring greater mass, its parts multiply and differentiate. It is thus with a society. At first the unlikenesses among its groups of units are inconspicuous in number and degree, but as population augments, divisions and subdivisions become more numerous and more decided. Further, in the social organism as in the individual organism, differentiations cease only with that completion of the type which marks maturity and precedes decay.

Though in inorganic aggregates also, as in the entire solar system and in each of its members, structural differentiations accompany the integrations, yet these are so relatively slow and so relatively simple, that they may be disregarded. The multiplication of contrasted parts in bodies politic and in living bodies is so great that it substantially constitutes another common character which marks them off from inorganic bodies.

This community will be more fully appreciated on observing that progressive differentiation of structures is accompanied by progressive differentiation of functions.

The divisions, primary, secondary, and tertiary, which arise in a developing animal, do not assume their major and minor unlikenesses to no purpose. Along with diversities in their shapes and compositions go diversities in the actions they perform: they grow into unlike organs having unlike duties. Assuming the entire function of absorbing nutriment at the same time that it takes on its structural characters, the alimentary system becomes gradually marked off into contrasted portions, each of which has a special function forming part of the general function. A limb, instrumental to locomotion or prehension, acquires divisions and subdivisions which perform their leading and their subsidiary shares in this office.

So is it with the parts into which a society divides. A dominant class arising does not simply become unlike the rest, but assumes control over the rest; when this class separates into the more and the less dominant, these again begin to discharge distinct parts of the entire control. With the classes whose actions are controlled it is the same. The various groups into which they fall have various occupations: each of such groups also, within itself, acquiring minor contrasts of parts along with minor contrasts of duties.

And here we see more clearly how the two classes of things we are comparing distinguish themselves from things of other classes, for such differences of structure as slowly arise in inorganic aggregates are not accompanied by what we can fairly call differences of function.

Why in a body politic and in a living body these unlike actions of unlike parts are properly regarded by us as functions, while we cannot so regard the unlike actions of unlike parts in an inorganic body, we shall perceive on turning to the next and most distinctive common trait.

Evolution establishes in them both, not differences simply, but definitely connected differences—differences such that each makes the others possible. The parts of an inorganic aggregate are so related that one may change greatly without appreciably affecting the rest. It is otherwise with the parts of an organic aggregate or of a social aggregate. In either of these, the changes in the parts are mutually determined, and the changed actions of the parts are mutually dependent. In both, too, this mutuality increases as the evolution advances. The lowest type of animal is all stomach, all respiratory surface, all limb. Development of a type having appendages by which to move about or lay hold of food can take place only if these appendages, losing power to absorb nutriment directly from surrounding bodies, are supplied with nutriment by parts which retain the power of absorption. A respiratory surface to which the circulating fluids are brought to be aerated can be formed only on condition that the concomitant loss of ability to supply itself with materials for repair and growth is made good by the development of a structure bringing these materials.

Similarly in a society. What we call with perfect propriety its organization, necessarily implies traits of the same kind. While rudimentary, a society is all warrior, all hunter, all hut-builder, all tool-maker; every part fulfils for itself all needs. Progress to a stage characterized by a permanent army can go on only as there arise arrangments for supplying that army with food, clothes, and munitions of war by the rest. If here the population occupies itself solely with agriculture and there with mining—if these manufacture goods while those distribute them —it must be on condition that in exchange for a special kind of service rendered by each part to other parts, these other parts severally give due proportions of their services.

This division of labor, first dwelt on by political economists as a social phenomenon, and thereupon recognized by biologists as a phenomenon of living bodies, which they called the "physiological division of labor," is that which in the society, as in the animal, makes it a living whole. Scarcely can I emphasize enough the truth that in respect of this fundamental trait a social organism and an individual organism are entirely alike. When we see that in a mammal arresting the lungs quickly brings the heart to a stand, that if the stomach fails absolutely in its office all other parts by-and-by cease to act, that paralysis of its limbs entails on the body at large death from want of food or inability to escape, that loss of even such small organs as the eyes deprives the rest of a service essential to their preservation, we cannot but admit that mutual dependence of parts is an essential characteristic. And when, in a society, we see that the workers in iron stop if the miners do not supply materials, that makers of clothes cannot carry on their business in the absence of those who spin and weave textile fabrics, that the manufacturing community will cease to act unless the food-producing and food-distributing agencies are acting, that the controlling powers, governments, bureaus, judicial officers, police, must fail to keep order when the necessaries of life are not supplied to them by the parts kept in order, we are obliged to say that this mutual dependence of parts is similarly rigorous. Unlike as the two kinds of aggregate otherwise are, they are alike in respect of this fundamental character, and the characters implied by it.

How the combined actions of mutually dependent parts constitute life of the whole, and how there hence results a parallelism between social life and animal life, we see still more clearly on learning that the life of every visible organism is constituted by the lives of units too minute to be seen by the unaided eye.

An undeniable illustration is furnished by the strange order *Myxomycetes*. The spores or germs produced by one of these forms become ciliated monads which, after a time of active locomotion, change into shapes like those of amoebae, move about, take in nutriment, grow, multiply by fission. Then these amoeba-form individuals swarm together, begin to coalesce into groups, and these groups to coalesce with one another, making a mass sometimes barely visible, sometimes as big as the hand. This *plasmodium*, irregular, mostly reticulated, and in substance gelatinous, itself exhibits movements of its parts like those of a gigantic rhizopod, creeping slowly over surfaces of decaying matters, and even up the stems of plants. Here, then, union of many minute living individuals to form a relatively vast aggregate in which their individualities are apparently lost but the life of which results from combination of their lives, is demonstrable. . . .

The relation between the lives of the units and the life of the aggregate has a further character common to the two cases. By a catastrophe the life of the aggregate may be destroyed without immediately destroying the lives of all its units, while, on the other hand, if no catastrophe abridges it, the life of the aggregate is far longer than the lives of its units.

In a cold-blooded animal, ciliated cells perform their motions with perfect regularity long after the creature they are part of has become motionless. Muscular fibers retain their power of contracting under stimulation. The cells of secreting organs go on pouring out their product if blood is artificially supplied to them. And the components of an entire organ, as the heart, continue their cooperation for many hours after its detachment.

Similarly, arrest of those commercial activities, governmental coordinations, etc., which constitute the corporate life of a nation may be caused, say by an inroad of barbarians, without immediately stopping the actions of all the units. Certain classes of these, especially the widely diffused ones engaged in food-production, may long survive and carry on their individual occupations.

On the other hand, the minute living elements composing a developed animal severally evolve, play their parts, decay, and are replaced, while the animal as a whole continues. In the deep layer of the skin, cells are formed by fission which, as they enlarge, are thrust outwards, and, becoming flattened to form the epidermis, eventually exfoliate, while the younger ones beneath take their places. Liver-cells, growing by imbibition of matters from which they separate the bile, presently die, and their vacant seats are occupied by another generation. Even bone, though so dense and seemingly inert, is permeated by blood vessels carrying materials to replace old components by new ones. And the replacement, rapid in some tissues and in others slow, goes on at such rate that during the continued existence of the entire body each portion of it has been many times over produced and destroyed.

Thus it is also with a society and its units. Integrity of the whole as of each large division is perennially maintained, notwithstanding the deaths of component citizens. The fabric of living persons which, in a manufacturing town, produces some commodity for national use, remains after a century as large a fabric, though all the masters and workers who a century ago composed it have long since disappeared. Even with minor parts of this industrial structure the like holds. A firm that dates from past generations, still carrying on business in the name of its founder, has had all its members and employees changed one by one, perhaps several times over, while the firm has continued to occupy the same place and to maintain like relations with buyers and sellers. Throughout we find this. Governing bodies, general and local, ecclesiastical corporations, armies, institutions of all orders down to guilds, clubs, philanthropic associations, etc., show us a continuity of life exceeding that of the persons constituting them. Nay, more. As part of the same law, we see that the existence of the society at large exceeds in duration that of some of the compound parts. Private unions, local public bodies, secondary national institutions, towns carrying on special industries, may decay, while the nation, maintaining its integrity, evolves in mass and structure.

In both cases, too, the mutually dependent functions of the various divisions being severally made up of the actions of many units, it results that these units dying one by one, are replaced without the function in which they share being sensibly affected. In a muscle, each sarcous element wearing out in its turn, is removed and a substitution made while the rest carry on their combined contractions as usual; the retirement of a public official or death of a shopman, perturbs inappreciably the business of the department, or activity of the industry, in which he had a share.

Hence arises in the social organism, as in the individual organism, a life of the whole quite unlike the lives of the units, though it is a life produced by them.

From these likenesses between the social organism and the individual organism we must now turn to an extreme unlikeness. The parts of an animal form a concrete whole, but the parts of a society form a whole which is discrete. While the living units composing the one are bound together in close contact, the living units composing the other are free, are not in contact, and are more or less widely dispersed. How, then, can there be any parallelism? . . .

Though coherence among its parts is a prerequisite to that cooperation by which the life of an individual organism is carried on, and though the members of a social organism, not forming a concrete whole, cannot maintain cooperation by means of physical influences directly propagated from part to part, yet they can and do maintain cooperation by another agency. Not in contact, they nevertheless affect one another through intervening spaces, both by emotional language and by the language, oral and written, of the intellect. For carrying on mutually dependent actions it is requisite that impulses, adjusted in their kinds, amounts, and times, shall be conveyed from part to part. This requisite is fulfilled in living bodies by molecular waves that are indefinitely diffused in low types and in high types are carried along definite channels (the function of which has been significantly called *internuncial*). It is fulfilled in societies by the signs of feelings and thoughts conveyed from person to person, at first in vague ways and only through short distances, but afterwards more definitely and through greater distances. That is to say, the internuncial function, not achievable by stimuli physically transferred, is nevertheless achieved by language—emotional and intellectual.

That mutual dependence of parts which constitutes organization is thus effectually established. Though discrete instead of concrete, the social aggregate is rendered a living whole. . . .

Let us now . . . sum up the reasons for regarding a society as an organism.

It undergoes continuous growth. As it grows, its parts become unlike: it exhibits increase of structure. The unlike parts simultaneously assume activities of unlike kinds. These activities are not simply different, but their differences are so related as to make one another possible. The reciprocal aid thus given causes mutual dependence of the parts. And the mutually dependent parts, living by and for one another, form an aggregate constituted on the same general principle as is an individual organism. The analogy of a society to an organism becomes still clearer on learning that every organism of appreciable size is a society, and on further learning that in both, the lives of the units continue for some time if the life of the aggregate is suddenly arrested, while if the aggregate is not destroyed by violence, its life greatly exceeds in duration the lives of its units. Though the two are contrasted as respectively discrete and concrete, and though there results a difference in the ends subserved by the organization, there does not result a difference in the laws of the organization: the required mutual influences of the parts, not transmissible in a direct way, being, in a society, transmitted in an indirect way.

Having thus considered in their most general forms the reasons for regarding a society as an organism, we are prepared for following out the comparison in detail.

8

WILLIAM GRAHAM SUMNER

On Folkways and Mores

William Graham Sumner (1840–1910) was an important voice in American sociology at the turn of the century.[1] *He is best remembered for his advocacy of unilinear and irreversible evolutionary process in human affairs, or Social Darwinism,*[2] *a position which caused him to espouse a strict laissez faire political and economic orientation, an approach based on the assumption that the survival of the fittest was the law of civilization.*[3]

Sumner was also responsible for the introduction of the terms folkways *and* mores *into sociology. The* folkways *of a society are those norms that dominate social life but are subject to change and can be purposely modified by men. On the other hand, the* mores *(the singular term is* mos*), are deemed essential for the maintenance of the group and can not be so easily changed. Folkways can become mores, and both can become institutionalized in the form of laws.*

Sumner was highly comparative in his perspective and he drew heavily upon the evidence and data in ethnology. His principal method was largely inductive; he tried to amass great bodies of verified facts, which he then largely allowed to tell their own story. His works are thus often fascinating in their wealth of description but organizationally weak. Nonetheless, it is this largely atheoretical element in his writings, this constant concern with empirical facts, that allows his writing to hold up very well for the modern reader. Sumner's emphasis on factual inventory, initiated by Herbert Spencer in his Descriptive Sociology *and exemplified today by the Human Relations Area Files originated by George Peter Murdock, plus the introduction of concepts based on such broad comparative compilation, constitute his primary contribution to contemporary sociological theory.*

Reprinted from William Graham Sumner, *Folkways* (Boston: Ginn & Company, 1906).

Bibliographical Notes

1. *Although Sumner's best known book is* Folkways *(Boston: Ginn, 1906), his great work, finished after his death by his student Albert G. Keller and published under their joint signatures, was the massive four-volume* The Science of Society *(New Haven, Conn.: Yale University Press, 1927). In addition to these major works, Sumner's bibliography consists of some 300 items, mostly essays. The best selection of the latter is to be found in: Albert G. Keller and Maurice R. Davie (eds.),* Essays of William Graham Sumner, *2 vols. (New Haven, Conn.: Yale University Press, 1940).*

2. *For an excellent discussion of this perspective, see: Richard Hofstadter,* Social Darwinism in American Thought, *rev. ed. (Boston: Beacon Press, 1955). Since Spencer's work preceded that of Darwin (in fact, Darwin acknowledged his debt to Spencer and dedicated* The Origin of the Species *to Spencer), it could be argued that Darwin's work might better have been termed* Biological Spencerianism.

3. *This position of Sumner's is well exemplified in his essay, "The Absurd Effect to Make the World Over," published in 1894. This essay is reprinted in Albert G. Keller and Maurice R. Davie (eds.),* Essays of William Graham Sumner, *2 vols. (New Haven, Conn.: Yale University Press, 1940).*

---

1. *Definition and mode of origin of the folkways.* If we put together all that we have learned from anthropology and ethnography about primitive men and primitive society, we perceive that the first task of life is to live. Men begin with acts, not with thoughts. Every moment brings necessities which must be satisfied at once. Need was the first experience, and it was followed at once by a blundering effort to satisfy it. It is generally taken for granted that men inherited some guiding instincts from their beast ancestry, and it may be true, although it has never been proved. If there were such inheritances, they controlled and aided the first efforts to satisfy needs. Analogy makes it easy to assume that the ways of beasts had produced channels of habit and predisposition along which dexterities and other psychophysical activities would run easily. Experiments with newborn animals show that

in the absence of any experience of the relation of means to ends, efforts to satisfy needs are clumsy and blundering. The method is that of trial and failure, which produces repeated pain, loss, and disappointments. Nevertheless, it is a method of rude experiment and selection. The earliest efforts of men were of this kind. Need was the impelling force. Pleasure and pain, on the one side and the other, were the rude constraints which defined the line on which efforts must proceed. The ability to distinguish between pleasure and pain is the only psychical power which is to be assumed. Thus ways of doing things were selected, which were expedient. They answered the purpose better than other ways, or with less toil and pain. Along the course on which efforts were compelled to go, habit, routine, and skill were developed. The struggle to maintain existence was carried on, not individually, but in groups. Each profited by the other's experience; hence there was concurrence towards that which proved to be most expedient. All at last adopted the same way for the same purpose; hence the ways turned into customs and became mass phenomena. Instincts were developed in connection with them. In this way folkways arise. The young learn them by tradition, imitation, and authority. The folkways, at a time, provide for all the needs of life then and there. They are uniform, universal in the group, imperative, and invariable. As time goes on, the folkways become more and more arbitrary, positive, and imperative. If asked why they act in a certain way in certain cases, primitive people always answer that it is because they and their ancestors always have done so. A sanction also arises from ghost fear. The ghosts of ancestors would be angry if the living should change the ancient folkways (see sec. 6).

2. *The folkways are a societal force.* The operation by which folkways are produced consists in the frequent repetition of petty acts, often by great numbers acting in concert or, at least, acting in the same way when face to face with the same need. The immediate motive is interest. It produces habit in the individual and custom in the group. It is, therefore, in the highest degree original and primitive. By habit and custom it exerts a strain on every individual within its range; therefore it rises to a societal force to which great classes of societal phenomena are due. Its earliest stages, its course, and laws may be studied; also its influence on individuals and their reaction on it. It is our present purpose so to study it. We have to recognize it as one of the chief forces by which a society is made to be what it is. Out of the unconscious experiment which every repetition of the ways includes, there issues pleasure or pain, and then, so far as the men are capable of reflection, convic-

tions that the ways are conducive to societal welfare. These two experiences are not the same. The most uncivilized men, both in the food quest and in war, do things which are painful, but which have been found to be expedient. Perhaps these cases teach the sense of social welfare better than those which are pleasurable and favorable to welfare. The former cases call for some intelligent reflection on experience. When this conviction as to the relation to welfare is added to the folkways they are converted into mores, and, by virtue of the philosophical and ethical element added to them, they win utility and importance and become the source of the science and the art of living.

3. *Folkways are made unconsciously.* It is of the first importance to notice that, from the first acts by which men try to satisfy needs, each act stands by itself, and looks no further than the immediate satisfaction. (From recurrent needs arise habits for the individual and customs for the group, but these results are consequences which were never conscious, and never foreseen or intended. They are not noticed until they have long existed, and it is still longer before they are appreciated.) Another long time must pass, and a higher stage of mental development must be reached, before they can be used as a basis from which to deduce rules for meeting, in the future, problems whose pressure can be foreseen. The folkways, therefore, are not creations of human purpose and wit. They are like products of natural forces which men unconsciously set in operation, or they are like the instinctive ways of animals, which are developed out of experience, which reach a final form of maximum adaptation to an interest, which are handed down by tradition and admit of no exception or variation, yet change to meet new conditions, still within the same limited methods, and without rational reflection or purpose. From this it results that all the life of human beings, in all ages and stages of culture, is primarily controlled by a vast mass of folkways handed down from the earliest existence of the race, having the nature of the ways of other animals, only the top most layers of which are subject to change and control, and have been somewhat modified by human philosophy, ethics, and religion, or by other acts of intelligent reflection. We are told of savages that "It is difficult to exhaust the customs and small ceremonial usages of a savage people. Custom regulates the whole of a man's actions,—his bathing, washing, cutting his hair, eating, drinking, and fasting. From his cradle to his grave he is the slave of ancient usage. In his life there is nothing free, nothing original, nothing spontaneous, no progress towards a higher and better life, and no attempt to improve his condition, men-

tally, morally, or spiritually." All men act in this way with only a little wider margin of voluntary variation.

. . .

5. *The strain of improvement and consistency.* The folkways, being ways of satisfying needs, have succeeded more or less well, and therefore have produced more or less pleasure or pain. Their quality always consisted in their adaptation to the purpose. If they were imperfectly adapted and unsuccessful, they produced pain, which drove men on to learn better. The folkways are, therefore, (1) subject to a strain of improvement towards better adaptation of means to ends, as long as the adaptation is so imperfect that pain is produced. They are also (2) subject to a strain of consistency with each other, because they all answer their several purposes with less friction and antagonism when they coöperate and support each other. The forms of industry, the forms of the family, the notions of property, the constructions of rights, and the types of religion show the strain of consistency with each other through the whole history of civilization. The two great cultural divisions of the human race are the oriental and the occidental. Each is consistent throughout; each has its own philosophy and spirit; they are separated from top to bottom by different mores, different standpoints, different ways, and different notions of what societal arrangements are advantageous. In their contrast they keep before our minds the possible range of divergence in the solution of the great problems of human life, and in the views of earthly existence by which life policy may be controlled. If two planets were joined in one, their inhabitants could not differ more widely as to what things are best worth seeking, or what ways are most expedient for well living.

6. *The aleatory interest.* If we should try to find a specimen society in which expedient ways of satisfying needs and interests were found by trial and failure, and by long selection from experience, as broadly described in sec. 1. above, it might be impossible to find one. Such a practical and utilitarian mode of procedure, even when mixed with ghost sanction, is rationalistic. It would not be suited to the ways and temper of primitive men. There was an element in the most elementary experience which was irrational and defied all expedient methods. One might use the best known means with the greatest care, yet fail of the result. On the other hand, one might get a great result with no effort at all. One might also incur a calamity without any fault of his own. This was the aleatory element in life, the element of risk and loss, good or

bad fortune. This element is never absent from the affairs of men. It has greatly influenced their life philosophy and policy. On one side, good luck may mean something for nothing, the extreme case of prosperity and felicity. On the other side, ill luck may mean failure, loss, calamity, and disappointment, in spite of the most earnest and well-planned endeavor. The minds of men always dwell more on bad luck. They accept ordinary prosperity as a matter of course. Misfortunes arrest their attention and remain in their memory. Hence the ills of life are the mode of manifestation of the aleatory element which has most affected life policy. Primitive men ascribed all incidents to the agency of men or of ghosts and spirits. Good and ill luck were attributed to the superior powers, and were supposed to be due to their pleasure or displeasure at the conduct of men. This group of notions constitutes goblinism. It furnishes a complete world philosophy. The element of luck is always present in the struggle for existence. That is why primitive men never could carry on the struggle for existence, disregarding the aleatory element and employing a utilitarian method only. The aleatory element has always been the connecting link between the struggle for existence and religion. It was only by religious rites that the aleatory element in the struggle for existence could be controlled. The notions of ghosts, demons, another world, etc., were all fantastic. They lacked all connection with facts, and were arbitrary constructions put upon experience. They were poetic and developed by poetic construction and imagination. The nexus between them and events was not cause and effect, but magic. They therefore led to delusive deductions in regard to life and its meaning, which entered into subsequent action as guiding faiths, and imperative notions about the conditions of success. The authority of religion and that of custom coalesced into one indivisible obligation. Therefore the simple statement of experiment and expediency in the first paragraph above is not derived directly from actual cases, but is a product of analysis and inference. It must also be added that vanity and ghost fear produced needs which man was as eager to satisfy as those of hunger or the family. Folkways resulted for the former as well as for the latter.

. . .

34. Definition of the mores. When the elements of truth and right are developed into doctrines of welfare, the folkways are raised to another plane. They then become capable of producing inferences, developing into new forms, and extending their constructive influence over men and society. Then we call them the mores. The mores are the folkways, including the philosophical and ethical generalizations as to societal welfare which are suggested by them, and inherent in them, as they grow.

35. *Taboos.* The mores necessarily consist, in a large part, of taboos, which indicate the things which must not be done. In part these are dictated by mystic dread of ghosts who might be offended by certain acts, but they also include such acts as have been found by experience to produce unwelcome results, especially in the food quest, in war, in health, or in increase or decrease of population. These taboos always contain a greater element of philosophy than the positive rules, because the taboos contain reference to a reason, as, for instance, that the act would displease the ghosts. The primitive taboos correspond to the fact that the life of man is environed by perils. His food quest must be limited by shunning poisonous plants. His appetite must be restrained from excess. His physical strength and health must be guarded from dangers. The taboos carry on the accumulated wisdom of generations, which has almost always been purchased by pain, loss, disease, and death. Other taboos contain inhibitions of what will be injurious to the group. The laws about the sexes, about property, about war, and about ghosts, have this character. They always include some social philosophy. They are both mystic and utilitarian, or compounded of the two.

Taboos may be divided into two classes, (1) protective and (2) destructive. Some of them aim to protect and secure, while others aim to repress or exterminate. Women are subject to some taboos which are directed against them as sources of possible harm or danger to men, and they are subject to other taboos which put them outside of the duties or risks of men. On account of this difference in taboos, taboos act selectively, and thus affect the course of civilization. They contain judgments as to societal welfare.

. . .

80. *The mores have the authority of facts.* The mores come down to us from the past. Each individual is born into them as he is born into the atmosphere, and he does not reflect on them, or criticise them any more than a baby analyzes the atmosphere before he begins to breathe it. Each one is subjected to the influence of the mores, and formed by them, before he is capable of reasoning about them. It may be objected that nowadays, at least, we criticise all traditions, and accept none just because they are handed down to us. If we take up cases of things which are still entirely or almost entirely in the mores, we shall see that this is not so. There are sects of free-lovers amongst us who want to

discuss pair marriage. They are not simply people of evil life. They invite us to discuss rationally our inherited customs and ideas as to marriage, which, they say, are by no means so excellent and elevated as we believe. They have never won any serious attention. Some others want to argue in favor of polygamy on grounds of expediency. They fail to obtain a hearing. Others want to discuss property. In spite of some literary activity on their part, no discussion of property, bequest, and inheritance has ever been opened. Property and marriage are in the mores. Nothing can ever change them but the unconscious and imperceptible movement of the mores. Religion was originally a matter of the mores. It became a societal institution and a function of the state. It has now to a great extent been put back into the mores. Since laws with penalties to enforce religious creeds or practices have gone out of use any one may think and act as he pleases about religion. Therefore it is not now "good form" to attack religion. Infidel publications are now tabooed by the mores, and are more effectually repressed than ever before. They produce no controversy. Democracy is in our American mores. It is a product of our physical and economic conditions. It is impossible to discuss or criticise it. It is rhetoric. No one treats it with complete candor and sincerity. No one dares to analyze it as he would aristocracy or autocracy. He would get no hearing and would only incur abuse. The thing to be noticed in all these cases is that the masses oppose a deaf ear to every argument against the mores. It is only in so far as things have been transferred from the mores into laws and positive institutions that there is discussion about them or rationalizing upon them. The mores contain the norm by which, if we should discuss the mores, we should have to judge the mores. We learn the mores as unconsciously as we learn to walk and eat and breathe. The masses never learn how we walk, and eat, and breathe, and they never know any reason why the mores are what they are. The justification of them is that when we wake to consciousness of life we find them facts which already hold us in the bonds of tradition, custom, and habit. The mores contain embodied in them notions, doctrines, and maxims, but they are facts. They are in the present tense. They have nothing to do with what ought to be, will be, may be, or once was, if it is not now.

. . .

83. *Inertia and rigidity of the mores.* We see that we must conceive of the mores as a vast system of usages, covering the whole of life, and serving all its interests; also containing in themselves their own justification by tradition and use and wont, and approved by mystic

sanctions until, by rational reflection, they develop their own philosophical and ethical generalizations, which are elevated into "principles" of truth and right. They coerce and restrict the newborn generation. They do not stimulate to thought, but the contrary. The thinking is already done and is embodied in the mores. They never contain any provision for their own amendment. They are not questions, but answers, to the problem of life. They present themselves as final and unchangeable, because they present answers which are offered as "the truth." No world philosophy, until the modern scientific world philosophy, and that only within a generation or two, has ever presented itself as perhaps transitory, certainly incomplete, and liable to be set aside tomorrow by more knowledge. No popular world philosophy or life policy ever can present itself in that light. It would cost too great a mental strain. All the groups whose mores we consider far inferior to our own are quite as well satisfied with theirs as we are with ours. The goodness or badness of mores consists entirely in their adjustment to the life conditions and the interests of the time and place. Therefore it is a sign of ease and welfare when no thought is given to the mores, but all coöperate in them instinctively. The nations of southeastern Asia show us the persistency of the mores, when the element of stability and rigidity in them becomes predominant. Ghost fear and ancestor worship tend to establish the persistency of the mores by dogmatic authority, strict taboo, and weighty sanctions. The mores then lose their naturalness and vitality. They are stereotyped. They lose all relation to expediency. They become an end in themselves. They are imposed by imperative authority without regard to interests or conditions (caste, child marriage, widows). When any society falls under the dominion of this disease in the mores it must disintegrate before it can live again. In that diseased state of the mores all learning consists in committing to memory the words of the sages of the past who established the formulæ of the mores. Such words are "sacred writings," a sentence of which is a rule of conduct to be obeyed quite independently of present interests, or of any rational considerations.

9

RALPH LINTON
On Status and Role

Ralph Linton (1893–1953), an eminent American anthropologist, proposed the distinction between status and role, one of the most influential ideas in contemporary sociology.[1] *Linton conceptualized a* status *as a collection of rights and duties*[2] *and a* role *as the dynamic aspect of a status.*[3] *In addition, Linton's discrimination between* achieved *and* ascribed *roles has also been highly influential.*[4] *The notion that social positions and roles constituted societal elements suggested new possibilities for the analysis of social structure. The concept that the behavior of an individual could be seen in terms of role performance implied that the role was a major link between individual behavior and social structure.*[5]

Linton's primary works were ethnological (dealing with Madagascar and Polynesia, particularly), but his writings covered a diversity of topics including primitive art, the relationship of psychiatry to anthropology, and general culture history. His general orientation in anthropology was largely psychological; he was greatly concerned with the meanings that cultural elements held for the people who manifested or used them. Linton is generally considered to be a key figure in the neo-Freudian culture and personality movement within anthropology.[6] *Despite his psychological preoccupation, however, his classic discussion of status and role is a cornerstone in the thinking of most modern Durkheimian sociologists. The power this formulation exerts results from the fact that these two concepts are not simply reducible to the individual (psychological) level. They refer instead to certain relationships between the individuals and are thus strictly sociological constructs.*

Bibliographical Notes

1. *Linton's major works include:* The Tanala: A Hill Tribe of Madagascar (*1933*); The Study of Man: An Introduction (*1936*); The Cultural Background of Personality (*1945*); The Tree of Culture (*1955*); Culture and Mental Disorders (*edited by George Devereux, 1956*). *Biographical information on Linton can be found in: John Gillin, "Ralph Linton,"* American Anthropologist, 56 (*1954*), *274–281; and Lauriston Sharp, "Linton, Ralph,"* International Encyclopedia of the Social Sciences, *Vol.* 9 (*New York: Macmillan and Free Press, 1968*), *pp.* 386–390. *A bibliography of Linton's works can be found in: Clyde Kluckhohn, "Ralph Linton," National Academy of Sciences,* Biographical Memoirs, 31 (*1958*), *pp.* 236–253.

2. *On contemporary uses of the term* status, *see: S. H. Jamerson, "Status of Status,"* Sociology and Social Research, 23 (*1939*), *360–372; Frederick C. Bates, "Position, Status, and Role: A Reformulation of Concepts,"* Social Forces, 34 (*1955*), *313–321; and Albert Pierce, "On the Concepts of Role and Status,"* Sociologus, 6 (*1956*), *29–34.*

3. *On the concept of role, see: Lionel J. Neiman and James W. Hughes, "The Problem of the Concept of Role—A Re-survey of the Literature,"* Social Forces, 30 (*1951*), *141–149; and Bruce J. Biddle,* the Present Status of Role Theory (*Columbia: University of Missouri, Social Psychology Laboratory, 1961*). *See also: Bruce J. Biddle and Edwin J. Thomas,* Role Theory: Concepts and Research (*New York: Wiley, 1966*); *Michael Blanton,* Roles: An Introduction to the Study of Social Relations (*New York: Basic Books, 1965*); *and Jerald Hage and Gerald Marwell, "Toward the Development of an Empirically Based Theory of Role Relationships,"* Sociometry, 31 (*1968*), 200–212.

4. *The distinction between achieved and ascribed roles forms the polar types for one of Talcott Parsons' major cultural dimensions known as the* pattern variables. *On this distinction, see: Irving S. Foladare, "A Clarification of 'Ascribed Status' and 'Achieved Status,'"* Sociological Quarterly, 10 (*1969*), *53–61.*

5. *For an example of a major theoretical work using the social role as a central construct, see: Hans Gerth and C. Wright Mills,* Character and Social Structure: The Psychology of Social Institutions (*New York: Harcourt Brace Jovanovich, 1953*).

6. *Cf., Marvin Harris,* The Rise of Anthropological Theory: A His-

tory of Theories of Culture (New York: Thomas Y. Crowell, 1968), p. 394.

. . . the functioning of societies depends upon the presence of patterns for reciprocal behavior between individuals or groups of individuals. The polar positions in such patterns of reciprocal behavior are technically known as *statuses*. The term *status*, like the term *culture*, has come to be used with a double significance. A *status*, in the abstract, is a position in a particular pattern. It is thus quite correct to speak of each individual as having many statuses, since each individual participates in the expression of a number of patterns. However, unless the term is qualified in some way, *the status* of any individual means the sum total of all the statuses which he occupies. It represents his position with relation to the total society. Thus the status of Mr. Jones as a member of his community derives from a combination of all the statuses which he holds as a citizen, as an attorney, as a Mason, as a Methodist, as Mrs. Jones's husband, and so on.

A status, as distinct from the individual who may occupy it, is simply a collection of rights and duties. Since these rights and duties can find expression only through the medium of individuals, it is extremely hard for us to maintain a distinction in our thinking between statuses and the people who hold them and exercise the rights and duties which constitute them. The relation between any individual and any status he holds is somewhat like that between the driver of an automobile and the driver's place in the machine. The driver's seat with its steering wheel, accelerator, and other controls is a constant with ever-present potentialities for action and control, while the driver may be any member of the family and may exercise these potentialities very well or very badly.

A *rôle* represents the dynamic aspect of a status. The individual is socially assigned to a status and occupies it with relation to other statuses. When he puts the rights and duties which constitute the status into effect, he is performing a rôle. Rôle and status are quite inseparable, and the distinction between them is of only academic interest. There are no rôles without statuses or statuses without rôles. Just as in the case of *status*, the term *rôle* is used with a double significance. Every individual has a series of rôles deriving from the various patterns in which he participates and at the same time *a rôle,* general, which represents the sum total of these rôles and determines what he does for his society and what he can expect from it.

Although all statuses and rôles derive from social patterns and are integral parts of patterns, they have an independent function with relation to the individuals who occupy particular statuses and exercise their rôles. To such individuals the combined status and rôle represent the minimum of attitudes and behavior which he must assume if he is to participate in the overt expression of the pattern. Status and rôle serve to reduce the ideal patterns for social life to individual terms. They become models for organizing the attitudes and behavior of the individual so that these will be congruous with those of the other individuals participating in the expression of the pattern. Thus if we are studying football teams in the abstract, the position of quarter-back is meaningless except in relation to the other positions. From the point of view of the quarter-back himself it is a distinct and important entity. It determines where he shall take his place in the line-up and what he shall do in various plays. His assignment to this position at once limits and defines his activities and establishes a minimum of things which he must learn. Similarly, in a social pattern such as that for the employer-employee relationship the statuses of employer and employee define what each has to know and do to put the pattern into operation. The employer does not need to know the techniques involved in the employee's labor, and the employee does not need to know the techniques for marketing or accounting.

It is obvious that, as long as there is no interference from external sources, the more perfectly the members of any society are adjusted to their statuses and rôles the more smoothly the society will function. In its attempts to bring about such adjustments every society finds itself caught on the horns of a dilemma. The individual's formation of habits and attitudes begins at birth, and, other things being equal, the earlier his training for a status can begin the more successful it is likely to be. At the same time, no two individuals are alike, and a status which will be congenial to one may be quite uncongenial to another. Also, there are in all social systems certain rôles which require more than training for their successful performance. Perfect technique does not make a great violinist, nor a thorough book knowledge of tactics an efficient general. The utilization of the special gifts of individuals may be highly important to society, as in the case of the general, yet these gifts usually show themselves rather late, and to wait upon their manifestation for the assignment of statuses would be to forfeit the advantages to be derived from commencing training early.

Fortunately, human beings are so mutable that almost any normal individual can be trained to the adequate performance of almost any rôle. Most of the business of living can be conducted on a basis of habit, with little need for intelligence and none for special gifts. Societies have met the dilemma by developing two types of statuses, the *ascribed* and the *achieved*. *Ascribed* statuses are those which are assigned to individuals without reference to their innate differences or abilities. They can be predicted and trained for from the moment of birth. The *achieved* statuses are, as a minimum, those requiring special qualities, although they are not necessarily limited to these. They are not assigned to individuals from birth but are left open to be filled through competition and individual effort. The majority of the statuses in all social systems are of the ascribed type and those which take care of the ordinary day-to-day business of living are practically always of this type.

In all societies certain things are selected as reference points for the ascription of status. The things chosen for this purpose are always of such a nature that they are ascertainable at birth, making it possible to begin the training of the individual for his potential statuses and rôles at once. The simplest and most universally used of these reference points is sex. Age is used with nearly equal frequency, since all individuals pass through the same cycle of growth, maturity, and decline, and the statuses whose occupation will be determined by age can be forecast and trained for with accuracy. Family relationships, the simplest and most obvious being that of the child to its mother, are also used in all societies as reference points for the establishment of a whole series of statuses. Lastly, there is the matter of birth into a particular socially established group, such as a class or caste. The use of this type of reference is common but not universal. In all societies the actual ascription of statuses to the individual is controlled by a series of these reference points which together serve to delimit the field of his future participation in the life of the group.

The division and ascription of statuses with relation to sex seems to be basic in all social systems. All societies prescribe different attitudes and activities to men and to women. Most of them try to rationalize these prescriptions in terms of the physiological differences between the sexes or their different rôles in reproduction. However, a comparative study of the statuses ascribed to women and men in different cultures seems to show that while such factors may have served as a starting point for the development of a division the actual ascriptions are almost entirely determined by culture. Even the psychological characteristics ascribed to men and women in different societies vary so much that they can have little physiological basis. Our own idea of women as ministering angels contrasts sharply with the ingenuity of women as torturers among the Iroquois and the sadistic delight they took in the process. Even the last two generations have seen a sharp change in the psychological patterns for women in our own society. The delicate, fainting lady of the middle eighteen-hundreds is as extinct as the dodo.

When it comes to the ascription of occupations, which is after all an integral part of status, we find the differences in various societies even more marked. Arapesh women regularly carry heavier loads than men "because their heads are so much harder and stronger." In some societies women do most of the manual labor; in others, as in the Marquesas, even cooking, housekeeping, and baby-tending are proper male occupations, and women spend most of their time primping. Even the general rule that women's handicap through pregnancy and nursing indicates the more active occupations as male and the less active ones as female has many exceptions. Thus among the Tasmanians seal-hunting was women's work. They swam out to the seal rocks, stalked the animals, and clubbed them. Tasmanian women also hunted opossums, which required the climbing of large trees.

Although the actual ascription of occupations along sex lines is highly variable, the pattern of sex division is constant. There are very few societies in which every important activity has not been definitely assigned to men or to women. Even when the two sexes coöperate in a particular occupation, the field of each is usually clearly delimited. Thus in Madagascar rice culture the men make the seed beds and terraces and prepare the fields for transplanting. The women do the work of transplanting, which is hard and back-breaking. The women weed the crop, but the men harvest it. The women then carry it to the threshing floors, where the men thresh it while the women winnow it. Lastly, the women pound the grain in mortars and cook it.

When a society takes over a new industry, there is often a period of uncertainty during which the work may be done by either sex, but it soon falls into the province of one or the other. In Madagascar, pottery is made by men in some tribes and by women in others. The only tribe in which it is made by both men and women is one into which the art has been introduced within the last sixty years. I was told that during the fifteen years preceding my visit there had been a marked decrease in the number of male potters, many men who had once practised the art having given it up. The factor of lowered wages, usually advanced as the reason for men leaving one of our own occupations when women enter it in force, certainly was not operative here. The field was not overcrowded, and the prices for men's and women's products were the same. Most of the men who had given up the trade were vague as to their reasons, but a few said frankly that they did not like to compete with women. Apparently the entry of women into the occupation had robbed it of a certain amount of prestige. It was no longer quite the thing for a man to be a potter, even though he was a very good one.

The use of age as a reference point for establishing status is as universal as the use of sex. All societies recognize three age groupings as a minimum: child, adult, and old. Certain societies have emphasized age as a basis for assigning status and have greatly amplified the divisions. Thus in certain African tribes the whole male population is divided into units composed of those born in the same years or within two- or three-year intervals. However, such extreme attention to age is unusual, and we need not discuss it here.

The physical differences between child and adult are easily recognizable, and the passage from childhood to maturity is marked by physiological events which make it possible to date it exactly for girls and within a few weeks or months for boys. However, the physical passage from childhood to maturity does not necessarily coincide with the social transfer of the individual from one category to the other. Thus in our own society both men and women remain legally children until long after they are physically adult. In most societies this difference between the physical and social transfer is more clearly marked than in our own. The child becomes a man not when he is physically mature but when he is formally recognized as a man by his society. This recognition is almost always given ceremonial expression in what are technically known as puberty rites. The most important element in these rites is not the determination of physical maturity but that of social maturity. Whether a boy is able to breed is less vital to his society than whether he is able to do a man's work and has a man's knowledge. Actually, most puberty ceremonies include tests of the boy's learning and fortitude, and if the aspirants are unable to pass these they are left in the child status until they can. For those who pass the tests, the ceremonies usually culminate in the transfer to them of certain secrets which the men guard from women and children.

The passage of individuals from adult to aged is harder to perceive. There is no clear physiological line for men, while even women may retain their full physical vigor and their ability to carry on all the activities of the adult status for several years after the menopause. The social transfer of men from the adult to the aged group is given ceremonial recognition in a few cultures, as when a father formally surrenders his official position and titles to his son, but such recognition is rare. As for women, there appears to be no society in which the menopause is given ceremonial recognition, although there are a few societies in which it does alter the individual's status. Thus Comanche women, after the menopause, were released from their disabilities with regard to the supernatural. They could handle sacred objects, obtain power through dreams and practice as shamans, all things forbidden to women of bearing age.

The general tendency for societies to emphasize the individual's first change in age status and largely ignore the second is no doubt due in part to the difficulty of determining the onset of old age. However, there are also psychological factors involved. The boy or girl is usually anxious to grow up, and this eagerness is heightened by the exclusion of children from certain activities and knowledge. Also, society welcomes new additions to the most active division of the group, that which contributes most to its perpetuation and well-being. Conversely, the individual who enjoys the thought of growing old is atypical in all societies. Even when age brings respect and a new measure of influence, it means the relinquishment of much that is pleasant. We can see among ourselves that the aging usually refuse to recognize the change until long after it has happened.

10

ALBION W. SMALL
On Interests

Albion Woodbury Small (1854–1926) was possibly the major figure who contributed to the rise of academic sociology in America. He published the first introductory textbook in sociology with George E. Vincent in 1894,[1] *and in 1895 founded the* American Journal of Sociology *(which he edited until his death). His greatest influence, however, came from his position as the head of the department of sociology at the University of Chicago, which he held beginning with the department's creation in 1892. The University of Chicago dominated American sociology during its formative period, and Small played a major role in determining the future direction of the field.*[2]

In his major work, General Sociology, *Small developed the concept of* interests *as the central feature of his sociology. Unlike his extensive personal influence, Small's writings have had little impact upon American sociology (though the concept of interests has had widespread use in political science). This discrepancy largely results from the fact that Small accepted the then prominent evolutionary emphasis of the Social Darwinists emanating from the works of Herbert Spencer. Nonetheless, Small's work is in line with a direction currently very fashionable in American sociology. His general framework for the analysis of society followed an organismic analogy (largely influenced by the work of the Austrian sociologist Gustav Ratzenhofer), which has many points of contact with the system emphasis in today's functionalist sociologies. In addition, his central concern with interests stressed the importance of conflict within the social system. Thus, his work represents an early synthesis of two major conflicting approaches in contemporary sociology, functionalism and conflict theory.*[3]

Reprinted from Albion W. Small, *General Sociology* (Chicago: University of Chicago Press, 1905), pp. 425–436.

Bibliographical Notes

1. An Introduction to the Study of Society (*New York: American Book, 1894*). *Small's major works include:* General Sociology (*1905*), *and* The Meaning of the Social Sciences (*1910*).

2. *For a description of this period, see: Harry Elmer Barnes, "Albion Woodbury Small: Promoter of American Sociology and Expositor of Social Interests," in H. E. Barnes (ed.),* An Introduction to the History of Sociology (*Chicago: University of Chicago Press, 1948*), *pp.* 766–792.

3. *For an excellent introduction to this dispute, see: N. J. Demerath, III, and Richard A. Peterson (eds.),* System Change and Conflict: A Reader on Contemporary Sociological Theory and the Debate over Functionalism (*New York: Free Press, 1967*).

Nature—i.e., the physical surroundings in which men come into existence and develop their endowment—is analyzed for us by the physical sciences. We do not know all its secrets, but in studying the social process we have to start with such knowledge of nature as the physical sciences have gained, and we have to search for similar knowledge of the human factor. Men have been analyzed much less successfully than nature. During the past generation, the conception of "the atom" has been of enormous use in physical discovery. Although no one has ever seen an atom, the supposition that there are ultimate particles of matter in which the "promise and potency" of all physical properties and actions reside, has served as a means of investigation during the most intensive period of research in the history of thought. Without the hypothesis of the atom, physics and chemistry, and in a secondary sense biology, would have lacked chart and compass upon their voyages of exploration. Although the notion of the atom is rapidly changing, and the tendency of physical science is to construe physical facts in terms of motion rather than of the traditional atom, it is probably as needless as it is useless for us to concern ourselves as laymen with this refinement. Although we cannot avoid speaking of the smallest parts into which matter can be divided, and although we cannot imagine, on the other hand, how any portions of matter can exist and not be divisible into parts, we are probably quite as incapable of saving ourselves from paradox by resort to the vortex hypothesis in any form. That is, these subtleties are too wonderful for most minds. Without pushing analysis too far, and without resting any theory upon analogy with the atom of physical theory, it is necessary to find some starting place from which to trace up the composition of sentient beings, just as the physicists assumed that they found their starting-place in the atom. The notion of interests is accordingly serving the same purpose in sociology which the notion of atoms has served in physical science. Interests are the stuff that men are made of. More accurately expressed, the last elements to which we can reduce the actions of human beings are units which we may conveniently name "interests." It is merely inverting the form of expression to say: *Interests are the simplest modes of motion which we can trace in the conduct of human beings.*

Now, it is evident that human beings contain one group of interests which are generically identical with the factors that compose plants and animals. They are those modes of motion which follow the laws of physics and chemistry and biology. The sociologist is not accountable for a metaphysics of those motions. They exist in trees and fishes and birds and quadrupeds and men alike. They are movements that exhibit the different forms of vital energy. These forces that work together in building living organisms are no other in men than in the lower organisms. These forces are incessantly displaying themselves in movements that arrive at certain similar types of result. Viz.: There is the building of living tissue. There is the growth and development of this tissue till it detaches itself from the parent stock and leads an independent life. There is, in turn, the parental action of this organism in giving life to other organisms like itself. All that goes forward in living organisms may be conceived as the working of a complex group of energies which we may call the health interest. In the form of a definition, we may generalize as follows: *The health interest is that group of motions which normally build and work the bodily organism.* That interest has one specific content in a clover plant, another in an oak tree, another in an insect, another in a man. In each case, however, it is an energetic pushing forward toward expression of power which proves to have different limits in the different types; but these puttings forth of power, so far as they go, consist of motions which all belong in one and the same group. Physical, chemical, and vital energies, variously mixed, attain to the life of the plant in one instance, of the insect in another, of the man in another. In short, the basal interest in every man is the impulse of all the physical energy deposited in his organism to work itself out to the limit. This is what we mean by the health interest. It is the impulsion and the propulsion of the frankly material in our composition. Before referring to other interests, we may illustrate in this connection what was said a little earlier about all men being variations of the same elemental factors.

Here is a black man committing a fiendish crime, and here are white men dragging him to a fiendish expiation, and here is a saintly man throwing the whole force of his life into horror-stricken protest against the inhumanity of both. Now, the point is that, in the first instance, the criminal, the avenger, and the saint are storage batteries of one and the same kind of physical energy. The vital processes of the one are precisely similar to those of the other. The same elementary physical motions occur in the life of each. It might even happen that precisely the same quantity of physical energy resided in each of the three. The criminal does not do something to the like of which nothing in the avenger or in the saint urges. On the contrary, the rudimentary energies in the average man move in the same direction as those that betray themselves in the criminal. The health interest is a term in the personal equation of each; but something in the avenger and in the saint inhibits the health interest from monopoly of the man in the two latter cases, while without such inhibition it rages to madness in the former. The saint is not a unit that contains no factor in common with the fiend. On the contrary, saint and fiend are terms which alike cover a certain quantity and quality of the brute. That the fiend is not a saint, and the saint is not a fiend, is not because the make-up of either utterly lacks components of the other character. It is because that which goes to make the fiend is, in the one case, not organized into other interests which modify its workings; in the other case other interests have so asserted themselves that the health interest has been reduced to a completely subordinate rôle.

In the lowest condition in which we find human beings, they present little to attract the attention of any scientific observer except the zoölogist. They are merely specimens of a higher order of animal. The differences which the comparative anatomist makes out are merely more complex details in the same series which he traces from the lowest orders in the animal kingdom. The horde of savage men is simply a mass of practically identical specimens of a species, just like a shoal of fish or a herd of buffaloes. That is, so long as the health interest alone is in working force, there is no such fact present as a human individual. The specimens in the aggregation are not individualized. Each presents the same dead level of characteristics that appear in all the rest. So far nothing but the animal kingdom is in sight. The properly human stage in world-evolution begins when the differentiation of other interests in some of the specimens of the *genus homo* produces human individuals. In other words, the individual who builds human society, as distinguished from packs of animals, is the human animal varied by the appearance and incessant modification of other than the health interest. In order to have an adequate theory of the human process, therefore, there is need of intimate acquaintance with the human individual, the ultimate molecular unit carrying on the process. This is to be insisted upon for its own sake, but also incidentally for the reason that certain critics of present tendencies in sociology insist that the sociologists are entirely on the wrong track, since they start by leaving individuals out of the account. These critics assert that the sociologist cares only about societies, but that the things which he thinks he knows about societies are necessarily wrong, because we cannot know societies without understanding the persons who compose the societies.

The criticism seriously misinterprets the sociologists. Instead of ignoring the individual, nobody has seen more clearly than the sociologists that we must stop taking a fictitious individual for granted, or still worse, assuming that it is unnecessary to take a real individual into the account at all. Nobody has more strenuously insisted that we must analyze human personality to the utmost limit in order to posit the real actor in association. The sociologists have therefore quite as often erred in the direction opposite to that alleged by these critics. They have invaded psychological and pedagogical territory, and usually without equipment to do respectable work. They have been tempted to this sort of foray by encountering in their own proper work the need of more knowledge of the individual than is available. It is true the sociologists think that, when division of labor is fully organized, study of the individual, as such, will fall to others. But the social fact and the social process will never be understood till we have better knowledge of the individual element in the fact and the process. Professor Baldwin spoke for sociology as truly as for psychology when he said:

> It is the first requirement of a theory of society that it shall have adequate views of the progress of the social whole, which shall be consistent with the psychology of the individual's personal growth. It is this requirement, I think, which has kept the science of society so long in its infancy; or, at least, this in part. Psychologists have not had sufficient genetic theory to use on their side; and what theory they had seemed to forbid any attempt to interpret social progress in its categories. As soon as we come to see, however, that the growth of the individual does not forbid this individual's taking part in the

larger social movement as well, and, moreover, reach the view that in his growth he is at once also growing into the social whole, and in so far aiding its further evolution—then we seem to have found a bridge on which it is safe to travel, and from which we can get vistas of the country on both sides.[1]

In this connection we may adopt another remark of Professor Baldwin:

. . . . one of the historical conceptions of man is, in its social aspects, mistaken. Man is not a person who stands up in his isolated majesty, meanness, passion, or humility, and sees, hits, worships, fights, or overcomes another man, who does the opposite things to him, each preserving his isolated majesty, meanness, passion, humility, all the while, so that he can be considered a "unit" for the compounding processes of social speculation. On the contrary, *a man is a social outcome rather than a social unit*. He is always, in his greatest part, also someone else. Social acts of his—that is, acts which may not prove anti-social—are his *because they are society's first;* otherwise he would not have learned them nor have had any tendency to do them. Everything that he learns is copied, reproduced, assimilated from his fellows; and what all of them, including him—all the fellows, the *socii*—do and think, they do and think because they have each been through the same course of copying, reproducing, assimilating that he has. When he acts quite privately, it is always with a boomerang in his hand; and every use he makes of his weapon leaves its indelible impression both upon the other and upon him.

It is on such truths as these, which recent writers have been bringing to light,[2] that the philosophy of society must be gradually built up. Only the neglect of such facts can account for the present state of social discussion. Once let it be our philosophical conviction, drawn from the more general results of pschology and anthropology, that man is not two, an *ego* and an *alter*, each in active and chronic protest against a third great thing, society; once dispel this hideous un-fact, and with it the remedies found by the egoists, back all the way from the Spencers to the Hobbeses and the Comtes—and I submit the main barrier to the successful understanding of society is removed.[3]

At the same time, there should be no difficulty in getting it understood that, while biology and psychology have to do with the individual when he is in the making, sociology wants to start with him as the finished product. There is a certain impossible antinomy about this, to be sure; for our fundamental conception is that the individual and his associations are contantly in the reciprocal making by each other. Nevertheless, there are certain constant aspects of the individual which furnish known terms for sociology. They are aspects which present their own problems to physiology and psychology, on the one hand,

and to sociology, on the other; but in themselves they must be assumed at the beginning of sociological inquiry.

To the psychologist the individual is interesting primarily as a center of knowing, feeling, and willing. To the sociologist the individual begins to be interesting when he is thought as knowing, feeling, and willing *something*. In so far as a mere trick of emphasis may serve to distinguish problems, this ictus indicates the sociological starting-point. The individual given in experience is thought to the point at which he is available for sociological assumption, when he is recognized as a center of activities which make for something outside of the psychical series in which volition is a term. These activities must be referred primarily to desires, but the desires themselves may be further referred to certain universal interests. In this character the individual becomes one of the known or assumed terms of sociology. The individual as a center of active interests may be thought both as the lowest term in the social equation and as a composite term whose factors must be understood. These factors are either the more evident desires, or the more remote interests which the individual's desires in some way represent. At the same time, we must repeat the admission that these assumed interests are like the atom of physics. They are the metaphysical recourse of our minds in accounting for concrete facts. We have never seen or touched them. They are the hypothetical substratum of those regularities of conduct which the activities of individuals display.

In this connection the term "interest" is to be understood, not in the psychological, but in a teleological sense.[4] The sense in which we use the term is antecedent to that which seems to be predominantly in Professor Baldwin's mind in the following passages:

> The very concept of interests, when one considers it with reference to himself, necessarily involves others, therefore, on very much the same footing as oneself. One's interests, the things he wants in life are the things which, by the very same thought, he allows others also the right to want; and if he insists upon the gratification of his own wants at the expense of the legitimate wants of the "other," then he in so far does violence to his sympathies and to his sense of justice. And this in turn must impair his satisfaction. For the very gratification of himself thus secured must, if it be accompanied with any reflection at all, involve the sense of the "other's" gratification also; and since this conflicts with the fact, a degree of discomfort must normally arise in the mind, varying with the development which the self has attained in the dialectical process described above. . . .
>
> On the one hand, we can get no doctrine of society but by getting the psychology of the *socius* with all his natural history; and, on the

> other hand, we can get no true view of the *socius* without describing the social conditions under which he normally lives, with the history of their action and reaction upon him. Or, to put the outcome in terms of the restriction which we have imposed upon ourselves—the only way to get a solid basis for social theory based upon human want or desire, is to work out first a descriptive and genetic psychology of desire in its social aspects; and, on the other hand, the only way to get an adequate psychological view of the rise and development of desire in its social aspects is by a patient tracing of the conditions of social environment in which the child and the race have lived and which they have grown up to reflect.[5]

The somewhat different concept of this element "interest" which we posit may be indicated at first with the least possible technicality. We may start with the familiar popular expressions, "the farming interest," "the railroad interest," "the packing interest," "the milling interest," etc., etc. Everyone knows what the expressions mean. Our use of the term "interest" is not co-ordinate with these, but it may be approached by means of them. All the "interests" that are struggling for recognition in business and in politics are highly composite. The owner of a flourmill, for example, is a man before he is a miller. He becomes a miller at last because he is a man; i.e., because he has interests—in a deeper sense than that of the popular expressions—which impel him to act in order to gain satisfactions. The clue to all social activity is in this fact of individual interests. Every act that every man performs is to be traced back to an interest. We eat because there is a desire for food; but the desire is set in motion by a bodily interest in replacing exhausted force. We sleep because we are tired; but the weariness is a function of the bodily interest in rebuilding used-up tissue. We play because there is a bodily interest in use of the muscles. We study because there is a mental interest in satisfying curiosity. We mingle with our fellow-men because there is a mental interest in matching our personality against that of others. We go to market to supply an economic interest, and to war because of some social interest of whatever mixed or simple form.

With this introduction, we may venture an extremely abstract definition of our concept "interest." In general, *an interest is an unsatisfied capacity, corresponding to an unrealized condition, and it is predisposition to such rearrangement as would tend to realize the indicated condition.*[6] Human needs and human wants are incidents in the series of events between the latent existence of human interests and the achievement of partial satisfaction. Human interests, then, are the ultimate terms of calculation in sociology. *The whole life-process, so far as we know it, whether viewed in its individual or in its social phase, is at last the process of developing, adjusting, and satisfying interests.*[7]

No single term is of more constant use in recent sociology than this term "interests." We use it in the plural partly for the sake of distinguishing it from the same term in the sense which has become so familiar in modern pedagogy. The two uses of the term are closely related, but they are not precisely identical. The pedagogical emphasis is rather on the voluntary attitude toward a possible object of attention. The sociological emphasis is on attributes of persons which may be compared to the chemical affinities of different elements.[8]

To distinguish the pedagogical from the sociological use of the term "interest," we may say pedagogically of a supposed case: "The boy has no *interest* in physical culture, or in shop-work, or in companionship with other boys, or in learning, or in art, or in morality." That is, attention and choice are essential elements of interest in the pedagogical sense. On the other hand, we may say of the same boy, in the sociological sense: "He has not discovered his health, wealth, sociability, knowledge, beauty, and rightness *interests*." We thus imply that interests, in the sociological sense, are not necessarily matters of attention and choice. They are affinities, latent in persons, pressing for satisfaction, whether the persons are conscious of them either generally or specifically, or not; they are indicated spheres of activity which persons enter into and occupy in the course of realizing their personality.

Accordingly, we have virtually said that interests are merely specifications in the make-up of the personal units. We have several times named the most general classes of interests which we find serviceable in sociology, viz.: *health, wealth, sociability, knowledge, beauty, and rightness.* We shall speak more in detail of the content of these interests in the next chapter.

We need to emphasize, in addition, several considerations about these interests which are the motors of all individual and social action: First, there is a subjective and an objective aspect of them all. It would be easy to use terms of these interests in speculative arguments in such a way as to shift the sense fallaciously from the one aspect to the other; e.g., moral conduct, as an actual adjustment of the person in question with other persons, is that person's "interest," in the objective sense. On the other hand, we are obliged to think of something in the person himself impelling him, however unconsciously, toward that moral conduct, i.e., interest as "unsatisfied capacity," in the subjective sense. So with each of the other interests. The fact that these two senses of the term are always concerned must never be ignored; but, until we reach refinements of analysis which demand use for these discriminations, they may be left out of sight. Second, human interests pass more and more from the latent, subjective, unconscious state to the active, objective, conscious form. That is, before the baby is self-conscious, the baby's essential interest in bodily well-being is operating in performance of the organic functions. A little later the baby is old enough to understand that certain regulation of his diet, certain kinds of work or play, will help to make and keep him well and strong. Henceforth there is in him a co-operation of interest in the fundamental sense, and interest in the derived, secondary sense, involving attention and choice. If we could agree upon the use of terms, we might employ the word "desire" for this development of interest; i.e., physiological performance of function is, strictly speaking, the health interest; the desires which men actually pursue within the realm of bodily function may be normal, or perverted, in an infinite scale of variety. So with each of the other interests. Third, with these qualifications provided for, resolution of human activities into pursuit of differentiated interests becomes the first clue to the combination that unlocks the mysteries of society. For our purposes in this argument we need not trouble ourselves very much about nice metaphysical distinctions between the aspects of interest, because we have mainly to do with interests in the same sense in which the man of affairs uses the term.[9] The practical politician looks over the lobby at Washington, and he classifies the elements that compose it. He says: "Here is the railroad interest, the sugar interest, the labor interest, the army interest, the canal interest, the Cuban interest, etc." He uses the term "interest" essentially in the sociological sense, but in a relatively concrete form, and he has in mind little more than variations of the wealth interest. He would explain the legislation of a given session as the final balance between these conflicting pecuniary interests. He is right, in the main; and every social action is, in the same way, an accommodation of the various interests which are represented in the society concerned.

NOTES

1. *Social and Ethical Interpretations*, p. 81.
2. E.g., Stephen, S. Alexander, Höffding, Tarde.
3. *Op. cit.*, p. 87.
4. Here again we have a term which has insensibly grown into force in sociology, and it would require long search to trace its history. It may be found almost indiscriminately among the sociologists. Its use sometimes leaves the impression that the author attaches to it very little importance. In other cases it seems to be cardinal. No writer has made more of it than Ratzenhofer, *Sociologische Erkenntniss*, chap. 2, *et passim*.
5. *Social and Ethical Intrepretations*, pp. 15, 16, 21, 22.
6. Professor Dewey's formula is: "*Interest is impulse functioning with reference to self-realization.*" Our formula attempts to express a conception of something back of consciousness, and operating more generally than in facts of consciousness. Whether this philosophical conceit is defensible or not, is unessential for the remainder of our analysis. All that is strictly necessary for sociology proper is the later analysis, which might be performed in terms of "interest," either in our own or in the psychological sense, or of "desires" in a more empirical sense. Indeed, the latter is the method to be applied in the following discussion.
7. Quite in harmony with this formula is the conclusion of Professor Ludwig Stein, *Die sociale Frage*, 2d ed., p. 519. Closely connected with this conception of the social process is Stein's formula of the ultimate social imperative: *ibid.*, p. 522.
8. Probably it is needless to say that the term "interest" in this connection, whether used in the singular or the plural, has nothing to do with the economic term "interest."
9. We might reserve the term "interest" strictly for the use defined above, applying the term "desire" to the subjective aspect of choice and "want" to the objective aspect, i.e., the thing desired. Precisely because the term "interest" is in current use for all these aspects of the case, we prefer to retain it.

11

FLORIAN ZNANIECKI

On Social Roles and Social Circles

Polish-born Florian Witold Znaniecki (1882–1958) represented an important international voice in contemporary sociology.[1] *His voice in American sociology, however, was often one of dissent.*[2] *He viewed sociology as a special rather than a general science, was highly concerned with the meaningfulness of social reality, and believed that sociology was destined to remain a qualitative rather than a quantitative science for the foreseeable future.*

One of the numerous constructs that Znaniecki introduced into sociology was that of social circles. *In his elegant volume* (The Social Role of the Man of Knowledge) *dealing with the social relations of those who produce knowledge, both among themselves and with their audiences, he described the social circles as giving social status to the actors who in turn perform services for their circle. In Znaniecki's view, these social circles are components of the social roles of the actors.*

Znaniecki was concerned with the study of organized and interdependent interaction among human beings, which he defined as social systems. *He believed such social systems could be divided into four basic categories:* social relations, social roles, social groups, *and* societies. *He attempted to achieve the inductive development of a taxonomy of such systems, which the sociologist could then use as the basis for making generalizations about man's social life.*

This excerpt is reprinted from Florian Znaniecki, *The Social Role of the Man of Knowledge* (New York: Columbia University Press, 1940), pp. 13–19, by permission of the publisher. Footnotes have been renumbered.

Bibliographical Notes

1\. *In addition to his best known work (in collaboration with W. I. Thomas), the five-volume classic* The Polish Peasant in Europe and America *(1918–1920), and his seven books in Polish, Znaniecki's major works include:* Cultural Reality *(1919),* The Laws of Social Psychology *(1925),* The Methods of Sociology *(1934),* Social Actions *(1936),* The Social Role of the Man of Knowledge *(1940),* Cultural Sciences *(1952),* Modern Nationalities: A Sociological Study *(1952), and his unfinished* Systematic Sociology *(published as* Social Relations and Social Roles *in 1965).*

Good treatments of Znaniecki's life and work can be found in: Joseph C. Gidijnski, "Florian Znaniecki: Original Thinker, Philosopher, and Sociologist," Polish Review, *3 (1958), 77–87; Eileen M. Znaniecki, "Polish Sociology," in G. Gurvitch and W. E. Moore (eds.),* Twentieth Century Sociology *(New York: Philosophical Library, 1945), pp. 703–717; and Robert Bierstedt, "Znaniecki, Florian,"* International Encyclopedia of the Social Sciences, *Vol. 16 (New York: Macmillan and Free Press, 1968), pp. 599–602.*

2\. *An excellent statement of Znaniecki's position in contrast to the positivistic emphasis in contemporary American sociology is: Franciszek Jakubczak, "Subjectivism and Objectivism in Sociology,"* Polish Sociological Bulletin, *18 (1968), 8–21. For other excellent discussions that contrast Znaniecki's position with that of others, see: Zbigniew Bokszanski, "Florian Znaniecki's Concept of Social Actions and the Theory of Action in Sociology,"* Polish Sociological Bulletin, *17 (1968), 18–29; and Pitirim A. Sorokin,* Sociological Theories of Today *(New York: Harper & Row, 1966), pp. 278–288.*

In sociology a conceptual framework for dealing with these problems has been gradually developing in the course of monographic investigations. In recent years the term "social role" has been used by many sociologists to denote the phenomena in question.[1] We say that a priest, a lawyer, a politician, a banker, a merchant, a physician, a farmer, a workman, a soldier, a housewife, a teacher performs a specific social role. Furthermore, the concept (with certain variations) has proved applicable not only to individuals who specialize in certain activities but also to individuals as members of certain groups: thus, an American, a Frenchman, a Methodist, a Catholic, a Communist, a Fascist, a club member, a member of the family (child, father, mother, grandparent) plays a certain social role.[2] An individual in the course of his life performs a number of different roles, successively or simultaneously; the synthesis of all the social roles he has ever performed from birth to death constitutes his social personality.

Every social role presupposes that between the individual performing the role, who may thus be called a "social person," and a smaller or larger set of people who participate in his performance and may be termed his "social circle" there is a common bond constituted by a complex of values which all of them appreciate positively. These are economic values in the case of a merchant or a banker and the circle formed by his clients; hygienic values for the physician and his patients; political values for a king and his subjects; religious values for the priest and his circle of lay believers; aesthetic values for the artist and the circle of his admirers and critics; a combination of various values which fill the content of family life between the child and his family circle. The person is an object of positive valuation on the part of his circle because they believe that they all need his coöperation for the realization of certain tendencies connected with these values. The banker's coöperation is presumably needed by those who tend to invest or borrow money; the physician's coöperation by those who wish to regain or to preserve their own health and the health of the people in whom they are interested; the child's coöperation by other family members for the maintenance of family life. On the other hand, the person obviously cannot perform his role without the coöperation of his circle—though not necessarily the coöperation of any particular individual within the circle. There can be no active banker without clients, no practicing physician without patients, no reigning king without subjects, no child-in-the-family without other family members.

The person is conceived by his circle as an organic and psychological entity who is a "self," conscious of his own existence as a body and a soul and aware of how others regard him. If he is to be the kind of person his social circle needs, his "self" must possess in the opinion of the circle certain qualities, physical and mental, and not possess certain other qualities. For instance, organic "health" or "sickness" affects his supposed capacity to perform most roles, but particularly occupational roles, such as the farmer's, the workman's, the soldier's, and the housewife's, which require certain bodily skills; while lack of training in the "proper" ways of moving and eating may exclude an individual from roles which require "society" manners. Some roles are limited to men, others to women; there are upper or lower age limits for every role; the majority of roles imply certain somatic racial characteristics and definite, though variable, standards of external appearance.

The psychological qualities ascribed to persons performing social roles are enormously diversified: in every Western language there are hundreds of words denoting supposed traits of "intelligence" and "character"; and almost every such trait has, or had in the past, an axiological significance, that is, is positively or negatively valued, either in all persons or in persons performing certain kinds of role. In naïve popular reflection, such psychological traits are real qualities of a substantial "mind" or "soul," whose existence is manifested by specific acts (including verbal statements) of the individual.

A person who is needed by a social circle and whose self possesses the qualities required for the role for which he is needed has a definite social *status*, that is, his circle grants him certain rights and enforces those rights, when necessary, against individual participants of the circle or outsiders. Some of those rights concern his bodily existence. For instance, he has an ecological position, the right to occupy a definite space (as home, room, office, seat) where he is safe from bodily injury, and the right to move safely over given territories. His economic position includes rights to use certain material values regarded as necessary for his subsistence on a level commensurate with his role. Other rights involve his "spiritual welfare": he has a fixed moral standing, can claim some recognition, social response, and participation in the nonmaterial values of his circle.

He, in turn, has a social *function* to fulfill; he is regarded as obliged to achieve certain tasks by which the supposed needs of his circle will be satisfied and to behave toward other individuals in his circle in a way that shows his positive valuation of them.

Such are the essential components which we believe, on the basis of previous studies, to be found in all social roles, although of course the specific composition of different kinds of social role varies considerably. But our knowledge of a social role is not complete if we know only its composition, for a role is a dynamic system and its components may be variously interconnected in the course of its performance. There are many different ways of performing a role, according to the dominant active tendencies of the performer. He may, for instance, be mainly interested in one of the components of his role—the social circle, his own self, the status, or the function—and tend to subordinate other components to it. And, whatever his main interest, he may tend to conform with the demands of his circle or else try to innovate, to become independent of those demands. And, again, in either case he may be optimistically confident in the opportunities offered by his role and tend to expand it or else he may mistrust its possibilities and tend to restrict it to a perfectly secure minimum.

The possibility of reaching such general conclusions about all social roles and more specific, though still widely applicable, generalizations about social roles of a certain kind—such as the role of peasant, priest, merchant, factory worker, or artist—points obviously to the existence of essential uniformities and also of important variations among these social phenomena. Social roles constitute one general class of social system, and this class may be subdivided into less general classes, these into subclasses, and so on; for instance, within the specific class of factory worker there are hundreds of subclasses of workers employed in particular trades and there is another line of differentiation according to the economic organization of the factories in which they are employed. Systematic sociology stands before a task similar to that of systematic biology with its still greater complication of classes and subclasses of living organisms; and here, as there, only uniformities of specific systems make possible a further search for static and dynamic laws. But, manifestly, the source of uniformities in the social field is different from that in the field of biology.

Although in both fields differentiation is due to variations of individual systems, biological uniformities are due in the main to heredity; whereas uniformities of social systems, like those of all cultural systems, are chiefly the result of a reflective or unreflective use of the same *cultural patterns* in many particular cases. There is obviously a fundamental and universal, though unreflective, cultural pattern in accordance with which all kinds of lasting relationships between individuals and their social milieus are normatively organized and which we denote by the term "social role." The genesis of this pattern is lost in an inaccessible past, and so are the origins of what are probably its earliest variations, that is, those which everywhere differentiate individual roles according to sex and age.

NOTES

1. Some sociologists prefer the term "personal role." The concept may be traced back to C. H. Cooley's *Human Nature and the Social Order* (1902). R. E. Park, E. W. Burgess, G. H. Mead, E. T. Hiller, and others have developed it since then. In the form here presented, it has been utilized in a series of monographic investigations based on first-hand materials and carried on for a number of years by myself and my assistants. These investigations covered the following classes of social role: peasant, peasant housewife, farm laborer, industrial worker, unemployed worker, child in family, pupil in school, youthful member of playgroup, soldier, teacher, artist. Materials have been drawn in each case from several national societies. Some of these studies have been published, mostly in Polish. The first outline of the present study was published in the *Polish Sociological Review*, 1937.
2. Cf. the author's "Social Groups as Products of Cooperating Individuals," *American Journal of Sociology*, May, 1939.

12

R. E. PARK AND E. W. BURGESS

On Competition, Conflict, Accommodation and Assimilation

Robert Ezra Park (1864–1944)[1] *and Ernest W. Burgess (1886–19)*[2] *have possibly been the most intellectually influential figures in American sociology. Their impact largely results from the tremendous popularity of their introductory textbook* An Introduction to the Science of Sociology (1921) *in which they introduced many concepts and ideas (as well as numerous European thinkers in the first translations of their work to be seen by Americans) that still permeate contemporary sociology texts today.*[3] *Among these influential concepts were the basic processes of* competition, conflict, accommodation, *and* assimilation.[4]

Both Park and Burgess are also noted for their independent work (Park for his work in race relations, social control, and collective behavior and Burgess for his work on the family).[4] *In addition, they—along with R. D. MacKenzie—are considered to be the founders of that area of sociology known as* human ecology, *the study of man's relationship to his environment. Following their period of collaboration, Burgess went on to develop the concept of natural areas within a city into a patterning of concentric zones. Park's later work included the elaboration of a theory of the natural history of the city through the processes of invasion and succession.*

Reprinted from Robert E. Park and Ernest W. Burgess, *Introduction to the Science of Sociology* by permission of The University of Chicago Press. Footnotes have been modified and renumbered.

Bibliographical Notes

1. *Park's major books include:* The Immigrant Press and Its Control (*1922*) *and* The City (*with E. W. Burgess and R. D. MacKenzie, with a bibliography by L. Wirth; 1925*). *Park's many papers can be found in Everett C. Hughes,* et al. (*eds.*), The Collected Papers of Robert Ezra Park (*Glencoe, Ill.: Free Press, 1950–1955*). *A bibliography of his writings can be found in: Ralph H. Turner* (*ed.*), Robert E. Park on Social Control and Collective Behavior (*Chicago: University of Chicago Press, 1967*), *pp. 269–274.*

2. *Burgess' major works include:* Predicting Success or Failure in Marriage (*with L. S. Cottrell, Jr.; 1939*); The Family: From Institution to Companionship (*1945*); *and* Engagement and Marriage (*with Paul Wallin; 1953*).

3. *For a brief overview of the perspectives taken by Park and Burgess, see: Alvin Boskoff,* Theory in American Sociology (*New York: Thomas Y. Crowell, 1969*), *pp. 94–111.*

4. *Criticisms of these four categories of social process can be found in: P. A. Sorokin,* Contemporary Sociological Theory (*New York: Harper Torchbooks, 1964*), *pp. 508–513.*

Competition

COMPETITION A PROCESS OF INTERACTION

Of the four great types of interaction—competition, conflict, accommodation, and assimilation—competition is the elementary, universal and fundamental form. Social contact, as we have seen, initiates interaction. But competition, strictly speaking, is *interaction without social contact.* If this seems, in view of what has already been said, something of a paradox, it is because in human society competition is always complicated with other processes, that is to say, with conflict, assimilation, and accommodation.

It is only in the plant community that we can observe the process of competition in isolation, uncomplicated with other social processes.

The members of a plant community live together in a relation of mutual interdependence which we call social probably because, while it is close and vital, it is not biological. It is not biological because the relation is a merely external one and the plants that compose it are not even of the same species. They do not interbreed. The members of a plant community adapt themselves to one another as all living things adapt themselves to their environment, but there is no conflict between them because they are not conscious. Competition takes the form of conflict or rivalry only when it becomes conscious, when competitors identify one another as rivals or as enemies.

This suggests what is meant by the statement that competition is interaction *without social contact.* It is only when minds meet, only when the meaning that is in one mind is communicated to another mind so that these minds mutually influence one another, that social contact, properly speaking, may be said to exist.

On the other hand, social contacts are not limited to contacts of touch or sense or speech, and they are likely to be more intimate and more pervasive than we imagine. Some years ago the Japanese, who are brown, defeated the Russians, who are white. In the course of the next few months the news of this remarkable event penetrated, as we afterward learned, uttermost ends of the earth. It sent a thrill through all Asia and it was known in the darkest corners of Central Africa. Everywhere it awakened strange and fantastic dreams. This is what is meant by social contact.

a) *Competition and Competitive Co-operation.* Social contact, which inevitably initiates conflict, accommodation, or assimilation, invariably creates also sympathies, prejudices, personal and moral relations which modify, complicate, and control competition. On the other hand, within the limits which the cultural process creates, and custom, law, and tradition impose, competition invariably tends to create an impersonal social order in which each individual, being free to pursue his own profit, and, in a sense, compelled to do so, makes every other individual a means to that end. In doing so, however, he inevitably contributes through the mutual exchange of services so established to the common welfare. It is just the nature of the trading transaction to isolate the motive of profit and make it the basis of business organization, and so far as this motive becomes dominant and exclusive, business relations inevitably assume the impersonal character so generally ascribed to them.

"Competition," says Walker, "is opposed to sentiment. Whenever any economic agent does or forbears anything under the influence of any sentiment other than the desire of giving the least and gaining the most he can in exchange, be that sentiment patriotism, or gratitude, or charity, or vanity, leading him to do otherwise than as self interest would prompt, in that case also, the rule of competition is departed from. Another rule is for the time substituted." [1]

This is the significance of the familiar sayings to the effect that one "must not mix business with sentiment," that "business is business" "corporations are heartless," etc. It is just because corporations are "heartless," that is to say impersonal, that they represent the most advanced, efficient, and responsible form of business organization. But it is for this same reason that they can and need to be regulated in behalf of those interests of the community that cannot be translated immediately into terms of profit and loss to the individual.

The plant community is the best illustration of the type of social organization that is created by competitive co-operation because in the plant community competition is unrestricted.

b) *Competition and Freedom.* The economic organization of society, so far as it is an effect of free competition, is an ecological organization. There is a human as well as a plant and an animal ecology.

If we are to assume that the economic order is fundamentally ecological, that is, created by the struggle for existence, an organization like that of the plant community in which the relations between individuals are conceivably at least wholly external, the question may be very properly raised why the competition and the organization it has created should be regarded as social at all. As a matter of fact sociologists have generally identified the social with the moral order, and Dewey, in his *Democracy and Education,* makes statements which suggest that the purely economic order, in which man becomes a means rather than an end to other men, is unsocial, if not antisocial.

The fact is, however, that this character of *externality* in human relations is a fundamental aspect of society and social life. It is merely another manifestation of what has been referred to as the distributive aspect of society. Society is made up of individuals spatially separated, territorially distributed, and capable of independent locomotion. This capacity of independent locomotion is the basis and the symbol of every other form of independence. Freedom is fundamentally freedom to move and individuality is inconceivable without the capacity and the opportunity to gain an individual experience as a result of independent action.

On the other hand, it is quite true that society may be said to exist only so far as this independent activity of the individual is *controlled* in the interest of the group as a whole. That is the reason why the problem of control, using that term in its evident significance, inevitably becomes the central problem of sociology.

c) *Competition and Control.* Conflict, assimilation and accommodation as distinguished from competition are all intimately related to control. Competition is the process through which the distributive and ecological organization of society is created. Competition determines the distribution of population territorially and vocationally. The division of labor and all the vast organized economic interdependence of individuals and groups of individuals characteristic of modern life are a product of competition. On the other hand, the moral and political order, which imposes itself upon this competitive organization, is a product of conflict, accommodation and assimilation.

Competition is universal in the world of living things. Under ordinary circumstances it goes on unobserved even by the individuals who are most concerned. It is only in periods of crisis, when men are making new and conscious efforts to control the conditions of their common life, that the forces with which they are competing get identified with persons, and competition is converted into conflict. It is in what has been described as the *political process* that society consciously deals with its crises. War is the political process par excellence. It is in war that the great decisions are made. Political organizations exist for the purpose of dealing with conflict situations. Parties, parliaments and courts, public discussion and voting are to be considered simply as substitutes for war.

d) *Accommodation, Assimilation, and Competition.* Accommodation, on the other hand, is the process by which the individuals and groups make the necessary internal adjustments to social situations which have been created by competition and conflict. War and elections change situations. When changes thus effected are decisive and are accepted, conflict subsides and the tensions it created are resolved in the process of accommodation into profound modifications of the competing units, i.e., individuals and groups. A man once thoroughly defeated is, as has often been noted, "never the same again." Conquest, subjugation, and defeat are psychological as well as social processes. They establish a new order by changing, not merely the status, but the attitudes of the parties involved. Eventually the new order gets itself fixed in habit and custom and is then transmitted as part of the established social order to succeeding generations. Neither the physical nor the social world is made to satisfy at once all the wishes of the natural man. The rights of property, vested interests of every sort, the family organization, slavery, caste and class, the whole social organization, in fact, represent accommodations, that is to say, limitations of the natural wishes of the individual. These socially inherited accommodations have presumably grown up in the pains and struggles of previous generations, but they have been transmitted to and accepted by succeeding generations as part of the natural, inevitable social order. All of these are forms of control in which competition is limited by status.

Conflict is then to be identified with the political order and with conscious control. Accommodation, on the other hand, is associated with the social order that is fixed and established in custom and the mores.

Assimilation, as distinguished from accommodation, implies a more thoroughgoing transformation of the personality—a transformation which takes place gradually under the influence of social contacts of the most concrete and intimate sort.

Accommodation may be regarded, like religious conversion, as a kind of mutation. The wishes are the same but their organization is different. Assimilation takes place not so much as a result of changes in the organization as in the content, i.e., the memories, of the personality. The individual units, as a result of intimate association, interpenetrate, so to speak; and come in this way into possession of a common experience and a common tradition. The permanence and solidarity of the group rest finally upon this body of common experience and tradition. It is the rôle of history to preserve this body of common experience and tradition, to criticise and reinterpret it in the light of new experience and changing conditions, and in this way to preserve the continuity of the social and political life.

The relation of social structures to the processes of competition, conflict, accommodation, and assimilation may be represented schematically as follows:

SOCIAL PROCESS	SOCIAL ORDER
Competition	The economic equilibrum
Conflict	The political order
Accommodation	Social organization
Assimilation	Personality and the cultural heritage

Conflict

THE CONCEPT OF CONFLICT

The distinction between competition and conflict has already been indicated. Both are forms of interaction, but competition is a struggle between individuals, or groups of individuals, who are not necessarily in contact and communication; while conflict is a contest in which contact is an indispensable condition. Competition, unqualified and uncontrolled as with plants, and in the great impersonal life-struggle of man with his kind and with all animate nature, is unconscious. Conflict is always conscious, indeed, it evokes the deepest emotions and strongest passions and enlists the greatest concentration of attention and of effort. Both competition and conflict are forms of struggle. Competition, however, is continuous and impersonal, conflict is intermittent and personal.

Competition is a struggle for position in an economic order. The distribution of populations in the world-economy, the industrial organization in the national economy, and the vocation of the individual in the division of labor—all these are determined, in the long run, by competition. The status of the individual, or a group of individuals, in the social order, on the other hand, is determined by rivalry, by war, or by subtler forms of conflict.

"Two is company, three is a crowd" suggests how easily the social equilibrium is disturbed by the entrance of a new factor in a social situation. The delicate nuances and grades of attention given to different individuals moving in the same social circle are the superficial reflections of rivalries and conflicts beneath the smooth and decorous surfaces of polite society.

In general, we may say that competition determines the position of the individual in the community; conflict fixes his place in society. Location, position, ecological interdependence—these are the characteristics of the community. Status, subordination and superordination, control—these are the distinctive marks of a society.

The notion of conflict, like the fact, has its roots deep in human interest. Mars has always held a high rank in the hierarchy of the gods. Whenever and wherever struggle has taken the form of conflict, whether of races, of nations, or of individual men, it has invariably captured and held the attention of spectators. And these spectators, when they did not take part in the fight, always took sides. It was this conflict of the non-combatants that made public opinion, and public opinion has always played an important rôle in the struggles of men. It is this that has raised war from a mere play of physical forces and given it the tragic significance of a moral struggle, a conflict of good and evil.

The result is that war tends to assume the character of litigation, a judicial procedure, in which custom determines the method of procedure, and the issue of the struggle is accepted as a judgment in the case.

The duello, as distinguished from the wager of battle, although it never had the character of a judicial procedure, developed a strict code which made it morally binding upon the individual to seek redress for wrongs, and determined in advance the methods of procedure by which such redress could and should be obtained. The penalty was a loss of status in the particular group of which the individual was a member.

It was the presence of the public, the ceremonial character of the proceedings, and the conviction that the invisible powers were on the side of truth and justice that gave the trial by ordeal and the trial by battle a significance that neither the duello nor any other form of private vengeance ever had.

It is interesting in this connection, also, that political and judicial forms of procedure are conducted on a conflict pattern. An election is a contest in which we count noses when we do not break heads. A trial by jury is a contest in which the parties are represented by champions, as in the judicial duels of an earlier time.

In general, then, one may say competition becomes conscious and personal in conflict. In the process of transition competitors are transformed into rivals and enemies. In its higher forms, however, conflict becomes impersonal—a struggle to establish and maintain rules of justice and a moral order. In this case the welfare not merely of individual men but of the community is involved. Such are the struggles of political parties and religious sects. Here the issues are not determined by the force and weight of the contestants immediately involved, but to a greater or less extent, by the force and weight of public opinion of the community, and eventually by the judgment of mankind.

Accommodation

ADAPTATION AND ACCOMMODATION

The term *adaptation* came into vogue with Darwin's theory of the origin of the species by natural selection. This theory was based upon the observation that no two members of a biological species or of a family are ever exactly alike. Everywhere there is variation and individuality. Darwin's theory assumed this variation and explained the species as the result of natural selection. The individuals best fitted to live under the conditions of life which the environment offered, survived and produced the existing species. The others perished and the species which they represented disappeared. The differences in the species were explained as the result of the accumulation and perpetuation of the individual variations which had "survival value." Adaptations were the variations which had been in this way selected and transmitted.

The term *accommodation* is a kindred concept with a slightly different meaning. The distinction is that adaptation is applied to organic modifications which are transmitted biologically; while accommodation is used with reference to changes in habit, which are transmitted, or may be transmitted, sociologically, that is, in the form of social tradition. The term first used in this sense by Baldwin is defined in the *Dictionary of Philosophy and Psychology.*

> In view of modern biological theory and discussion, two modes of adaptation should be distinguished: (*a*) adaptation through variation [hereditary]; (*b*) adaptation through modification [acquired]. For the functional adjustment of the individual to its environment [(*b*) above] J. Mark Baldwin has suggested the term "accommodation," recommending that adaptation be confined to the structural adjustments which are congenital and heredity [(*a*) above]. The term "accommodation" applies to any acquired alteration of function resulting in better adjustment to environment and to the functional changes which are thus effected.[2]

The term accommodation, while it has a limited field of application in biology, has a wide and varied use in sociology. All the social heritages, traditions, sentiments, culture, technique, are accommodations—that is, acquired adjustments that are socially and not biologically transmitted. They are not a part of the racial inheritance of the individual, but are acquired by the person in social experience. The two conceptions are further distinguished in this, that adaptation is an effect of competition, while accommodation, or more properly social accommodation, is the result of conflict.

The outcome of the adaptations and accommodations, which the struggle for existence enforces, is a state of relative equilibrium among the competing species and individual members of these species. The equilibrium which is established by adaptation is biological, which means that, in so far as it is permanent and fixed in the race or the species, it will be transmitted by biological inheritance.

The equilibrium based on accommodation, however, is not biological; it is economic and social and is transmitted, if at all, by tradition. The nature of the economic equilibrium which results from competition has been fully described in chapter viii. The plant community is this equilibrium in its absolute form.

In animal and human societies the community has, so to speak, become incorporated in the individual members of the group. The individuals are adapted to a specific type of communal life, and these adaptations, in animal as distinguished from human societies, are represented in the division of labor between the sexes, in the instincts which secure the protection and welfare of the young, in the so-called gregarious instinct, and all these represent traits that are transmitted biologically. But human societies, although providing for the expression of original tendencies, are organized about tradition, mores, collective representations, in short, *consensus*. And consensus represents, not biological adaptations, but social accommodations.

Social organization, with the exception of the order based on competition and adaptation, is essentially an accommodation of differences through conflicts. This fact explains why diverse-mindedness rather than like-mindedness is characteristic of human as distinguished from animal society. Professor Cooley's statement of this point is clear:

> The unity of the social mind consists not in agreement but in organization, in the fact of reciprocal influence or causation among its parts, by virtue of which everything that takes place in it is connected with everything else, and so is an outcome of the whole.[3]

The distinction between accommodation and adaptation is illustrated in the difference between domestication and taming. Through domestication and breeding man has modified the original inheritable traits of plants and animals. He has changed the character of the species. Through taming, individuals of species naturally in conflict with man have become accommodated to him. Eugenics may be regarded as a program of biological adaptation of the human race in conscious realization of social ideals. Education, on the other hand, represents a program of accommodation or an organization, modification, and culture of original traits.

Every society represents an organization of elements more or less antagonistic to each other but united for the moment, at least, by an arrangement which defines the reciprocal relations and respective spheres of action of each. This accommodation, this *modus vivendi*, may be relatively permanent as in a society constituted by castes, or quite transitory as in societies made up of open classes. In either case, the accommodation, while it is maintained, secures for the individual or for the group a recognized status.

Accommodation is the natural issue of conflicts. In an accommodation the antagonism of the hostile elements is, for the time being, regulated, and conflict disappears as overt action, although it remains latent as a potential force. With a change in the situation, the adjustment that had hitherto successfully held in control the antagonistic forces fails. There is confusion and unrest which may issue in open conflict. Conflict, whether a war or a strike or a mere exchange of polite innuendoes, invariably issues in a new accommodation or social order, which in general involves a changed status in the relations among the participants. It is only with assimilation that this antagonism, latent in the organization of individuals or groups, is likely to be wholly dissolved.

Assimilation

I. POPULAR CONCEPTIONS OF ASSIMILATION

The concept assimilation, so far as it has been defined in popular usage, gets its meaning from its relation to the problem of immigration. The more concrete and familiar terms are the abstract noun Americanization and the verbs Americanize, Anglicize, Germanize, and the like.

All of these words are intended to describe the process by which the culture of a community or a country is transmitted to an adopted citizen. Negatively, assimilation is a process of denationalization and this is, in fact, the form it has taken in Europe.

The difference between Europe and America, in relation to the problem of cultures, is that in Europe difficulties have arisen from the forcible incorporation of minor cultural groups, i.e., nationalities, within the limits of a larger political unit, i.e., an empire. In America the problem has arisen from the voluntary migration to this country of peoples who have abandoned the political allegiances of the old country and are gradually acquiring the culture of the new. In both cases the problem has its sources in an effort to establish and maintain a political order in a community that has no common culture. Fundamentally the problem of maintaining a democratic form of government in a southern village composed of whites and blacks, and the problem of maintaining an international order based on anything but force are the same. The ultimate basis of the existing moral and political order is still kinship and culture. Where neither exist, a political order, not based on caste or class, is at least problematic.

Assimilation, as popularly conceived in the United States, was expressed symbolically some years ago in Zangwill's dramatic parable of *The Melting Pot*. William Jennings Bryan has given oratorical expression to the faith in the beneficent outcome of the process: "Great has been the Greek, the Latin, the Slav, the Celt, the Teuton, and the Saxon; but greater than any of these is the American, who combines the virtues of them all."

Assimilation, as thus conceived, is a natural and unassisted process, and practice, if not policy, has been in accord with this laissez faire conception, which the outcome has apparently justified. In the United States, at any rate, the tempo of assimilation has been more rapid than elsewhere.

Closely akin to this "magic crucible" notion of assimilation is the theory of "like-mindedness." This idea was partly a product of Professor Giddings' theory of sociology, partly an outcome of the popular notion that similarities and homogeneity are identical with unity. The ideal of assimilation was conceived to be that of feeling, thinking, and acting alike. Assimilation and socialization have both been described in these terms by contemporary sociologists.

Another and a different notion of assimilation or Americanization is based on the conviction that the immigrant has contributed in the past and may be expected in the future to contribute something of his own in temperament, culture, and philosophy of life to the future American civilization. This conception had its origin among the immigrants themselves, and has been formulated and interpreted by persons who are, like residents in social settlements, in close contact with them. This recognition of the diversity in the elements entering into the cultural process is not, of course, inconsistent with the expectation of an ultimate homogeneity of the product. It has called attention, at any rate, to the fact that the process of assimilation is concerned with differences quite as much as with likenesses.

II. THE SOCIOLOGY OF ASSIMILATION

Accommodation has been described as a process of adjustment, that is, an organization of social relations and attitudes to prevent or to reduce conflict, to control competition, and to maintain a basis of security in the social order for persons and groups of divergent interests and types to carry on together their varied life-activities. Accommodation in the sense of the composition of conflict is invariably the goal of the political process.

Assimilation is a process of interpenetration and fusion in which persons and groups acquire the memories, sentiments, and attitudes of other persons or groups, and, by sharing their experience and history, are incorporated with them in a common cultural life. In so far as assimilation denotes this sharing of tradition, this intimate participation in common experiences, assimilation is central in the historical and cultural processes.

This distinction between accommodation and assimilation, with reference to their rôle in society, explains certain significant formal differences between the two processes. An accommodation of a conflict, or an accommodation to a new situation, may take place with rapidity. The more intimate and subtle changes involved in assimilation are more gradual. The changes that occur in accommodation are frequently not only sudden but revolutionary, as in the mutation of attitudes in conversion. The modifications of attitudes in the process of assimilation are not only gradual, but moderate, even if they appear considerable in their accumulation over a long period of time. If mutation is the symbol for accommodation, growth is the metaphor for assimilation. In accommodation the person or the group is generally, though not always, highly conscious of the occasion, as in the peace treaty that ends the war, in the arbitration of an industrial controversy, in the adjustment of the person to the formal requirements of life in a new social world. In assimilation the process is typically unconscious; the person is incorporated into the common life of the group before he is aware and with little conception of the course of events which brought this incorporation about.

James has described the way in which the attitude of the person changes toward certain subjects, woman's sufferage, for example, not as the result of conscious reflection, but as the outcome of the unreflective responses to a series of new experiences. The intimate associations of the family and of the play group, participation in the ceremonies of religious worship and in the celebrations of national holidays, all these activities transmit to the immigrant and to the alien a store of memories and sentiments common to the native-born, and these memories are the basis of all that is peculiar and sacred in our cultural life.

As social contact initiates interaction, assimilation is its final perfect product. The nature of the social contacts is decisive in the process. Assimilation naturally takes place most rapidly where contacts are primary, that is, where they are the most intimate and intense, as in the area of touch relationship, in the family circle and in intimate congenial groups. Secondary contacts facilitate accommodations, but do not greatly promote assimilation. The contacts here are external and too remote.

A common language is indispensable for the most intimate association of the members of the group; its absence is an insurmountable barrier to assimilation. The phenomenon "that every group has its own language," its peculiar "universe of discourse," and its cultural symbols is evidence of the interrelation between communication and assimilation.

Through the mechanisms of imitation and suggestion, communication effects a gradual and unconscious modification of the attitudes and sentiments of the members of the group. The unity thus achieved is not necessarily or even normally like-mindedness; it is rather a unity of experience and of orientation, out of which may develop a community of purpose and action.

NOTES

1. Walker, Francis A., *Political Economy*, p. 92. (New York, 1887.)
2. *Dictionary of Philosophy and Psychology*, I, 15, 8.
3. *Social Organization*, p. 4.

3

Dimensions of Social Organization

13

ÉMILE DURKHEIM

On the Division of Labor

Émile Durkheim (whose views on the nature of social facts we discussed earlier), like Ferdinand Tönnies before him, was concerned with the varieties of social relationships that welded individuals into a cohesive group. According to Durkheim, a small society contains a homogeneity of social individuals who are bound together by what Durkheim called mechanical solidarity, *a unity based on the strong unanimity of public opinion, mentality, and morality (very similar to the* Gemeinschaft *condition described by Tönnies). As the population of the group increases, this homogeneity vanishes and is replaced by increasing division of labor. This division of labor becomes a new social tie insofar as individuals need one another's cooperation for survival, and these new social bonds constitute what Durkheim termed* organic solidarity.[1]

Bibliographical Note

1. The literature showing Durkheim's influence on the general question of division of labor and group solidarity is immense. A few relevant recent studies of special interest include: W. A. Faunce, *"Automation and the Division of Labor,"* Social Problems, 13 *(1965); 149–160; J. P. Gibbs and H. L. Browning, "Division of Labor, Technology, and the Organization of Production in Twelve Countries,"* American Sociological Review, 31 *(1966), 81–92; and M. L. Myers, "Division of Labor as a Principle of Social Cohesion,"* Canadian Journal of Economics, 33 *(1967), 127–139. For a recent attempt to modify*

Durkheim's position, see: Richard D. Schwartz and James Miller, "Legal Evolution and Societal Complexity," American Journal of Sociology, 70 (1965), *159–169, and the debate on this piece in* 70 (1965), *625–628.*
For a listing of the major works by and about Durkheim, see the introduction to his first statement in this volume, pp. 55–57.

[We] shall recognize only two kinds of positive solidarity which are distinguishable by the following qualities:

1. The first binds the individual directly to society without any intermediary. In the second, he depends upon society, because he depends upon the parts of which it is composed.

2. Society is not seen in the same aspect in the two cases. In the first, what we call society is a more or less organized totality of beliefs and sentiments common to all the members of the group: this is the collective type. On the other hand, the society in which we are solidary in the second instance is a system of different, special functions which definite relations unite. These two societies really make up only one. They are two aspects of one and the same reality, but none the less they must be distinguished.

3. From this second difference there arises another which helps us to characterize and name the two kinds of solidarity.

The first can be strong only if the ideas and tendencies common to all the members of the society are greater in number and intensity than those which pertain personally to each member. It is as much stronger as the excess is more considerable. But what makes our personality is how much of our own individual qualities we have, what distinguishes us from others. This solidarity can grow only in inverse ratio to personality. There are in each of us, as we have said, two consciences: one which is common to our group in its entirety, which, consequently, is not ourself, but society living and acting within us; the other, on the contrary, represents that in us which is personal and distinct, that which makes us an individual.[1] Solidarity which comes from likenesses is at its maximum when the collective conscience completely envelops our whole conscience and coincides in all points with it. But, at that moment, our individuality is nil. It can be born only if the community takes smaller toll of us. There are, here, two contrary forces, one centripetal, the other centrifugal, which cannot flourish at the same time. We cannot, at one and the same time, develop ourselves in two opposite senses. If we have a lively desire to think and act for ourselves, we cannot be strongly inclined to think and act as others do. If our ideal is to present a singular and personal appearance, we do not want to resemble everybody else. Moreover, at the moment when this solidarity exercises its force, our personality vanishes, as our definition permits us to say, for we are no longer ourselves, but the collective life.

The social molecules which can be coherent in this way can act together only in the measure that they have no actions of their own, as the molecules of inorganic bodies. That is why we propose to call this type of solidarity mechanical. The term does not signify that it is produced by mechanical and artificial means. We call it that only by analogy to the cohesion which unites the elements of an inanimate body, as opposed to that which makes a unity out of the elements of a living body. What justifies this term is that the link which thus unites the individual to society is wholly analogous to that which attaches a thing to a person. The individual conscience, considered in this light, is a simple dependent upon the collective type and follows all of its movements, as the possessed object follows those of its owner. In societies where this type of solidarity is highly developed, the individual does not appear, as we shall see later. Individuality is something which the society possesses. Thus, in these social types, personal rights are not yet distinguished from real rights.

It is quite otherwise with the solidarity which the division of labor produces. Whereas the previous type implies that individuals resemble each other, this type presumes their difference. The first is possible only in so far as the individual personality is absorbed into the collective personality; the second is possible only if each one has a sphere of action which is peculiar to him; that is, a personality. It is necessary, then, that the collective conscience leave open a part of the individual conscience in order that special functions may be established there, functions which it cannot regulate. The more this region is extended, the stronger is the cohesion which results from this solidarity. In effect, on the one hand, each one depends as much more strictly on society as labor is more divided; and, on the other, the activity of each is as much more personal as it is more specialized. Doubtless, as circumscribed as it is, it is never completely original. Even in the exercise of our occupation, we conform to usages, to practices which are common to our whole professional brotherhood. But, even in this instance, the yoke that we submit to is much less heavy than when society completely controls us, and it leaves much more place open for the free play of our initiative. Here, then, the individuality of all grows at the same time as that of its parts. Society becomes more capable of collective movement, at the same time that each of its elements has more freedom of movement. This solidarity resembles that which we observe among the higher animals. Each organ, in effect, has its special physiognomy, its autonomy. And, moreover, the unity of the organism is as great as the individuation of the parts is more marked. Because of this analogy, we propose to call the solidarity which is due to the division of labor, organic.

. . .

In determining the principal cause of the progress of the division of labor, we have at the same time determined the essential factor of what is called civilization.

Civilization is itself the necessary consequence of the changes which are produced in the volume and in the density of societies. If science, art, and economic activity develop it is in accordance with a necessity which is imposed upon men. It is because there is, for them, no other way of living in the new conditions in which they have been placed. From the time that the number of individuals among whom social relations are established begins to increase, they can maintain themselves only by greater specialization, harder work, and intensification of their faculties. From this general stimulation, there inevitably results a much higher degree of culture. From this point of view, civilization appears, not as an end which moves people by its attraction for them, not as a good foreseen and desired in advance, of which they seek to assure themselves the largest possible part, but as the effect of a cause, as the necessary resultant of a given state. It is not the pole towards which historic development is moving and to which men seek to get nearer in order to be happier or better, for neither happiness nor morality necessarily increases with the intensity of life. They move because they must move, and what determines the speed of this march is the more or less strong pressure which they exercise upon one another, according to their number.

This does not mean that civilization has no use, but that it is not the services that it renders that make it progress. It develops because it cannot fail to develop. Once effectuated, this development is found to be generally useful, or, at least, it is utilized. It responds to needs formed at the same time because they depend upon the same causes. But this is an adjustment after the fact. Yet, we must notice that the good it renders in this direction is not a positive enrichment, a growth in our stock of happiness, but only repairs the losses that it has itself caused. It is because this superactivity of general life fatigues and weakens our nervous system that it needs reparations proportionate to its expenditures, that is to say, more varied and complex satisfactions. In that, we see even better how false it is to make civilization the function of the division of labor; it is only a consequence of it. It can explain neither the existence nor the progress of the division of labor, since it has, of itself, no intrinsic or absolute value, but, on the contrary, has a reason for existing only in so far as the division of labor is itself found necessary.

We shall not be astonished by the importance attached to the numerical factor if we notice the very capital role it plays in the history of organisms. In effect, what defines a living being is the double property it has of nourishing itself and reproducing itself, and reproduction is itself only a consequence of nourishment. Therefore, the intensity of organic life is proportional, all things being equal, to the activity of nourishment, that is, to the number of elements that the organism is capable of incorporating. Hence, what has not only made possible, but even necessitated the appearance of complex organisms is that, under certain conditions, the more simple organisms remain grouped together in a way to form more voluminous aggregates. As the constitutive parts of the animal are more numerous, their relations are no longer the same, the conditions of social life are changed, and it is these changes which, in turn, determine both the division of labor, polymorphism, and the concentration of vital forces and their greater energy. The growth of organic substance is, then, the fact which dominates all zoological development. It is not surprising that social development is submitted to the same law.

Moreover, without recourse to arguments by analogy, it is easy to explain the fundamental role of this factor. All social life is made up of a system of facts which come from positive and durable relations established between a plurality of individuals. It is, thus, as much more intense as the reactions exchanged between the component units are themselves more frequent and more energetic. But, upon what does this frequency and this energy depend? Upon the nature of the elements present, upon their more or less great vitality? But . . . individuals are much more a product of common life than they are determinants of it. If from each of them we take away everything due to social action, the residue that we obtain, besides being picayune, is not capable of presenting much variety. Without the diversity of social conditions upon which they depend, the differences which separate them would be inexplicable. It is not, then, in the unequal aptitudes of men that we must seek the cause for the unequal development of societies. Will it be in the unequal duration of these relations? But time, by itself, produces nothing. It is only necessary in bringing latent energies to light. There remains no other variable factor than the number of individuals in relation and their material and moral proximity, that is to say, the volume and density of society. The more numerous they are and the more they act upon one another, the more they react with force and rapidity; consequently, the more intense social life becomes. But it is this intensification which constitutes civilization.[2]

But, while being an effect of necessary causes, civilization can become an end, an object of desire, in short, an ideal. Indeed, at each moment of a society's history, there is a certain intensity of the collective life which is normal, given the number and distribution of the social units. Assuredly, if everything happens normally, this state will be realized of itself, but we cannot bring it to pass that things will happen normally. If health is in nature, so is sickness. Health is, indeed, in societies as in individual organisms, only an ideal type which is nowhere entirely realized. Each healthy individual has more or less numerous traits of it, but there is none that unites them all. Thus, it is an end worthy of pursuit to seek to bring society to this degree of perfection.

Moreover, the direction to follow in order to attain this end can be laid out. If, instead of letting causes engender their effects by chance and according to the energy in them, thought intervenes to direct the course, it can spare men many painful efforts. The development of the individual reproduces that of the species in abridged fashion; he does not pass through all the stages that it passed through; there are some he omits and others he passes through more quickly because the experiences of the race help him to accelerate them. But thought can produce analogous results, for it is equally a utilization of anterior experience, with a view to facilitating future experience. By thought, moreover, one must not understand exclusively scientific knowledge of means and ends. Sociology, in its present state, is hardly in a position to lead us efficaciously to the solution of these practical problems. But beyond these clear representations in the milieu in which the scholar moves, there are obscure ones to which tendencies are linked. For need to stimulate the will, it is not necessary that it be clarified by science. Obscure gropings are enough to teach men that there is something lacking, to awaken their aspirations and at the same time make them feel in what direction they ought to bend their efforts.

Hence, a mechanistic conception of society does not preclude ideals, and it is wrong to reproach it with reducing man to the status of an inactive witness of his own history. What is an ideal, really, if not an anticipated representation of a desired result whose realization is possible only thanks to this very anticipation? Because things happen in accordance with laws, it does not follow that we have nothing to do. We shall perhaps find such an objective mean, because, in sum, it is only a question of living in a state of health. But this is to forget that, for the cultivated man, health consists in regularly satisfying his most elevated needs as well as others, for the first are no less firmly rooted in his nature than the second. It is true that such an ideal is near, that the horizons it opens before us have nothing unlimited about them. In any event, it cannot consist in exalting the forces of society beyond measure, but only in developing them to the limit marked by the definite state of the social milieu. All excess is bad as well as all insufficiency. But what other ideal can we propose? To seek to realize a civilization superior to that demanded by the nature of surrounding conditions is to desire to turn illness loose in the very society of which we are part, for it is not possible to increase collective activity beyond the degree determined by the state of the social organism without compromising health. In fact, in every epoch there is a certain refinement of civilization whose sickly character is attested by the uneasiness and restlessness which accompanies it. But there is never anything desirable about sickness.

But if the ideal is always definite, it is never definitive. Since progress is a consequence of changes in the social milieu, there is no reason for supposing that it must ever end. For it to have a limit, it would be necessary for the milieu to become stationary at some given moment. But such an hypothesis is contrary to the most legitimate inductions. As long as there are distinct societies, the number of social units will necessarily be variable in each of them. Even supposing that the number of births ever becomes constant, there will always be movements of population from one country to another, through violent conquests or slow and unobtrusive infiltrations. Indeed, it is impossible for the strongest peoples not to tend to incorporate the feeblest, as the most dense overflow into the least dense. That is a mechanical law of social equilibrium not less necessary than that which governs the equilibrium of liquids. For it to be otherwise, it would be necessary for all human societies to have the same vital energy and the same density. What is irrepresentable would only be so because of the diversity of habitats.

It is true that this source of variations would be exhausted if all humanity formed one and the same society. But, besides our not knowing whether such an ideal is realizable, in order for progress to cease it would still be necessary for the relations between social units in the interior of this gigantic society to be themselves recalcitrant to all change. It would be necessary for them always to remain distributed in the same way, for not only the total aggregate but also each of the elementary aggregates of which it would be formed, to keep the same dimensions. But such a uniformity is impossible, solely because these partial groups do not all have the same extent nor the same vitality. Population cannot be concentrated in the same way at all points; it is inevitable that the greatest centres, those where life is most intense, exercise an attraction for the others proportionate to their importance. The migrations which are thus produced result in further concentrating social units in certain regions, and, consequently, in determining new advances there which irradiate little by little from the homes in which they were born into the rest of the country. Moreover, these changes call forth others, without it being possible to say where the repercussions stop. In fact, far from societies approaching a stationary position in proportion to their development, they become, on the contrary, more mobile and more plastic.

. . .

With societies, individuals are transformed in accordance with the changes produced in the number of social units and their relations.

First, they are made more and more free of the yoke of the organism. An animal is almost completely under the influence of his physical environment; its biological constitution predetermines its existence. Man, on the contrary, is dependent upon social causes. Of course, animals also form societies, but, as they are very restricted, collective life is very simple. They are also stationary because the equilibrium of such small societies is necessarily stable. For these two reasons, it easily fixes itself in the organism. It not only has its roots in the organism, but it is entirely enveloped in it to such a point that it loses its own characteristics. It functions through a system of instincts, of reflexes which are not essentially distinct from those which assure the functioning of organic life. They present, it is true, the particular characteristic of adapting the individual to the social environment, not to the physical environment, and are caused by occurrences of the common life. They are not of different nature, however, from those which, in certain cases, determine without any previous education the necessary movements in locomotion. It is quite otherwise with man, because the societies he forms are much vaster. Even the smallest we know of are more extensive than the majority of animal societies. Being more complex, they also change more, and these two causes together see to it that social life with man is not congealed in a biological form. Even where it is most simple, it clings to its specificity. There are always beliefs and practices common to men which are not inscribed in their tissues. But this character is more manifest as the social mass and density grow. The more people there are in association, and the more they react upon one another, the more also does the product of these reactions pass beyond the bounds of the organism. Man thus finds himself placed under the sway of causes *sui generis* whose relative part in the constitution of human nature becomes ever more considerable.

Moreover, the influence of this factor increases not only in relative value, but also in absolute value. The same cause which increases the importance of the collective environment weakens the organic environment in such a manner as to make it accessible to the action of social causes and to subordinate it to them. Because there are more individuals living together, common life is richer and more varied, but for this variety to be possible, the organic type must be less definite to be able to diversify itself. We have seen, in effect, that the tendencies and aptitudes transmitted by heredity became ever more general and more indeterminate, more refractory consequently, to assuming the form of instincts. Thus, a phenomenon is produced which is exactly the inverse of that which we observe at the beginning of evolution. With animals, the organism assimilates social facts to it, and, stripping them of their special nature, transforms them into biological facts. Social life is materialized. In man, on the contrary, and particularly in higher societies, social causes substitute themselves for organic causes. The organism is spiritualized.

The individual is transformed in accordance with this change in dependence. Since this activity which calls forth the special action of social causes cannot be fixed in the organism, a new life, also *sui generis*, is superimposed upon that of the body. Freer, more complex, more independent of the organs which support it, its distinguishing characteristics become ever more apparent as it progresses and becomes solid. From this description we can recognize the essential traits of psychic life. To be sure, it would be exaggerating to say that psychic life begins only with societies, but certainly it becomes extensive only as societies develop. That is why, as has often been remarked, the progress of conscience is in inverse ratio to that of instinct. Whatever may be said of them, it is not the first which breaks up the second. Instinct, the product of the accumulated experience of generations, has a much greater resistive force to dissolution simply because it becomes conscious. Truly, conscience only invades the ground which instinct has ceased to occupy, or where instinct cannot be established. Conscience does not make instinct recede; it only fills the space instinct leaves free. Moreover, if instinct regresses rather than extends as general life extends, the greater importance of the social factor is the cause of this. Hence, the great difference which separates man from animals, that is, the greater development of his psychic life, comes from his greater sociability. To understand why psychic functions have been carried, from the very beginnings of the human species, to a degree of perfection unknown among animal species, one would first have to know why it is that men, instead of living in solitude or in small bands, were led to form more extensive societies. To put it in terms of the classical definition, if man is a reasonable animal, that is because he is a sociable animal, or at least infinitely more sociable than other animals.[3]

This is not all. In so far as societies do not reach certain dimensions nor a certain degree of concentration, the only psychic life which may be truly developed is that which is common to all the members of the group, which is found identical in each. But, as societies become more vast and, particularly, more condensed, a psychic life of a new sort appears. Individual diversities, at first lost and confused amidst the mass of social likenesses, become disengaged, become conspicuous, and multiply. A multitude of things which used to remain outside consciences because they did not affect the collective being become objects of representations. Whereas individuals used to act only by involving one another, except in cases where their conduct was determined by physical needs, each of them becomes a source of spontaneous activity. Particular personalities become constituted, take conscience of themselves. Moreover, this growth of psychic life in the individual does not obliterate the psychic life of society, but only transforms it. It becomes freer, more extensive, and as it has, after all, no other bases than individual consciences, these extend, become complex, and thus become flexible.

Hence, the cause which called forth the differences separating man from animals is also that which has forced him to elevate himself above himself. The ever growing distance between the savage and the civilized man has no other source. If the faculty of ideation is slowly disengaged from the confused feeling of its origin, if man has learned to formulate concepts and laws, if his spirit has embraced more and more extensive portions of space and time, if, not content with clinging to the past, he has trespassed upon the future, if his emotions and his tendencies, at first simple and not very numerous, have multiplied and diversified, that is because the social milieu has changed without interruption. In effect, unless these transformations were born from nothing, they can have had for causes only the corresponding transformations of surrounding milieux. But, man depends only upon three sorts of milieux: the organism, the external world, society. If one leaves aside the accidental variations due to combinations of heredity,—and their role in human progress is certainly not very considerable,—the organism is not automatically modified; it is necessary that it be impelled by some external cause. As for the physical world, since the beginning of history it has remained sensibly the same, at least if one does not take account of novelties which are of social origin.[4] Consequently, there is only society which has changed enough to be able to explain the parallel changes in individual nature.

It is not, then, audacious to affirm that, from now on, whatever progress is made in psycho-physiology will never represent more than a fraction of psychology, since the major part of psychic phenomena does not come from organic causes. This is what spiritualist philosophers have learned, and the great service that they have rendered science has been to combat the doctrines which reduce psychic life merely to an efflorescence of physical life. They have very justly felt that the first, in its highest manifestations, is much too free and complex to be merely a prolongation of the second. Because it is partly independent of the organism, however, it does not follow that it depends upon no natural cause, and that it must be put outside nature. But all these facts whose explanation we cannot find in the constitution of tissues derive from properties of the social milieu. This hypothesis assumes, at least, very great probability from what has preceded. But the social realm is not less natural than the organic realm. Consequently, because there is a vast region of conscience whose genesis is unintelligible through psycho-physiology alone, we must not conclude that it has been formed of itself and that it is, accordingly, refractory to scientific investigation, but only that it derives from some other positive science which can be called socio-psychology. The phenomena which would constitute its matter are, in effect, of a mixed nature. They have the same essential characters as other psychic facts, but they arise from social causes.

NOTES

1. However, these two consciences are not in regions geographically distinct from us, but penetrate from all sides.
2. We do not here have to look to see if the fact which determines the progress of the division of labor and civilization, growth in social mass and density, explains itself automatically; if it is a necessary product of efficient causes, or else an imagined means in view of a desired end or of a very great foreseen good. We content ourselves with stating this law of gravitation in the social world without going any farther. It does not seem, however, that there is a greater demand here than elsewhere for a teleological explanation. The walls which separate different parts of society are torn down by the force of things, through a sort of natural usury, whose effect can be further enforced by the action of violent causes. The movements of population thus become more numerous and rapid and the passage-lines through which these movements are effected—the means of communication—deepen. They are more particularly active at points where several of these lines cross; these are cities. Thus social density grows. As for the growth in volume, it is due to causes of the same kind. The barriers which separate peoples are analogous to those which separate the different cells of the same society and they disappear in the same way.
3. The definition of de Quatrefages which makes man a religious animal is a particular instance of the preceding, for man's religiosity is a consequence of his eminent sociability. See *supra*, pp. 168ff.
4. Transformations of the soil, of streams, through the art of husbandry, engineers, etc.

14

FERDINAND TÖNNIES

On Gemeinschaft and Gesellschaft

The German sociologist Ferdinand Tönnies (1855–1936) was a major contributor to theory and field studies in sociology.[1] *He is best remembered for his distinction between two basic types of social groups.*[2] *Tönnies argued that there are two basic forms of human will: the* essential will, *which is the underlying, organic, or instinctive driving force; and* arbitrary will, *which is deliberative, purposive, and future (goal) oriented. Groups that form around essential will, in which membership is self-fulfilling, Tönnies called* Gemeinschaft *(often translated as* community*). Groups in which membership was sustained by some instrumental goal or definite end he termed* Gesellschaft *(often translated as* society*).* Gemeinschaft *was exemplified by the family or neighborhood;* Gesellschaft, *by the city or the state.*[3]

Bibliographical Notes

1. *Tönnies' major work,* Gemeinschaft und Gesellschaft *(first published in 1887), is available in English translation (edited and translated by Charles P. Loomis) as* Community and Society *(1957). It is also available in an earlier edition, which also contained some of Tönnies' later essays, as* Fundamental Concepts of Sociology *(1940). Tönnies ten other books, of which the major work dealing with sociology is his 1931* Einführung in die Soziologie (An Introduction to Sociology), *plus most of his essays, still await English translations. A full bibliography of Tönnies' work can be found in:* American Journal of Sociology, 42 *(1937), 100–101.*

Reprinted from *Community and Society: Gemeinschaft und Gesellschaft* by Ferdinand Tönnies, translated and edited by Charles P. Loomis, pp. 223–231.

2. *Brief critiques of Tönnies' works include: Louis Wirth, "The Sociology of Ferdinand Tönnies,"* American Journal of Sociology, *32 (1927), 412–422; and Rudolf Heberle, "The Sociological System of Ferdinand Tönnies: 'Community' and 'Society'," in Harry Elmer Barnes (ed.),* An Introduction to the History of Sociology *(Chicago: University of Chicago Press, 1948), pp. 227–248.*

3. *Modern applications of Tönnies' typology can be found in: Linton C. Freeman and Robert F. Winch, "Societal Complexity: An Empirical Test of a Typology of Societies,"* American Journal of Sociology, *62 (1957), 461–466; and Charles P. Loomis and John C. McKinney, "Systematic Differences between Latin-American Communities of Family Farms and Large Estates,"* American Journal of Sociology, *61 (1956), 404–412.*

---

1. Order—Law—Mores

There is a contrast between a social order which—being based upon consensus of wills—rests on harmony and is developed and ennobled by folkways, mores, and religion, and an order which—being based upon a union of rational wills—rests on convention and agreement, is safeguarded by political legislation, and finds its ideological justification in public opinion.

There is, further, in the first instance a common and binding system of positive law, of enforcible norms regulating the interrelation of wills. It has its roots in family life and is based on land ownership. Its forms are in the main determined by the code of the folkways and mores. Religion consecrates and glorifies these forms of the divine will, i.e., as interpreted by the will of wise and ruling men. This system of norms is in direct contrast to a similar positive law which upholds the separate identity of the individual rational wills in all their interrelations and entanglements. The latter derives from the conventional order of trade and similar relations but attains validity and binding force only through the sovereign will and power of the state. Thus, it becomes one of the most important instruments of policy; it sustains, impedes, or furthers social trends; it is defended or contested publicly by doctrines and opinions and thus is changed, becoming more strict or more lenient.

There is, further, the dual concept of morality as a purely ideal or mental system of norms for community life. In the first case, it is mainly an expression and organ of religious beliefs and forces, by necessity intertwined with the conditions and realities of family spirit and the folkways and mores. In the second case, it is entirely a product and instrument of public opinion, which encompasses all relations arising out of contractual sociableness, contacts, and political intentions.

Order is natural law, law as such = positive law, mores = ideal law. Law as the meaning of what may or ought to be, of what is ordained or permitted, constitutes an object of social will. Even the natural law, in order to attain validity and reality, has to be recognized as positive and binding. But it is positive in a more general or less definite way. It is general in comparison with special laws. It is simple compared to complex and developed law.

2. *Dissolution*

The substance of the body social and the social will consists of concord, folkways, mores, and religion, the manifold forms of which develop under favorable conditions during its lifetime. Thus, each individual rcccives his share from this common center, which is manifest in his own sphere, i.e., in his sentiment, in his mind and heart, and in his conscience as well as in his environment, his possessions, and his activities. This is also true of each group. It is in this center that the individdual's strength is rooted, and his rights derive, in the last instance, from the one original law which, in its divine and natural character, encompasses and sustains him, just as it made him and will carry him away. But under certain conditions and in some relationships, man appears as a free agent (person) in his self-determined activities and has to be conceived of as an independent person. The substance of the common spirit has become so weak or the link connecting him with the others worn so thin that it has to be excluded from consideration. In contrast to the family and co-operative relationship, this is true of all relations among separate individuals where there is no common understanding, and no time-honored custom or belief creates a common bond. This means war and the unrestricted freedom of all to destroy and subjugate one another, or, being aware of possible greater advantage, to conclude agreements and foster new ties. To the extent that such a relationship exists between closed groups or communities or between their individuals or between members and nonmembers of a community, it does not come within the scope of this study. In this connection we see a community organization and social conditions in which the individuals remain in isolation and veiled hostility toward each other so that only fear of clever retaliation restrains them from attacking one another, and, therefore, even peaceful and neighborly relations are in reality based upon a warlike situation. This is, according to our concepts, the condition of Gesellschaft-like civilization, in which peace and commerce are maintained through conventions and the underlying mutual fear. The state protects this civilization through legislation and politics. To a certain extent science and public opinion, attempting to conceive it as necessary and eternal, glorify it as progress toward perfection.

But it is in the organization and order of the Gemeinschaft that folk life and folk culture persist. The state, which represents and embodies Gesellschaft, is opposed to these in veiled hatred and contempt, the more so the further the state has moved away from and become estranged from these forms of community life. Thus, also in the social and historical life of mankind there is partly close interrelation, partly juxtaposition and opposition of natural and rational will.

3. *The People* (*Volkstum*) *and the State* (*Staatstum*)

In the same way as the individual natural will evolves into pure thinking and rational will, which tends to dissolve and subjugate its predecessors, the original collective forms of Gemeinschaft have developed into Gesellschaft and the rational will of the Gesellschaft. In the course of history, folk culture has given rise to the civilization of the state.

The main features of this process can be described in the following way. The anonymous mass of the people is the original and dominating power which creates the houses, the villages, and the towns of the country. From it, too, spring the powerful and self-determined individuals of many different kinds: princes, feudal lords, knights, as well as priests, artists, scholars. As long as their economic condition is determined by the people as a whole, all their social control is conditioned by the will and power of the people. Their union on a national scale, which alone could make them dominant as a group, is dependent on economic conditions. And their real and essential control is economic control, which before them and with them and partly against them the merchants attain by harnessing the labor force of the nation. Such economic control is achieved in many forms, the highest of which is planned capitalist production or large-scale industry. It is through the merchants that the technical conditions for the national union of independent individuals and for capitalistic production are created. This merchant class is by nature, and mostly also by origin, international as well as national and urban, i.e., it belongs to Gesellschaft, not Gemeinschaft. Later all social groups and dignitaries and, at least in tendency, the whole people acquire the characteristics of the Gesellschaft.

Men change their temperaments with the place and conditions of their daily life, which becomes hasty and changeable through restless striving. Simultaneously, along with this revolution in the social order, there takes place a gradual change of the law, in meaning as well as in form. The contract as such becomes the basis of the entire system, and rational will of Gesellschaft, formed by its interests, combines with authoritative will of the state to create, maintain and change the legal system. According to this conception, the law can and may completely change the Gesellschaft in line with its own discrimination and purpose; changes which, however, will be in the interest of the Gesellschaft, making for usefulness and efficiency. The state frees itself more and more from the traditions and customs of the past and the belief in their importance. Thus, the forms of law change from a product of the folkways and mores and the law of custom into a purely legalistic law, a product of policy. The state and its departments and the individuals are the only remaining agents, instead of numerous and manifold fellowships, communities, and commonwealths which have grown up organically. The characters of the people, which were influenced and determined by these previously existing institutions, undergo new changes in adaptation to new and arbitrary legal constructions. These earlier institutions lose the firm hold which folkways, mores, and the conviction of their infallibility gave to them.

Finally, as a consequence of these changes and in turn reacting upon them, a complete reversal of intellectual life takes place. While originally rooted entirely in the imagination, it now becomes dependent upon thinking. Previously, all was centered around the belief in invisible beings, spirits and gods; now it is focalized on the insight into visible nature. Religion, which is rooted in folk life or at least closely related to it, must cede supremacy to science, which derives from and corresponds to consciousness. Such consciousness is a product of learning and culture and, therefore, remote from the people. Religion has an immediate contact and is moral in its nature because it is most deeply related to the physical-spiritual link which connects the generations of men. Science receives its moral meaning only from an observation of the laws of social life, which leads it to derive rules for an arbitrary and reasonable order of social organization. The intellectual attitude of the individual becomes gradually less and less influenced by religion and more and more influenced by science. Utilizing the research findings accumulated by the preceding industrious generation, we shall investigate the tremendous contrasts which the opposite poles of this dichotomy and these fluctuations entail. For this presentation, however, the following few remarks may suffice to outline the underlying principles.

4. *Types of Real Community Life*

The exterior forms of community life as represented by natural will and Gemeinschaft were distinguished as house, village, and town. These are the lasting types of real and historical life. In a developed Gesellschaft, as in the earlier and middle stages, people live together in these different ways. The town is the highest, viz., the most complex, form of social life. Its local character, in common with that of the village, contrasts with the family character of the house. Both village and town retain many characteristics of the family; the village retains more, the town less. Only when the town develops into the city are these characteristics almost entirely lost. Individuals or families are separate identities, and their common locale is only an accidental or deliberately chosen place in which to live. But as the town lives on within the city, elements of life in the Gemeinschaft, as the only real form of life, persist within the Gesellschaft, although lingering and decaying. On the other hand, the more general the condition of Gesellschaft becomes in the nation or a group of nations, the more this entire "country" or the entire "world" begins to resemble one large city. However, in the city and therefore where general conditions characteristic of the Gesellschaft prevail, only the upper strata, the rich and the cultured, are really active and alive. They set up the standards to which the lower strata have to conform. These lower classes conform partly to supersede the others, partly in imitation of them in order to attain for themselves social power and independence. The city consists, for both groups (just as in the case of the "nation" and the "world"), of free persons who stand in contact with each other, exchange with each other and cooperate without any Gemeinschaft or will thereto developing among them except as such might develop sporadically or as a leftover from former conditions. On the contrary, these numerous external contacts, contracts, and contractual relations only cover up as many inner hostilities and antagonistic interests. This is especially true of the antagonism between the rich or the so-called cultured class and the poor or the servant class, which try to obstruct and destroy each other. It is this contrast which, according to Plato, gives the "city" its dual character and makes it divide in itself. This itself, according to our concept, constitutes the city, but the same contrast is also manifest in every large-scale relationship between capital and labor. The common town life remains within the Gemeinschaft of family and rural life; it is devoted to some agricultural pursuits but concerns itself especially with art and handicraft which evolve from these natural needs and habits. City life, however, is sharply distinguished from that; these basis activities are used only as means and tools for the special purposes of the city.

The city is typical of Gesellschaft in general. It is essentially a commercial town and, in so far as commerce dominates its productive labor, a factory town. Its wealth is capital wealth which, in the form of trade, usury, or industrial capital, is used and multiplies. Capital is the means for the appropriation of products of labor or for the exploitation of workers. The city is also the center of science and culture, which always go hand in hand with commerce and industry. Here the arts must make a living; they are exploited in a capitalistic way. Thoughts spread and change with astonishing rapidity. Speeches and books through mass distribution become stimuli of far-reaching importance.

The city is to be distinguished from the national capital, which, as residence of the court or center of government, manifests the features of the city in many respects although its population and other conditions have not yet reached that level. In the synthesis of city and capital, the highest form of this kind is achieved: the metropolis. It is the essence not only of a national Gesellschaft, but contains representatives from a whole group of nations, i.e., of the world. In the metropolis, money and capital are unlimited and almighty. It is able to produce and supply goods and science for the entire earth as well as laws and public opinion for all nations. It represents the world market and world traffic; in it world industries are concentrated. Its newspapers are world papers, its people come from all corners of the earth, being curious and hungry for money and pleasure.

5. *Counterpart of Gemeinschaft*

Family life is the general basis of life in the Gemeinschaft. It subsists in village and town life. The village community and the town themselves can be considered as large families, the various clans and houses representing the elementary organisms of its body; guilds, corporations, and offices, the tissues and organs of the town. Here original kinship and inherited status remain an essential, or at least the most important, condition of participating fully in common property and other rights. Strangers may be accepted and protected as serving-members or guests either temporarily or permanently. Thus, they can belong to the Gemeinschaft as objects, but not easily as agents and representatives of the Gemeinschaft. Children are, during minority, dependent members of the family, but according to Roman custom they are called free because it is anticipated that under possible and normal conditions they will certainly be masters, their own heirs. This is true neither of guests nor of servants, either in the house or in the community. But honored guests can approach the position of children. If they are adopted or civic rights are granted to them, they fully acquire this position with the right to inherit. Servants can be esteemed or treated as guests or even, because of the value of their functions, take part as members in the activities of the group. It also happens sometimes that they become natural or appointed heirs. In reality there are many gradations, lower or higher, which are not exactly met by legal formulas. All these relationships can, under special circumstances, be transformed into merely interested and dissolvable interchange between independent contracting parties. In the city such change, at least with regard to all relations of servitude, is only natural and becomes more and more widespread with its development. The difference between natives and strangers becomes irrelevant. Everyone is what he is, through his personal freedom, through his wealth and his contracts. He is a servant only in so far as he has granted certain services to someone else, master in so far as he receives such services. Wealth is, indeed, the only effective and original differentiating characteristic; whereas in Gemeinschaften property it is considered as participation in the common ownership and as a specific legal concept is entirely the consequence and result of freedom or ingenuity, either original or acquired. Therefore, wealth, to the extent that this is possible, corresponds to the degree of freedom possessed.

In the city as well as in the capital, and especially in the metropolis, family life is decaying. The more and the longer their influence prevails, the more the residuals of family life acquire a purely accidental character. For there are only few who will confine their energies within such a narrow circle; all are attracted outside by business, interests, and pleasures, and thus separated from one another. The great and mighty, feeling free and independent, have always felt a strong inclination to break through the barriers of the folkways and mores. They know that they can do as they please. They have the power to bring about changes in their favor, and this is positive proof of individual arbitrary power. The mechanism of money, under usual conditions and if working under high pressure, is means to overcome all resistance, to obtain everything wanted and desired, to eliminate all dangers and to cure all evil. This does not hold always. Even if all controls of the Gemeinschaft are eliminated, there are nevertheless controls in the Gesellschaft to which the free and independent individuals are subject. For Gesellschaft (in the narrower sense), convention takes to a large degree the place of the folkways, mores, and religion. It forbids much as detrimental to the common interest which the folkways, mores, and religion had condemned as evil in and of itself.

The will of the state plays the same role through law courts and police, although within narrower limits. The laws of the state apply equally to everyone; only children and lunatics are not held responsible to them. Convention maintains at least the appearance of morality; it is still related to the folkways, mores, and religious and aesthetic feeling, although this feeling tends to become arbitrary and formal. The state is hardly directly concerned with morality. It has only to suppress and punish hostile actions which are detrimental to the common weal or seemingly dangerous for itself and society. For as the state has to administer the common weal, it must be able to define this as it pleases. In the end it will probably realize that no increase in knowledge and culture alone will make people kinder, less egotistic, and more content and that dead folkways, mores, and religions cannot be revived by coercion and teaching. The state will then arrive at the conclusion that in order to create moral forces and moral beings it must prepare the ground and fulfill the necessary conditions, or at least it must eliminate counteracting forces. The state, as the reason of Gesellschaft, should decide to destroy Gesellschaft or at least to reform or renew it. The success of such attempts is highly improbable.

6. *The Real State*

Public opinion, which brings the morality of Gesellschaft into rules and formulas and can rise above the state, has nevertheless decided tendencies to urge the state to use its irresistible power to force everyone to do what is useful and to leave undone what is damaging. Extension of the penal code and the police power seems the right means to curb the evil impulses of the masses. Public opinion passes easily from the demand for freedom (for the upper classes) to that of despotism (against the lower classes). The makeshift, convention, has but little influence over the masses. In their striving for pleasure and entertainment they are limited only by the scarcity of the means which the capitalists furnish them as price for their labor, which condition is as general as it is natural in a world where the interests of the capitalists and merchants anticipated all possible needs and in mutual competition incite to the most varied expenditures of money. Only through fear of discovery and punishment, that is, through fear of the state, is a special and large group, which encompasses far more people than the professional criminals, restrained in its desire to obtain the key to all necessary and unnecessary pleasures. The state is their enemy. The state, to them, is an alien and unfriendly power; although seemingly authorized by them and embodying their own will, it is nevertheless opposed to all their needs and desires, protecting property which they do not possess, forcing them into military service for a country which offers them hearth and altar only in the form of a heated room on the upper floor or gives them, for native soil, city streets where they may stare at the glitter and luxury in lighted windows forever beyond their reach! Their own life is nothing but a constant alternative between work and leisure, which are both distorted into factory routine and the low pleasure of the saloons. City life and Gesellschaft down the common people to decay and death; in vain they struggle to attain power through their own multitude, and it seems to them that they can use their power only for a revolution if they want to free themselves from their fate. The masses become conscious of this social position through the education in schools and through newspapers. They proceed from class consciousness to class struggle. This class struggle may destroy society and the state which is its purpose to reform. The entire culture has been transformed into a civilization of state and Gesellschaft, and this transformation means the doom of culture itself if none of its scattered seeds remain alive and again bring forth the essence and idea of Gemeinschaft, thus secretly fostering a new culture amidst the decaying one.

15

HOWARD BECKER

On the Sacred and the Secular

Howard Becker (1899–1960), best known as a sociological theorist and methodologist,[1] *focused his sociology upon the study of values. His work was greatly influenced by the German sociologists Max Weber and Leopold von Wiese and the American sociologists Robert E. Park and George Herbert Mead. Becker's basic procedure involved the development of what he called* constructive typology. *Essentially, this procedure consists of (1) framing some provisional hypotheses about the relations between some phenomena one wishes to study, and then (2) looking at an empirical case (or series of cases) and abstracting a "typical set of typical personalities, processes, and structures" that appear to explain the case(s) studied. Although these abstracted types are not necessarily found in their pure state in reality, they are not what Weber called ideal types nor are they fictions. The validity of the constructed type is determined by a third step in the procedure: using the type as an explanatory device to apply to new empirical cases.*[2]

The major constructive types developed by Becker are those of the sacred *and the* secular society. *These are social and cultural contexts in which there are differential systems of values, and these value systems determine the nature and variety of the social action that will take place.*

Reprinted from Howard Becker, "Current Sacred-Secular Theory and Its Development," in *Modern Sociological Theory*, edited by Howard Becker and Alvin Boskoff (New York: Holt, Rinehart and Winston, 1966), pp. 140–149. Footnotes have been renumbered.

Bibliographical Notes

1. *Becker's major works include:* Social Thought from Lore to Science, *with Harry Elmer Barnes (1938, final revision in 1961)*; Contemporary Social Theory, *edited with H. E. Barnes and F. B. Becker (1940)*; Marriage and the Family, *edited with Reuben Hill (1942)*; German Youth: Bond or Free (*1946*); Through Values to Social Interpretation: Essays on Social Contexts, Actions, Types and Prospects (*1950*); Man in Reciprocity (*1956*); Modern Sociological Theory in Continuity and Change, *edited with* A. *Boskoff (1957); and a translation, adaptation, and amplification of Leopold von Wiese's* Systematic Sociology (*1932*).

2. *For a full analysis and discussion of these problems and the method, see: John C. McKinney,* Constructive Typology and Social Theory (*New York: Appleton-Century-Crofts, 1966*). *A negative appraisal of Becker's contribution can be found in: Pitirim* A. *Sorokin,* Sociological Theories of Today (*New York: Harper & Row, 1966*), *pp. 333–341.*

The Nature of Values and Evaluation

The digressions have now served their immediate purpose; let us turn to the values and value-systems to be treated as sacred and secular. The digressions have perhaps called attention to the fact that there is a certain ambiguity in the term "value" as hitherto used.[1] From all that is now known about human beings, it is evident that mere knowing-and-desiring is not characteristically human; the crucial differential is limitation, through culture, of permissibility. Less abstractly stated, all "takens" are subjected to judgments, with awareness or without, of right-wrong, good-bad, proper-improper, convenient-inconvenient, and so on, and these normative judgments involve more than a single actor. In other words, the range of values that may be known-and-desired is far wider than those issuing in actual conduct; perhaps nowhere, to speak popularly, does man do what he *could* wish to do.[2]

In discussing values at the human level, therefore, it would be possible to handle the issues involved in such a way as to require frequent use of the term "norms." Indeed, if it were not so cumbrous a way of putting it, it would be quite proper always to speak of human activity as essentially "knowing-desiring-norming." [3]

Beyond question, the persons engaged in such activity often are not even dimly aware of the fact that their "takens" have been strained through a normative mesh; their choosing has been done for them by predecessors in such ways that no genuine alternatives are perceived. Only the sophisticated observer, presumably holding in view more evidence of the varieties of conduct that could be engaged in than any subject under observation possesses, can state what might or might not be chosen. Again resorting to simpler but not necessarily inaccurate phraseology, it may be a case of "Those fellows just don't know what's good for 'em"—or bad for them, for that matter. Nature and nurture, then, limit the scope of "knowing-desiring-norming" in ways that are at times quite drastic where particular subjects are concerned.

Further, to call an observer "sophisticated" is not to assume that he is omniscient; he too operates within confines, wide though they may be, of permissibility, which is to say that he wittingly or unwittingly imposes normative judgments on what is observed. In the case of the predictively oriented social scientist *qua* scientist, his norms lead to the exclusion of esthetic, playful, religious, and like considerations except as they promise to yield greater predictive power. He consistently makes judgments to the following effect: "All value-judgments other than the supreme value-judgment that prediction is in and of itself worth while are to be set aside by the social scientist in his strictly scientific role." If the predictive statements resulting from the social scientist's activity are verified, he still has no warrant for assuming that he possesses Truth in any final sense; he has merely selected and properly handled those kinds of evidence that have a crucial bearing on the achievement of his supreme value. The difference between the sophisticated social-scientific observer and the persons he observes is in essence the difference between the adherent of a predictive value-system and persons yielding allegiance to other kinds.[4]

Note now that in the previous paragraph the *general* usage has returned to "values." As any object of any need, a value is the outcome of knowing-desiring-norming; what is known is a value, what is desired is a value, what is normed is a value. Similarly, "evaluating" or "evaluation" may and should be used to designate *any* human activity that defines values in terms of needs and *vice versa.*[5] Accordingly, we are back where we began; values and value-systems have once more come into focus.

The Comprehensiveness of Sacred and Secular

Sacred and secular values and value-systems represent a quite abstract level of formulation, although they inductively derive from very substantial bodies of empirical evidence. In the later part of this chapter, dealing with some of the history of sacred-secular constructs, the close interplay of induction-deduction is made reasonably clear; the constructs progressively emerged when certain perplexities arose, and were not set up in advance. But here the writer anticipates unduly; it seems best to continue with substantive presentation.

Reluctance and readiness to accept or initiate social change provide the construction lines of what may be called a sacred-secular scale or continuum. Any society or part thereof that imparts to or elicits from its members evaluations that can be altered, if at all, only in the face of definite emotionalized reluctance is a sacred society—a shorthand term for a society bearing a cultural system making for the reluctance indicated. Conversely, any society or part thereof that imparts to or elicits from its members evaluations leading to well-marked readiness to change is a secular society in a similar shorthand sense. Problems relating to social and cultural change [see Chap. 9, by Alvin Boskoff, in *Modern Sociological Theory*], therefore, are built into the sacred-secular scale, as are also what in some ways are their counterparts, problems of social control.

Given such considerations, and the empirical evidence relating to them, sacred values must be treated as comprising far more than the religious, divine, spiritual, and so on.[6] Any conduct whatsoever may be viewed as hinging on sacred considerations when it is accompanied by a characteristic reluctance to change values and/or their related needs. Putting it differently, unwillingness or inability or both—linked with distress or similar signs of tension—to alter any aspect of one's "way of life" is sacred evaluation. The person who makes such evaluation has certain needs so interwoven with certain values that he feels and acts in an "upset" manner when change in those needs and values is even suggested, let alone demanded.

Culture Is Crucial

Whether sacred or secular, all values are culturally defined in some manner and degree. What is sacred to any people in eating, mating, fighting, and worshiping is what they have been taught in some fashion or another to hold sacred. In discernibly different but similar ways, the same is true of secular values, for although the secular is not merely the reverse of the sacred, it is still safe to say that readiness for and liking of change must be learned. Ability or willingness to change are, like their opposites, acquired capacities. The learning of secular conduct is clearly, from what has been said above, much more than the acquisition of avowedly or unavowedly non-religious, profane, or skeptical needs and values.[7] These are all secular, of course, but the designation reaches far beyond them. Any sort of conduct may be viewed as centering on values designable in secular terms when well-marked needs to seek those values, whatever the changes entailed, are in some way evident. Persons so evaluating have learned to concentrate on certain ends, tangible or intangible as the case may be, in a manner such that they may even be unable to refrain from pursuing them by any means available and regardless of the disapproval, however severely expressed, of their fellows.

Here likewise culture is powerfully at work. No innovation ever is entirely without a "cultural base," and from such a standpoint all innovations are culturally conditioned, but over and above this it is obvious that if they are not to disappear when their introducers die, they must be passed on to others who have come to accept or, in some cases, to welcome them. Stated otherwise, changes in culture must be imparted to at least one succeeding generation if they are to become more than merely private variations or deviations; communication over time is indispensable. Cultural changes must be transmitted, learned, and shared quite as definitely as must cultural continuities. Sacred and secular value-systems, then, are both products and producers of culture, particularly when viewed as embodied in evaluative actions leading subsequent actors to evaluate similarly.

From Reluctance to Readiness

The writer earlier remarked that the major theoretical task now under survey is the constructing of a sacred-secular continuum along which evaluations can be ranged. Such a continuum, if it is formalized as a scale, should have specified end-points. The present state of our knowledge makes specification of this kind rather venturesome or even somewhat arbitrary, but it cannot be avoided. Therefore, let us array several types of evaluation along a line leading from estimated maximum reluctance to change old values to estimated maximum readiness to seek new values. (Incidentally, "old" and "new" must be assigned the definitions offered, in whatever ways, by the *subjects* concerned; it makes no difference for present purposes whether the values involved are "really" old or new.) As long as unduly precise connotations are not thereby introduced, the scale in question may be constructed algebraically—that is, from maximum plus to maximum minus, with a zero or transitional point somewhere about the middle.[8]

What Is Holy Must Be Kept Holy

Starting with maximum plus as the strongest empirically manifested reluctance to change, we may give appropriate attention to the frequent embracing of martyrdom for oneself or the inflicting of it on others that men have time out of mind practiced for the sake of preserving religious needs and values. Their orientation toward what they have regarded as supernatural forces or beings has frequently been so compulsive that they have sacrificed themselves or their fellows rather than permit changes in the evaluation of those orientations, or supernatural agencies, or both. Now and then, it may be admitted, there prevails a conception that impious innovators are supernaturally punished, and that hence the pious need not themselves take action. "Vengeance is mine; I will repay, saith the Lord." When this is the case, the heretical deviant merely becomes an outcast or, less frequently, may be allowed to remain a member of the society, albeit at the lower levels. But in spite of this and other exceptions noted later, holy evaluation in one or another form bringing sacrificial extinction with it has so often been evident that there seems considerable warrant for placing it at the maximum-plus pole of the sacred-secular scale.

Indulging in terminological comment: "Holy" is expressly limited, following established precedent, to evaluations bound up with supernaturalism, which is to say with religion as here viewed. Much confusion has resulted, and will probably continue to result, from the loose use of "religion" to designate non-supernaturalistic evaluations of compelling kind—for example "Communism as a religion." Similar confusion comes about when the sacred and the religious are treated as coterminous; religion *per se* is but one aspect of the sacred. A very large amount of sacred conduct has little or nothing to do with the supernaturalistically oriented—which is to say, with the religious. The holy, on the other hand, has long been properly restricted in English to religious manifestations in the narrow and only suitable sense: holy water, holy days, holy wedlock, holy communion, holy orders, the Holy Land, His Holiness the Pope, the Holy Bible, and so on.[9] Attention to the holy as a kind of evaluation inseparably linked with supernaturalism was taken as a matter of course by anthropologists and sociologists until well beyond Tylor's time—in fact, until Durkheim and Sumner (to name only the more prominent) befogged significant distinctions by using all-inclusive and vague categories. Only in the second quarter of the present century, with Otto and other students of comparative religion, was the importance of the holy again recognized. Even now only a few sociological investigators such as Goode seem to have kept abreast of the newer evidence and emphasis;[10] for the most part, anthropologists as well as sociologists seem confused and out of date. Unless religion, which is to say holy evaluation, which is to say conduct oriented toward objects regarded as supernatural, is analytically distinguished from other varieties of the sacred, little predictive worth attaches to it as a category.

Nobody Loves a Traitor

Having at least provisionally placed the holy at the plus extreme of the evaluation scale, it must nevertheless be noted that the basic criterion, action involving martyrdom or its equivalents, is also present in several other kinds of sacredness. The loyalistic, for example, comprising clan allegiance, patriotism, identification with one or another race, class, faction, party, or what not, calls forth everything from "altruistic suicide" to murder—or shall we say "liquidation"? It is easy to bring to mind instance after instance of the terrific power of loyalism; multitudes of men have perished because of their own or their opponents' devotion to groups of one or another kind. So numerous are the instances, in fact, that loyalistic sacredness seems closely to rival and now and again to surpass the holy variety as a contender for the maximum-plus position on the scale.[11]

The historical record is by no means clear, and it may well be that supernaturalism is not the most important source, numerically speaking, of "supreme sacrifice." The obscurity enshrouding much of the past is increased by the fact that the holy and the loyalistic are often difficult if not virtually impossible to separate, not only empirically but also analytically. Just where the line can be appropriately drawn between Hindu religious belief, practice, and feeling as such, on the one hand,

and the intermeshing evaluative conduct constituting the structure of Hindu castes, guilds, village councils, and similar loyalty-eliciting groups on the other, baffles the most thoroughly informed students of such matters.

Moreover, there is a substantial amount of evidence showing that it may occasionally be far safer openly to denounce a god than to assert independence of a group, much less to become traitor to it. A researcher, in his work among the Winnebago, found that one skeptic boldly expressed contempt for the holiest of the tribal deities and that, when the deity in question appeared in order to inflict lethal disease as punishment, his impious critic remained immune. The consequence was that the diety, hoping to escape ridicule, begged the man to succumb, but in vain. The same researcher also found that non-observance or defiance of established social relations carried far more serious consequences than did religious dissent; those unable or unwilling to conform socially faced banishment or death. In short, religious heretics sometimes held their own, but social mavericks never did.[12]

In spite of this and like evidence, however, the writer feels that although the loyalistically sacred, together with several other varieties to be mentioned later, may come very close indeed to the holy in life-or-death power, the holy has probably been stronger in a somewhat greater number of cases. This feeling arises from a considerable amount of reading in the relevant sources, but proof or disproof would require elaborate and costly research.

The Bonds of Intimacy

Thus far we have dealt only with the holy and the loyalistic, but several other kinds of sacredness must be discussed, among them that connected with what have long been called primary groups. Intimate sacredness, represented by ties with playfellows, friends, comrades, mates, and partners, is encountered on every hand. Intimacy, once well and favorably established, is usually regarded as not lightly to be terminated or even altered in slight degree.

Manifestly, the grounds of intimacy, as of all other aspects of the sacred and the secular, differ strikingly from one society to another, but the world over we encounter evidence of the supreme devotion that it calls forth; it also often rivals the holy in the sacrificial zeal it evokes. Cooley's praise of democracy had little realistic reference to the mass political phenomena apparent to other than Pollyanna observers even in his day, but what he had to say about kindly give-and-take, shared responsibility, good faith, willingness to cooperate, and neighborliness was warranted for what he saw among face-to-face and relatively small groupings practicing—however short of perfection—a kind of rural and small-town American version of nineteenth-century Protestant Christianity. The core of his sociology was a cheerful exaggeration of the scope and power of the intimately sacred, but he did validly point to its importance.[13]

The Moralistic and Its Qualifications

Proceeding further along the scale, it seems that moralistic sacredness may be assigned the next section of the continuum. This variety has a range more limited than that of the familiar mores, for the latter has been so loosely used, from the very beginning, that it takes in everything from the holy to the fitting and has been applied to some aspects of secular conduct as well. What is here meant by the moralistic covers evaluations referring directly to enjoined or forbidden types of conduct specifically distinguishable from the total personalities of those engaged therein. Concretely, a man may be viewed as having bad morals but not as being a hopelessly bad man; further, his morals can be improved piecemeal, as it were. In contrast, grave breaches of the holy, loyalistic, and intimate put the offender beyond the pale in many societies; condemnation is complete.

In the case of the moralistic, to be sure, the "manners and customs" concerned are often so entrenched that marked indignation is the immediate consequence of even the mere suggestion that they should be changed. Nevertheless, the potential or actual violator is not exterminated, cast out, or wholly ostracized; there is some possibility of making amends. This may be illustrated by the fact that in American society, particularly of almost bygone rural type, violations of sexual morals among the unmarried could be remedied by the "shotgun wedding." With moralistic requirements thus satisfied, the ensuing conduct of the once outraged guardian of the moral code was ordinarily the reverse of violent; the son-in-law acquired by threat was frequently treated as though no major deviation had occurred. Obviously, this example also serves to indicate that on occasion the moralistically sacred carries with it the ultimate sanction of death—but usually as alternative, not as inevitability.

Placing the moralistic at a considerable remove from the maximum-plus end of the scale therefore seems warranted. Again, however, there must be inserted the proviso that the wide variations between one culture and another may bring about *notable shifts* in scale position, not only of the moralistic, but also of other types of sacredness.

Still another qualification must be imposed with regard to the ethical, viewed as the moralistic at a more general level. Ethical sacredness, as is well known, often engenders exalted and passionate devotion. That is to say, abstract ethical precepts may approximate the holy in the zeal they call forth. Further, in form they are often highly rational (in the formal, discursive sense), although in content they are usually, at least with regard to origin, quite as nonrational as the moralistic. Moreover, ethical precepts may be held with such intensity as to lead to rejection of ritual; take the example of the Hebrew prophets who declared that Yahveh desired justice rather than burnt offerings. Ethical demands, in other words, may be closely linked with the transcendent claims of the holy. Consequently, the treatment of the ethical as merely the moralistic at a more abstract level may beg some questions in favor of the present scaling procedure. Let it be understood, then, that there is nothing sacred about this procedure. If it proves predictively useful, well and good; if not, alterations are certainly advisable.

"It Jest Ain't Fittin'!"

Next along the scale comes a kind of evaluation of distinctly lower intensity than any of those thus far considered. This may be called the fittingly sacred; it occupies the hazy band between the moralistic and the merely appropriate. Designations for conduct falling in this band are many; a short list includes proper–improper, "done"–"not done," "good form"–"bad form," mannerly–unmannerly, decent–vulgar, and the like. This list draws on the vast fund of what is viewed as etiquette in the formal sense, but there are equivalents, likewise representing a low intensity of the sacred, for all other forms of the fitting. Few persons would regard the custom, observed in some circles, of not immediately picking up one's change on the bar when a drink has been served as in the realm of etiquette, for example; but it may nevertheless be viewed as eminently fitting even by those not conversant with Emily Post.

One of the most convenient ways of distinguishing the fittingly sacred from closely related varieties is to take account of the conduct attending its violation. Moralistic offenses evoke indignation, whereas failure to observe the fitting elicits little if anything more than contempt. The almost imperceptible shrug of the shoulders, the raised eyebrow or the curled lip, the sudden and noticeably continued silence when the obtrusive newcomer enters the clubroom frequented only by the long-established members, are all unspoken but nevertheless definite judgments that the fitting is being disregarded in a culpable way.[14]

Reference has been made to the low intensity of the fitting, yet there may be a high degree of reluctance to change even in what those of us inclined toward informality call "mere manners." Men seldom die for the sake of the fitting, but they may undergo extreme discomfort and sometimes danger. Those of us who have watched Britishers quietly finish their tea-drinking before proceeding to air-raid shelters, even though the noise of bursting bombs was to be heard all through teatime, have gained some notion of the fact that though the fitting is not oriented toward holiness, it represents a reluctance to change that can hardly be viewed as other than sacred.

"Dinner Jackets Would Be Approppropriate"

The sacred on the fringe of fadeout has sometimes been placed in the realm of the folkways; but like the mores, the folkways take in too much of both sacred and secular. It here seems best to make use of a more limited term such as the appropriate. There is a minimum of any controls savoring of indignation or contempt, but resort to ridicule is still possible. "Suitable," "customary," "regular," "expected," "normal," "usual," and similar more or less interchangeable words often have a sacred tinge; they indicate that "right" and "wrong" ways of doing things are not matters of indifference, and that there is some reluctance to relinquish, or to see others relinquish, the appropriate ways.

At the same time, those who wittingly or unwittingly perpetrate the inappropriate are not viewed as unworthy, but rather as uninstructed. Their remediable ignorance, indifference, or impatience may be viewed with nothing more than mild and courteously concealed amusement. The man who wears yellow-tan shoes and bright blue socks with a green suit and a pictorial necktie at a garden party will, it is assumed, learn better after a while. In the interval, the temptation to smile in his presence remains only a temptation. Defense of the appropriate, which is to say of the sacred almost at the vanishing point, here amounts to no more than an inadvertent twitch at the corners of the mouth;[15] the shift to the secular is close at hand.

The Pervasiveness of Ceremonial

Discussion of this shift must be delayed, however, until some reference is made to an aspect of sacred conduct evident in all its varieties, from the holy to the merely appropriate, that may be labeled the ceremonially sacred. Its importance is readily perceived when we focus on the holy, for ritual, in the sense of religious ceremonial *per se*, is often the most obvious mark of supernaturalistic orientation. In fact, Jane Harrison and others have pointed out that *dromena*—"things done" rather than "things believed"—may be overwhelmingly more evident in some kinds of religion than are doctrines and creeds. Ritual in the strict sense, as set forms of worship, may be performed when the worshipers have only the vaguest of notions as to what the supernaturalistic forces or beings worshiped may be like. The misty outlines of the supernaturalistic object may fluctuate tremendously, as it were, in accordance with the hazily defined and therefore fluctuating needs of the worshiper, while the ritual varies little if at all. Stock ejaculations in ancient tongues, dimly comprehended but rote-learned formulas, elaborate genuflections, and intricate processions may be accurately repeated again and again by men who have achieved no *explicit* orientation toward a *definite* supernaturalistic object.

Ceremonial as bound up with the holy, which is to say as ritual in the strict sense, is clearly of great importance, but there are many other significant kinds of ceremonial. This fact is usually overlooked, and confusion between ritual and other ceremonial is induced and increased,[16] because we lack terms for distinguishing these other varieties, except for a few such as "commencement" for graduation ceremonial, "commemoration" for anniversary or otherwise time-defined ceremonial, and the like.[17]

NOTES

1. The same is, of course, true of the term "need."
2. See *TVTSI* [Howard Becker, *Through Values to Social Interpretation*], p. 21, note 26.
3. Clearly, it is quite possible to lay stress on any act of "knowing-desiring-norming" in such a way that one aspect is emphasized to the *apparent* exclusion of the others. Thus conduct may be primarily cognitive, conative, or normative. But *pure* knowing, desiring, or norming are nowhere to be found empirically.
4. See *TVTSI*, Chap. 6.
5. Implicit throughout this treatment of needs and values is what has come to be known, since the days of Max Weber, as the means-ends schema. See the presentation of this in *MIR* [Howard Becker, *Man in Reciprocity*], pp. 111–136, and especially pp. 190–196. It is also dealt with in *TVTSI;* use index for "ends" and "means."
6. This is discussed at greater length in *TVTSI*, pp. 43–44, 248–250, including notes, and in *MIR*, pp. 137–144.
7. See references immediately above; also *TVTSI*, pp. 68–69, 277–278 (note 47); and *MIR*, pp. 169–170.
8. This is not the proper context for discussion of the properties that a suitable scale should possess, but certainly the mere specification of end-points is not sufficient. The writer does not here wish to take a position regarding unidimensionality, cumulativeness, etc., especially as a forthcoming paper by a colleague, Robert B. McGinnis, raises a number of issues casting doubt on some of the accepted conceptions.
9. See especially *The New Century Dictionary* (New York, 1940), section on "Synonyms, Antonyms, and Discriminations," p. 2319. Cf. also Howard Becker and H. E. Barnes, *Social Thought from Lore to Science* (2nd ed., New York, 1952, or reissue), hereinafter referred to as STFLTS (1952), "1951 Appendix on Value-System Terminology," pp. iii–x.
10. W. J. Goode, *Religion Among the Primitives* (Glencoe, 1951), *passim.*
11. Here in particular see Howard Becker, *Systematic Sociology on the Basis of the* Beziehungslehre *and* Gebildelehre *of Leopold von Wiese*, hereinafter *WBSS* (New York, 1932, and Gary, Ind., 1950 ed. with new preface). For discussion of abstract collectivities, use index, but especially pp. 556–642. See also *MIR*, pp. 434–435.
12. Paul Radin, *The Method and Theory of Ethnology* (New York, 1933), pp. 42–43, 50–51.
13. C. H. Cooley, *Human Nature and the Social Order* (New York, 1902); *Social Organization* (New York, 1909); and *Social Process* (New York, 1918).
14. Violation of the fitting, as noted, elicits negative sanction primarily as contempt, etc. Whether or not the baring of the teeth, or tendencies thereto, in the sneer represents an attenuated inclination to use physical violence in defense of the fitting, is debatable, beyond question, but the possibility should be mentioned. If the mere suggestion seems to involve too much biological preoccupation, the writer asks, "Is man a disembodied spirit?"
15. Note 14 is also relevant here. There are many theories of laughter and its derivatives, but among them are several stressing the quasi-sadistic enjoyment of discomfiture. See Max Eastman, *The Enjoyment of Laughter* (New York, 1936), especially the notes. In view of such theories, we can at least suggest that our basic criterion is not irrelevant.
16. This distinction is not observed, unfortunately, in the otherwise excellent

book by J. H. S. Bossard and Elinor H. Boll, *Ritual in Family Living* (Philadelphia, 1950). However, as recently as 1955 the present writer failed to make the distinction; see Howard Becker and Reuben Hill, *Family, Marriage, and Parenthood* (2nd ed., Boston, 1955), p. 20.

17. See the classic treatment, Herbert Spencer, *Principles of Sociology*, II, I (2nd ed., reprinted, New York, 1897), chapter on "Ceremonial Institutions."

16

MAX WEBER

The Three Types of Legitimate Rule

Max Weber has generally been acclaimed the greatest of the German sociologists.[1] *In addition to his prime influence on the "value-free" position dominant in contemporary American sociology (which we examined earlier), Weber has had tremendous impact in a wide variety of specialized substantive areas.*[2] *Probably his most impressive influence has come from his seminal work on power in social organizations. Central to his writings in this area is his concern with the types of authority and the sources of their legitimation.*

Weber set forth three types of legitimate authority, which he called ideal types; *that is, they are never found in a pure form empirically. They are developed for analytical purposes—to be used in the analysis of real cases through a process of comparison.*

Bibliographical Notes

1. *See, for example, Raymond Aron (translated by Mary and Thomas Bottomore),* German Sociology *(New York: Free Press, 1964) p. 67.*

2. *For a listing of works by and about Weber, see the introduction to the earlier statement by Weber in this volume, p. 16.*

3. *Among the many works stimulated by Weber's writings on types of authority and their sources of legitimation, see: Herbert Goldhamer and Edward A. Shils, "Types of Power and Status,"* American Journal of Sociology, *45 (1940), 171–182; and P. M. Harrison, "Weber's Categories of Authority and Voluntary Associations,"* American Sociological Review, *25 (1960), 232–237.*

Translated by Hans Gerth. Reprinted from the *Berkeley Journal of Sociology*, IV (1958), 1–11 by permission.

Authority means the probability that a specific command will be obeyed. Such obedience may feed on diverse motives. It may be determined by sheer interest situation, hence by the compliant actor's calculation of expediency; by mere custom, that is, the actor's inarticulate habituation to routine behavior; or by mere affect, that is, purely personal devotion of the governed. A structure of power, however, if it were to rest on such foundations alone, would be relatively unstable. As a rule both rulers and rules uphold the internalized power structure as "legitimate" by right, and usually the shattering of this belief in legitimacy has far-reaching ramifications.

There are but three clear-cut grounds on which to base the belief in legitimate authority. Given pure types each is connected with a fundamentally different sociological structure of executive staff and means of administration.

I

Legal authority rests on enactment; its pure type is best represented by bureaucracy. The basic idea is that laws can be enacted and changed at pleasure by formally correct procedure. The governing body is either elected or appointed and constitutes as a whole and in all its sections rational organizations. A heteronomous and heterocephalous sub-unit we shall call "public authorities" (Behörde). The administrative staff consists of officials appointed by the ruler; the law-abiding people are members of the body politic ("fellow citizens").

Obedience is not owed to anybody personally but to enacted rules and regulations which specify to whom and to what rule people owe obedience. The person in authority, too, obeys a rule when giving an order, namely, "the law," or "rules and regulations" which represent abstract norms. The person in command typically is the "superior" within a functionally defined "competency" or "jurisdiction," and his right to govern is legitimized by enactment. Specialization sets limits with regard to functional purpose and required skill of the office incumbent.

The typical official is a trained specialist whose terms of employment are contractual and provide a fixed salary scaled by rank of office, not by amount of work, and the right to a pension according to fixed rules of advancement. His administration represents vocational work by virtue of impersonal duties of office; ideally the administrator proceeds *sine ira et studio*, not allowing personal motive or temper to influence conduct, free of arbitrariness and unpredictability; especially he proceeds "without regard to person," following rational rules with strict formality. And where rules fail he adheres to "functional" considerations of expediency. Dutiful obedience is channeled through a hierarchy of offices which subordinates lower to higher offices and provides a regular procedure for lodging complaints. Technically, operation rests on organizational discipline.

1. Naturally this type of "legal" rule comprises not only the modern structure of state and city government but likewise the power relations in private capitalist enterprise, in public corporations and voluntary associations of all sorts, provided that an extensive and hierarchically organized staff of functionaries exists. Modern political bodies merely represent the type pre-eminently. Authority of private capitalist organization is partially heteronomous, its order is partly prescribed by the state, and it is completely heterocephalous as regards the machinery of coercion. Normally the courts and police take care of these functions. Private enterprise, however, is autonomous in its increasingly bureaucratic organization of management. The fact that, formally speaking, people enter into the power relationship (*Herrschaftsverband*) voluntarily and are likewise "free" to give notice does not affect the nature of private enterprise as a power structure since conditions of the labor market normally subject the employees to the code of the organization. Its sociological affinity to modern state authority will be clarified further in the discussion of the economic bases of power and authority. The "contract" as constitutive for the relations of authority in capitalist enterprise makes this a pre-eminent type of "legal authority."

2. Technically, bureaucracy represents the purest type of legal authority. No structure of authority, however, is exclusively bureaucratic, to wit, is managed by contractually hired and appointed officials alone. That is quite impossible. The top positions of the body politic may be held by "monarchs" (hereditary charismatic rulers), or by popularly elected "presidents" (hence plebiscitarian charismatic rulers), or by parliamentary elected presidents. In the latter case the actual rulers are members of parliament or rather the leaders of the prevailing parliamentary parties. These leaders in turn may stand close to the type of charismatic leadership or to that of notabilities. More of this below.

Likewise the administrative staff is almost never exclusively bureaucratic but usually notables and agents of interest groups participate in administration in manifold ways. This holds most of all for the so-called self-government. It is decisive that regular administrative work is predominantly and increasingly performed by bureaucratic forces. The historical development of the modern state is identical indeed with that of modern officialdom and bureaucratic organization (cf. below), just as the development of modern capitalism is identical with the increasing bureaucratization of economic enterprise. The part played by bureaucracy becomes bigger in all structures of power.

3. Bureaucracy does not represent the only type of legal authority. Other types comprise rotating office holders or office holders chosen by lot or popularly elected officers. Parliamentary and committee administration and all sorts of collegiate and administrative bodies are included under the type if and when their competency rests on enacted rules and if the use they make of their prerogative follows the type of legal administration. During the rise of the modern state collegiate bodies have made essential contributions to the development of legal authority, especially the concept of "public authorities" (Behörde) originated with them. On the other hand, elected officialdom has played an important role in the pre-history of the modern civil service and still does so today in the democracies.

II

Traditional authority rests on the belief in the sacredness of the social order and its prerogatives as existing of yore. Patriarchal authority represents its pure type. The body politic is based on communal relationships, the man in command is the "lord" ruling over obedient "subjects." People obey the lord personally since his dignity is hallowed by tradition; obedience rests on piety. Commands are substantively bound by tradition, and the lord's inconsiderate violation of tradition would endanger the legitimacy of his personal rule, which rests merely upon the sacredness of tradition. The creation of new law opposite traditional norms is deemed impossible in principle. Actually this is done by way of "recognizing" a sentence as "valid of yore" (the *Weistum* of ancient Germanic law). Outside the norms of tradition, however, the lord's sway in a given case is restricted only by sentiments of equity, hence by quite elastic bonds. Consequently the rule of the lord divides into a strictly tradition-bound sphere and one of free favor and arbitrariness where he rules at pleasure as sympathy or antipathy move him; following purely personal considerations subject especially to the influence of "good turns."

So far as principles are followed in administration and settlement of disputes, they rest on substantive considerations of ethical equity, justice, or utilitarian expediency, not on formal considerations characteristic of the rule of law. The lord's administrative staff proceeds in the same way. It consists of personally dependent men (members of the household or domestic officials), of relatives, of personal friends (favorites), or associates bound by personal allegiance (vassals, tributory princes). The bureaucratic concept of "competency" as a functionally delimited jurisdictional sphere is absent. The scope of the "legitimate" prerogatives of the individual servant is defined from case to case at the pleasure of the lord on whom the individual servant is completely dependent as regards his employment in more important or high ranking roles. Actually this depends largely on what the servant may dare do opposite the more or less docile subjects. Personal loyalty of the faithful servant, not functional duty of office and office discipline, control the interrelationship of the administrative staff.

One may, however, observe two characteristically different forms of positional relationships, the patriarchal structure and that of estates.

1. In the purely patriarchal structure of administration the servants are completely and personally dependent on the lord; they are either purely patrimonially recruited as slaves, bondsmen-serfs, eunuchs, or extra patrimonially as favorites and plebeians from among strata lacking all rights. Their administration is entirely heteronomous and heterocephalous, the administrators have no personal right to their office, there is neither merit selection nor status honor; the material means of administration are managed under, and on account of, the lord. Given the complete dependency of the administrative staff on the lord, there is no guarantee against the lord's arbitrariness, which in this set-up can therefore have its greatest possible sway. Sultanistic rule represents the pure type. All genuine "despotism" was of this nature. Prerogatives are considered . . . ordinary property rights of the lord.

2. In the estate system the servants are not personal servants of the lord but independent men whose social position makes them presumably socially prominent. The lord, actually or according to the legitimacy fiction, bestows office on them by privilege or concession; or they have contractually, by purchase, tenancy or lease, acquired a title to their office which cannot be arbitrarily taken away from them; hence within limits, their administration is autocephalous and autonomous. Not the lord but they dispose over the material means of administration. This represents estate rule.

The competition of the officeholders for larger bailiwicks (and income) then determines the mutual delimitation of their actual bailiwicks and takes the place of "competency." Privilege often breaks through the hierarchic structure (*de non evocando, non apellando*). The category of "discipline" is absent. Tradition, privilege, feudal or patrimonial bonds of allegiance, status honor and "good will" regulate the web of inter-relations. The power prerogatives of the lord hence are divided between the lord and the privileged administrative staff, and this division of powers among the estates brings about a high degree of stereotypy in the nature of administration.

Patriarchal rule (of the family father, sib chief, father of his people [*Landesvater*]) represents but the purest type of traditionalist rule. Any "authorities" who claim legitimacy successfully by virtue of mere habituation represent the most typical contrast, on the one hand, to the position of a contractually employed worker in business enterprise; on the other, to the way a faithful member of a religious community emotionally relates to a prophet. Actually the domestic group [*Hausverband*] is the nucleus of traditionalist power structures. The typical "officials" of the patrimonial and feudal state are domestic officers with originally purely domestic tasks (dapifer, chamberlain, marshall, cupbearer, seneschal, major domo).

The co-existence of the strictly tradition-bound and the free sphere of conduct is a common feature of all traditionalistic forms of authority. Within the free sphere, action of the lord or of his administrative staff must be bought or earned by personal relations. (This is one of the origins of the institution of fees.) It is decisive that formal law is absent and that substantive principles of administration and arbitration take its place. This likewise is a common feature of all traditionalist power structures and has far-reaching ramifications, especially for economic life.

The patriarch, like the patrimonial ruler, governs and decides according to the principles of "cadi justice": on the one hand, decisions are strictly bound by tradition; however, where these fetters give leeway, decisions follow juristically informal and irrational considerations of equity and justice from case to case, also taking individual differences into account. All codifications and laws of patrimonial rulers embody the spirit of the so-called "welfare state." A combination of social ethical with social utilitarian principles prevails, breaking through all rigor of formal law.

The sociological distinction between the patriarchal power structure and that of the estates in traditionalist rule is fundamental for all states of the pre-bureaucratic epoch. (The contrast will become fully clear only in connection with its economic aspect, that is, with the separation of the administrative staff from the material means of administration or with their appropriation by the staff.) This has been historically decisive for the question whether and what status groups existed as champions of ideas and culture values.

Patrimonial dependents (slaves, bondsmen) as administrators are to be found throughout the Mideastern orient and in Egypt down to the time of the Mamelukes; they represent the most extreme and what would seem to be the most consistent type of the purely patriarchal rule devoid of estates. Plebeian freemen as administrators stand relatively close to rational officialdom. The administration by literati can vary greatly in accordance with their nature: typical is the contrast between Brahmins and Mandarins, and both in turn stand opposite Buddhist and Christian clerics—yet their administration always approximates the estate type of power structure.

The rule of estates is most clearly represented by aristocracy, in purest form by feudalism, which puts in the place of the functional and rational duty of office the personal allegiance and the appeal to status honor of the enfeoffed.

In comparison to patriarchalism, all estate rule, based upon more or less stable appropriation of administrative power, stands closer to legal authority as the guarantees surrounding the prerogatives of the privileged assume the form of special "rights" (a result of the "division of power" among the estates). This rationale is absent in patriarchal structures, with their administration completely dependent on the lord's arbitrary sway. On the other hand, the strict discipline and the lack of rights of the administrative staff within patriarchalism is more closely related to the discipline of legal authority than is the administration of estates, which is fragmented and stereotyped through the appropriation of the means of administration by the staff. Plebeians (used as jurists) in Europe's princely service have been pacemarkers of the modern state.

III

Charismatic authority rests on the affectual and personal devotion of the follower to the lord and his gifts of grace (charisma). They comprise especially magical abilities, revelations of heroism, power of the mind and of speech. The eternally new, the non-routine, the unheard of and the emotional rapture from it are sources of personal devotion. The purest types are the rule of the prophet, the warrior hero, the great demagogue. The body politic consists in the communal relationship of a religious group or following. The person in command is typically the "leader"; he is obeyed by the "disciple." Obedience is given exclusively to the leader as a person, for the sake of his non-routine qualities, not because of enacted position or traditional dignity. Therefore obedience is forthcoming only so long as people ascribe these qualities to him, that is, so long as his charisma is proven by evidence. His rule falls if he is "forsaken" by his god [1] or deprived of his heroic strength, or if the masses lose faith in his leadership capacity. The administrative staff is selected according to charisma and personal devotion, hence selection does not consider special qualification (as in the case of the civil servant) nor rank and station (as in the case of administration by estates) nor domestic or other forms of personal dependency (as, in contrast to the above, holds for the patriarchal administrative staff). The rational concept of "competency" is lacking as is the status idea of "privilege." Decisive for the legitimation of the commissioned follower or disciple is alone the mission of the lord and his followers' personal charismatic qualification. The administration—so far as this word is adequate—lacks all orientation to rules and regulations whether enacted or traditional. Spontaneous revelation or creation, deed and example, decision from case to case, that is—at least measured against enacted order—irrational decisions are characteristic of charismatic authority. It is not bound to tradition: "It is written but I say unto you" holds for the prophet. For the warrior hero the legitimate orders vanish opposite new creations by power of the sword, for the demagogue by virtue of his annunciation or suggestion of revolutionary "natural law." In the genuine form of charismatic justice and arbitration the lord or "sage" speaks the law and the (military or religious) following gives it recognition, which is obligatory, unless somebody raises a counter claim to charismatic validity. This case presents a struggle of leaders which in the last analysis can solely be decided by the confidence of the community; only one side can be right; the other side must be wrong and be obliged to make amends.

A. The type of charismatic authority has first been developed brilliantly by R. Sohm in his *Kirchenrecht* for the early Christian community without his recognizing that it represents a type of authority. The term has since been used repeatedly without recognition of its bearing.

Early history shows alongside a few beginnings of "enacted" authority, which are by no means entirely absent, the division of all power relationships under tradition and charisma. Besides the "economic chief" (sachem) of the Indians, an essentially traditional figure, stands the charismatic warrior prince (corresponding to the Germanic "duke") with his following. Hunting and war campaigns, both demanding a leader of extraordinary personal endowments, are the secular; magic is the "sacred" place of charismatic leadership. Throughout the ages charismatic authority exercised by prophets and warrior princes has held sway over men. The charismatic politician—the "demagogue"—is the product of the occidental city state. In the city state of Jerusalem he emerged only in religious costume as a prophet. The constitution of Athens, however, was completely cut out for his existence after the innovations of Pericles and Ephialtes, since without the demagogue the state machine would not function at all.

B. Charismatic authority rests on the "faith" in the prophet, on the "recognition" which the charismatic warrior hero, the hero of the street or the demagogue, finds personally, and this authority falls with him. Yet, charismatic authority does not derive from this recognition by the subjects. Rather the reverse obtains: the charismatically legitimized leader considers faith in the acknowledgement of his charisma obligatory and punishes their violation. Charismatic authority is even one of the great revolutionary forces in history, but in pure form it is thoroughly authoritarian and lordly in nature.

C. It should be understood that the term "charisma" is used here in a completely value-neutral sense. For the sociologist the manic seizure and rage of the Nordic berserk, the miracles and revelations of any pettifogging prophecy, the demogogic talents of Cleon are just as much "charisma" as the qualities of a Napoleon, Jesus, Pericles. Decisive for us is only whether they were considered charismatics and whether they were effective, that is, gained recognition. Here, "proof" is the basic prerequisite. The charismatic lord has to prove his being sent "by the grace of god" by performing miracles and being successful in securing the good life for his following or subjects. Only as long as he can do so will he be recognized. If success fails him, his authority falters. Wherever this charismatic concept of rule by the grace of god has existed, it has had decisive ramifications. The Chinese monarch's position was threatened as soon as drought, floods, military failure or other misfortune made it appear questionable whether he stood in the grace of Heaven. Public self-impeachment and penance, in cases of stubborn misfortune, removal and possible sacrifice threatened him. Certification by miracles was demanded of every prophet (the Zwickau people demanded it still from Luther).

So far as the belief in legitimacy matters for the stability of basically legal structures of authority, this stability rests mostly on mixed foundations. Traditional habituation of "prestige" (charisma) fuse with the belief in formal legality which in the last analysis is also a matter of habit. The belief in the legitimacy of authority is shattered alike through extraordinary misfortunes whether this exacts unusual demands from the subjects in the light of tradition, or destroys the prestige or violates the usual formal legal correctness. But with all structures of authority the obedience of the governed as a stable condition depends above all on the availability of an administrative staff and especially its continuous operation to maintain order and (directly or indirectly) enforce submission to the rule. The term "organization" means to guarantee the pattern of conduct which realizes the structure of authority. The solidarity of its (ideal and material) interests with those of the lord is decisive for the all important loyalty of the staff to the lord. For the relation of the lord to the executive staff it generally holds that the lord is the stronger opposite the resisting individual because of the isolation of the individual staff member and his solidarity with the lord. The lord is weak opposite the staff members as a whole then they band themselves together, as has happened occasionally in the past and present. Deliberate agreement of the staff is requisite in order to frustrate the lord's action and rule through obstruction or deliberate counter action. Likewise the opposition requires an administrative staff of its own.

D. Charismatic rule represents a specifically extraordinary and purely personal relationship. In the case of continued existence, however, at least when the personal representative of charisma is eliminated, the authority structure has the tendency to routinize. This is the case when the charisma is not extinguished at once but continues to exist in some form and the authority of the lord, hence, is transferred to successors. This routinization of charisma proceeds through

1. Traditionalization of the orders. The authority of precedents takes the place of the charismatic leader's or his staff's charismatic creativity in law and administration. These precedents either protect the successors or are attributed to them.

2. The charismatic staff of disciples or followers changes into a legal or estate-like staff by taking over internal prerogatives or those appropriated by privilege (fiefs, prebends).

3. The meaning of charisma itself many undergo a change. Decisive in this is the way in which the problem of successorship is solved, which is a burning question for ideological and indeed often material reasons. This question can be solved in various ways: the merely passive tarrying for a new charismatically certified or qualified master usually gives

way to an active search for a successor, especially if none readily appears and if any strong interests are vested in the continuity of the authority structure.

NOTE

1. Translator's note: This allusion to Jesus' death and its interpretation as a downfall of his charismatic authority comes out more strongly in Weber's "Sociology of Charismatic Authority" ("Charismatismus," *Wirtschaft und Gesellschaft*, in *From Max Weber: Essays in Sociology*, H. H. Gerth and C. Wright Mills, trans.) (New York: Oxford, 1946), p. 248. In his later work, *Ancient Judaism*, Hans H. Gerth and Don Martindale, trans. (New York: Free Press 1952), p. 376, Weber reversed his position.

17

R. M. MacIVER and C. H. PAGE

On Associations

Robert Morrison MacIver (1882–   ), the author of numerous works on political science, philosophy, and economics, as well as on sociology,[1] *presented his general sociological theory in his 1931 textbook* Society, *later twice revised in collaboration with Charles H. Page (1909–   ),*[2] *in 1937 and in 1949. It has been said that MacIver's greatest power lay in his ability to interpret and synthesize diverse contributions from the vast heritage of social science and to shape from them a coherent system of social theory.*[3] *This contention is well documented in the following passage, which presents an analysis of* interests *(in part built upon the works of Albion Small) and* associations *(largely based on Ferdinand Tönnies' concept of* Gesellschaft*).*

Bibliographical Notes

1. *MacIver's major sociological works include:* Community *(1917),* Society *(1931), and* Social Causation *(1942). For excellent and sympathetic overviews of MacIver's sociology, see: Harry Alpert (ed.),* Robert M. MacIver: Teacher and Sociologist *(Northampton, Mass.: Metcalf, 1953); Harry Alpert, "Robert MacIver's Contributions to Sociological Theory," in M. Berger, T. Abel, and C. H. Page (eds.),* Freedom and Control in Modern Society *(New York: Van Nostrand, 1954), pp. 286–292; Alvin Boskoff,* Theory in American Sociology *(New York: Thomas Y. Crowell, 1969), pp. 112–121; and the small piece by Charles H. Page, "MacIver," in N. S. Timasheff,* Sociological

---

From: *Society: An Introductory Analysis* by Robert M. MacIver and Charles H. Page, pp. 443–452. Footnotes have been renumbered.

Theory: Its Nature and Growth, *3rd ed. (New York: Random House, 1967), pp. 250–255.*

2. *Page's major works include:* Class and American Sociology: From Ward to Ross *(1940, revised 1970); and his edited* Sociology and Contemporary Education *(1964).*

3. *Charles H. Page, "MacIver," in N. S. Timasheff,* Sociological Theory: Its Nature and Growth, *3rd ed., (New York: Random House, 1967), p. 251.*

The Classification of Associations

ASSOCIATIONS IN A COMPLEX SOCIETY

In a complex society, associations tend to be specialized so that each stands for a particular type of interest or interest complex. In primitive society, where there is less division of labor and where change is slower, there are few associations and they are more inclusive. They are communal or semicommunal in the range of their interest. A newly developed interest does not so often create, as with us, a new association, but is incorporated in the general body of interests pursued by the existing organization. Thus in primitive life, associations lack the specific, limited functional character which our own possess. They take such forms as age-groups, kin-groups, sex-groups, groups for the performance of communal rites and ceremonies, secret societies, rather than the economic or professional or political or cultural varieties familiar to ourselves. . . . The functional differentiation of modern organized groups makes it possible for us to classify them according to the characteristic interests they severally pursue.

SOME SPECIFIC PROBLEMS OF CLASSIFICATION

In classifying associations in terms of the nature of their interests, however, we are confronted with certain difficulties. There are four particularly important precautions we should have in mind in depicting the interest characteristic of any organized group.

[1] *The professed interest not always the determinant interest:* The group's ostensible interest is not always determinant; the professed or formulated aims of an association do not necessarily reveal the full or even the true character of the goal that it chiefly seeks. But at least a part of this difficulty disappears when we take as the basis of classification the immediate field of interest rather than the remote objectives or purposes, when in particular we avoid the confusion of interests and motivations. It would indeed be a hazardous task to classify associations in terms of professed objectives or ulterior aims. For one thing, a disparity not infrequently arises because the association, passing through historical changes, clings traditionally to older formulations—as religious bodies are particularly apt to do—or because the leaders idealize its aims, in the desire to broaden its appeal, to strengthen its public position, to secure funds, and so forth. Such idealization is seen not only in the platforms of political parties but also in the pronouncements of many other organizations. Often an organization will stress the more altruistic of the objects which lie within the field of its interest. A department store will proclaim that it exists to serve the community. A professional organization will emphasize the necessity of rigid qualifications for membership on the ground that the service of the public must be safeguarded while it is more or less silent on the competitive economic advantage thereby gained.

[2] *Professed interest modified by variant conditions:* We should also observe that we are far from expressing the distinctive character of any individual association when we have placed it in its interest category. The character of an individual association is often very subtle, and it is only in the light of a considerable study of its activities that its actual purpose and proper distinctiveness can be found. Moreover, in every case the interest it pursues is colored or modified by the personalities of the constituents and the social make-up of the community in which it functions. Often certain features of organizations are not brought into the focus of consciousness by the members or even by the leaders. For example, an organization which has gradually abandoned a traditional basis of solidarity may gropingly move in a new direction and gain a new kind of solidarity, related to but different from that which its leaders believe and certainly state that it possesses. This situation is illustrated in the history of certain semireligious organizations such as the Y.M.C.A. and the Y.W.C.A. Shall we classify them as religious or recreational or generally educational or in a broad sense as "social" clubs? What element is focal or dominant in the interest com-

plex? For reasons just suggested it is difficult to answer. The Y.M.C.A. or the Y.W.C.A. is a characteristic association, a certain "kind" of association with its own social "flavor." But it is a different kind in a rural area and in, say, a metropolitan area. In each region it has responded to certain social exigencies, seeking in the face of competing social agencies still to represent something, something in some way different from the rest, for when an organization loses its specific identity it loses its most important reason for existence in our highly organized society.

An associated problem of classification, arising out of the changing relation of associations to interests, is revealed in the struggle to survive of those interests which have fulfilled their original *raison d'être*. Organizations of people, like the individuals themselves, are tenacious of life. They refuse to die when their day is past. New interests are thus sought within them which will justify their existence in a continuing purpose. This organizational "will to live" centers in the officials, in the occupants of the "bureaucratic structure." A political association is organized to achieve some piece of legislation; it is attained but the association lingers on. Thus a league for the enfranchisement of women turns into a party organization when the women gain the vote; or a reform movement to eliminate the "machine" becomes itself a machine after achieving its initial goal. An ancient guild is rendered obsolete by industrial change, yet it survives as an "honorable company," to perpetuate traditional ceremonies at annual dinners—once an economic organization, it has passed over into another category. This list can be easily extended—patriotic societies, veterans' groups, hooded organizations, and many others have sought and found new interests when the old have disappeared.

[3] *The main interest sometimes hard to determine:* A more important obstacle to a satisfactory classification is presented by those organizations which stand for a variety of different interests in such a way that it is hard to designate any one as dominant. Shall we classify a denominational college as a religious organization? Sometimes religion is the primary interest, sometimes merely the historical matrix. Shall we assign an organization for workers' education as economic or as cultural? It may exist to train union leaders or to inculcate the principles of Marx or to provide a general education—and it may combine all these interests in one. Shall we call a businessmen's club an association for social intercourse or an economic association? One aspect may be dominant at one time, the other at another. These are examples of the difficulty which frequently occurs when we seek to place associations in

the categories described below. This difficulty leads up to our final caution.

[4] *Some important interests do not create specific associations:* We are making interests the basis of our classification, but the correspondence of interest and association is not, even in our specialized society, a simple one. There are some strong interests, such as the interest of power and of distinction, which do not normally create specific associations but ramify through associations of every kind. The dynastic state might be termed a "power organization," but the quest of power in some form invades every political system, underlies the interest of wealth which is the direct object of economic association, and in fact is found wherever organization of any kind exists. We might call certain kinds of clubs "prestige organizations," but as the interest of prestige is fostered no less in many other kinds of association, and particularly as men do not pursue prestige except through the medium of other interests, such an attribution would only confuse our classification. Again, the interest of companionship or of social intercourse is so pervasive that it is in some degree satisfied by every association and thus it is often dubious whether or not it is the main determinant. In our classification below, we take the club as the type-form association corresponding to this interest, but social intercourse is not the focus of all bodies called clubs and, on the other hand, there are various groups ostensibly established for other objects, from library associations to spelling bees, from charity leagues to sewing meetings, which are sustained mainly by this interest. The main interest of a group cannot be inferred from the name we apply to it. A gang, for example, may be little more than a boys' brotherhood, or it may be essentially an economic organization, exploiting a neighborhood by illegal means for economic ends.

ASSOCIATIONS CLASSIFIED BY INTERESTS

We may now turn to the classification as set forth in Chart I. We suggest that the reader consult this chart as he considers the following explanation.

[1] *Explanation of our general classification:* We first divide associations into *unspecialized* and *specialized.* Here we refer to the fact that they may stand for the total interests of a group or class or, on the

other hand, they may represent either a particular interest or a particular method of pursuing interests. We include the state among specialized associations because, in spite of the vast range of its interests, it works through the special agencies of law and government. As we have already pointed out, unspecialized associations are less characteristic of modern society—and less effective within it—than specialized associations.

The latter are classified in terms of the distinction between *primary* and *secondary* interests. By the former we mean those interests which have for men a final value, which are *ends* in themselves. By the latter we mean those interests which by their intrinsic nature are *means* to other interests. We do *not* mean that primary interests are more pervasive or necessarily even more significant in social life than secondary interests, or that the one or the other type functions in isolation from the other . . .

Our distinction is one of ends and means. One difficulty in applying the distinction lies in the fact that *any* object we seek can become the "end" of our search, so that we look for no utility beyond it. We may seek wealth merely to possess it and not for its ulterior services; we may construct instruments or mechanisms (perhaps even social mechanisms) because we enjoy doing so and not because they will aid us to achieve other objects. But this is a problem of individual motivations, not of social organization. As aspects of the latter, the economic system would not exist but for the interests which underlie it, and technological mechanisms would be idle and soon forgotten toys but for their service as man's instruments. We divide these secondary or *utilitarian* interests into three classes, the *economic*, the *political*, and the *technological*. We have placed another large group of interests, the *educational*, in an intermediate position between secondary and primary, since they involve both means and ends, since they are both utilitarian and cultural. All genuine education, elementary or higher, technical or "liberal," is at the same time an instrumental equipment for living and itself a cultural mode of life. We set the cultural or primary interests over against the secondary interests. We pursue the cultural goals apart from external pressure or necessity. Again, cultural interests may serve us merely as means, but, sociologically, their utilitarian service is incidental to the fact that we, or some of us, pursue them for their own sakes, because, that is, they bring us some *direct* satisfaction.

[2] *Other modes of classification in terms of interests:* While the specific nature of the interest is the main clue to the character of the

CHART 1

General Classification of Interests and Associations

INTERESTS	ASSOCIATIONS
A. *Unspecialized*	Class and caste organizations Tribal and quasi-political organizations of simpler societies Age-groups and sex-groups The patriarchal family (Perhaps also such organizations as vigilante groups, civic welfare associations, etc.)
B. *Specialized*	
I. *Secondary* (civilizational or utilitarian)	
(a) Economic interests	Type form: *The business* Industrial, financial, and agricultural organizations, including unions Occupational and professional associations[a] Protective and insurance societies Charity and philanthropic societies[b] Gangs, "rackets," etc.
(b) Political interests	Type form: *The state* Municipal and other territorial divisions of the state Parties, lobbies, propagandist groups
(c) Technological interests	Associations for technical research, and for the solution of practical problems of many kinds[c]
II. *Intermediate*	
Educational interests	Type form: *The school* Colleges, universities, study groups, reformatories, etc.
III. *Primary* (cultural)	
(a) Social intercourse	Type form: *The club* Various organizations ostensibly for the pursuit of other interests
(b) Health and recreation	Associations for sports, games, dancing, etc.[d]
(c) Sex and reproduction	Type form: *The family*
(d) Religion	Type form: *The church* Religious propagandist associations Monasteries, etc.[e]
(e) Aesthetic interests, art, etc.	Corresponding associations
(f) Science and philosophy	Learned societies

[a] These combine economic and technological interest; where the latter are dominant the associations fall in I (c).

[b] The economic interest is usually, though by no means always, the focus of these associations. The fact that it is the economic welfare of others than the members which is sought does not affect the classification.

[c] The technological interest is generally subordinate to the economic, i.e., it is a means to a means. Hence it is usually pursued through subagencies of the economic order. Sometimes it is organized, under political auspices, through such divisions as a department of agriculture, bureau of standards, atomic commissions, etc.

[d] The interest of health and of recreation may of course be entirely dissociated. The interest of recreation is, on the other hand, often associated with the aesthetic interests, so that various associations could be classified under III (b) or under III (e).

[e] The monastery is a quasi-community, but if religion is the main determinant of its activities as well as the basis of organization, we can retain it under III (d).

CHART 2
Associations Classified According to the Durability of the Interest

INTERESTS	ASSOCIATIONS
(a) Interests realizable once for all—definite temporary objectives	Associations for the achievement of a specific reform, reconstruction, etc., political or other (e.g., anti-slavery); for a celebration, erection of a memorial, etc., for an emergency such as a flood, economic crisis, war
(b) Interests peculiar to a definite number of original or potential members—the "broken plate" situation[a]	Groups composed of the members of a school or college class or year, of army veterans, of the survivors of a shipwreck, etc.
(c) Interests limited to age-periods of a relatively short range	School and college teams, debating societies, etc.; boy scouts, junior leagues, etc.—associations continuous as individual structures but with rapidly successive memberships
(d) Interests limited by the tenure or life span of some original or present members[c]	Partnerships of various kinds; groups of friends; the family—permanent as a social system embodied in successive individual associations[b]
(e) Interests unlimited by a time span	The corporation; most large-scale organizations, state, church, occupational associations, scientific associations, etc.—associations individually continuous through the recruitment and incorporation of new members

[a] The reference here is to an illustration given by G. Simmel in *Soziologie* (Munich, 1923), p. 60. A group of industrialists were seated at a banquet when a plate was dropped and shattered into fragments. It was observed that the number of pieces corresponded to the number of those present. Each received one fragment, and the group agreed that at the death of any member his fragment was to be returned, the plate being thus gradually pieced together until the last surviving member fitted in the last fragment and shattered again the whole plate.
[b] The larger patriarchal family or the "joint family" does not fall within this class, but the modern individual family does. We speak of the family in another sense, as when we say that a person is a member of an "old" family, but in this sense the family is not an association. See Chapter XI [of *Society: An Introductory Analysis*].
[c] Observe particularly the difference between the groups under (b) and under (d). The interest which creates an association under (b) is unique, peculiar to the members, and dies with the association. It has therefore little significance for the social structure. The interest under (d) is universal in its appeal and particularizes itself in a multitude of individual associations. The interest under (b) is in fact the social bond itself, whereas the interest under (d) is the perennial source of the social bond.

corresponding association, as set out in Chart 2, there are other ways of classifying interests that throw further light on the relation between them and associations. Thus the direct social interest in *persons* is the distinguishing feature of *primary groups,* whereas the interest in the *impersonal* means and ends of living characterizes the *large-scale association*. . . . Again, we can distinguish interests according to their degree of duration in the life history of their members. In terms of this criterion, associations within the same field may be transient, rapidly successive, or permanent. They may be permanent, as established *forms* of social organization like the family, though the individual instances are mortal, or they may be long-lived, potentially immortal, as individual structures, like the corporation. In Chart 2 we neglect the types of interest in order to classify associations according to their *durability*.

The classification in our first chart (1) is meant to serve as an introduction to the organized aspects of the social structure. The task in this study, which we undertake in the concluding four chapters of this division of Book Two, is to reveal the distinctive types of association that enter into the social structure—distinctive with respect to the kinds of social relationship they exhibit—and at the same time to show their place and function in the social order, their relation to one another and to the whole.

Intra-Associational Conflict of Interests

SOCIAL COHESION AND CONFLICT

The interest for which an association stands is the primary ground of its unity, the basis of its particular cohesion or solidarity. This unity is reinforced by other bonds, by the shared tradition and prestige of the association or the associates, by the sustenance of the general need of social relationships that it may provide, by the particular habituations and attitudes that it supports, by the other common interests the members share in whole or in part. But at the same time forces are generated or revealed within the association that cause tensions and strains in its solidarity.

Conflicts develop in the field of the particular interest the association promotes and conflicts arise from oppositions between that interest and other interests of the members. Like the greater communal manifestations of social cohesion—class, ethnic and racial group, and crowd, as well as the community itself—the unity of the association is imperfect and unstable, representing, while it endures, the victory of integrative over disintegrative processes. A study of the conflicts and harmonies of interest that appear within the life of associations could be for the student an excellent preparation for the investigation of that greater unstable equilibrium which is the social order itself.

TYPES OF INTEREST-CONFLICT WITHIN ASSOCIATIONS

Here we select for brief discussion three main types of interest-conflict. These three types occur persistently in the history of organized groups, especially in the variety of associations that grow up in modern complex society.

[1] *Conflicts within the interest-complex:* The first arises from a lack of harmony between the objectives that fall within the interest-complex. A clear illustration is frequently presented within professional or occupational associations. The economic interest, the maintenance or enhancement of the emoluments of the service they render, is often difficult to reconcile with the professional interest proper, the quality and extent of the professional service.

The medical profession offers a peculiarly interesting situation. If it could achieve its professional ideal, it would thereby reduce to a minimum the need for its therapeutic service while enlarging greatly its preventive service. The former is mainly private practice, the latter is largely socialized, provided through clinics, hospitals, state departments, public and semi-public institutions of various kinds. Here a dilemma is apt to arise not only because private practice is more in accord with the traditions of the profession but also because it tends, under prevailing conditions, to be more remunerative. If economic interest alone determined the policy of a professional organization, whether medical or other, we would have simply a conflict between the associational interest and the public interest. But the members of a medical association, like those of other professional groups, are concerned with the efficacy of the service the group represents. Hence there arises a conflict of interests within the association itself in the attempt to work out a policy that will reconcile or adjust the economic interest and the professional ideal. The problem has a peculiar character in this case, since under competitive conditions the livelihood of the physician depends on the length of treatment, on the seriousness of cases, and generally on the amount of disease prevalent in the community.[1]

Similar problems of the adjustment of interests arise within bar associations, educational organizations, business firms, labor unions, and other bodies. The conflict is seen very clearly in political groups. It is only in the extreme exploitative political organizations, such as that centering round a "boss," that the economic interest drives out almost altogether the professional interest, that of the standard of service. When this happens any "professional" organization becomes an association of another and frequently of a socially detrimental type.[2]

[2] *Conflicts between relevant and irrelevant interests:* The second type of conflict arises where the specific interest of the association demands a course of action which is opposed to some other interests not relevant to the association as such but nevertheless entertained by some members of the group. A highly qualified Negro, let us say, seeks admission to a university. He possesses the requisite qualifications, for racial difference is no bar to scholarship. But other considerations that have nothing to do with the express purpose of the association enter in and create within the association a conflict concerning policy. In one form or another such conflicts are constantly occurring. Outside interests prevent the association from pursuing with single-mindedness its stated objectives. Group prejudices modify the devotion of the association to its avowed purpose. Individual jealousies and predilections thwart the interest which is the *raison d'être* of the organization. Thus confusion and disharmony appear within its councils.

We may include in the same general category the conflict which arises owing to the fact that the interests of the officials or leaders are not identical with those of the other members, or cease to be identical once they have enjoyed the fruits of office. The officials may be anxious to enhance their authority, though this course may lead to policies detrimental to the general associational interest. Or they may have an economic interest at variance with the interest, economic or other, of the group. The degree of maladjustment varies not only with the personalities involved, but also with the nature of the interest. A particularly significant illustration is furnished by groups founded on principles of equality, whether economic, political, or religious. Organization is essential to each and hence a bureaucratic structure emerges. It has even been maintained that officials, as soon as they acquire power, are driven by the logic of their position to antidemocratic attitudes, and thus no democratic or socialist organization can ever translate its principles into effective practice.[3] The argument is too sweeping, but the numerous instances adduced by the proponents of this "iron law of oligarchy" sufficiently illustrate the serious conflicts and confusions created by the dilemma of leadership.

[3] *Conflicts between alternative policies in the pursuit of interests:* A third source of conflict is found in the constant necessity of the new adaptation of means to ends. By the end we here understand the provisional basis of agreement regarding the interest of the association, which has to be translated into action by means of a policy. A group meets to decide a course of action in a given situation. The group interest has already been defined and redefined by past decisions, has been canalized in the series of adjustments which the group has undergone. But a new occasion often demands more than a routine following of the channel. Being different, it demands a fresh decision, a new expression of policy. The members meet on the assumption that all are agreed regarding the end—the problem is the appropriate means. A business must decide how to deal with a new competitive threat. A club must raise funds to meet a deficit. A church must decide how to act in the face of a declining membership. A settlement house must adapt itself to a changing neighborhood or to the "competition" of state agencies. A political party, say a revolutionary party, must adjust its strategy to changing historical circumstances.

In these situations, the agreement on ends is implicit, taken for granted. But the agreement on means must be explicit. This necessity inevitably evokes differences of temperament and viewpoint within the group. Shall the club raise the necessary funds by an extension of membership or by a levy on its present members? Shall the church popularize its regular services or undertake additional social activities? Shall the national revolutionary party support a program of military preparedness in its own country or advocate a policy of peace at all costs? Some members answer one way, some another—the interplay of divergent personal factors and divergent policies is very complex. The sense of solidarity may prevail, an adjustment may be reached, and a generally acceptable policy formed. But in the process acute differences may emerge sufficient to disrupt or even to end the life of the association.

THE TYPE OF ASSOCIATION AND INTERNAL CONFLICT

In conclusion, we may point out that if the association stands for a broad cultural interest or one strongly charged with emotional elements there is greater danger that difference will lead to schism. For here differences on matters of policy are apt to extend down into differences regarding the *implicit end* which the policy is meant to serve. The interest of a business firm is relatively simple. The end to which its policy must be adapted is accepted and understood without dispute. But it is otherwise with the interest of a church, of an artist group, or, in some cases, of a political party. Dissension over means may here reveal the inadequacy of the more basic agreement over ends. The end itself, at some level, is brought into the arena of conflict, and thus the solidarity of the organization may be shaken. When a church faces a declining membership it may be forced to raise the further question concerning its proper mission. When the business faces declining sales, its endeavor to restore profits raises no similar question regarding the appropriate definition of its quest. Such considerations help to explain the tendency to schism exhibited by churches which do not adhere strongly to authoritative interpretations, by left-wing parties generally, by artistic and other bodies united around some cultural conviction. The particular case of the political association we shall discuss in the following chapter.

NOTES

1. See, for example, J. Rorty, *American Medicine Mobilizes* (New York, 1937); C. Binger, *The Doctor's Job* (New York, 1945); and for brief reviews of the question, R. H. Shrylock, "Freedom and Interference in Medicine," *The Annals of the American Academy of Political and Social Science*, Nov., 1938; W. T. Foster, *Doctors, Dollars, and Disease*, Public Affairs Pamphlet No. 10 (rev., New York, 1944).
2. The conflict of interests in the professions is stressed in a large literature. Many illustrations may be found, for example, in A. M. Carr-Saunders and P. A. Wilson, *The Professions* (New York, 1933); E. L. Brown, *Lawyers and the Promotion of Justice* (New York, 1938); and L. Wilson, *The Academic Man* (New York, 1942).
3. R. Michels, *Political Parties* (Eng. tr., New York, 1915).

4

Dimensions of Social Organization

Stratification

18

MAX WEBER

On Class, Status, and Party

As in so many other areas of sociology, the influence of Max Weber on stratification theory has been substantial. His consideration of the ordering of power was a continuation and a natural extension of his other formulations. According to Weber, the stratification of persons and social units is essentially a problem in the allocation of power, the mechanisms of which parallel those we have already discussed in connection with his consideration of the sources of legitimacy in systems of authority. Power distribution within the economic sphere, position within the market, is a rational *process of* class *differentiation. The distribution of social prestige follows a nonrational and* traditional *process referred to as* status *differentiation. Mixing the* rational-purposeful *and the* value-rational *forms of social action, ability to influence communal or societal actions constitutes some relative degree of* party *differentiation. This breakdown of Weber's represented, in part, an attempt to broaden the vision of the existing dimensions of social heirarchy, thus counteracting Marx's over-emphasis upon economic interest. Much of Weber's work strives for the development of a broader and more comprehensive system for social analysis, a reaction against a simple economic determinism.*[1]

Bibliographical Note

1. For a critical appraisal of Weber's views on stratification and a defense of them, see: O. C. Cox, "Max Weber on Social Stratification:

Reprinted from H. H. Gerth and C. Wright Mills, translators and editors, *From Max Weber: Essays in Sociology* (New York: Oxford University Press, 1958 Galaxy edition), pp. 181–183, 186–188, and 194–195. Copyright 1946 by Oxford University Press, Inc. Excerpt from Weber's *Wirtschaft und Gesellschaft*, part III, chapter 4. Reprinted by permission of the publisher.

A Critique," American Sociological Review, 15 *(1951), 223–227; and H. Gerth, "Max Weber Versus Oliver C. Cox,"* American Sociological Review, 15 *(1951), 557–558. For a listing of the main works by and about Weber, see the introduction to his first statement in this volume, p. 16.*

[*Class*]

We may speak of a 'class' when (1) a number of people have in common a specific causal component of their life chances, in so far as (2) this component is represented exclusively by economic interests in the possession of goods and opportunities for income, and (3) is represented under the conditions of the commodity or labor markets. [These points refer to 'class situation,' which we may express more briefly as the typical chance for a supply of goods, external living conditions, and personal life experiences, in so far as this chance is determined by the amount and kind of power, or lack of such, to dispose of goods or skills for the sake of income in a given economic order. The term 'class' refers to any group of people that is found in the same class situation.]

It is the most elemental economic fact that the way in which the disposition over material property is distributed among a plurality of people, meeting competitively in the market for the purpose of exchange, in itself creates specific life chances. According to the law of marginal utility this mode of distribution excludes the non-owners from competing for highly valued goods; it favors the owners and, in fact, gives to them a monopoly to acquire such goods. Other things being equal, this mode of distribution monopolizes the opportunities for profitable deals for all those who, provided with goods, do not necessarily have to exchange them. It increases, at least generally, their power in price wars with those who, being propertyless, have nothing to offer but their services in native form or goods in a form constituted through their own labor, and who above all are compelled to get rid of these products in order barely to subsist. This mode of distribution gives to the propertied a monopoly on the possibility of transferring property from the sphere of use as a 'fortune,' to the sphere of 'capital goods'; that is, it gives them the entrepreneurial function and all chances to share directly or indirectly in returns on capital. All this holds true within the area in which pure market conditions prevail. 'Property' and 'lack of property' are, therefore, the basic categories of all class situations. It does not matter whether these two categories become effective in price wars or in competitive struggles.

Within these categories, however, class situations are further differentiated: on the one hand, according to the kind of property that is usable for returns; and, on the other hand, according to the kind of services that can be offered in the market. Ownership of domestic buildings; productive establishments; warehouses; stores; agriculturally usable land, large and small holdings—quantitative differences with possibly qualitative consequences—; ownership of mines; cattle; men (slaves); disposition over mobile instruments of production, or capital goods of all sorts, especially money or objects that can be exchanged for money easily and at any time; disposition over products of one's own labor or of others' labor differing according to their various distances from consumability; disposition over transferable monopolies of any kind—all these distinctions differentiate the class situations of the propertied just as does the 'meaning' which they can and do give to the utilization of property, especially to property which has money equivalence. Accordingly, the propertied, for instance, may belong to the class of rentiers or to the class of entrepreneurs.

Those who have no property but who offer services are differentiated just as much according to their kinds of services as according to the way in which they make use of these services, in a continuous or discontinuous relation to a recipient. But always this is the generic connotation of the concept of class: that the kind of chance in the *market* is the decisive moment which presents a common condition for the individual's fate. 'Class situation' is, in this sense, ultimately 'market situation.' The effect of naked possession *per se*, which among cattle breeders gives the non-owning slave or serf into the power of the cattle owner, is only a forerunner of real 'class' formation. However, in the cattle loan and in the naked severity of the law of debts in such communities, for the first time mere 'possession' as such emerges as decisive for the fate of the individual. This is very much in contrast to the agricultural communities based on labor. The creditor-debtor relation becomes the basis of 'class situations' only in those cities where a 'credit market,' however primitive, with rates of interest increasing according to the extent of dearth and a factual monopolization of credits, is developed by a plutocracy. Therewith 'class struggles' begin.

Those men whose fate is not determined by the chance of using goods or services for themselves on the market, e.g. slaves, are not, however, a 'class' in the technical sense of the term. They are, rather, a 'status group.' . . .

[*Status*]

In contrast to classes, *status groups* are normally communities. They are, however, often of an amorphous kind. In contrast to the purely economically determined 'class situation' we wish to designate as 'status situation' every typical component of the life fate of men that is determined by a specific, positive or negative, social estimation of *honor*. This honor may be connected with any quality shared by a plurality, and, of course, it can be knit to a class situation: class distinctions are linked in the most varied ways with status distinctions. Property as such is not always recognized as a status qualification, but in the long run it is, and with extraordinary regularity. In the subsistence economy of the organized neighborhood, very often the richest man is simply the chieftain. However, this often means only an honorific preference. For example, in the so-called pure modern 'democracy,' that is, one devoid of any expressly ordered status privileges for individuals, it may be that only the families coming under approximately the same tax class dance with one another. This example is reported of certain smaller Swiss cities. But status honor need not necessarily be linked with a 'class situation.' On the contrary, it normally stands in sharp opposition to the pretensions of sheer property.

Both propertied and propertyless people can belong to the same status group, and frequently they do with very tangible consequences. This 'equality' of social esteem may, however, in the long run become quite precarious. The 'equality' of status among the American 'gentlemen,' for instance, is expressed by the fact that outside the subordination determined by the different functions of 'business,' it would be considered strictly repugnant—wherever the old tradition still prevails—if even the richest 'chief,' while playing billiards or cards in his club in the evening, would not treat his 'clerk' as in every sense fully his equal in birthright. It would be repugnant if the American 'chief' would bestow upon his 'clerk' the condescending 'benevolence' marking a distinction of 'position,' which the German chief can never dissever from his attitude. This is one of the most important reasons why in America the German 'clubby-ness' has never been able to attain the attraction that the American clubs have.

GUARANTEES OF STATUS STRATIFICATION

In content, status honor is normally expressed by the fact that above all else a specific *style of life* can be expected from all those who wish to belong to the circle. Linked with this expectation are restrictions on 'social' intercourse (that is, intercourse which is not subservient to economic or any other of business's 'functional' purposes). These restrictions may confine normal marriages to within the status circle and may lead to complete endogamous closure. As soon as there is not a mere individual and socially irrelevant imitation of another style of life, but an agreed-upon communal action of this closing character, the 'status' development is under way.

In its characteristic form, stratification by 'status groups' on the basis of conventional styles of life evolves at the present time in the United States out of the traditional democracy. For example, only the resident of a certain street ('the street') is considered as belonging to 'society,' is qualified for social intercourse, and is visited and invited. Above all, this differentiation evolves in such a way as to make for strict submission to the fashion that is dominant at a given time in society. This submission to fashion also exists among men in America to a degree unknown in Germany. Such submission is considered to be an indication of the fact that a given man *pretends* to qualify as a gentleman. This submission decides, at least *prima facie*, that he will be treated as such. And this recognition becomes just as important for his employment chances in 'swank' establishments, and above all, for social intercourse and marriage with 'esteemed' families, as the qualification for dueling among Germans in the Kaiser's day. As for the rest: certain families resident for a long time, and, of course, correspondingly wealthy, e.g. 'F. F. V., i.e. First Families of Virginia,' or the actual or alleged descendants of the 'Indian Princess' Pocahontas, of the Pilgrim fathers, or of the Knickerbockers, the members of almost inaccessible sects and all sorts of circles setting themselves apart by means of any other characteristics and badges . . . all these elements usurp 'status' honor. The development of status is essentially a question of stratification resting upon usurpation. Such usurpation is the normal origin of almost all status honor. But the road from this purely conventional situation to legal privilege, positive or negative, is easily traveled as soon as a certain stratification of the social order has in fact been 'lived in' and has achieved stability by virtue of a stable distribution of economic power. . . .

[*Parties*]

Whereas the genuine place of 'classes' is within the economic order, the place of 'status groups' is within the social order, that is, within the sphere of the distribution of 'honor.' From within these spheres, classes and status groups influence one another and they influence the legal order and are in turn influenced by it. But 'parties' live in a house of 'power.'

Their action is oriented toward the acquisition of social 'power,' that is to say, toward influencing a communal action no matter what its content may be. In principle, parties may exist in a social 'club' as well as in a 'state.' As over against the actions of classes and status groups, for which this is not necessarily the case, the communal actions of 'parties' always mean a societalization. For party actions are always directed toward a goal which is striven for in planned manner. This goal may be a 'cause' (the party may aim at realizing a program for ideal or material purposes), or the goal may be 'personal' (sinecures, power, and from these, honor for the leader and the followers of the party). Usually the party action aims at all these simultaneously. Parties are, therefore, only possible within communities that are societalized, that is, which have some rational order and a staff of persons available who are ready to enforce it. For parties aim precisely at influencing this staff, and if possible, to recruit it from party followers.

In any individual case, parties may represent interests determined through 'class situation' or 'status situation,' and they may recruit their following respectively from one or the other. But they need be neither purely 'class' nor purely 'status' parties. In most cases they are partly class parties and partly status parties, but sometimes they are neither. They may represent ephemeral or enduring structures. Their means of attaining power may be quite varied, ranging from naked violence of any sort to canvassing for votes with coarse or subtle means: money, social influence, the force of speech, suggestion, clumsy hoax, and so on to the rougher or more artful tactics of obstruction in parliamentary bodies.

The sociological structure of parties differs in a basic way according to the kind of communal action which they struggle to influence. Parties also differ according to whether or not the community is stratified by status or by classes. Above all else, they vary according to the structure of domination within the community. For their leaders normally deal with the conquest of a community. They are, in the general concept which is maintained here, not only products of specially modern forms of domination. We shall also designate as parties the ancient and medieval 'parties,' despite the fact that their structure differs basically from the structure of modern parties. By virtue of these structural differences of domination it is impossible to say anything about the structure of parties without discussing the structural forms of social domination *per se*. Parties, which are always structures struggling for domination, are very frequently organized in a very strict 'authoritarian' fashion. . . .

Concerning 'classes,' 'status groups,' and 'parties,' it must be said in general that they necessarily presuppose a comprehensive societalization, and especially a political framework of communal action, within which they operate. This does not mean that parties would be confined by the frontiers of any individual political community. On the contrary, at all times it has been the order of the day that the societalization (even when it aims at the use of military force in common) reaches beyond the frontiers of politics. This has been the case in the solidarity of interests among the Oligarchs and among the democrats in Hellas, among the Guelfs and among Ghibellines in the Middle Ages, and within the Calvinist party during the period of religious struggles. It has been the case up to the solidarity of the landlords (international congress of agrarian landlords), and has continued among princes (holy alliance, Karlsbad decrees), socialist workers, conservatives (the longing of Prussian conservatives for Russian intervention in 1850). But their aim is not necessarily the establishment of new international political, i.e. *territorial*, dominion. In the main they aim to influence the existing dominion.

19

KARL MARX AND FRIEDRICH ENGELS

On Class Conflict

Karl Marx (1818–1883)[1] *and Friedrich Engels (1820–1895)*[2] *are best known in their roles as ideologues and originators of the rationale for the political-economic movement of international communism.*[3] *Aside from their symbolic significance in that movement, many of their (especially Marx's) ideas have had great impact upon many theoretic areas in contemporary sociology.*[4] *A central concern for Marx and Engels was the historical pattern that they believed produced inevitable conflicts between social classes. Though this conceptualization has been severely criticized by contemporary sociologists,*[5] *the work of Marx and Engels has recently played a very important part in redirecting attention to the problems of conflicting interests and the strains of social change. These topics had been neglected by many sociological theorists who had been concerned predominantly with questions of societal consensus, integration, and social order. Marx's early writings on the problems of worker alienation in the industrial society have also attracted renewed attention.*[6]

Bibliographical Notes

1. *Marx's major writings with Engels include:* The German Ideology *(1845–1846)*; The Holy Family *(1845)*; The Communist Manifesto *(1848)*; The First Indian War of Independence *(1857–1859)*; The Civil War in the United States *(1861–1866)*; *and* Critique of the Gotha Programme *(1875)*. *Marx's own principal writings include:* Economic and Philosophic Manuscripts of 1844 *(1844)*; The Poverty

---

Reprinted from Karl Marx and Friedrich Engels, *Manifesto of the Communist Party* (Chicago: Charles H. Kerr, 1888). Footnotes have been abridged.

of Philosophy (*1847*); The Class Struggles in France: 1848–1850 (*1850*); The Eighteenth Brumaire of Louis Bonaparte (*1852*); Secret Diplomatic History of the Eighteenth Century (*1856*); Pre-capitalist Economic Formations (*1857–1858*); A Contribution to the Critique of Political Economy (*1859*); Theories of Surplus Value: Selections (*1861–1863*); Capital: A Critique of Political Economy, *3 vols.* (*1867–1879*); *and* The Civil War in France (*1871*). *For sociological writings by Marx, the reader is referred to the excellent collection of T. B. Bottomore and Maximilien Rubel (eds.)*, Karl Marx: Selected Writings in Sociology and Social Philosophy (*London: Watts, 1956*). *The biographical literature on Marx is immense. For a recent sociological examination of his work, see: Irving M. Zeitlin*, Marxism: A Re-examination (*Princeton, N.J.: Van Nostrand, 1967*).

2. *In addition to the works with Marx, the principal works of Engels that have been translated into English include:* The Condition of the Working Class in England (*1845*); Principles of Communism (*1847*); The Peasant War in Germany (*1850*); Germany: Revolution and Counterrevolution (*1851–1852*); Notes on the War (*1870–1871*); Dialectics of Nature (*1873–1883*); Socialism: Utopian and Scientific (*1880*); The Origin of the Family, Private Property and the State (*1884*); *and* Ludwig Feurbach and the Outcome of Classical German Philosophy (*1886*). *For the details of Engels' life, see: Gustav Mayer*, Friedrich Engels: A Biography (*London: Chapman, 1936*).

3. *Marx himself was much less doctrinaire than many of his "followers" have made him appear. He himself once said, "I am not a Marxist."*

4. *For an excellent discussion, see: T. B. Bottomore and Maximilien Rubel, "The Influence of Marx's Sociological Thought" in T. B. Bottomore and Maximilien Rubel (eds.)*, Karl Marx: Selected Writings in Sociology and Social Philosophy (*London: Watts, 1956*), *pp. 29–48; or T. B. Bottomore, "Marxist Sociology,"* International Encyclopedia of Social Sciences, *Vol. 10* (*New York: Macmillan and Free Press, 1968*), *pp. 46–53.*

5. *E.g.: Ralf Dahrendorf*, Class and Class Conflict in an Industrial Society (*Stanford, Calif.: Stanford University Press, 1959*).

6. *E.g.: Erich Fromm (ed.)*, Marx's Concept of Man (*New York: Ungar, 1961*), *and Irving M. Zeitlin*, Ideology and the Development of Sociological Theory (*Englewood Cliffs, N.J.: Prentice-Hall, 1968*), *pp. 103–108.*

I. *Bourgeois and Proletarians*[1]

The history of all hitherto existing society[2] is the history of class struggles.

Freeman and slave, patrician and plebeian, lord and serf, guildmaster[3] and journeyman, in a word, oppressor and oppressed stood in constant opposition to one another, carried on an uninterrupted, now hidden, now open fight, a fight that each time ended, either in a revolutionary reconstitution of society at large, or in the common ruin of the contending classes.

In the earlier epochs of history, we find almost everywhere a complicated arrangement of society into various orders, a manifold gradation of social rank. In ancient Rome we have patricians, knights, plebeians, slaves; in the Middle Ages, feudal lords, vassals, guild-masters, journeymen, apprentices, serfs; in almost all of these classes, again, subordinate gradations.

The modern bourgeois society that has sprouted from the ruins of feudal society has not done away with class antagonisms. It has but established new classes, new conditions of oppression, new forms of struggle in place of the old ones.

Our epoch, the epoch of the bourgeoisie, possesses, however, this distinctive feature: It has simplified the class antagonisms. Society as a whole is more and more splitting up into two great hostile camps, into two great classes directly facing each other—bourgeoisie and proletariat.

From the serfs of the Middle Ages sprang the chartered burghers of the earliest towns. From these burgesses the first elements of the bourgeoisie were developed.

The discovery of America, the rounding of the Cape, opened up fresh ground for the rising bourgeoisie. The East-Indian and Chinese markets, the colonisation of America, trade with the colonies, the increase in the means of exchange and in commodities generally, gave to commerce, to navigation, to industry, an impulse never before known, and thereby, to the revolutionary element in the tottering feudal society, a rapid development.

The feudal system of industry, in which industrial production was monopolised by closed guilds, now no longer sufficed for the growing wants of the new markets. The manufacturing system took its place. The guildmasters were pushed aside by the manufacturing middle class; division of labour between the different corporate guilds vanished in the face of division of labor in each single workshop.

Meantime the markets kept ever growing, the demand ever rising. Even manufacture no longer sufficed. Thereupon, steam and machinery revolutionised industrial production. The place of manufacture was taken by the giant, modern industry, the place of the industrial middle class by industrial millionaires, the leaders of whole industrial armies, the modern bourgeois.

Modern industry has established the world market, for which the discovery of America paved the way. This market has given an immense development to commerce, to navigation, to communication by land. This development has, in its turn, reacted on the extension of industry; and in proportion as industry, commerce, navigation, railways extended, in the same proportion the bourgeoisie developed, increased its capital, and pushed into the background every class handed down from the Middle Ages.

We see, therefore, how the modern bourgeoisie is itself the product of a long course of development, of a series of revolutions in the modes of production and of exchange.

Each step in the development of the bourgeoisie was accompanied by a corresponding political advance of that class. An oppressed class under the sway of the feudal nobility, an armed and self-governing association in the mediæval commune[4]; here independent urban republic (as in Italy and Germany), there taxable "third estate" of the monarchy (as in France); afterwards, in the period of manufacture proper, serving either the semi-feudal or the absolute monarchy as a counterpoise against the nobility, and, in fact, corner-stone of the great monarchies in general—the bourgeoisie has at last, since the establishment of modern industry and of the world market, conquered for itself, in the modern representative state, exclusive political sway. The executive of the modern state is but a committee for managing the common affairs of the whole bourgeoisie.

The bourgeoisie, historically, has played a most revolutionary part.

The bourgeoisie, wherever it has got the upper hand, has put an end to all feudal, patriarchal, idyllic relations. It has pitilessly torn asunder the motley feudal ties that bound man to his "natural superiors," and has left no other nexus between man and man than naked self-interest, than callous "cash payment." It has drowned the most heavenly ecstasies of religious fervour, of chivalrous enthusiasm, of philistine sentimentalism, in the icy water of egotistical calculation. It has resolved a personal worth into exchange value, and in place of the numberless indefeasible chartered freedoms, has set up that single, unconscionable freedom—Free Trade. In one word, for exploitation, veiled by religious and political illusions, it has substituted naked, shameless, direct, brutal exploitation.

The bourgeoisie has stripped of its halo every occupation hitherto honoured and looked up to with reverent awe. It has converted the physician, the lawyer, the priest, the poet, the man of science, into its paid wage labourers.

The bourgeoisie has torn away from the family its sentimental veil, and has reduced the family relation to a mere money relation.

The bourgeoisie has disclosed how it came to pass that the brutal display of vigour in the Middle Ages, which reactionaries so much admire, found its fitting complement in the most slothful indolence. It has been the first to show what man's activity can bring about. It has accomplished wonders far surpassing Egyptian pyramids, Roman aqueducts, and Gothic cathedrals; it has conducted expeditions that put in the shade all former exoduses of nations and crusades.

The bourgeoisie cannot exist without constantly revolutionising the instruments of production, and thereby the relations of production, and with them the whole relations of society. Conservation of the old modes of production in unaltered form, was, on the contrary, the first condition of existence for all earlier industrial classes. Constant revolutionising of production, uninterrupted disturbance of all social conditions, everlasting uncertainty and agitation distinguish the bourgeois epoch from all earlier ones. All fixed, fast frozen relations, with their train of ancient and venerable prejudices and opinions, are swept away, all new-formed ones become antiquated before they can ossify. All that is solid melts into air, all that is holy is profaned, and man is at last compelled to face with sober senses his real conditions of life and his relations with his kind.

The need of a constantly expanding market for its products chases the bourgeoisie over the whole surface of the globe. It must nestle everywhere, settle everywhere, establish connections everywhere.

The bourgeoisie has through its exploitation of the world market given a cosmopolitan character to production and consumption in every country. To the great chagrin of reactionaries, it has drawn from under the feet of industry the national ground on which it stood. All old-established national industries have been destroyed or are daily being destroyed. They are dislodged by new industries, whose introduction becomes a life and death question for all civilised nations, by industries that no longer work up indigenous raw material, but raw material drawn from the remotest zones; industries whose products are consumed, not only at home, but in every quarter of the globe. In place of the old wants, satisfied by the production of the country, we find new wants, requiring for their satisfaction the products of distant lands and climes. In place of the old local and national seclusion and self-sufficiency, we have intercourse in every direction, universal inter-dependence of nations. And as in material, so also in intellectual production. The intellectual creations of individual nations become common property. National one-sidedness and narrow-mindedness become more and more impossible, and from the numerous national and local literatures there arises a world literature.

The bourgeoisie, by the rapid improvement of all instruments of production, by the immensely facilitated means of communication, draws all, even the most barbarian, nations into civilisation. The cheap prices of its commodities are the heavy artillery with which it batters down all Chinese walls, with which it forces the barbarians' intensely obstinate hatred of foreigners to capitulate. It compels all nations, on pain of extinction, to adopt the bourgeois mode of production; it compels them to introduce what it calls civilisation into their midst, *i.e.*, to become bourgeois themselves. In one word, it creates a world after its own image.

The bourgeois has subjected the country to the rule of the towns. It has created enormous cities, has greatly increased the urban population as compared with the rural, and has thus rescued a considerable part of the population from the idiocy of rural life. Just as it has made the country dependent on the towns, so it has made barbarian and semi-barbarian countries dependent on the civilised ones, nations of peasants on nations of bourgeois, the East on the West.

The bourgeoisie keeps more and more doing away with the scattered state of the population, of the means of production, and of property. It has agglomerated population, centralised means of production, and has concentrated property in a few hands. The necessary consequence of this was political centralisation. Independent, or but loosely connected provinces, with separate interests, laws, governments and systems of taxation, became lumped together into one nation, with one government, one code of laws, one national class interest, one frontier and one customs tariff.

The bourgeoisie, during its rule of scarce one hundred years, has created more massive and more colossal productive forces than have all preceding generations together. Subjection of nature's forces to man, machinery, application of chemistry to industry and agriculture, steam navigation, railways, electric telegraphs, clearing of whole continents for cultivation, canalisation of rivers, whole populations conjured out of the ground—what earlier century had even a presentiment that such productive forces slumbered in the lap of social labour?

We see then: the means of production and of exchange, on whose foundation the bourgeoisie built itself up, were generated in feudal society. At a certain stage in the development of these means of production and of exchange, the conditions under which feudal society produced and exchanged, the feudal organisation of agriculture and manufacturing industry, in one word, the feudal relations of property became no longer compatible with the already developed productive forces; they became so many fetters. They had to be burst asunder; they were burst asunder.

Into their place stepped free competition, accompanied by a social and political constitution adapted to it, and by the economic and political sway of the bourgeois class.

A similar movement is going on before our own eyes. Modern bourgeois society with its relations of production, of exchange and of property, a society that has conjured up such gigantic means of production and of exchange, is like the sorcerer who is no longer able to control the powers of the nether world whom he has called up by his spells. For many a decade past the history of industry and commerce is but the history of the revolt of modern productive forces against modern conditions of production, against the property relations that are the conditions for the existence of the bourgeoisie and of its rule. It is enough to mention the commercial crises that by their periodical return put the existence of the entire bourgeois society on its trial, each time more threateningly. In these crises a great part not only of the existing products, but also of the previously created productive forces, are periodically destroyed. In these crises there breaks out an epidemic that, in all earlier epochs, would have seemed an absurdity—the epidemic of overproduction. Society suddenly finds itself put back into a state of momentary barbarism; it appears as if a famine, a universal war of devastation had cut off the supply of every means of subsistence; industry and commerce seems to be destroyed. And why? Because there is too much civilisation, too much means of subsistence, too much industry, too much commerce. The productive forces at the disposal of society no longer tend to further the development of the conditions of bourgeois property; on the contrary, they have become too powerful for these conditions, by which they are fettered, and so soon as they overcome these fetters, they bring disorder into the whole of bourgeois society, endanger the existence of bourgeois property. The conditions of bourgeois society are too narrow to comprise the wealth created by them. And how does the bourgeoisie get over these crises? On the one hand, by enforced destruction of a mass of productive forces; on the other, by the conquest of new markets, and by the more thorough exploitation of the old ones. That is to say, by paving the way for more extensive and more destructive crises, and by diminishing the means whereby crises are prevented.

The weapons with which the bourgeoisie felled feudalism to the ground are now turned against the bourgeoisie itself.

But not only has the bourgeoisie forged the weapons that bring death to itself; it has also called into existence the men who are to wield those weapons—the modern working class—the proletarians.

In proportion as the bourgeoisie, *i.e.*, capital, is developed, in the same proportion is the proletariat, the modern working class, developed—a class of labourers, who live only so long as they find work, and who find work only so long as their labour increases capital. These labourers, who must sell themselves piecemeal, are a commodity, like every other article of commerce, and are consequently exposed to all the vicissitudes of competition, to all the fluctuations of the market.

Owing to the extensive use of machinery and to division of labour, the work of the proletarians has lost all individual character, and, consequently, all charm for the workman. He becomes an appendage of the machine, and it is only the most simple, most monotonous, and most easily acquired knack, that is required of him. Hence, the cost of production of a workman is restricted, almost entirely, to the means of subsistence that he requires for his maintenance, and for the propagation of his race. But the price of a commodity, and therefore also of labour, is equal to its cost of production. In proportion, therefore, as the repulsiveness of the work increases, the wage decreases. Nay more, in proportion as the use of machinery and division of labour increases, in the same proportion the burden of toil also increases, whether by prolongation of the working hours, by increase of the work exacted in a given time, or by increased speed of the machinery, etc.

Modern industry has converted the little workshop of the patriarchal master into the great factory of the industrial capitalist. Masses of labourers, crowded into the factory, are organised like soldiers. As privates of the industrial army they are placed under the command of a perfect hierarchy of officers and sergeants. Not only are they slaves of the bourgeois class, and of the bourgeois state; they are daily and hourly enslaved by the machine, by the overlooker, and, above all, by the individual bourgeois manufacturer himself. The more openly this despotism proclaims gain to be its end and aim, the more petty, the more hateful and the more embittering it is.

The less the skill and exertion of strength implied in manual labour, in other words, the more modern industry becomes developed, the more is the labour of men superseded by that of women. Differences of age and sex have no longer any distinctive social validity for the working class. All are instruments of labour, more or less expensive to use, according to their age and sex.

No sooner is the exploitation of the labourer by the manufacturer, so far at an end, that he receives his wages in cash, than he is set upon by the other portions of the bourgeoisie, the landlord, the shopkeeper, the pawnbroker, etc.

The lower strata of the middle class—the small tradespeople, shopkeepers, and retired tradesmen generally, the handicraftsmen and peasants—all these sink gradually into the proletariat, partly because their diminutive capital does not suffice for the scale on which modern industry is carried on, and is swamped in the competition with the large capitalists, partly because their specialized skill is rendered worthless by new methods of production. Thus the proletariat is recruited from all classes of the population.

The proletariat goes through various stages of development. With its birth begins its struggle with the bourgeoisie. At first the contest is carried on by individual labourers, then by the work people of a factory, then by the operatives of one trade, in one locality, against the individual bourgeois who directly exploits them. They direct their attacks not against the bourgeois conditions of production, but against the instruments of production themselves; they destroy imported wares that compete with their labour, they smash to pieces machinery, they set factories ablaze, they seek to restore by force the vanished status of the workman of the Middle Ages.

At this stage the labourers still form an incoherent mass scattered over the whole country, and broken up by their mutual competition. If anywhere they unite to form more compact bodies, this is not yet the consequence of their own active union, but of the union of the bourgeoisie, which class, in order to attain its own political ends, is compelled to set the whole proletariat in motion, and is moreover yet, for a time, able to do so. At this stage, therefore, the proletarians do not fight their enemies, but the enemies of their enemies, the remnants of absolute monarchy, the landowners, the non-industrial bourgeois, the petty bourgeoisie. Thus the whole historical movement is concentrated in the hands of the bourgeoisie; every victory so obtained is a victory for the bourgeoisie.

But with the development of industry the proletariat not only increases in number; it becomes concentrated in greater masses, its strength grows, and it feels that strength more. The various interests and conditions of life within the ranks of the proletariat are more and more equalised, in proportion as machinery obliterates all distinctions of labour, and nearly everywhere reduces wages to the same low level. The growing competition among the bourgeois, and the resulting commercial crises, make the wages of the workers ever more fluctuating. The unceasing improvement of machinery, ever more rapidly developing, makes their livelihood more and more precarious; the collisions between individual workmen and individual bourgeois take more and more the character of collisions between two classes. Thereupon the workers begin to form combinations (trades unions) against the bourgeois; they club together in order to keep up the rate of wages; they found permanent associations in order to make provisions beforehand for these occasional revolts. Here and there the contest breaks out into riots.

Now and then the workers are victorious, but only for a time. The real fruit of their battles lies, not in the immediate result, but in the ever expanding union of the workers. This union is helped on by the improved means of communication that are created by modern industry, and that place the workers of different localities in contact with one another. It was just this contact that was needed to centralise the numerous local struggles, all of the same character, into one national struggle between classes. But every class struggle is a political struggle. And that union, to attain which the burghers of the Middle Ages, with their miserable highways, required centuries, the modern proletarians, thanks to railways, achieve in a few years.

This organization of the proletarians into a class, and consequently into a political party, is continually being upset again by the competition between the workers themselves. But it ever rises up again, stronger, firmer, mightier. It compels legislative recognition of particular interests of the workers, by taking advantage of the divisions among the bourgeoisie itself. Thus the ten-hours' bill in England was carried.

Altogether, collisions between the classes of the old society further in many ways the course of development of the proletariat. The bourgeoisie finds itself involved in a constant battle. At first with the aristocracy; later on, with those portions of the bourgeoisie itself, whose interests have become antagonistic to the progress of industry; at all times with the bourgeoisie of foreign countries. In all these battles it sees itself compelled to appeal to the proletariat, to ask for its help, and thus, to drag it into the political arena. The bourgeoisie itself, therefore, supplies the proletariat with its own elements of political and general education, in other words, it furnishes the proletariat with weapons for fighting the bourgeoisie.

Further, as we have already seen, entire sections of the ruling classes are, by the advance of industry, precipitated into the proletariat, or are at least threatened in their conditions of existence. These also supply the proletariat with fresh elements of enlightenment and progress.

Finally, in times when the class struggle nears the decisive hour, the process of dissolution going on within the ruling class, in fact within the whole range of old society, assumes such a violent, glaring character, that a small section of the ruling class cuts itself adrift, and joins the revolutionary class, the class that holds the future in its hands. Just as, therefore, at an earlier period, a section of the nobility went over to the bourgeoise, so now a portion of the bourgeoisie goes over to the proletariat, and in particular, a portion of the bourgeois ideologists, who have raised themselves to the level of comprehending theoretically the historical movement as a whole.

Of all the classes that stand face to face with the bourgeoisie today, the proletariat alone is a really revolutionary class. The other classes decay and finally disappear in the face of modern industry; the proletariat is its special and essential product. The lower middle class, the small manufacturer, the shopkeeper, the artisan, the peasant, all these fight against the bourgeoisie, to save from extinction their existence as fractions of the Middle Class. They are therefore not revolutionary, but conservative. Nay more, they are reactionary, for they try to roll back the wheel of history. If by chance they are revolutionary, they are so only in view of their impending transfer into the proletariat; they thus defend not their present, but their future interests; they desert their own standpoint to place themselves at that of the proletariat.

The "dangerous class," the social scum, that passively rotting mass thrown off by the lowest layers of old society, may, here and there, be swept into the movement by a proletarian revolution; its conditions of life, however, prepare it far more for the part of a bribed tool of reactionary intrigue.

In the conditions of the proletariat, those of old society at large are already virtually swamped. The proletarian is without property; his relation to his wife and children has no longer anything in common with the bourgeois family relations: modern industrial labour, modern subjection to capital, the same in England as in France, in America as in Germany, has stripped him of every trace of national character. Law, morality, religion, are to him so many bourgeois prejudices, behind which lurk in ambush just as many bourgeois interests.

All the preceding classes that got the upper hand, sought to fortify their already acquired status by subjecting society at large to their conditions of appropriation. The proletarians cannot become masters of the productive forces of society, except by abolishing their own previous mode of appropriation, and thereby also every other previous mode of appropriation. They have nothing of their own to secure and to fortify: their mission is to destroy all previous securities for, and insurances of, individual property.

All previous historical movements were movements of minorities, or in the interest of minorities. The proletarian movement is the self-conscious, independent movement of the immense majority, in the interest of the immense majority. The proletariat, the lowest stratum of our present society, cannot stir, cannot raise itself up, without the whole superincumbent strata of official society being sprung into the air.

Though not in substance, yet in form, the struggle of the proletariat with the bourgeoisie is at first a national struggle. The proletariat of each country must, of course, first of all settle matters with its own bourgeoisie.

In depicting the most general phases of the development of the proletariat, we traced the more or less veiled civil war, raging within existing society, up to the point where that war breaks out into open revolution, and where the violent overthrow of the bourgeoisie lays the foundation for the ways of the proletariat.

Hitherto, every form of society has been based, as we have already seen, on the antagonism of oppressing and oppressed classes. But in order to oppress a class, certain conditions must be assured to it under which it can, at least, continue its slavish existence. The serf, in the period of serfdom, raised himself to membership in the commune, just as the petty bourgeois, under the yoke of feudal absolutism, managed to develop into a bourgeois. The modern labourer, on the contrary, instead of rising with the progress of industry, sinks deeper and deeper below the conditions of existence of his own class. He becomes a pauper, and pauperism develops more rapidly than population and wealth. And here it becomes evident, that the bourgeoisie is unfit any longer to be the ruling class in society, and to impose its conditions of existence upon society as an over-riding law. It is unfit to rule because it is incompetent to assure an existence to its slave within his slavery, because it cannot help letting him sink into such a state, that it has to feed him, instead of being fed by him. Society can no longer live under this bourgeoisie, in other words, its existence is no longer compatible with society.

The essential condition for the existence and for the sway of the bourgeois class, is the formation and augmentation of capital; the condition for capital is wage labour. Wage labour rests exclusively on competition between the labourers. The advance of industry, whose involuntary promoter is the bourgeoisie, replaces the isolation of the labourers, due to competition, by their revolutionary combination, due to association. The development of modern industry, therefore, cuts from under its feet the very foundation on which the bourgeoisie produces and appropriates products. What the bourgeoisie therefore produces, above all, are its own grave-diggers. Its fall and the victory of the proletariat are equally inevitable.

II. Proletarians and Communists

In what relation do the Communists stand to the proletarians as a whole?

The Communists do not form a separate party opposed to other working class parties.

They have no interests separate and apart from those of the proletariat as a whole.

They do not set up any sectarian principles of their own, by which to shape and mould the proletarian movement.

The Communists are distinguished from the other working class parties by this only: 1. In the national struggles of the proletarians of the different countries, they point out and bring to the front the common interests of the entire proletariat, independently of all nationality. 2. In the various stages of development which the struggle of the working class against the bourgeoisie has to pass through, they always and everywhere represent the interests of the movement as a whole.

The Communists, therefore, are on the one hand, practically, the most advanced and resolute section of the working class parties of every country, that section which pushes forward all others; on the other hand, theoretically, they have over the great mass of the proletariat the advantage of clearly understanding the line of march, the conditions, and the ultimate general results of the proletarian movement.

The immediate aim of the Communists is the same as that of all the other proletarian parties: Formation of the proletariat into a class, overthrow of the bourgeois supremacy, conquest of political power by the proletariat.

The theoretical conclusions of the Communists are in no way based on ideas or principles that have been invented, or discovered, by this or that would-be universal reformer.

They merely express, in general terms, actual relations springing from an existing class struggle, from a historical movement going on under our very eyes. The abolition of existing property relations is not at all a distinctive feature of communism.

All property relations in the past have continually been subject to historical change consequent upon the change in historical conditions.

The French Revolution, for example, abolished feudal property in favour of bourgeois property.

The distinguishing feature of communism is not the abolition of property generally, but the abolition of bourgeois property. But modern bourgeois private property is the final and most complete expression of the system of producing and appropriating products that is based on class antagonisms, on the exploitation of the many by the few.

In this sense, the theory of the Communists may be summed up in the single sentence: Abolition of private property.

We Communists have been reproached with the desire of abolishing the right of personally acquiring property as the fruit of a man's own labour, which property is alleged to be the groundwork of all personal freedom, activity and independence.

Hard-won, self-acquired, self-earned property! Do you mean the property of the petty artisan and of the small peasant, a form of property that preceded the bourgeois form? There is no need to abolish that: the development of industry has to a great extent already destroyed it, and is still destroying it daily.

Or do you mean modern bourgeois private property?

But does wage labour create any property for the labourer? Not a bit. It creates capital, *i.e.*, that kind of property which exploits wage labour, and which cannot increase except upon condition of begetting a new supply of wage labour for fresh exploitation. Property, in its present form, is based on the antagonism of capital and wage labour. Let us examine both sides of this antagonism.

To be a capitalist is to have not only a purely personal, but a social, *status* in production. Capital is a collective product, and only by the united action of many members, nay, in the last resort, only by the united action of all members of society, can it be set in motion.

Capital is therefore not a personal, it is a social power.

When, therefore, capital is converted into common property, into the property of all members of society, personal property is not thereby transformed into social property. It is only the social character of the property that is changed. It loses its class character.

Let us now take wage labour.

The average price of wage labour is the minimum wage, *i.e.*, that quantum of the means of subsistence which is absolutely requisite to keep the labourer in bare existence as a labourer. What, therefore, the wage labourer appropriates by means of his labour, merely suffices to prolong and reproduce a bare existence. We by no means intend to abolish this personal appropriation of the products of labour, an appropriation that is made for the maintenance and reproduction of human life, and that leaves no surplus wherewith to command the labour of others. All that we want to do away with is the miserable character of this appropriation, under which the labourer lives merely to increase capital, and is allowed to live only in so far as the interest of the ruling class requires it.

In bourgeois society, living labour is but a means to increase accumulated labour. In communist society, accumulated labour is but a means to widen, to enrich, to promote the existence of the labourer.

In bourgeois society, therefore, the past dominates the present; in communist society, the present dominates the past. In bourgeois society capital is independent and has individuality, while the living person is dependent and has no individuality.

And the abolition of this state of things is called by the bourgeois, abolition of individuality and freedom! And rightly so. The abolition of bourgeois individuality, bourgeois independence, and bourgeois freedom is undoubtedly aimed at.

By freedom is meant, under the present bourgeois conditions of production, free trade, free selling and buying.

But if selling and buying disappears, free selling and buying disappears also. This talk about free selling and buying, and all the other "brave words" of our bourgeoisie about freedom in general, have a meaning, if any, only in contrast with restricted selling and buying, with the fettered traders of the Middle Ages, but have no meaning when opposed to the communist abolition of buying and selling, of the bourgeois conditions of production, and of the bourgeoisie itself.

You are horrified at our intending to do away with private property. But in your existing society, private property is already done away with for nine-tenths of the population; its existence for the few is solely due to its non-existence in the hands of those nine-tenths. You reproach us, therefore, with intending to do away with a form of property, the necessary condition for whose existence is the non-existence of any property for the immense majority of society.

In one word, you reproach us with intending to do away with your property. Precisely so; that is just what we intend.

From the moment when labour can no longer be converted into capital, money, or rent, into a social power capable of being monopolised, *i.e.*, from the moment when individual property can no longer be transformed into bourgeois property, into capital, from that moment, you say, individuality vanishes.

You must, therefore, confess that by "individual" you mean no other person than the bourgeois, than the middle-class owner of property. This person must, indeed, be swept out of the way, and made impossible.

Communism deprives no man of the power to appropriate the products of society; all that it does is to deprive him of the power to subjugate the labour of others by means of such appropriation.

It has been objected, that upon the abolition of private property all work will cease, and universal laziness will overtake us.

According to this, bourgeois society ought long ago to have gone to the dogs through sheer idleness; for those of its members who work, acquire nothing, and those who acquire anything, do not work. The whole of this objection is but another expression of the tautology: There can no longer be any wage labour when there is no longer any capital.

All objections urged against the communistic mode of producing and appropriating material products, have, in the same way, been urged against the communistic modes of producing and appropriating intellectual products. Just as to the bourgeois, the disappearance of class property is the disappearance of production itself, so the disappearance of class culture is to him identical with the disappearance of all culture.

That culture, the loss of which he laments, is, for the enormous majority, a mere training to act as a machine.

But don't wrangle with us so long as you apply, to our intended abolition of bourgeois property, the standard of your bourgeois notions of freedom, culture, law, etc. Your very ideas are but the outgrowth of the conditions of your bourgeois production and bourgeois property, just as your jurisprudence is but the will of your class made into a law for all, a will whose essential character and direction are determined by the economical conditions of existence of your class.

The selfish misconception that induces you to transform into eternal laws of nature and of reason, the social forms springing from your present mode of production and form of property—historical relations that rise and disappear in the progress of production—this misconception you share with every ruling class that has preceded you. What you see clearly in the case of ancient property, what you admit in the case of feudal property, you are of course forbidden to admit in the case of your own bourgeois form of property.

Abolition of the family! Even the most radical flare up at this infamous proposal of the Communists.

On what foundation is the present family, the bourgeois family, based? On capital, on private gain. In its completely developed form this family exists only among the bourgeoisie. But this state of things finds its complement in the practical absence of the family among the proletarians, and in public prostitution.

The bourgeois family will vanish as a matter of course when its complement vanishes, and both will vanish with the vanishing of capital.

Do you charge us with wanting to stop the exploitation of children by their parents? To this crime we plead guilty.

But, you will say, we destroy the most hallowed of relations, when we replace home education by social.

And your education! Is not that also social, and determined by the social conditions under which you educate, by the intervention direct or indirect, of society, by means of schools, etc.? The Communists have not invented the intervention of society in education; they do but seek to alter the character of that intervention, and to rescue education from the influence of the ruling class.

The bourgeois claptrap about the family and education, about the hallowed correlation of parent and child, becomes all the more disgusting, the more, by the action of modern industry, all family ties among the proletarians are torn asunder, and their children transformed into simple articles of commerce and instruments of labour.

But you Communists would introduce community of women, screams the whole bourgeoisie in chorus.

The bourgeois sees in his wife a mere instrument of production. He hears that the instruments of production are to be exploited in common, and, naturally, can come to no other conclusion than that the lot of being common to all will likewise fall to the women.

He has not even a suspicion that the real point aimed at is to do away with the status of women as mere instruments of production.

For the rest, nothing is more ridiculous than the virtuous indignation of our bourgeois at the community of women which, they pretend, is to be openly and officially established by the Communists. The Communists have no need to introduce community of women; it has existed almost from time immemorial.

Our bourgeois, not content with having the wives and daughters of their proletarians at their disposal, not to speak of common prostitutes, take the greatest pleasure in seducing each other's wives.

Bourgeois marriage is in reality a system of wives in common and thus, at the most, what the Communists might possibly be reproached with is that they desire to introduce, in substitution for a hypocritically concealed, an openly legalised community of women. For the rest, it is self-evident, that the abolition of the present system of production must bring with it the abolition of the community of women springing from that system, *i.e.*, of prostitution both public and private.

The Communists are further reproached with desiring to abolish countries and nationality.

The workingmen have no country. We cannot take from them what they have not got. Since the proletariat must first of all acquire political supremacy, must rise to be the leading class of the nation, must constitute itself *the* nation, it is, so far, itself national, though not in the bourgeois sense of the word.

National differences and antagonism between peoples are daily more and more vanishing, owing to the development of the bourgeoisie, to freedom of commerce, to the world market, to uniformity in the mode of production and in the conditions of life corresponding thereto.

The supremacy of the proletariat will cause them to vanish still faster. United action of the leading civilised countries at least, is one of the first conditions for the emancipation of the proletariat.

In proportion as the exploitation of one individual by another is put an end to, the exploitation of one nation by another will also be put an end to. In proportion as the antagonism between classes within the nation vanishes, the hostility of one nation to another will come to an end.

The charges against communism made from a religious, a philosophical and, generally, from an ideological standpoint, are not deserving of serious examination.

Does it require deep intuition to comprehend that man's ideas, views, and conceptions, in one word, man's consciousness, changes with every change in the conditions of his material existence, in his social relations and in his social life?

What else does the history of ideas prove, than that intellectual production changes its character in proportion as material production is changed? The ruling ideas of each age have ever been the ideas of its ruling class.

When people speak of ideas that revolutionise society, they do but express the fact, that within the old society, the elements of a new one have been created, and that the dissolution of the old ideas keeps even pace with the dissolution of the old conditions of existence.

When the ancient world was in its last throes, the ancient religions were overcome by Christianity. When Christian ideas succumbed in the eighteenth century to rationalist ideas, feudal society fought its death battle with the then revolutionary bourgeoisie. The ideas of religious liberty and freedom of conscience, merely gave expression to the sway of free competition within the domain of knowledge.

"Undoubtedly," it will be said, "religious, moral, philosophical and juridical ideas have been modified in the course of historical development. But religion, morality, philosophy, political science, and law, constantly survived this change."

"There are, besides, eternal truths, such as Freedom, Justice, etc., that are common to all states of society. But communism abolishes eternal truths, it abolishes all religion, and all morality, instead of constituting them on a new basis; it therefore acts in contradiction to all past historical experience."

What does this accusation reduce itself to? The history of all past society has consisted in the development of class antagonisms, antagonisms that assumed different forms at different epochs.

But whatever form they may have taken, one fact is common to all past ages, *viz.*, the exploitation of one part of society by the other. No wonder, then, that the social consciousness of past ages, despite all the multiplicity and variety it displays, moves within certain common forms, or general ideas, which cannot completely vanish except with the total disappearance of class antagonisms.

The communist revolution is the most radical rupture with traditional property relations; no wonder that its development involves the most radical rupture with traditional ideas.

But let us have done with the bourgeois objections to communism.

We have seen above, that the first step in the revolution by the working class, is to raise the proletariat to the position of ruling class, to win the battle of democracy.

The proletariat will use its political supremacy to wrest, by degrees, all capital from the bourgeoisie, to centralise all instruments of production in the hands of the state, *i.e.*, of the proletariat organised as the ruling class; and to increase the total of productive forces as rapidly as possible.

Of course, in the beginning, this cannot be effected except by means of despotic inroads on the rights of property, and on the conditions of bourgeois production; by means of measures, therefore, which appear economically insufficient and untenable, but which, in the course of the movement, outstrip themselves, necessitate further inroads upon the old social order, and are unavoidable as a means of entirely revolutionising the mode of production.

These measures will of course be different in different countries.

Nevertheless in the most advanced countries, the following will be pretty generally applicable.

1. Abolition of property in land and application of all rents of land to public purposes.
2. A heavy progressive or graduated income tax.
3. Abolition of all right of inheritance.
4. Confiscation of the property of all emigrants and rebels.
5. Centralisation of credit in the hands of the state, by means of a national bank with state capital and an exclusive monopoly.
6. Centralisation of the means of communication and transport in the hands of the state.
7. Extension of factories and instruments of production owned by the state; the bringing into cultivation of waste lands, and the improvement of the soil generally in accordance with a common plan.
8. Equal obligation of all to work. Establishment of industrial armies, especially for agriculture.
9. Combination of agriculture with manufacturing industries; gradual abolition of the distinction between town and country, by a more equable distribution of the population over the country.
10. Free education for all children in public schools. Abolition of children's factory labour in its present form. Combination of education with industrial production, etc.

When, in the course of development, class distinctions have disappeared, and all production has been concentrated in the hands of a vast association of the whole nation, the public power will lose its political character. Political power, properly so called, is merely the organised power of one class for oppressing another. If the proletariat during its contest with the bourgeoisie is compelled, by the force of circumstances, to organise itself as a class; if, by means of a revolution, it makes itself the ruling class, and, as such, sweeps away by force the old conditions of production, then it will, along with these conditions, have swept away the conditions for the existence of class antagonisms and of classes generally, and will thereby have abolished its own supremacy as a class.

In place of the old bourgeois society, with its classes and class antagonisms, we shall have an association, in which the free development of each is the condition for the free development of all.

NOTES

1. By bourgeoisie is meant the class of modern capitalists, owners of the means of social production and employers of wage labour. By proletariat, the class of modern wage labourers who, having no means of production of their own, are reduced to selling their labour power in order to live.
2. That is, all *written* history. In 1847 the pre-history of society, the social organisation existing previous to recorded history, was all but unknown. Since then Haxthausen [August von, 1792–1866] discovered common ownership of land in Russia, Maurer [Georg Ludwig von] proved it to be the social foundation from which all Teutonic races started in history, and, by and by, village communities were found to be, or to have been, the primitive form of society everywhere from India to Ireland. The inner organisation of this primitive communistic society was laid bare, in its typical form, by Morgan's [Lewis Henry, 1818–81] crowning discovery of the true nature of the *gens* and its relation to the *tribe*. With the dissolution of these primæval communities, society begins to be differentiated into separate and finally antagonistic classes. I have attempted to retrace this process of dissolution in *Der Ursprung der Familie, des Privateigenthums und des Staats* [*The Origin of the Family, Private Property and the State*], second edition, Stuttgart, 1886.
3. Guild-master, that is a full member of a guild, a master within, not a head of a guild.
4. "Commune" was the name taken in France by the nascent towns even before they had conquered from their feudal lords and masters local self-government and political rights as the "Third Estate." Generally speaking, for the economical development of the bourgeoisie, England is here taken as the typical country, for its political development, France.

20

PITIRIM A. SOROKIN

On Social Mobility

Pitirim A. Sorokin made theoretic or empirical contributions to almost every specialization within sociology. Although his contributions were not always cited or acknowledged by those who adopted them, his ideas continue to create reverberations in the work of many American sociologists. Much of Sorokin's work was highly controversial. His classic work in stratification, Social and Cultural Mobility (1927), *represented one such explosive pioneering effort. The conceptual distinctions first made in this volume quickly became part of the vocabulary of those writing on stratification, although often they failed to give recognition to the source. As Hans Speier, one of Sorokin's more severe critics, has acknowledged: "The wealth of quantitative data and the rich historical documentation of the volume have made it an indispensable textbook for anyone interested in social stratification."*

Bibliographical Notes

1. A very good brief discussion of Sorokin's contributions to the literature of social stratification can be found in: Alvin Boskoff, Theory in American Sociology *(New York: Thomas Y. Crowell, 1969), pp. 145–149. A more general review can be found in: Gösta Carlsson, "Sorokin's Theory of Social Mobility," in Philip J. Allen (ed.),* Pitirim A. Sorokin in Review *(Durham, N.C.: Duke University Press, 1963), pp. 122–139, which also includes Sorokin's responses, pp. 449–454. A listing of major works by and about Sorokin can be found in the introduction to his earlier statement in this volume, pp. 3–4.*

2. Hans Speier, "The Sociological Ideas of Pitirim Alexandrovitch

---

Sorokin: 'Integralist' Sociology," in Harry Elmer Barnes (ed.), An Introduction to the History of Sociology *(Chicago: University of Chicago Press, 1948), p. 887.*

---

1. *Conception of Social Mobility and Its Forms*

By social mobility is understood any transition of an individual or social object or value—anything that has been created or modified by human activity—from one social position to another. There are two principal types of social mobility, *horizontal* and *vertical.* By horizontal social mobility or shifting, is meant the transition of an individual or social object from one social group to another situated on the same level. Transitions of individuals, as from the Baptist to the Methodist religious group, from one citizenship to another, from one family (as a husband or wife) to another by divorce and remarriage, from one factory to another in the same occupational status, are all instances of social mobility. So too are transitions of social objects, the radio, automobile, fashion, Communism, Darwin's theory, within the same social stratum, as from Iowa to California, or from any one place to another. In all these cases, "shifting" may take place without any noticeable change of the social position of an individual or social object in the vertical direction. By *vertical* social mobility is meant the relations involved in a transition of an individual (or a social object) from one social stratum to another. According to the direction of the transition there are two types of vertical social mobility: *ascending* and *descending,* or *social climbing* and *social sinking.* According to the nature of the stratification, there are ascending and descending currents of economic, political, and occupational mobility, not to mention other less important types. The ascending currents exist in two principal forms: as an *infiltration* of the individuals of a lower stratum into an existing higher one; and as a *creation of a new group by such individuals, and the insertion of such a group into a higher stratum instead of, or side by side with, the existing groups of this stratum.* Correspondingly, the descending current has also two principal forms: the first consists in a dropping of individuals from a higher social position into an existing lower one, without a degradation or disintegration of the higher group to which they belonged; the second is manifested in *a degradation of a social group as a whole, in an abasement of its rank among other groups, or in its disintegration as a social unit.* The first case of "sinking" reminds one of an individual falling from a ship; the second of the sinking of the ship itself with all on board, or of the ship as a wreck breaking itself to pieces.

The cases of individual infiltration into an existing higher stratum or of individuals dropping from a higher social layer into a lower one are relatively common and comprehensible. They need no explanation. The second form of social ascending and descending, the rise and fall of groups, must be considered more carefully.

The following historical examples may serve to illustrate. The historians of India's caste-society tell us that the caste of the Brahmins did not always hold the position of indisputable superiority which it has held during the last two thousand years. In the remote past, the caste of the warriors and rulers, or the caste of the Kshatriyas, seems to have been not inferior to the caste of the Brahmins; and it appears that only after a long struggle did the latter become the highest caste.[1] If this hypothesis be true, then this elevation of the rank of the Brahmin caste as a whole through the ranks of other castes is an example of the second type of social ascent. The group as a whole being elevated, all its members, *in corpore*, through this very fact, are elevated also. Before the recognition of the Christian religion by Constantine the Great, the position of a Christian Bishop, or the Christian clergy, was not a high one among other social ranks of Roman society. In the next few centuries the Christian Church, as a whole, experienced an enormous elevation of social position and rank. Through this wholesale elevation of the Christian Church, the members of the clergy, and especially the high Church dignitaries, were elevated to the highest ranks of medieval society. And, contrariwise, a decrease in the authority of the Christian Church during the last two centuries has led to a relative abasement of the social ranks of the high Church dignitaries within the ranks of the present society. The position of the Pope or a cardinal is still high, but undoubtedly it is lower than it was in the Middle Ages.[2] The group of the legists in France is another example. In the twelfth century, this group appeared in France, as a group, and began to grow rapidly in significance and rank. Very soon, in the form of the judicial aristocracy, it inserted itself into the place of the previously existing nobility. In this way, its members were raised to a much higher social position. During the seventeenth, and especially the eighteenth centuries, the group, as a whole, began to "sink," and finally disappeared in the conflagration of the Revolution. A similar process took place in the elevation of the Communal *Bourgeoisie* in the Middle Ages, in the privileged Six Corps or the *Guilda Mercatoria*, and in the aristocracy of many royal courts. To have a high position at the court of the Romanoffs, Hapsburgs, or Hohenzollerns before the revolutions meant to have one of the highest social ranks in the corresponding countries. The "sinking" of the dynasties led to a "social sinking" of all ranks connected with them. The group of the Communists in Russia, before the Revolution, did not have any high rank socially recognized. During the Revolution the group climbed an enormous social distance and occupied the highest strata in Russian society. As a result, all its members have been elevated *en masse* to the place occupied by the Czarist aristocracy. Similar cases are given in a purely economic stratification. Before the "oil" and "automobile" era, to be a prominent manufacturer in this field did not mean to be a captain of industry and finance. A great expansion of these industries has transformed them into some of the most important kinds of industry. Correspondingly, to be a leading manufacturer in these fields now means to be one of the most important leaders of industry and finance. These examples illustrate the second collective form of ascending and descending currents of social mobility.

The situation is summed up in the following scheme:

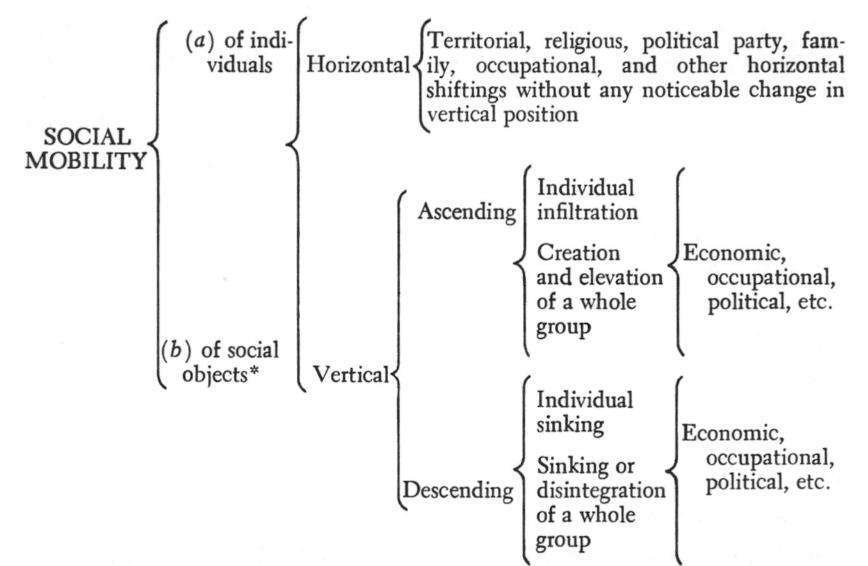

* The mobility of social objects and values and the horizontal mobility, in spite of the great importance of the problem, is not an object of this study.

2. *Intensiveness or Velocity and Generality of Vertical Social Mobility*

From the quantitative point of view, a further distinction must be made between the intensiveness and the generality of the vertical mobility. By its *intensiveness* is meant the vertical social distance, or the number of strata—economic or occupational or political—crossed by an individual in his upward or downward movement in a definite period of time. If, for instance, one individual in one year climbed from the position of a man with a yearly income of $500 to a position with an income of $50,000, while another man in the same period succeeded in increasing his income only from $500 to $1,000, in the first case the intensiveness of the economic climbing would be fifty times greater than in the second case. For a corresponding change, the intensiveness of the vertical mobility may be measured in the same way in the field of the political and occupational stratifications. By the generality of the vertical mobility, is meant the number of individuals who have changed their social position in the vertical direction in a definite period of time. The absolute number of such individuals gives the *absolute generality* of the vertical mobility in a given population; the proportion of such individuals to the total number of a given population gives *the relative generality of the vertical mobility.*

Finally, combining the data of intensiveness and relative generality of the vertical mobility in a definite field (*e.g.*, in the economic), *the aggregate index of the vertical economic mobility of a given society* may be obtained. In this way a comparison of one society with another, or of the same society at different periods may be made, to find in which of them, or at what period, the aggregate mobility is greater. The same may be said about the aggregate index of the political and occupational vertical mobility.

3. *Immobile and Mobile Types of Stratified Societies*

On the basis of the above, it is easy to see that a social stratification of the same height and profile may have a different inner structure caused by the difference in the intensiveness and generality of the (horizontal and) vertical social mobility. Theoretically, there may be a stratified society in which the vertical social mobility is nil. This means that within it there is no ascending or descending, no circulation of its members; that every individual is forever attached to the social stratum in which he was born; that the membranes or hymens which separate one stratum from another are absolutely impenetrable, and do not have any "holes" through which, nor any stairs and elevators with which, the dwellers of the different strata may pass from one floor to another. *Such a type of stratification may be styled as absolutely closed, rigid, impenetrable, or immobile.* The opposite theoretical type of the inner structure of the stratification of the same height and profile is that in which the vertical mobility is very intensive and general; here the membranes between the strata are very thin and have the largest holes to pass from one floor to another. Therefore, though the social building is as stratified as the immobile one, nevertheless, the dwellers of its different strata are continually changing; they do not stay a very long time in the same "social story," and with the help of the largest staircases and elevators are *en masse* moving "up and down." *Such a type of social stratification may be styled open, plastic, penetrable, or mobile.* Between these two extreme types there may be many middle or intermediary types of stratification.

Having indicated these types and the types of the vertical mobility, turn now to an analysis of the different kinds of societies and the same society at different times, from the standpoint of the vertical mobility and penetrability of their strata.

4. *Democracy and Vertical Social Mobility*

One of the most conspicuous characteristics of the so-called "democratic societies" is a more intensive vertical mobility compared with that of the non-democratic groups. In democratic societies the social position of an individual, at least theoretically, is not determined by his birth; all positions are open to everybody who can get them; there are no judicial or religious obstacles to climbing or going down. All this facilitates a "greater vertical mobility" (capillarity, according to the expression of Dumont) in such societies. This greater mobility is probably one of the causes of the belief that the social building of democratic societies is not stratified, or is less stratified, than that of autocratic societies. We have seen that this opinion is not warranted by the facts. Such a belief is a kind of mental aberration, due to many causes, and among them to the fact that the strata in democratic groups are more open, have more holes and "elevators" to go up and down. This produces the illusion that there are no strata, even though they exist.

In pointing out this considerable mobility of the democratic societies, a reservation must be made at the same time, for not always, and not in all "democratic" societies, is the vertical mobility greater than in the "autocratic" ones.[3] In some of the non-democratic groups mobility has been greater than in the democracies. This is not often seen because the "channels" and the methods of climbing and sinking in such societies are not "the elections," as in democracies, but other and somewhat different ones. While "elections" are conspicuous indications of mobility, its other outlets and channels are often overlooked. Hence the impression of the stagnant and immobile character of all "non-electoral" societies. That this impression is far from being always true will be shown.

5. *General Principles of Vertical Mobility*

1. *First Proposition.—There has scarcely been any society whose strata were absolutely closed, or in which vertical mobility in its three forms—economic, political and occupational—was not present.* That the strata of primitive tribes have been penetrable follows from the fact that within many of them there is no hereditary high position; their leaders often have been elected, their structures have been far from being quite rigid, and the personal qualities of an individual have played a decisive rôle in social ascent or descent. The nearest approach to an absolutely rigid society, without any vertical mobility, is the so-called caste-society. Its most conspicuous type exists in India. Here, indeed, vertical social mobility is very weak. But even here it has not been absolutely absent. Historical records show that in the past, when the caste-system had already been developed, it did happen that members of the highest Brahmin caste, or the king and his family, were overthrown or cast out for crimes. "Through a want of modesty many kings have perished, together with their belongings; through modesty even hermits in the forest have gained kingdoms. Through a want of humility Vena perished, likewise king Nahusha, Sudâs, Sumukha and Nevi," etc.[4] On the other hand, the outcasts, after a suitable repentance, might be reinstated, or individuals born in a lower social stratum might succeed in entering the Brahmin caste, the top of the social cone of India. "By humility Prithu and Manu gained sovereignty, Kubera

the position of the Lord of wealth and the son of Gâdhi, the rank of a Brâhmana." [5] Because of the mixed intercaste marriages, it was possible slowly to climb or sink from caste to caste in several generations. Here are the juridical texts corroborating these statements. In *Gautama* we read: "From a marriage of Brâhmana and Kshatriya springs a Savarna, from a Brâhmana and Vaisya a Nishada, from a Brâhmana and Sûdra a Parasava." In this way intercaste subdivision was appearing. But "In the seventh generation men obtain a change of caste either being raised to a higher or being degraded to a lower one." [6] "By the power of austerities and of the seed from which they sprang the mixed races obtain here among men more exalted or lower rank in successive birth." [7] Articles concerning the degradation and casting-out for the transgression of the caste rule are scattered throughout all the Sacred Books of India.[8] The existence of the process of social climbing is certainly vouched for, too. At least, in the period of Early Buddhism, we find "many cases of Brahmans and Princes doing manual work and manual occupations. Among the middle classes we find not a few instances revealing anything but castebound heredity and groove, to wit, parents discussing the best profession for their son—no reference being made to the father's trade." "Social divisions and economic occupations were very far from being coinciding." "Labor was largely hereditary, yet there was, withal, a mobility and initiative anything but rigid revealed in the exercise of it." Moreover, at different periods, "slave-born kings are known in history but tabooed in Law." "The spectacle of the low-born man in power was never a rarity in India." The case of Chandragupta, a low-born son of Mura who became the founder of the great dynasty of the Maurya and the creator of the great and powerful Maurya Empire (321 to 297 B.C.) is only one conspicuous example among many.[9]

For the last few decades we see a similar picture. The weak current of the vertical mobility has been active in different ways: "through enrolling in one of the more distinguished castes" by those who became wealthy and could obtain a sanction from the Brahmins; through creation of a new caste; through change of occupation; through intercaste marriages; through migration; and so on.[10] Quite recently a considerable rôle began to be played by education, and by political and religious factors.[11] It is evident, therefore, that, in spite of the fact that the caste-society of India is apparently the most conspicuous example of the most impenetrable and rigidly stratified body, nevertheless, even within it, the weak and slow currents of vertical mobility have been constantly present. If such is the case with the India caste-society, it is clear that in all other social bodies vertical mobility to this or that degree, must obviously be present. This statement is warranted by the facts. The histories of Greece, Rome, Egypt,[12] China, Medieval Europe, and so on show the existence of a vertical mobility much more intensive than that of the Indian caste-society. The absolutely rigid society is a myth which has never been realized in history.

2. *The Second Proposition.—There has never existed a society in which vertical social mobility has been absolutely free and the transition from one social stratum to another has had no resistance.* This proposition is a mere corollary to the premises established above, that every organized society is a stratified body. If vertical mobility were absolutely free, in the resultant society there would be no strata. It would remind us of a building having no floors separating one story from another. But all societies have been stratified. This means that within them there has been a kind of "sieve" which has sifted the individuals, allowing some to go up, keeping others in the lower strata, and contrariwise.

Only in periods of anarchy and great disorder, when the entire social structure is broken and where the social strata are considerably demolished, do we have anything reminding us of a chaotic and disorganized vertical mobility *en masse*.[13] But even in such periods, there are some hindrances to unlimited social mobility, partly in the form of the remnants of the "sieve" of the old régime, partly in the form of a rapidly growing "new sieve." After a short period, if such an anarchic society does not perish in anarchy, a modified "sieve" rapidly takes the place of the old one and, incidentally, becomes as tight as its predecessor. What is to be understood by the "sieve" will be explained further on. Here it is enough to say that it exists and functions in this or that form in any society. The proposition is so evident and in the future we shall indicate so many facts which warrant it, that there is no need to dwell on it longer here.

3. *The Third Proposition.—The intensiveness, as well as the generality of the vertical social mobility, varies from society to society (fluctuation of mobility in space).* This statement is quite evident also. It is enough to compare the Indian caste-society with the American society to see that. If the highest ranks in the political, or economic, or occupational cone of both societies are taken, it is seen that in India almost all these ranks are determined by birth, and there are very few "upstarts" who climbed to these positions from the lowest strata. Meanwhile, in the United States, among its captains of industry and finance, 38.8 per cent in the past and 19.6 per cent in the present generation started

poor; 31.5 per cent among the deceased and 27.7 per cent among the living multimillionaires started their careers neither rich nor poor;[14] among the twenty-nine presidents of the United States 14, or 48.3 per cent, came from poor and humble families.[15] The differences in the generality of the vertical mobility of both countries are similar. In India a great majority of the occupational population inherit and keep throughout their lives the occupational status of their fathers; in the United States the majority of the population change their occupations at least once in a lifetime. The study of occupational shifting by Dr. Dublin has shown that among the policyholders of the Metropolitan Life Insurance Company 58.5 per cent have changed their occupation between the moment of issuance of the policy and death.[16] My own study of the transmission of occupation from father to son among different groups of the American population has shown that among the present generation the shifting from occupation to occupation is high. The same may be said about the generality of the vertical economic mobility.

Furthermore, the differences in the intensity and generality of the vertical political mobility in different societies may be seen from the following figures which show what per cent among the monarchs and executives of the different countries were "newcomers" who climbed to this highest position from the lower social strata. (See following table.)

These figures may be taken as an approximate indication of the intensiveness and generality of the vertical political mobility from the bottom of the political structure to its top. The great variation of the figures is an indication of the great fluctuation of the political mobility from country to country.

4. *The Fourth Proposition.—The intensiveness and the generality of the vertical mobility—the economic, the political and the occupational —fluctuate in the same society at different times.* In the course of the history of a whole country, as well as of any social group, there are periods when the vertical mobility increases from the quantitative as

COUNTRY	PER CENT OF "UPSTARTS" AMONG THE MONARCHS AND PRESIDENTS
Western Roman Empire	45.6
Eastern Roman Empire	27.7
Russia	5.5
France	3.9
England	5.0
United States of America	48.3
Presidents of France and Germany	23.1

well as from the qualitative viewpoint, and there are the periods when it decreases.

Though accurate statistical material to prove this proposition is very scarce and fragmentary, nevertheless, it seems to me that these data, together with different forms of historical testimony, are enough to make the proposition safe. . . .

5. *The Fifth Proposition.—As far as the corresponding historical and other materials permit seeing, in the field of vertical mobility, in its three fundamental forms, there seems to be no definite perpetual trend toward either an increase or a decrease of the intensiveness and generality of mobility. This is proposed as valid for the history of a country, for that of a large social body, and, finally, for the history of mankind.* . . . It is evident that the tendency to social seclusion and rigidity in the later stages of development of many social bodies has been rather common. While not trying to claim for this tendency a permanent trend, it is mentioned only to oppose the alleged tendency of an increase of social mobility in the course of time.

What has been said seems to be enough to challenge the alleged trend theories.

Summary

1. The principal forms of social mobility of individuals and social objects are: horizontal and vertical. Vertical mobility exists in the form of ascending and descending currents. Both have two varieties: individual infiltration and collective ascent or descent of the whole group within the system of other groups.

2. According to the degree of the circulation, it is possible to discriminate between immobile and mobile types of society.

3. There scarcely has existed a society whose strata were absolutely closed.

4. There scarcely has existed a society where vertical mobility was absolutely free from obstacles.

5. The intensiveness and the generality of vertical mobility vary from group to group, from time to time (fluctuation in space and in time). In the history of a social body there is a rhythm of comparatively immobile and mobile periods.

6. In these fluctuations there seems to be no perpetual trend toward either an increase or decrease of vertical mobility.

7. Though the so-called democratic societies are often more mobile

than autocratic ones, nevertheless, the rule is not general and has many exceptions.

NOTES

1. See Bouglé, C., "Remarques sur le régime des castes," pp. 53 *et seq.*; *The Cambridge History of India*, pp. 92 *et seq*.
2. See Guizot, F., *The History of Civilization*, Vol. I, pp. 50–54, New York, 1874.
3. This is natural because under the signboard "democracy" are usually put societies of the most different types. The same is true of "autocracy." Both terms are very vague and scientifically defective.
4. *Laws of Manu*, VII, 40–42; see also XI, 183–199.
5. *Laws of Manu*, VII, 42, XI, 187–199.
6. Guautama, Chap. IV, pp. 8–21.
7. *Laws of Manu*, X, 42; see also 5–56.
8. See also Lilly, W. S., *India and Its Problems*, pp. 200 *et seq*., London, 1922.
9. *The Cambridge History of India*, Vol. 1, pp. 208ff., 223, 268–269, 288, 480, New York, 1922.
10. See *The Imperial Gazetteer of India*, Vol. I, pp. 311–331.
11. See Woodburne, A. S., *Decline of Caste in India*, in Case, C., *Outlines of Introductory Sociology*.
12. See Breasted, J. H., *op. cit*., pp. 120, 173, 289, 333, 360.
13. See Sorokin, P., *Sociology of Revolution*, Pt. III.
14. Sorokin, P., "American Millionaires and Multimillionaires," *Journal of Social Forces*, p. 638, May, 1925.
15. Sorokin, P., "The Monarchs and the Rulers," *Journal of Social Forces*, March, 1926.
16. Dublin, L. J., "Shifting of Occupations Among Wage Earners," *Monthly Labor Review*, April, 1924.

21

THORSTEIN VEBLEN

On Conspicuous Consumption

Thorstein Bunde Veblen (1857–1929), an economist, has had a measurable influence on sociology. His major impact, however, did not so much derive from his general social theory, a form of evolutionism in which the progress of technology shaped and led society. Instead, sociology has been most greatly affected by Veblen's ironic and biting insights into the patterns of social competition that involve those individuals whose positions allowed them membership in what he called the leisure class.[1] *In their essence, many of his incisive observations concerned what are today called status symbols.*[2] *Though his emphasis on technology as a major social variable had important consequences for the work of later sociologists, for example, William F. Ogburn, it is for his trenchant observations on American life that Veblen has been best remembered.*[3]

Bibliographical Notes

1. *Veblen's major works include:* The Theory of the Leisure Class (*1899*); The Theory of Business Enterprise (*1904*); The Instinct of Workmanship (*1914*); Imperial Germany and the Industrial Revolution (*1915*); The Higher Learning in America (*1918*); The Place of Science in Modern Civilization (*1919*); The Engineers and the Price System (*1921*); Absentee Ownership and Business Enterprise in Recent Times (*1923*); *and (edited by L. Ardzrooni)* Essays in Our Changing Order (*1934*). *The definitive work on Veblen, which contains a complete bibliography of his works, is: Joseph Dorfman,* Thorstein Veblen and His America (*New York: Viking, 1934*). *Among the*

Reprinted from Thorstein Veblen, *The Theory of the Leisure Class: An Economic Study of Institutions* (New York: Macmillan, 1902), pp. 68–101.

numerous other works on Veblen, I recommend: David Riesman, Thorstein Veblen: A Critical Interpretation *(New York: Scribners, 1953); and Douglas Dowd,* Thorstein Veblen *(New York: Washington Square Press, 1964).*

2. *An excellent work that could be considered an extension of Veblen's on the subject of status symbols is: Erving Goffman, "Symbols of Class Status,"* British Journal of Sociology, *2 (1951), 294–304.*

3. *A very critical review of Veblen's* The Theory of the Leisure Class, *written in grand satirical manner is: H. L. Mencken, "Professor Veblen," in his* Prejudices, First Series *(New York: Knopf, 1919), pp. 59–82. This review represents a literary curiosity to some extent since it attacks the Veblen style (which itself has become an object of great admiration by many sociologists, e.g., the late C. Wright Mills).*

In what has been said of the evolution of the vicarious leisure class and its differentiation from the general body of the working classes, reference has been made to a further division of labour,—that between different servant classes. One portion of the servant class, chiefly those persons whose occupation is vicarious leisure, come to undertake a new, subsidiary range of duties—the vicarious consumption of goods. The most obvious form in which this consumption occurs is seen in the wearing of liveries and the occupation of spacious servants' quarters. Another, scarcely less obtrusive or less effective form of vicarious consumption, and a much more widely prevalent one, is the consumption of food, clothing, dwelling, and furniture by the lady and the rest of the domestic establishment.

But already at a point in economic evolution far antedating the emergence of the lady, specialised consumption of goods as an evidence of pecuniary strength had begun to work out in a more or less elaborate system. The beginning of a differentiation in consumption even antedates the appearance of anything that can fairly be called pecuniary strength. It is traceable back to the initial phase of predatory culture, and there is even a suggestion that an incipient differentiation in this respect lies back of the beginnings of the predatory life. . . .

In the earlier phases of the predatory culture the only economic differentiation is a broad distinction between an honourable superior class made up of the able-bodied men on the one side, and a base inferior class of labouring women on the other. According to the ideal scheme of life in force at that time it is the office of the men to consume what the women produce. Such consumption as falls to the women is merely incidental to their work; it is a means to their continued labour, and not a consumption directed to their own comfort and fullness of life. Unproductive consumption of goods is honourable, primarily as a mark of prowess and a perquisite of human dignity; secondarily it becomes substantially honourable in itself, especially the consumption of the more desirable things. The consumption of choice articles of food, and frequently also of rare articles of adornment, becomes tabu to the women and children; and if there is a base (servile) class of men, the tabu holds also for them. With a further advance in culture this tabu may change into simple custom of a more or less rigorous character; but whatever be the theoretical basis of the distinction which is maintained, whether it be a tabu or a larger conventionality, the features of the conventional scheme of consumption do not change easily. When the quasi-peaceable stage of industry is reached, with its fundamental institution of chattel slavery, the general principle, more or less rigorously applied, is that the base, industrious class should consume only what may be necessary to their subsistence. In the nature of things, luxuries and the comforts of life belong to the leisure class. Under the tabu, certain victuals, and more particularly certain beverages, are strictly reserved for the use of the superior class.

The ceremonial differentiation of the dietary is best seen in the use of intoxicating beverages and narcotics. If these articles of consumption are costly, they are felt to be noble and honorific. Therefore the base classes, primarily the women, practise an enforced continence with respect to these stimulants, except in countries where they are obtainable at a very low cost. From archaic times down through all the length of the patriarchical régime it has been the office of the women to prepare and administer these luxuries, and it has been the perquisite of the men of gentle birth and breeding to consume them. Drunkenness and the other pathological consequences of the free use of stimulants therefore tend in their turn to become honorific, as being a mark, at the second remove, of the superior status of those who are able to afford the indulgence. Infirmities induced by over-indulgence are among some peoples freely recognised as manly attributes. It has even happened that the name for certain diseased conditions of the body arising from such an origin has passed into everyday speech as a synonym for "noble" or "gentle." It is only at a relatively early stage of culture that the symptoms of expensive vice are conventionally accepted as marks of a superior status, and so tend to become virtues and command the deference of the community; but the reputability that attaches to certain expensive vices long retains so much of its force as to appreciably lessen the disapprobation visited upon the men of the wealthy or noble class for any excessive indulgence. The same invidious distinction adds force to the current disapproval of any indulgence of this kind on the part of women, minors, and inferiors. This invidious traditional distinction has not lost its force even among the more advanced peoples of to-day. Where the example set by the leisure class retains its imperative force in the regulation of the conventionalities, it is observable that the women still in great measure practise the same traditional continence with regard to stimulants.

. . .

During the earlier stages of economic development, consumption of goods without stint, especially consumption of the better grades of goods,—ideally all consumption in excess of the subsistence minimum, —pertains normally to the leisure class. This restriction tends to disappear, at least formally, after the later peaceable stage has been reached, with private ownership of goods and an industrial system based on wage labour or on the petty household economy. But during the earlier quasi-peaceable stage, when so many of the traditions through which the institution of a leisure class has affected the economic life of later times were taking form and consistency, this principle has had the force of a conventional law. It has served as the norm to which consumption has tended to conform, and any appreciable departure from it is to be regarded as an aberrant form, sure to be eliminated sooner or later in the further course of development.

The quasi-peaceable gentleman of leisure, then, not only consumes of the staff of life beyond the minimum required for subsistence and physical efficiency, but his consumption also undergoes a specialisation as regards the quality of the goods consumed. He consumes freely and of the best, in food, drink, narcotics, shelter, services, ornaments, apparel, weapons and accoutrements, amusements, amulets, and idols or divinities. In the process of gradual amelioration which takes place in the articles of his consumption, the motive principle and the proximate aim of innovation is no doubt the higher efficiency of the improved and more elaborate products for personal comfort and well-being. But that does not remain the sole purpose of their consumption. The canon of reputability is at hand and seizes upon such innovations as are, according to its standard, fit to survive. Since the consumption of these more excellent goods is an evidence of wealth, it becomes honorific; and conversely, the failure to consume in due quantity and quality becomes a mark of inferiority and demerit.

This growth of punctilious discrimination as to qualitative excellence in eating, drinking, etc., presently affects not only the manner of life, but also the training and intellectual activity of the gentleman of leisure. He is no longer simply the successful, aggressive male,—the man of strength, resource, and intrepidity. In order to avoid stultification he must also cultivate his tastes, for it now becomes incumbent on him to discriminate with some nicety between the noble and the ignoble in consumable goods. He becomes a connoisseur in creditable viands of various degrees of merit, in manly beverages and trinkets, in seemly apparel and architecture, in weapons, games, dancers, and the narcotics. This cultivation of the aesthetic faculty requires time and application, and the demands made upon the gentleman in this direction therefore tend to change his life of leisure into a more or less arduous application to the business of learning how to live a life of ostensible leisure in a becoming way. Closely related to the requirement that the gentleman must consume freely and of the right kind of goods, there is the requirement that he must know how to consume them in a seemly manner. His life of leisure must be conducted in due form. Hence arise good manners in the way pointed out in an earlier chapter. High-bred manners and ways of living are items of conformity to the norm of conspicuous leisure and conspicuous consumption.

Conspicuous consumption of valuable goods is a means of reputability to the gentleman of leisure. As wealth accumulates on his hands, his own unaided effort will not avail to sufficiently put his opulence in evidence by this method. The aid of friends and competitors is therefore brought in by resorting to the giving of valuable presents and expensive feasts and entertainments. Presents and feasts had probably another origin than that of naïve ostentation, but they acquired their utility for this purpose very early, and they have retained that character to the present; so that their utility in this respect has now long been the substantial ground on which these usages rest. Costly entertainments, such as the potlatch or the ball, are peculiarly adapted to serve this end. The competitor with whom the entertainer wishes to institute a comparison is, by this method, made to serve as a means to the end. He consumes vicariously for his host at the same time that he is a witness to the consumption of that excess of good things which his host is unable to dispose of single-handed, and he is also made to witness his host's facility in etiquette.

. . .

As wealth accumulates, the leisure class develops further in function and structure, and there arises a differentiation within the class. There is a more or less elaborate system of rank and grades. This differentiation is furthered by the inheritance of wealth and the consequent inheritance of gentility. With the inheritance of gentility goes the inheritance of obligatory leisure; and gentility of a sufficient potency to entail a life of leisure may be inherited without the complement of wealth required to maintain a dignified leisure. Gentle blood may be transmitted without goods enough to afford a reputably free consumption at one's ease. Hence results a class of impecunious gentlemen of leisure, incidentally referred to already. These half-caste gentlemen of leisure fall into a system of hierarchical gradations. Those who stand near the higher and the highest grades of the wealthy leisure class, in point of birth, or in point of wealth, or both, outrank the remoter-born and the pecuniarily weaker. These lower grades, especially the impecunious, or marginal, gentlemen of leisure, affiliate themselves by a system of dependence or fealty to the great ones; by so doing they gain an increment of repute, or of the means with which to lead a life of leisure, from their patron. They become his courtiers or retainers, servants; and being fed and countenanced by their patron they are indices of his rank and vicarious consumers of his superfluous wealth. Many of these affiliated gentlemen of leisure are at the same time lesser men of substance in their own right; so that some of them are scarcely at all, others only partially, to be rated as vicarious consumers. So many of them, however, as make up the retainers and hangers-on of the patron may be classed as vicarious consumers without qualification. Many of these again, and also many of the other aristocracy of less degree, have in turn attached to their persons a more or less comprehensive group of vicarious consumers in the persons of their wives and children, their servants, retainers, etc.

. . .

With the disappearance of servitude, the number of vicarious consumers attached to any one gentleman tends, on the whole, to decrease. The like is of course true, and perhaps in a still higher degree, of the number of dependents who perform vicarious leisure for him. In a general way, though not wholly nor consistently, these two groups coincide. The dependent who was first delegated for these duties was the wife, or the chief wife; and, as would be expected, in the later development of the institution, when the number of persons by whom these duties are customarily performed gradually narrows, the wife remains the last. In the higher grades of society a large volume of both these kinds of service is required; and here the wife is of course still assisted in the work by a more or less numerous corps of menials. But as we descend the social scale, the point is presently reached where the duties of vicarious leisure and consumption devolve upon the wife alone. In the communities of the Western culture, this point is at present found among the lower middle class.

And here occurs a curious inversion. It is a fact of common observation that in this lower middle class there is no pretence of leisure on the part of the head of the household. Through force of circumstances it has fallen into disuse. But the middle-class wife still carries on the business of vicarious leisure, for the good name of the household and its master. In descending the social scale in any modern industrial community, the primary fact—the conspicuous leisure of the master of the household—disappears at a relatively high point. The head of the middle-class household has been reduced by economic circumstances to turn his hand to gaining a livelihood by occupations which often partake largely of the character of industry, as in the case of the ordinary business man of to-day. But the derivative fact—the vicarious leisure and consumption rendered by the wife, and the auxiliary vicarious performance of leisure by menials—remains in vogue as a conventionality which the demands of reputability will not suffer to be slighted. It is by no means an uncommon spectacle to find a man applying himself to work with the utmost assiduity, in order that his wife may in due form render for him that degree of vicarious leisure which the common sense of the time demands.

The leisure rendered by the wife in such cases is, of course, not a simple manifestation of idleness or indolence. It almost invariably occurs disguised under some form of work or household duties or social amenities, which prove on analysis to serve little or no ulterior end beyond showing that she does not and need not occupy herself with anything that is gainful or that is of substantial use. As has already been noticed under the head of manners, the greater part of the customary round of domestic cares to which the middle-class housewife gives her time and effort is of this character. Not that the results of her attention to household matters, of a decorative and mundificatory character, are not pleasing to the sense of men trained in middle-class proprieties; but the taste to which these effects of household adornment and tidiness appeal is a taste which has been formed under the selective guidance of a canon of propriety that demands just these evidences of wasted effort.

The effects are pleasing to us chiefly because we have been taught to find them pleasing. There goes into these domestic duties much solicitude for a proper combination of form and colour, and for other ends that are to be classed as aesthetic in the proper sense of the term; and it is not denied that effects having some substantial aesthetic value are sometimes attained. Pretty much all that is here insisted on is that, as regards these amenities of life, the housewife's efforts are under the guidance of traditions that have been shaped by the law of conspicuously wasteful expenditure of time and substance. If beauty or comfort is achieved,—and it is a more or less fortuitous circumstance if they are,—they must be achieved by means and methods that commend themselves to the great economic law of wasted effort. The more reputable, "presentable" portion of middle-class household paraphernalia are, on the one hand, items of conspicuous consumption, and on the other hand, apparatus for putting in evidence the vicarious leisure rendered by the housewife.

The requirement of vicarious consumption at the hands of the wife continues in force even at a lower point in the pecuniary scale than the requirement of vicarious leisure. At a point below which little if any pretence of wasted effort, in ceremonial cleanness and the like, is observable, and where there is assuredly no conscious attempt at ostensible leisure, decency still requires the wife to consume some goods conspicuously for the reputability of the household and its head. So that, as the latter-day outcome of this evolution of an archaic institution, the wife, who was at the outset the drudge and chattel of the man, both in fact and in theory,—the producer of goods for him to consume,—has become the ceremonial consumer of goods which he produces. But she still quite unmistakably remains his chattel in theory; for the habitual rendering of vicarious leisure and consumption is the abiding mark of the unfree servant.

This vicarious consumption practised by the household of the middle and lower classes can not be counted as a direct expression of the leisure-class scheme of life, since the household of this pecuniary grade does not belong within the leisure class. It is rather that the leisure-class scheme of life here comes to an expression at the second remove. The leisure class stands at the head of the social structure in point of reputability; and its manner of life and its standards of worth therefore afford the norm of reputability for the community. The observance of these standards, in some degree of approximation, becomes incumbent upon all classes lower in the scale. In modern civilized communities the lines of demarcation between social classes have grown vague and transient, and wherever this happens the norm of reputability imposed by the upper class extends its coercive influence with but slight hindrance down through the social structure to the lowest strata. The result is that the members of each stratum accept as their ideal of decency the scheme of life in vogue in the next higher stratum, and bend their energies to live up to that ideal. On pain of forfeiting their good name and their self-respect in case of failure, they must conform to the accepted code, at least in appearance.

The basis on which good repute in any highly organised industrial community ultimately rests is pecuniary strength; and the means of showing pecuniary strength, and so of gaining or retaining a good name, are leisure and a conspicuous consumption of goods. Accordingly, both of these methods are in vogue as far down the scale as it remains possible; and in the lower strata in which the two methods are employed, both offices are in great part delegated to the wife and children of the household. Lower still, where any degree of leisure, even ostensible, has become impracticable for the wife, the conspicuous consumption of goods remains and is carried on by the wife and children. The man of the household also can do something in this direction, and, indeed, he commonly does; but with a still lower descent into the levels of indigence—along the margin of the slums—the man, and presently also the children, virtually cease to consume valuable goods for appearances, and the woman remains virtually the sole exponent of the household's pecuniary decency. No class of society, not even the most abjectly poor, foregoes all customary conspicuous consumption. The last items of this category of consumption are not given up except under stress of the direst necessity. Very much of squalor and discomfort will be endured before the last trinket or the last pretence of pecuniary decency is put away. There is no class and no country that has yielded so abjectly before the pressure of physical want as to deny themselves all gratification of this higher or spiritual need.

From the foregoing survey of the growth of conspicuous leisure and consumption, it appears that the utility of both alike for the purposes of reputability lies in the element of waste that is common to both. In the one case it is a waste of time and effort, in the other it is a waste of goods. Both are methods of demonstrating the possession of wealth, and the two are conventionally accepted as equivalents. The choice between them is a question of advertising expediency simply, except so far as it may be affected by other standards of propriety, springing from a different source. On grounds of expediency the preference may be given to the one or the other at different stages of the economic development. The question is, which of the two methods will most effectively reach the persons whose convictions it is desired to affect. Usage has answered this question in different ways under different circumstances.

So long as the community or social group is small enough and compact enough to be effectually reached by common notoriety alone,—that is to say, so long as the human environment to which the individual is required to adapt himself in respect of reputability is comprised within his sphere of personal acquaintance and neighbourhood gossip,—so long the one method is about as effective as the other. Each will therefore serve about equally well during the earlier stages of social growth. But when the differentiation has gone farther and it becomes necessary to reach a wider human environment, consumption begins to hold over leisure as an ordinary means of decency. This is especially true during the later, peaceable economic stage. The means of communication and the mobility of the population now expose the individual to the observation of many persons who have no other means of judging of his reputability than the display of goods (and perhaps of breeding) which he is able to make while he is under their direct observation.

The modern organisation of industry works in the same direction also by another line. The exigencies of the modern industrial system frequently place individuals and households in juxtaposition between whom there is little contact in any other sense than that of juxtaposition. One's neighbours, mechanically speaking, often are socially not one's neighbours, or even acquaintances; and still their transient good opinion has a high degree of utility. The only practicable means of impressing one's pecuniary ability on these unsympathetic observers of one's everyday life is an unremitting demonstration of ability to pay. In the modern community there is also a more frequent attendance at large gatherings of people to whom one's everyday life is unknown; in such places as churches, theatres, ballrooms, hotels, parks, shops, and the like. In order to impress these transient observers, and to retain one's self-complacency under their observation, the signature of one's pecuniary strength should be written in characters which he who runs may read. It is evident, therefore, that the present trend of the development is in the direction of heightening the utility of conspicuous consumption as compared with leisure.

It is also noticeable that the serviceability of consumption as a means of repute, as well as the insistence on it as an element of decency, is at its best in those portions of the community where the human contact of the individual is widest and the mobility of the population is greatest. Conspicuous consumption claims a relatively larger portion of the income of the urban than of the rural population, and the claim is also more imperative. The result is that, in order to keep up a decent appearance, the former habitually live hand-to-mouth to a greater extent than the latter. So it comes, for instance, that the American farmer and his wife and daughters are notoriously less modish in their dress, as well as less urbane in their manners, than the city artisan's family with an equal income. It is not that the city population is by nature much more eager for the peculiar complacency that comes of a conspicuous consumption, nor has the rural population less regard for pecuniary decency. But the provocation to this line of evidence, as well as its transient effectiveness, are more decided in the city. This method is therefore more readily resorted to, and in the struggle to outdo one another the city population push their normal standard of conspicuous consumption to a higher point, with the result that a relatively greater expenditure in this direction is required to indicate a given degree of pecuniary decency in the city. The requirement of conformity to this higher conventional standard becomes mandatory. The standard of decency is higher , class for class, and this requirement of decent appearance must be lived up to on pain of losing caste.

Consumption becomes a larger element in the standard of living in the city than in the country. Among the country population its place is to some extent taken by savings and home comforts known through the medium of neighbourhood gossip sufficiently to serve the like general purpose of pecuniary repute. These home comforts and the leisure indulged in—where the indulgence is found—are of course also in great part to be classed as items of conspicuous consumption; and much the same is to be said of the savings. The smaller amount of the savings laid by by the artisan class is no doubt due, in some measure, to the fact that in the case of the artisan the savings are a less effective means of advertisement, relative to the environment in which he is placed, than are the savings of the people living on farms and in the small villages. Among the latter, everybody's affairs, especially everybody's pecuniary status, are known to everybody else. Considered by itself simply—taken in the first degree—this added provocation to which the artisan and the urban labouring classes are exposed may not very seriously decrease the amount of savings; but in its cumulative action, through raising the standard of decent expenditure, its deterrent effect on the tendency to save cannot but be very great.

. . .

But there are other standards of repute and other, more or less imperative, canons of conduct, besides wealth and its manifestation, and some of these come in to accentuate or to qualify the broad, fundamental canon of conspicuous waste. Under the simple test of effectiveness for advertising, we should expect to find leisure and the conspicuous consumption of goods dividing the field of pecuniary emulation pretty evenly between them at the outset. Leisure might then be expected gradually to yield ground and tend to obsolescence as the economic development goes forward, and the community increases in size; while the conspicuous consumption of goods should gradually gain in importance, both absolutely and relatively, until it had absorbed all the available product, leaving nothing over beyond a bare livelihood. But the actual course of development has been somewhat different from this ideal scheme. Leisure held the first place at the start, and came to hold a rank very much above wasteful consumption of goods, both as a direct exponent of wealth and as an element in the standard of decency, during the quasi-peaceable culture. From that point onward, consumption has gained ground, until, at present, it unquestionably holds the primacy, though it is still far from absorbing the entire margin of production above the subsistence minimum.

. . .

Throughout the entire evolution of conspicuous expenditure, whether of goods or of services or human life, runs the obvious implication that in order to effectually mend the consumer's good fame it must be an expenditure of superfluities. In order to be reputable it must be wasteful. No merit would accrue from the consumption of the bare necessaries of life, except by comparison with the abjectly poor who fall short even of the subsistence minimum; and no standard of expenditure could result from such a comparison, except the most prosaic and unattractive level of decency. A standard of life would still be possible which should admit of invidious comparison in other respects than that of opulence; as, for instance, a comparison in various directions in the manifestation of moral, physical, intellectual, or aesthetic force. Comparison in all these directions is in vogue to-day; and the comparison made in these respects is commonly so inextricably bound up with the pecuniary comparison as to be scarcely distinguishable from the latter. This is especially true as regards the current rating of expressions of intellectual and aesthetic force or proficiency; so that we frequently interpret as aesthetic or intellectual a difference which in substance is pecuniary only.

The use of the term "waste" is in one respect an unfortunate one. As used in the speech of everyday life the word carries an undertone of deprecation. It is here used for want of a better term that will adequately describe the same range of motives and of phenomena, and it is not to be taken in an odious sense, as implying an illegitimate expenditure of human products or of human life. In the view of economic theory the expenditure in question is no more and no less legitimate than any other expenditure. It is here called "waste" because this expenditure does not serve human life or human well-being on the whole, not because it is waste or misdirection of effort or expenditure as viewed from the standpoint of the individual consumer who chooses it. If he chooses it, that disposes of the question of its relative utility to him, as compared with other forms of consumption that would not be deprecated on account of their wastefulness. Whatever form of expenditure the consumer chooses, or whatever end he seeks in making his choice, has utility to him by virtue of his preference. As seen from the point of view of the individual consumer, the question of wastefulness does not arise within the scope of economic theory proper. The use of the word "waste" as a technical term, therefore, implies no deprecation of the motives or of the ends sought by the consumer under this canon of conspicuous waste.

. . .

It is obviously not necessary that a given object of expenditure should be exclusively wasteful in order to come in under the category of conspicuous waste. An article may be useful and wasteful both, and its utility to the consumer may be made up of use and waste in the most varying proportions. Consumable goods, and even productive goods, generally show the two elements in combination, as constituents of their utility; although, in a general way, the element of waste tends to predominate in articles of consumption, while the contrary is true of articles designed for productive use. Even in articles which appear at first glance to serve for pure ostentation only, it is always possible to detect the presence of some, at least ostensible, useful purpose; and on the other hand, even in special machinery and tools contrived for some particular industrial process, as well as in the rudest appliances of human industry, the traces of conspicuous waste, or at least of the habit of ostentation, usually become evident on a close scrutiny. It would be hazardous to assert that a useful purpose is ever absent from the utility of any article or of any service, however obviously its prime purpose and chief element is conspicuous waste; and it would be only less hazardous to assert of any primarily useful product that the element of waste is in no way concerned in its value, immediately or remotely.

22

W. L. WARNER, M. MEEKER, AND K. EELLS

On Social Class in America

The American anthoropologist William Lloyd Warner (1898–1970) directed a six-volume report of a small New England city known as the Yankee City Series.[1] *In this study, Warner used what is generally termed the* reputational *approach to the study of stratification: individuals were asked how they saw their community and its members in relation to one another. To use the terms Weber used in the preceding reading, this approach represents an investigation of the status rather than of the class structure of the community. Though Warner's work has been severely criticized,*[2] *its ethnographic value is largely indisputable,*[3] *and its influence has been immense. The following selection is a general statement on social class in America by Warner in collaboration with Marcia Meeker (1916–) and Kenneth Eells (1913–).*

Bibliographical Notes

1. *These volumes included:* The Social Life of a Modern Community, *with P. S. Lunt (1941)*; The Status System of a Modern Community, with *P. S. Lunt (1942)*; The Social Systems of American Ethnic Groups, *with Leo Srole (1946)*; The Social System of the Modern Factory. The Strike: A Social Analysis, *with J. O. Low (1947), and* Social Class in America, *with M. Meeker and K. Eells (1949). These have been condensed into a single volume,* Yankee City *(1963). Other*

Reprinted from W. Lloyd Warner, Marcia Meeker and Kenneth Eells, *Social Class in America: A Manual of Procedure for the Measurement of Social Status* (Chicago: Science Research Associates, 1949), pp. 11–24. Copyright 1949 by Science Research Associates, Inc., Chicago, Ill. Reprinted by permission of Harper & Row, Publishers. Footnotes have been renumbered.

works of Warner include: A Black Civilization (*1937*); Color and Human Nature, *with B. H. Junker and W. A. Adams* (*1941*); Who Shall Be Educated? The Challenge of Universal Opportunities, *with R. J. Havighurst and M. B. Loeb* (*1944*); The Radio Day Time Serial, a Symbolic Analysis, *with W. E. Henry* (*1948*); Democracy in Jonesville, *with W. C. Bailey*, et al. (*1949*); American Life: Dream and Reality (*1953*); What You Should Know about Social Class, *with M. H. Warner* (*1953*); Big Business in America, *with J. C. Abegglen* (*1955*); Occupational Mobility in American Business and Industry 1928–1952, *with J. C. Abegglen* (*1955*); The Living and the Dead (*1959*); Industrial Man, *edited with N. H. Martin* (*1959*); The Family of God (*1961*); The Corporation in the Emergent American Society (*1962*); The American Federal Executive, *with P. P. Van Riper*, et al. (*1963*); *and* The Emergent American Society, *edited with D. B. Unwalla and J. H. Trimm* (*1967*).

2. *Major criticisms include: Harold W. Pfautz and Otis Dudley Duncan, "A Critical Evaluation of Warner's Work in Community Stratification,"* American Sociological Review, 15 (*1950*), *205–215; C. Wright Mills, "Review of* The Social Life of a Modern Community," American Sociological Review, 7 (*1942*), *263–271; and Oscar Handlin, "Review of* The Social Life of a Modern Community *and* The Status System of a Modern Community," New England Quarterly, 15 (*1942*), *554–557.*

3. *One of his most severe critics said, "their value consists of the descriptions of some of the traits of the various organized groups in Yankee City, not in their statistical explorations of the relationships they 'discovered.'" P. A. Sorokin,* Sociological Theories of Today *(New York: Harper & Row, 1966), p. 121.*

Class Among the New England Yankees

Studies of communities in New England clearly demonstrate the presence of a well-defined social-class system.[1] At the top is an aristocracy of birth and wealth. This is the so-called "old family" class. The people of Yankee City say the families who belong to it have been in the community for a long time—for at least three generations and preferably many generations more than three. "Old family" means not only old to the community but old to the class. Present members of the class were born into it; the families into which they were born can trace their lineage through many generations participating in a way of life characteristic of the upper class back to a generation marking the lowly beginnings out of which their family came. Although the men of this level are occupied gainfully, usually as large merchants, financiers, or in the higher professions, the wealth of the family, inherited from the husband's or the wife's side, and often from both, has been in the family for a long time. Ideally, it should stem from the sea trade when Yankee City's merchants and sea captains made large fortunes, built great Georgian houses on elm-lined Hill Street, and filled their houses and gardens with the proper symbols of their high position. They became the 400, the Brahmins, the Hill Streeters to whom others looked up; and they, well-mannered or not, looked down on the rest. They counted themselves, and were so counted, equals of similar levels in Salem, Boston, Providence, and other New England cities. Their sons and daughters married into the old families from these towns and at times, when family fortune was low or love was great, they married wealthy sons and daughters from the newly rich who occupied the class level below them. This was a happy event for the fathers and mothers of such fortunate young people in the lower half of the upper class, an event well publicized and sometimes not too discreetly bragged about by the parents of the lower-upper-class children, an occasion to be explained by the mothers from the old families in terms of the spiritual demands of romantic love and by their friends as "a good deal and a fair exchange all the way around for everyone concerned."

The new families, the lower level of the upper class, came up through the new industries—shoes, textiles, silverware—and finance. Their fathers were some of the men who established New England's trading and financial dominance throughout America. When New York's Wall Street rose to power, many of them transferred their activities to this new center of dominance. Except that they aspire to old-family status, if not for themselves then for their children, these men and their families have a design for living similar to the old-family group. But they are consciously aware that their money is too new and too recently earned to have the sacrosanct quality of wealth inherited from a long line of ancestors. They know, as do those about them, that, while a certain amount of wealth is necessary, birth and old family are what really matter. Each of them can cite critical cases to prove that particular individuals have no money at all, yet belong to the top class because they have the right lineage and right name. While they recognize the worth and importance of birth, they feel that somehow their family's achievements should be better rewarded than by a mere second place in relation to those who need do little more than be born and stay alive.

The presence of an old-family class in a community forces the newly rich to wait their turn if they aspire to "higher things." Meanwhile, they must learn how to act, fill their lives with good deeds, spend their money on approved philanthropy, and reduce their arrogance to manageable proportions.

The families of the upper and lower strata of the upper classes are organized into social cliques and exclusive clubs. The men gather fortnightly in dining clubs where they discuss matters that concern them. The women belong to small clubs or to the Garden Club and give their interest to subjects which symbolize their high status and evoke those sentiments necessary in each individual if the class is to maintain itself. Both sexes join philanthropic organizations whose good deeds are an asset to the community and an expression of the dominance and importance of the top class to those socially beneath them. They are the members of the Episcopalian and Unitarian and, occasionally, the Congregational and Presbyterian churches.

Below them are the members of the solid, highly respectable upper-middle class, the people who get things done and provide the active front in civic affairs for the classes above them. They aspire to the classes above and hope their good deeds, civic activities, and high moral principles will somehow be recognized far beyond the usual pat on the back and that they will be invited by those above them into the intimacies of upper-class cliques and exclusive clubs. Such recognition might increase their status and would be likely to make them members of the lower-upper group. The fact that this rarely happens seldom stops members of this level, once activated, from continuing to try. The men tend to be owners of stores and belong to the large proprietor and professional levels. Their incomes average less than those of the lower-upper class, this latter group having a larger income than any other group, including the old-family level.

These three strata, the two upper classes and the upper-middle, constitute the levels above the Common Man. There is a considerable distance socially between them and the mass of the people immediately below them. They comprise three of the six classes present in the community. Although in number of levels they constitute half the community, in population they have no more than a sixth, and sometimes less, of the Common Man's population. The three levels combined include approximately 13 per cent of the total population.

The lower-middle class, the top of the Common Man level, is composed of clerks and other white-collar workers, small tradesmen, and a fraction of skilled workers. Their small houses fill "the side streets" down from Hill Street, where the upper classes and some of the upper-middle live, and are noticeably absent from the better suburbs where the upper-middle concentrate. "Side Streeter" is a term often used by those above them to imply an inferior way of life and an inconsequential status. They have accumulated little property but are frequently home owners. Some of the more successful members of ethnic groups, such as the Italians, Irish, French-Canadians, have reached this level. Only a few members of these cultural minorities have gone beyond it; none of them has reached the old-family level.

The old-family class (upper-upper) is smaller in size than the new-family class (lower-upper) below them. It has 1.4 per cent, while the lower-upper class has 1.6 per cent, of the total population. Ten per cent of the population belongs to the upper-middle class, and 28 per cent to the lower-middle level. The upper-lower is the most populous class, with 34 per cent, and the lower-lower has 25 per cent of all the people in the town.

The prospects of the upper-middle-class children for higher education are not as good as those of the classes above. One hundred per cent of the children of the two upper classes take courses in the local high school that prepare them for college, and 88 per cent of the upper-middle do; but only 44 per cent of the lower-middle take these courses, 28 per cent of the upper-lower, and 26 per cent of the lower-lower. These percentages provide a good index of the position of the lower-middle class, ranking it well below the three upper classes, but placing it well above the upper-lower and the lower-lower.[2]

The upper-lower class, least differentiated from the adjacent levels and hardest to distinguish in the hierarchy, but clearly present, is composed of the "poor but honest workers" who more often than not are only semi-skilled or unskilled. Their relative place in the hierarchy of class is well portrayed by comparing them with the classes superior to them and with the lower-lower class beneath them in the category of how they spend their money.

A glance at the ranking of the proportion of the incomes of each class spent on ten items (including such things as rent and shelter, food, clothing, and education, among others) shows, for example, that this class ranks second for the percentage of the money spent on food, the lower-lower class being first and the rank order of the other classes following lower-middle according to their place in the social hierarchy.

The money spent on rent and shelter by upper-lower class is also second to the lower-lower's first, the other classes' rank order and position in the hierarchy being in exact correspondence. To give a bird's-eye view of the way this class spends its money, the rank of the upper-lower, for the percentage of its budget spent on a number of common and important items, has been placed in parentheses after every item in the list which follows: food (2), rent (2), clothing (4), automobiles (5), taxes (5), medical aid (5), education (4), and amusements (4–5). For the major items of expenditure the amount of money spent by this class out of its budget corresponds fairly closely with its place in the class hierarchy, second to the first of the lower-lower class for the major necessities of food and shelter, and ordinarily, but not always, fourth or fifth to the classes above for the items that give an opportunity for cutting down the amounts spent on them. Their feelings about doing the right thing, of being respectable and rearing their children to do better than they have, coupled with the limitations of their income, are well reflected in how they select and reject what can be purchased on the American market.[3]

The lower-lower class, referred to as "Riverbrookers" or the "low-down Yankees who live in the clam flats," have a "bad reputation" among those who are socially above them. This evaluation includes beliefs that they are lazy, shiftless, and won't work, all opposites of the good middle-class virtues belonging to the essence of the Protestant ethic. They are thought to be improvident and unwilling or unable to save their money for a rainy day and, therefore, often dependent on the philanthropy of the private or public agency and on poor relief. They are sometimes said to "live like animals" because it is believed that their sexual mores are not too exacting and that pre-marital intercourse, post-marital infidelity, and high rates of illegitimacy, sometimes too publicly mixed with incest, characterize their personal and family lives. It is certain that they deserve only part of this reputation. Research shows many of them guilty of no more than being poor and lacking in the desire to get ahead, this latter trait being common among those above them. For these reasons and others, this class is ranked in Yankee City below the level of the Common Man (lower-middle and upper-lower). For most of the indexes of status it ranks sixth and last.

Class in the Democratic Middle West and Far West

Cities large and small in the states west of the Alleghenies sometimes have class systems which do not possess an old-family (upper-

upper) class. The period of settlement has not always been sufficient for an old-family level, based on the security of birth and inherited wealth, to entrench itself. Ordinarily, it takes several generations for an old-family class to gain and hold the prestige and power necessary to impress the rest of the community sufficiently with the marks of its "breeding" to be able to confer top status on those born into it. The family, its name, and its lineage must have had time to become identified in the public mind as being above ordinary mortals.

While such identification is necessary for the emergence of an old-family (upper-upper) class and for its establishment, it is also necessary for the community to be large enough for the principles of exclusion to operate. For example, those in the old-family group must be sufficiently numerous for all the varieties of social participation to be possible without the use of new-family members; the family names must be old enough to be easily identified; and above all there should always be present young people of marriageable age to become mates of others of their own class and a sufficient number of children to allow mothers to select playmates and companions of their own class for their children.

When a community in the more recently settled regions of the United States is sufficiently large, when it has grown slowly and at an average rate, the chances are higher that it has an old-family class. If it lacks any one of these factors, including size, social and economic complexity, and steady and normal growth, the old-family class is not likely to develop.

One of the best tests of the presence of an old-family level is to determine whether members of the new-family category admit, perhaps grudgingly and enviously and with hostile derogatory remarks, that the old-family level looks down on them and that it is considered a mark of advancement and prestige by those in the new-family group to move into it and be invited to the homes and social affairs of the old families. When a member of the new-family class says, "We've only been here two generations, but we still aren't old-family," and when he or she goes on to say that "they (old family) consider themselves better than people like us and the poor dopes around here let them get away with it," such evidence indicates that an old-family group is present and able to enforce recognition of its superior position upon its most aggressive and hostile competitors, the members of the lower-upper, or new-family, class.

When the old-family group is present and its position is not recognized as superordinate to the new families, the two tend to be coordinate and view each other as equals. The old-family people adroitly let it be known that their riches are not material possessions alone but are old-family lineage; the new families display their wealth, accent their power, and prepare their children for the development of a future lineage by giving them the proper training at home and later sending them to the "right" schools and marrying them into the "right" families.

Such communities usually have a five-class pyramid, including an upper class, two middle, and two lower classes.[4]

Jonesville, located in the Middle West, approximately a hundred years old, is an example of a typical five-class community. The farmers around Jonesville use it as their market, and it is the seat of government for Abraham County. Its population of over 6,000 people is supported by servicing the needs of the farmers and by one large and a few small factories.

At the top of the status structure is an upper class commonly referred to as "the 400." It is composed of old-family and new-family segments. Neither can successfully claim superiority to the other. Below this level is an upper-middle class which functions like the same level in Yankee City and is composed of the same kind of people, the only difference being the recognition that the distance to the top is shorter for them and the time necessary to get there much less. The Common Man level, composed of lower-middle- and upper-lower-class people, and the lower-lower level are replicas of the same classes in Yankee City. The only difference is that the Jonesville ethnics in these classes are Norwegian Lutherans and Catholic Poles, the Catholic Irish and Germans having been absorbed for the most part in the larger population; whereas in Yankee City the ethnic population is far more heterogeneous, and the Catholic Irish are less assimilated largely because of more opposition to them, and because the church has more control over their private lives.

The present description of Jonesville's class order can be brief and no more than introductory because all the materials used to demonstrate how to measure social class are taken from Jonesville. The interested reader will obtain a clear picture in the chapters which follow of what the classes are, who is in them, the social and economic characteristics of each class, and how the people of the town think about their status order.

The communities of the mountain states and Pacific Coast are new, and many of them have changed their economic form from mining to other enterprises; consequently, their class orders are similar to those found in the Middle West. The older and larger far western communities which have had a continuing, solid growth of population which has not destroyed the original group are likely to have the old-family level at the top with the other classes present; the newer and smaller communities and those disturbed by the destruction of their original status structure by large population gains are less likely to have an old-family class reigning above all others. San Francisco is a clear example of the old-family type; Los Angeles, of the more amorphous, less well-organized class structure.

Class in the Deep South

Studies in the Deep South demonstrate that, in the older regions where social changes until recently have been less rapid and less disturbing to the status order, most of the towns above a few thousand population have a six-class system in which an old-family elite is socially dominant.

For example, in a study of a Mississippi community, a market town for a cotton-growing region around it, Davis and the Gardners found a six-class system.[5] Perhaps the southern status order is best described by Chart I on page 258 which gives the names used by the people of the community for each class and succinctly tells how the members of each class regard themselves and the rest of the class order.

The people of the two upper classes make a clear distinction between an old aristocracy and an aristocracy which is not old. There is no doubt that the first is above the other; the upper-middle class views the two upper ones much as the upper classes do themselves but groups them in one level with two divisions, the older level above the other; the lower-middle class separates them but considers them co-ordinate; the bottom two classes, at a greater social distance than the others, group all the levels above the Common Man as "society" and one class. An examination of the terms used by the several classes for the other classes shows that similar principles are operating.

The status system of most communities in the South is further complicated by a color-caste system which orders and systematically controls the relations of those categorized as Negroes and whites.

Although color-caste in America is a separate problem and the present volume does not deal with this American status system, it is necessary that we describe it briefly to be sure a clear distinction is made between it and social class. Color-caste is a system of values and behavior which places all people who are thought to be white in a superior

CHART 1

The Social Perspectives of the Social Classes*

UPPER-UPPER CLASS		LOWER-UPPER CLASS
"Old aristocracy"	UU	"Old aristocracy"
"Aristocracy," but not "old"	LU	**"Aristocracy," but not "old"**
"Nice, respectable people"	UM	"Nice, respectable people"
"Good people, but 'nobody' "	LM	"Good people, but 'nobody' "
"Po' whites"	UL LL	"Po' whites"

UPPER-MIDDLE CLASS			LOWER-MIDDLE CLASS	
"Society"	"Old families"	UU	"Old aristocracy" (older)	"Broken-down aristocracy" (younger)
	"Society" but not "old families"	LU		
"People who should be upper class"		UM	"People who think they are somebody"	
"People who don't have much money"		LM	**"We poor folk"**	
"No 'count lot"		UL	"People poorer than us"	
		LL	"No 'count lot"	

UPPER-LOWER CLASS		LOWER-LOWER CLASS
"Society" or the "folks with money"	UU LU UM	"Society" or the "folks with money"
"People who are up because they have a little money"	LM	"Way-high-ups," but not "Society"
"Poor but honest folk"	UL	"Snobs trying to push up"
"Shiftless people"	LL	**"People just as good as anybody"**

* Allison Davis, Burleigh B. Gardner, and Mary R. Gardner, *Deep South* (Chicago: University of Chicago Press, 1941), p. 65.

position and those who are thought of as black in an inferior status.

Characteristics of American Negroes vary from very dark hair and skin and Negroid features to blond hair, fair skin, and Caucasian features, yet all of them are placed in the "racial" category of Negro. The skin and physical features of American Caucasians vary from Nordic blond types to the dark, swarthy skin and Negroid features of some eastern Mediterranean stocks, yet all are classed as socially white, despite the fact that a sizable proportion of Negroes are "whiter" in appearance than a goodly proportion of whites. The members of the two groups are severely punished by the formal and informal rules of our society if they intermarry, and when they break this rule of "caste endogamy," their children suffer the penalties of our caste-like system by being placed in the lower color caste. Furthermore, unlike class, the rules of this system forbid the members of the lower caste from climbing out of it. Their status and that of their children are fixed forever. This is true no matter how much money they have, how great the prestige and power they may accumulate, or how well they have acquired correct manners and proper behavior. There can be no social mobility out of the lower caste into the higher one. (There may, of course, be class mobility within the Negro or white caste.) The rigor of caste rules varies from region to region in the United States.[6]

The Mexicans, Spanish Americans, and Orientals occupy a somewhat different status from that of the Negro, but many of the characteristics of their social place in America are similar.[7]

The social-class and color-caste hypotheses, inductively established as working principles for understanding American society, were developed in the researches which were reported in the "Yankee City" volumes, *Deep South*, and *Caste and Class in a Southern Town*. Gunnar Myrdal borrowed them, particularly color-caste, and made them known to a large, non-professional American audience.[8]

The Generalities of American Class

It is now time to ask what are the basic characteristics of social status common to the communities of all regions in the United States and, once we have answered this question, to inquire what the variations are among the several systems. Economic factors are significant and important in determining the class position of any family or person, influencing the kind of behavior we find in any class, and contributing their share to the present form of our status system. But, while significant and necessary, the economic factors are not sufficient to predict where a particular family or individual will be or to explain completely the phenomena of social class. Something more than a large income is necessary for high social position. Money must be translated into socially approved behavior and possessions, and they in turn must be translated into intimate participation with, and acceptance by, members of a superior class.

This is well illustrated by what is supposed to be a true story of what happened to a Mr. John Smith, a newly rich man in a far western community. He wanted to get into a particular social club of some distinction and significance in the city. By indirection he let it be known, and was told by his friends in the club they had submitted his name to the membership committee.

Mr. Abner Grey, one of the leading members of the club and active on its membership committee, was a warm supporter of an important philanthropy in this city. It was brought to his attention that Mr. Smith, rather than contributing the large donation that had been expected of him, had given only a nominal sum to the charity.

When Mr. Smith heard nothing more about his application, he again approached one of the board members. After much evasion, he was told that Mr. Grey was the most influential man on the board and he would be wise to see that gentleman. After trying several times to make an appointment with Mr. Grey, he finally burst into Grey's offices unannounced.

"Why the hell, Abner, am I being kept out of the X club?"

Mr. Grey politely evaded the question. He asked Mr. Smith to be seated. He inquired after Mr. Smith's health, about the health of his wife, and inquired about other matters of simple convention.

Finally, Mr. Smith said, "Ab, why the hell am I being kept out of your club?"

"But, John, you're not. Everyone in the X club thinks you're a fine fellow."

"Well, what's wrong?"

"Well, John, we don't think you've got the *kind* of money necessary for being a good member of the X club. We don't think you'd be happy in the X club."

"Like hell I haven't. I could buy and sell a half dozen of some of your board members."

"I know that, John, but that isn't what I said. I did not say the amount of money. I said the kind of money."

"What do you mean?"

"Well, John, my co-workers on the charity drive tell me you only gave a few dollars to our campaign, and we had you down for a few thousand."

For a moment Mr. Smith was silent. Then he grinned. So did Mr.

Grey. Smith took out his fountain pen and checkbook. "How much?"

At the next meeting of the X club Mr. Smith was unanimously elected to its membership.

Mr. Smith translated his money into philanthropy acceptable to the dominant group, he received their sponsorship, and finally became a participant in the club. The "right" kind of house, the "right" neighborhood, the "right" furniture, the proper behavior—all are symbols that can ultimately be translated into social acceptance by those who have sufficient money to aspire to higher levels than they presently enjoy.

To belong to a particular level in the social-class system of America means that a family or individual has gained acceptance as an equal by those who belong in the class. The behavior in this class and the participation of those in it must be rated by the rest of the community as being at a particular place in the social scale.

Although our democratic heritage makes us disapprove, our class order helps control a number of important functions. It unequally divides the highly and lowly valued things of our society among the several classes according to their rank. Our marriage rules conform to the rules of class, for the majority of marriages are between people of the same class. No class system, however, is so rigid that it completely prohibits marriages above and below one's own class. Furthermore, an open class system such as ours permits a person during his lifetime to move up or down from the level into which he was born. Vertical social mobility for individuals or families is characteristic of all class systems. The principal forms of mobility in this country are through the use of money, education, occupation, talent, skill, philanthropy, sex, and marriage. Although economic mobility is still important, it seems likely now that more people move to higher positions by education than by any other route. We have indicated before this that the mere possession of money is insufficient for gaining and keeping a higher social position. This is equally true of all other forms of mobility. In every case there must be social acceptance.

Class varies from community to community. The new city is less likely than an old one to have a well-organized class order; this is also true for cities whose growth has been rapid as compared with those which have not been disturbed by huge increases in population from other regions or countries or by the rapid displacement of old industries by new ones. The mill town's status hierarchy is more likely to follow the occupational hierarchy of the mill than the levels of evaluated participation found in market towns or those with diversified industries.

Suburbs of large metropolises tend to respond to selective factors which reduce the number of classes to one or a very few. They do not represent or express all the cultural factors which make up the social pattern of an ordinary city.

Yet systematic studies (see Chapter 15 [in *Social Class* in America]) from coast to coast, in cities large and small and of many economic types, indicate that, despite the variations and diversity, class levels do exist and that they conform to a particular pattern of organization.

NOTES

1. See Chapter 15 [in *Social Class in America*] for a description of the several volumes of "Yankee City Series." New and poorly organized towns sometimes have class systems which have no old-family (upper-upper) class.
2. See W. Lloyd Warner and Paul S. Lunt, *The Social Life of a Modern Community*, Vol. I, "Yankee City Series" (New Haven: Yale University Press, 1941), pp. 58–72.
3. The evidence for the statements in this paragraph can be found in *The Social Life of a Modern Community*, pp. 287–300.
4. It is conceivable that in smaller communities there may be only three, or even two, classes present.
5. Allison Davis, Burleigh B. Gardner, and Mary R. Gardner, *Deep South* (Chicago: University of Chicago Press, 1941). Also read: John Dollard, *Caste and Class in a Southern Town* (New Haven: Yale University Press, 1937); Mozell Hill, "The All-Negro Society in Oklahoma" (Unpublished Ph.D. dissertation, University of Chicago, 1936); Harry J. Walker, "Changes in Race Accommodation in a Southern Community" (Unpublished Ph.D. dissertation, University of Chicago, 1945).
6. See St. Clair Drake and Horace R. Cayton, *Black Metropolis* (New York: Harcourt, Brace & Co., 1945), for studies of two contrasting caste orders; read the "Methodological Note" by Warner in *Black Metropolis* for an analysis of the difference between the two systems.
7. See W. Lloyd Warner and Leo Srole, *The Social Systems of American Ethnic Groups*, Vol. III, "Yankee City Series" (New Haven: Yale University Press, 1945). Chapter X discusses the similarities and differences and presents a table of predictability on their probable assimilation and gives the principles governing these phenomena.
8. Gunnar Myrdal, *An American Dilemma* (New York: Harper & Bros., 1944). For an early publication on color-caste, see W. Lloyd Warner, "American Caste and Class," *American Journal of Sociology*, XLII, No. 2 (September, 1936), 234–37, and "Formal Education and the Social Structure," *Journal of Educational Sociology*, IX (May, 1936), 524–531.

5

Social Processes

I. Microprocesses

23

G. H. MEAD

On Mind As the Product of Social Interaction

George Herbert Mead (1863–1931), a major pragmatist philosopher, exerted great influence upon the direction of current social thought through a course he taught in social psychology at the University of Chicago during the period in which that school dominated American sociology. Though Mead wrote a great many articles,[1] *he wrote no books. However, as a result of the great personal devotion of his students, his lectures were carefully assembled from a collection of student notes plus a few stenographic transcripts and edited for publication in the form of four posthumous volumes.*[2]

Mead called his position Social Behaviorism. His emphasis upon the social genesis of self through interaction with significant others, together with his concern with the mediating importance of symbols for social action, formed the basis for a major school of social psychology known as Symbolic Interactionism.[3]

For Mead, meaning and mind have their origins in the social act and are made possible by language. Mead believed that a self-concept is possible only through the use of language. Men evidence behavior through gestures. *A mutually understood gesture is a* significant symbol. *Language is a significant symbol group. Through the process of* role taking, *especially during play, the social process as a whole enters into the experience of the individual. He becomes self-conscious and then develops what we usually call* mind. *Thus, according to Mead, the self emerges as a product of social interaction.*

Reprinted from *Mind, Self & Society from the Standpoint of a Social Behaviorist,* edited by Charles W. Morris, by permission of The University of Chicago Press and Charles W. Morris. Footnotes have been renumbered.

Bibliographical Notes

1. *Mead's major articles can be found in: Andrew J. Reck (ed.),* Selected Writings: George Herbert Mead *(Indianapolis: Bobbs-Merrill, 1964).*

2. *The volumes were:* The Philosophy of the Present *(1932); Mind,* Self, and Society *(1934);* Movements of Thought in the Nineteenth Century *(1936); and* The Philosophy of the Act *(1938). An excellent brief introduction to Mead's social psychology can be found in an edited abridgement of his works: Anselm Strauss (ed.),* The Social Psychology of George Herbert Mead *(Chicago: University of Chicago Press, 1956). The major critical work dealing with Mead's position is: Maurice Natanson,* The Social Dynamics of George H. Mead *(Washington, D.C. Public Affairs Press, 1956).*

3. *Several varieties of Symbolic Interactionism exist today; cf., Manford Kuhn, "Major Trends in Symbolic Interaction Theory,"* Sociological Quarterly, 5 *(1964), 61–84; and Bernard Meltzer and John W. Petras, "The Chicago and Iowa Schools of Symbolic Interactionism," in T. Shibutani (ed.),* Human Nature and Collective Behavior: Papers in Honor of Herbert Blumer *(Englewood Cliffs, N.J.: Prentice-Hall, 1970). The best known variety of symbolic interactionism today is represented by the position of Mead's student Herbert Blumer; cf., Herbert Blumer, "Sociological Implications of the Thought of George Herbert Mead,"* American Journal of Sociology, 71 *(1966), 534–544; and Herbert Blumer,* Symbolic Interactionism: Perspective and Method *(Englewood Cliffs, N.J.: Prentice-Hall, 1969). For a variety of studies done by members of this school, see: Arnold Rose (ed.),* Human Behavior and Social Processes *(Boston: Houghton Mifflin, 1962); J. G. Manis and B. N. Meltzer (eds.),* Symbolic Interaction: A Reader in Social Psychology *(Boston: Allyn and Bacon, 1967); and Gregory P. Stone (ed.),* Social Psychology through Symbolic Interaction *(Waltham, Mass.: Ginn-Blaisdell, 1970). Numerous modern theoretical approaches also owe a great debt to the work of Mead, for example, Walter Coutu,* Emergent Human Nature: A New Social Psychology *(New York: Knopf, 1949).*

Social Attitudes and the Physical World

The self is not so much a substance as a process in which the conversation of gestures has been internalized within an organic form. This process does not exist for itself, but is simply a phase of the whole social organization of which the individual is a part. The organization of the social act has been imported into the organism and becomes then the mind of the individual. It still includes the attitudes of others, but now highly organized, so that they become what we call social attitudes rather than rôles of separate individuals. This process of relating one's own organism to the others in the interactions that are going on, in so far as it is imported into the conduct of the individual with the conversation of the "I" and the "me," constitutes the self.[1] The value of this importation of the conversation of gestures into the conduct of the individual lies in the superior co-ordination gained for society as a whole, and in the increased efficiency of the individual as a member of the group. It is the difference between the process which can take place in a group of rats or ants or bees, and that which can take place in a human community. The social process with its various implications is actually taken up into the experience of the individual so that that which is going on takes place more effectively, because in a certain sense it has been rehearsed in the individual. He not only plays his part better under those conditions but he also reacts back on the organization of which he is a part.

The very nature of this conversation of gestures requires that the attitude of the other is changed through the attitude of the individual to the other's stimulus. In the conversation of gestures of the lower forms the play back and forth is noticeable, since the individual not only adjusts himself to the attitude of others, but also changes the attitudes of the others. The reaction of the individual in this conversation of gestures is one that in some degree is continually modifying the social process itself. It is this modification of the process which is of greatest interest in the experience of the individual. He takes the attitude of the other toward his own stimulus, and in taking that he finds it modified in that his response becomes a different one, and leads in turn to further change.

Fundamental attitudes are presumably those that are only changed gradually, and no one individual can reorganize the whole society; but one is continually affecting society by his own attitude because he does bring up the attitude of the group toward himself, responds to it, and through that response changes the attitude of the group. This is, of course, what we are constantly doing in our imagination, in our thought; we are utilizing our own attitude to bring about a different situation in the community of which we are a part; we are exerting ourselves, bringing forward our own opinion, criticizing the attitudes of others, and approving or disapproving. But we can do that only in so far as we can call out in ourselves the response of the community; we only have ideas in so far as we are able to take the attitude of the community and then respond to it.

. . .

Mind as the Individual Importation of the Social Process

I have been presenting the self and the mind in terms of a social process, as the importation of the conversation of gestures into the conduct of the individual organism, so that the individual organism takes these organized attitudes of the others called out by its own attitude, in the form of its gestures, and in reacting to that response calls out other organized attitudes in the others in the community to which the individual belongs. This process can be characterized in a certain sense in terms of the "I" and the "me," the "me" being that group of organized attitudes to which the individual responds as an "I."

What I want particularly to emphasize is the temporal and logical pre-existence of the social process to the self-conscious individual that arises in it.[2] The conversation of gestures is a part of the social process which is going on. It is not something that the individual alone makes possible. What the development of language, especially the significant symbol, has rendered possible is just the taking over of this external social situation into the conduct of the individual himself. There follows from this the enormous development which belongs to human society, the possibility of the prevision of what is going to take place in the response of other individuals, and a preliminary adjustment to this by the individual. These, in turn, produce a different social situation which is again reflected in what I have termed the "me," so that the individual himself takes a different attitude.

Consider a politician or a statesman putting through some project in which he has the attitude of the community in himself. He knows how the community reacts to this proposal. He reacts to this expression of the community in his own experience—he feels with it. He has a set of organized attitudes which are those of the community. His own contribution, the "I" in this case, is a project of reorganization, a project which he brings forward to the community as it is reflected in himself. He himself changes, of course, in so far as he brings this project forward and makes it a political issue. There has now arisen a new social situation as a result of the project which he is presenting. The whole procedure takes place in his own experience as well as in the general experience of the community. He is successful to the degree that the final "me" reflects the attitude of all in the community. What I am pointing out is that what occurs takes place not simply in his own mind, but rather that his mind is the expression in his own conduct of this social situation, this great co-operative community process which is going on.

I want to avoid the implication that the individual is taking something that is objective and making it subjective. There is an actual process of living together on the part of all members of the community which takes place by means of gestures. The gestures are certain stages in the co-operative activities which mediate the whole process. Now, all that has taken place in the appearance of the mind is that this process has been in some degree taken over into the conduct of the particular individual. There is a certain symbol, such as the policeman uses when he directs traffic. That is something that is out there. It does not become subjective when the engineer, who is engaged by the city to examine its traffic regulations, takes the same attitude the policeman takes with reference to traffic, and takes the attitude also of the drivers of machines. We do imply that he has the driver's organization; he knows that stopping means slowing down, putting on the brakes. There is a definite set of parts of his organism so trained that under certain circumstances he brings the machine to a stop. The raising of the policeman's hand is the gesture which calls out the various acts by means of which the machine is checked. Those various acts are in the expert's own organization; he can take the attitude of both the policeman and the driver. Only in this sense has the social process been made "subjective." If the expert just did it as a child does, it would be play; but if it is done for the actual regulation of traffic, then there is the operation of what we term mind. Mind is nothing but the importation of this external process into the conduct of the individual so as to meet the problems that arise.

This peculiar organization arises out of a social process that is logically its antecedent. A community within which the organism acts in such a co-operative fashion that the action of one is the stimulus to the other to respond, and so on, is the antecedent of the peculiar type of organization we term a mind, or a self. Take the simple family relation, where there is the male and the female and the child which has to be cared for. Here is a process which can only go on through interactions within this group. It cannot be said that the individuals come first and the community later, for the individuals arise in the very process itself, just as much as the human body or any multi-cellular form is one in which differentiated cells arise. There has to be a life-process going on in order to have the differentiated cells; in the same way there has to be a social process going on in order that there may be individuals. It is just as true in society as it is in the physiological situation that there could not be the individual if there was not the process of which he is a part. Given such a social process, there is the possibility of human intelligence when this social process, in terms of the conversation of gestures, is taken over into the conduct of the individual—and then there arises, of course, a different type of individual in terms of the responses now possible. There might conceivably be an individual who simply plays as the child does, without getting into a social game; but the human individual is possible because there is a social process in which it can function responsibly. The attitudes are parts of the social reaction; the cries would not maintain themselves as vocal gestures unless they did call out certain responses in the others; the attitude itself could only exist as such in this interplay of gestures.

The mind is simply the interplay of such gestures in the form of significant symbols. We must remember that the gesture is there only in its relationship to the response, to the attitude. One would not have words unless there were such responses. Language would never have arisen as a set of bare arbitrary terms which were attached to certain stimuli. Words have arisen out of a social interrelationship. One of Gulliver's tales was of a community in which a machine was created into which the letters of the alphabet could be mechanically fed in an endless number of combinations, and then the members of the community gathered around to see how the letters arranged after each rotation, on the theory that they might come in the form of an Iliad or one of Shakespeare's plays, or some other great work. The assumption back of this would be that symbols are entirely independent of what we term their meaning. The assumption is baseless: there cannot be symbols unless there are responses. There would not be a call for assistance if there was not a tendency to respond to the cry of distress. It is such significant symbols, in the sense of a sub-set of social stimuli initiating a co-operative response, that do in a certain sense constitute our mind, provided that not only the symbol but also the responses are in our own nature. What the human being has succeeded in doing is in organizing the response to a certain symbol which is a part of the social act, so that he takes the attitude of the other person who co-operates with him. It is that which gives him a mind.

The sentinel of a herd is that member of the herd which is more sensitive to odor or sound than the others. At the approach of danger, he starts to run earlier than the others, who then follow along, in virtue of a herding tendency to run together. There is a social stimulus, a gesture, if you like, to which the other forms respond. The first form gets the odor earlier and starts to run, and its starting to run is a stimulus to the others to run also. It is all external; there is no mental process involved. The sentinel does not regard itself as the individual who is to give a signal; it just runs at a certain moment and so starts the others to run. But with a mind, the animal that gives the signal also takes the attitude of the others who respond to it. He knows what his signal means. A man who calls "fire" would be able to call out in himself the reaction he calls out in the other. In so far as the man can take the attitude of the other—his attitude of response to fire, his sense of terror—that response to his own cry is something that makes of his conduct a mental affair, as over against the conduct of the others.[3] But the only thing that has happened here is that what takes place externally in the herd has been imported into the conduct of the man. There is the same signal and the same tendency to respond, but the man not only can give the signal but also can arouse in himself the attitude of the terrified escape, and through calling that out he can come back upon his own tendency to call out and can check it. He can react upon himself in taking the organized attitude of the whole group in trying to escape from danger. There is nothing more subjective about it than that the response to his own stimulus can be found in his own conduct, and that he can utilize the conversation of gestures that takes place to determine his own conduct. If he can so act, he can set up a rational control, and thus make possible a far more highly organized society than otherwise. The process is one which does not utilize a man endowed with a consciousness where there was no consciousness before, but rather an individual who takes over the whole social process into his own conduct. That ability, of course, is dependent first of all on the symbol being one to which he can respond; and so far as we know, the vocal gesture has been the condition for the development of that type of symbol. Whether it can develop without the vocal gesture I cannot tell.

I want to be sure that we see that the content put into the mind is only a development and product of social interaction. It is a development which is of enormous importance, and which leads to complexities and complications of society which go almost beyond our power to trace, but originally it is nothing but the taking over of the attitude of the other. To the extent that the animal can take the attitude of the other and utilize that attitude for the control of his own conduct, we have what is termed mind; and that is the only apparatus involved in the appearance of the mind.

I know of no way in which intelligence or mind could arise or could have arisen, other than through the internalization by the individual of social processes of experience and behavior, that is, through this internalization of the conversation of significant gestures, as made possible by the individual's taking the attitudes of other individuals toward himself and toward what is being thought about. And if mind or thought has arisen in this way, then there neither can be nor could have been any mind or thought without language; and the early stages of the development of language must have been prior to the development of mind or thought.

NOTES

1. According to this view, conscious communication develops out of unconscious communication within the social process; conversation in terms of significant gestures out of conversation in terms of non-significant gestures; and the development in such fashion of conscious communication is coincident with the development of minds and selves within the social process.
2. The relation of mind and body is that lying between the organization of the self in its behavior as a member of a rational community and the bodily organism as a physical thing.

   The rational attitude which characterizes the human being is then the relationship of the whole process in which the individual is engaged to himself as reflected in his assumption of the organized rôles of the others in stimulating himself to his response. This self as distinguished from the others lies within the field of communication, and they lie also within this field. What may be indicated to others or one's self and does not respond to such gestures of indication is, in the field of perception, what we call a physical thing. The human body is, especially in its analysis, regarded as a physical thing.

   The line of demarcation between the self and the body is found, then, first of all in the social organization of the act within which the self arises, in its contrast with the activity of the physiological organism (MS).

   The legitimate basis of distinction between mind and body is between the social patterns and the patterns of the organism itself. Education must bring the two closely together. We have, as yet, no comprehending category. This does not mean to say that there is anything logically against it; it is merely a lack of our apparatus or knowledge (1927).

3. Language as made up of significant symbols is what we mean by mind. The content of our minds is (1) inner conversation, the importation of conversation from the social group to the individual (2) . . . . imagery. Imagery should be regarded in relation to the behavior in which it functions (1931).

   Imagery plays just the part in the act that hunger does in the food process (1912).

24

W. I. THOMAS

On the Definition of the Situation

William Isaac Thomas (1863–1947), unlike most of the authors represented in this collection, was primarily an empiricist rather than a theorist.[1] *Most of his contributions towards a systematic sociology grew out of his particular researches into various sociological and social-psychological data.*[2] *W. I. Thomas is today best remembered for his work with Florian Znaniecki published in the massive five-volume study* The Polish Peasant in Europe and America, *for his classification of human motives into what are commonly termed the Four Wishes (the needs for new experience, security, response, and recognition),*[3] *and for his widely quoted dictum: "If men define situations as real, they are real in their consequences."* [4] *Although Thomas gave a high priority to statistical verification of sociological hypotheses, he always insisted that any interpretation be made in light of unmeasured (e.g., subjective) factors and in terms of the total situation. Unlike some of his contemporaries, however, Thomas realized that the scientist could never truly enter an actor's mind and thus was always limited to inferences from behavioral data.*[5]

Bibliographical Notes

1. *For excellent surveys of Thomas's work and intellectual development, see: Kimball Young,* The Contribution of William Isaac Thomas to Sociology *(Evanston, Ill.: Student Book Exchange, n.d.); and Morris Janowitz (ed.),* W. I. Thomas on Social Organization and Social Personality *(Chicago: University of Chicago Press, 1966), pp. vii–lviii.*

2. *Thomas' major works include:* Sex and Society *(1907);* Source Book for Social Origins *(1909);* The Polish Peasant in Europe and

Reprinted from *The Unadjusted Girl* by W. I. Thomas (Boston: Little, Brown, and Co., 1923), by permission of the Social Science Research Council.

America, *5 volumes with F. Znaniecki (1918);* Old World Traits Transplanted, *with R. E. Park and H. A. Miller (1921);* The Unadjusted Girl *(1923);* The Child in America *(1928); and* Primitive Behavior *(1937).*

3. *The Four Wishes have come under criticism (e.g., W. B. Cameron and T. C. McCormick, "Concepts of Security and Insecurity,"* American Journal of Sociology, 55 *(1950), 556–564); however, Thomas often stated that they were clearly arbitrary categories. He even stated them differently in his earlier work,* The Polish Peasant in Europe and America, *presenting them as desires for new experience, recognition, mastery or power, and security.*

4. *Though his major statement on this topic is the one included here from* The Unadjusted Girl, *this famous quotation appears in* The Child in America *(New York: Knopf, 1928), p. 572. Thomas's work on this topic has recently been greatly expanded both conceptually and experimentally by Peter McHugh, see: Peter McHugh, "Defining the Situation: The Organization of Meaning" in* Social Interaction *(Indianapolis: Bobbs-Merrill, 1968). See, also: Robert B. Stebbins: "Studying the Definition of the Situation: Theory and Field Research Strategies,"* Canadian Review of Sociology and Anthropology, 6 *(1969), 193–211.*

5. *Cf., Kimball Young,* The Contribution of William Isaac Thomas to Sociology *(Evanston, Ill.: Student Book Exchange, n.d.), p. 73.*

One of the most important powers gained during the evolution of animal life is the ability to make decisions from within instead of having them imposed from without. Very low forms of life do not make decisions, as we understand this term, but are pushed and pulled by chemical substances, heat, light, etc., much as iron filings are attracted or repelled by a magnet. They do tend to behave properly in given conditions—a group of small crustaceans will flee as in a panic if a bit of strychnia is placed in the basin containing them and will rush toward a drop of beef juice like hogs crowding around swill—but they do this as an expression of organic affinity for the one substance and repugnance for the other, and not as an expression of choice or "free will." There are, so to speak, rules of behavior but these represent a sort of fortunate mechanistic adjustment of the organism to typically recurring situations, and the organism cannot change the rule.

On the other hand, the higher animals, and above all man, have the power of refusing to obey a stimulation which they followed at an earlier time. Response to the earlier stimulation may have had painful consequences and so the rule or habit in this situation is changed. We call this ability the power of inhibition, and it is dependent on the fact that the nervous system carries memories or records of past experiences. At this point the determination of action no longer comes exclusively from outside sources but is located within the organism itself.

Preliminary to any self-determined act of behavior there is always a stage of examination and deliberation which we may call *the definition of the situation*. And actually not only concrete acts are dependent on the definition of the situation, but gradually a whole life-policy and the personality of the individual himself follow from a series of such definitions.

But the child is always born into a group of people among whom all the general types of situation which may arise have already been defined and corresponding rules of conduct developed, and where he has not the slightest chance of making his definitions and following his wishes without interference. Men have always lived together in groups. Whether mankind has a true herd instinct or whether groups are held together because this has worked out to advantage is of no importance. Certainly the wishes in general are such that they can be satisfied only in a society. But we have only to refer to the criminal code to appreciate the variety of ways in which the wishes of the individual may conflict with the wishes of society. And the criminal code takes no account of the many unsanctioned expressions of the wishes which society attempts to regulate by persuasion and gossip.

There is therefore always a rivalry between the spontaneous definitions of the situation made by the member of an organized society and the definitions which his society has provided for him. The individual tends to a hedonistic selection of activity, pleasure first; and society to a utilitarian selection, safety first. Society wishes its member to be laborious, dependable, regular, sober, orderly, self-sacrificing; while the individual wishes less of this and more of new experience. And organized society seeks also to regulate the conflict and competition inevitable between its members in the pursuit of their wishes. The desire to have wealth, for example, or any other socially sanctioned wish, may not be accomplished at the expense of another member of the society,—by murder, theft, lying, swindling, blackmail, etc.

It is in this connection that a moral code arises, which is a set of rules or behavior norms, regulating the expression of the wishes, and which is built up by successive definitions of the situation. In practice the abuse arises first and the rule is made to prevent its recurrence. Morality is thus the generally accepted definition of the situation, whether expressed in public opinion and the unwritten law, in a formal legal code, or in religious commandments and prohibitions.

The family is the smallest social unit and the primary defining agency. As soon as the child has free motion and begins to pull, tear, pry, meddle, and prowl, the parents begin to define the situation through speech and other signs and pressures: "Be quiet", "Sit up straight", "Blow your nose", "Wash your face", "Mind your mother", "Be kind to sister", etc. This is the real significance of Wordsworth's phrase, "Shades of the prison house begin to close upon the growing child." His wishes and activities begin to be inhibited, and gradually, by definitions within the family, by playmates, in the school, in the Sunday school, in the community, through reading, by formal instruction, by informal signs of approval and disapproval, the growing member learns the code of his society.

In addition to the family we have the community as a defining agency. At present the community is so weak and vague that it gives us no idea of the former power of the local group in regulating behavior. Originally the community was practically the whole world of its members. It was composed of families related by blood and marriage and was not so large that all the members could not come together; it was a face-to-face group. I asked a Polish peasant what was the extent of an "*okolica*" or neighborhood—how far it reached. "It reaches," he said, "as far as the report of a man reaches—as far as a man is talked about." And it was in communities of this kind that the moral code which we now recognize as valid originated. The customs of the community are "folkways", and both state and church have in their more formal codes mainly recognized and incorporated these folkways.

The typical community is vanishing and it would be neither possible nor desirable to restore it in its old form. It does not correspond with the present direction of social evolution and it would now be a distressing condition in which to live. But in the immediacy of relationships and the participation of everybody in everything, it represents an element which we have lost and which we shall probably have to restore in some form of coöperation in order to secure a balanced and normal society,—some arrangement corresponding with human nature.

25

CHARLES HORTON COOLEY

On Primary Groups

Charles Horton Cooley (1864–1929), through his numerous works,[1] *emphasized the importance of the* self *as a social product. His analyses of the* primary group *constitute a landmark in the growth of sociology, especially psychological sociology. The* primary group, *in the form of the family, neighborhood, and play groups, is defined as a collection of persons characterized by affectional motives, face-to-face or intimate contact, and small size. It is primary in that it constitutes the nursery of human nature. Other and later encountered groups were termed* secondary. *Although the expression was initiated earlier,*[2] *Cooley was the first to elevate the term to a meaningful conception that soon permeated all sociological literature.*[3] *Though the concept has come under severe criticism,*[4] *S. C. Lee has recently argued that a careful examination of Cooley's meaning would still make it viable for current sociological analysis.*[5] *As interpreted by Lee, there are four properties, as originally envisaged by Cooley, that together identify the primary group. Each of these properties is* necessary *but only all four together are* sufficient *to constitute a primary group. These indispensible properties are: (1) the temporal priority of the group in experience; (2) the presence of personal and intimate association in the group; (3) the psychological unity of the group as expressed by a feeling of "we-ness"; and (4) a dissemination and sharing of the primary ideals of the group.*[6]

This excerpt is taken from Charles Horton Cooley, *Social Organization: A Study of the Larger Mind* (New York: Charles Scribner's Sons, 1909), pp. 25–31. Footnotes have been renumbered.

Bibliographical Notes

1. *Cooley's major works include:* Human Nature and the Social Order (*1902*); Social Organization (*1909*); Social Process (*1918*); *and* Life and the Student: Roadside Notes on Human Nature, Society, and Letters (*1927*). *A collection of his papers was published after his death, entitled* Sociological Theory and Social Research (*1930*).

2. *The term was probably first used as the chapter title "The Primary Social Group" by A. W. Small and G. E. Vincent in their* An Introduction to the Study of Society (*1894*).

3. *For a general survey, see: Edward A. Shils, "The Study of the Primary Group," in D. Lerner,* et al. (*eds.*), The Policy Sciences (*Stanford, Calif.: Stanford University Press, 1951*), *pp. 44–69.*

4. *See, for example, A. P. Bates and N. Babchuck, "The Primary Group: A Reappraisal,"* Sociological Quarterly, 2 (*1961*), *181–191; E. Faris, "The Primary Group: Essence and Accident,"* American Journal of Sociology, 37 (*1932*), *41–50; and T. D. Eliot, "Group, Primary," in H. P. Fairchild* (*ed.*), Dictionary of Sociology (*New York: Philosophical Library, 1944*), *p. 135.*

5. *S. C. Lee, "The Primary Group as Cooley Defines it,"* Sociological Quarterly, 5 (*1964*), *23–34. For an example of modern research emanating from Cooley's work, see: G. E. Swanson, "To Live in Concord with a Society: Two Empirical Studies of Primary Relations," in A. J. Reiss, Jr.* (*ed.*), Cooley and Sociological Analysis (*Ann Arbor: University of Michigan Press, 1968*), *pp. 87–150 and 165–172.*

6. *For a biographical statement and appraisal of Cooley, the reader is referred to: Edward C. Jandy,* Charles Horton Cooley: His Life and His Social Theory (*New York: Dryden, 1942*).

By primary groups I mean those characterized by intimate face-to-face association and coöperation. They are primary in several senses, but chiefly in that they are fundamental in forming the social nature and ideals of the individual. The result of intimate association, psychologically, is a certain fusion of individualities in a common whole, so that one's very self, for many purposes at least, is the common life and purpose of the group. Perhaps the simplest way of describing this wholeness is by saying that it is a "we"; it involves the sort of sympathy and mutual identification for which "we" is the natural expression. One lives in the feeling of the whole and finds the chief aims of his will in that feeling.

It is not to be supposed that the unity of the primary group is one of mere harmony and love. It is always a differentiated and usually a competitive unity, admitting of self-assertion and various appropriative passions; but these passions are socialized by sympathy, and come, or tend to come, under the discipline of a common spirit. The individual will be ambitious, but the chief object of his ambition will be some desired place in the thought of the others, and he will feel allegiance to common standards of service and fair play. So the boy will dispute with his fellows a place on the team, but above such disputes will place the common glory of his class and school.

The most important spheres of this intimate association and coöperation—though by no means the only ones—are the family, the play-group of children, and the neighborhood or community group of elders. These are practically universal, belonging to all times and all stages of development; and are accordingly a chief basis of what is universal in human nature and human ideals. The best comparative studies of the family, such as those of Westermarck[1] or Howard,[2] show it to us as not only a universal institution, but as more alike the world over than the exaggeration of exceptional customs by an earlier school had led us to suppose. Nor can any one doubt the general prevalence of play-groups among children or of informal assemblies of various kinds among their elders. Such association is clearly the nursery of human nature in the world about us, and there is no apparent reason to suppose that the case has anywhere or at any time been essentially different.

As regards play, I might, were it not a matter of common observation, multiply illustrations of the universality and spontaneity of the group discussion and coöperation to which it gives rise. The general fact is that children, especially boys after about their twelfth year, live in fellowships in which their sympathy, ambition and honor are engaged even more, often, than they are in the family. Most of us can recall examples of the endurance by boys of injustice and even cruelty, rather than appeal from their fellows to parents or teachers—as, for instance, in the hazing so prevalent at schools, and so difficult, for this very reason, to repress. And how elaborate the discussion, how cogent the public opinion, how hot the ambitions in these fellowships.

Nor is this facility of juvenile association, as is sometimes supposed, a trait peculiar to English and American boys; since experience among our immigrant population seems to show that the offspring of the more restrictive civilizations of the continent of Europe form self-governing play-groups with almost equal readiness. Thus Miss Jane Addams, after pointing out that the "gang" is almost universal, speaks of the interminable discussion which every detail of the gang's activity receives, remarking that "in these social folk-motes, so to speak, the young citizen learns to act upon his own determination." [3]

Of the neighborhood group it may be said, in general, that from the time men formed permanent settlements upon the land, down, at least, to the rise of modern industrial cities, it has played a main part in the primary, heart-to-heart life of the people. Among our Teutonic forefathers the village community was apparently the chief sphere of sympathy and mutual aid for the commons all through the "dark" and middle ages, and for many purposes it remains so in rural districts at the present day. In some countries we still find it with all its ancient vitality, notably in Russia, where the mir, or self-governing village group, is the main theatre of life, along with the family, for perhaps fifty millions of peasants.

In our own life the intimacy of the neighborhood has been broken up by the growth of an intricate mesh of wider contacts which leaves us strangers to people who live in the same house. And even in the country the same principle is at work, though less obviously, diminishing our economic and spiritual community with our neighbors. How far this change is a healthy development, and how far a disease, is perhaps still uncertain.

Besides these almost universal kinds of primary association, there are many others whose form depends upon the particular state of civilization; the only essential thing, as I have said, being a certain intimacy and fusion of personalities. In our own society, being little bound by place, people easily form clubs, fraternal societies and the like, based on congeniality, which may give rise to real intimacy. Many such relations are formed at school and college, and among men and women brought together in the first instance by their occupations—as workmen in the same trade, or the like. Where there is a little common interest and activity, kindness grows like weeds by the roadside.

But the fact that the family and neighborhood groups are ascendant in the open and plastic time of childhood makes them even now incomparably more influential than all the rest.

Primary groups are primary in the sense that they give the individual his earliest and completest experience of social unity, and also in the sense that they do not change in the same degree as more elaborate relations, but form a comparatively permanent source out of which the latter are ever springing. Of course they are not independent of the larger society, but to some extent reflect its spirit; as the German family and the German school bear somewhat distinctly the print of German militarism. But this, after all, is like the tide setting back into creeks, and does not commonly go very far. Among the German, and still more among the Russian, peasantry are found habits of free coöperation and discussion almost uninfluenced by the character of the state; and it is a familiar and well-supported view that the village commune, self-governing as regards local affairs and habituated to discussion, is a very widespread institution in settled communities, and the continuator of a similar autonomy previously existing in the clan. "It is man who makes monarchies and establishes republics, but the commune seems to come directly from the hand of God." [4]

In our own cities the crowded tenements and the general economic and social confusion have sorely wounded the family and the neighborhood, but it is remarkable, in view of these conditions, what vitality they show; and there is nothing upon which the conscience of the time is more determined than upon restoring them to health.

These groups, then, are springs of life, not only for the individual but for social institutions. They are only in part moulded by special traditions, and, in larger degree, express a universal nature. The religion or government of other civilizations may seem alien to us, but the children or the family group wear the common life, and with them we can always make ourselves at home.

By human nature, I suppose, we may understand those sentiments and impulses that are human in being superior to those of lower animals, and also in the sense that they belong to mankind at large, and not to any particular race or time. It means, particularly, sympathy and the innumerable sentiments into which sympathy enters, such as love, resentment, ambition, vanity, hero-worship, and the feeling of social right and wrong.[5]

Human nature in this sense is justly regarded as a comparatively permanent element in society. Always and everywhere men seek honor and dread ridicule, defer to public opinion, cherish their goods and their children, and admire courage, generosity, and success. It is always safe to assume that people are and have been human.

It is true, no doubt, that there are differences of race capacity, so great that a large part of mankind are possibly incapable of any high kind of social organization. But these differences, like those among individuals of the same race, are subtle, depending upon some obscure intellectual deficiency, some want of vigor, or slackness of moral fibre, and do not involve unlikeness in the generic impulses of human nature. In these all races are very much alike. The more insight one gets into the life of savages, even those that are reckoned the lowest, the more human, the more like ourselves, they appear. Take for instance the natives of Central Australia, as described by Spencer and Gillen,[6] tribes having no definite government or worship and scarcely able to count to five. They are generous to one another, emulous of virtue as they understand it, kind to their children and to the aged, and by no means harsh to women. Their faces as shown in the photographs are wholly human and many of them attractive.

And when we come to a comparison between different stages in the development of the same race, between ourselves, for instance, and the Teutonic tribes of the time of Caesar, the difference is neither in human nature nor in capacity, but in organization, in the range and complexity of relations, in the diverse expression of powers and passions essentially much the same.

There is no better proof of this generic likeness of human nature than in the ease and joy with which the modern man makes himself at home in literature depicting the most remote and varied phases of life—in Homer, in the Nibelung tales, in the Hebrew Scriptures, in the legends of the American Indians, in stories of frontier life, of soldiers and sailors, of criminals and tramps, and so on. The more penetratingly any phase of human life is studied the more an essential likeness to ourselves is revealed.

To return to primary groups: the view here maintained is that human nature is not something existing separately in the individual, but a *group-nature or primary phase of society*, a relatively simple and general condition of the social mind. It is something more, on the one hand, than the mere instinct that is born in us—though that enters into it—and something less, on the other, than the more elaborate development of ideas and sentiments that makes up institutions. It is the nature which is developed and expressed in those simple, face-to-face groups that are somewhat alike in all societies; groups of the family, the playground, and the neighborhood. In the essential similarity of these is to be found the basis, in experience, for similar ideas and sentiments in the human mind. In these, everywhere, human nature comes into existence. Man does not have it at birth; he cannot acquire it except through fellowship, and it decays in isolation.

If this view does not recommend itself to common sense I do not know that elaboration will be of much avail. It simply means the application at this point of the idea that society and individuals are inseparable phases of a common whole, so that wherever we find an individual fact we may look for a social fact to go with it. If there is a universal nature in persons there must be something universal in association to correspond to it.

What else can human nature be than a trait of primary groups? Surely not an attribute of the separate individual—supposing there were any such thing—since its typical characteristics, such as affection, ambition, vanity, and resentment, are inconceivable apart from society. If it belongs, then, to man in association, what kind or degree of association is required to develop it? Evidently nothing elaborate, because elaborate phases of society are transient and diverse, while human nature is comparatively stable and universal. In short the family and neighborhood life is essential to its genesis and nothing more is.

Here as everywhere in the study of society we must learn to see mankind in psychical wholes, rather than in artificial separation. We must see and feel the communal life of family and local groups as immediate facts, not as combinations of something else. And perhaps we shall do this best by recalling our own experience and extending it through sympathetic observation. What, in our life, is the family and the fellowship; what do we know of the we-feeling? Thought of this kind may help us to get a concrete perception of that primary group-nature of which everything social is the outgrowth.

NOTES

1. *The History of Human Marriage.*
2. *A History of Matrimonial Institutions.*
3. *Newer Ideals of Peace,* 177.
4. De Tocqueville, *Democracy in America,* vol. 1, chap. 5.
5. These matters are expounded at some length in the writer's *Human Nature and the Social Order.*
6. *The Native Tribes of Central Australia.* Compare also Darwin's views and examples given in chap. 7 of his *Descent of Man.*

26

WILLIAM GRAHAM SUMNER

On In-Groups and Out-Groups

In William Graham Sumner's classic volume Folkways, *the author developed a number of new concepts which have been highly influential in determining many theoretical directions for contemporary sociology.*[1] *Among these was his significant discussion of the importance of ethnocentricity and in-group perspectives as a source of social cohesion. Consideration of this topic has, in one way or another, permeated much contemporary consideration of group cohesion and exclusion processes*[2] *and has been very important in social psychological studies of authoritarianism and dogmatism.*[3]

Bibliographical Notes

1. *For a listing of major works by and about Sumner, see the introduction to his first statement in this volume, pp. 81–82.*

2. *E.g., Harrison White, "Management Conflict and Sociometric Structure,"* American Journal of Sociology, 67 *(1962), 185–199; J. H. Burma, "Cliques and Popularity among Freshman Girls,"* Sociology and Social Research, 34 *(1949), 21–24; or M. Sherif, "Superordinate Goals in the Reduction of Intergroup Conflict,"* American Journal of Sociology, 63 *(1958), 349–356.*

3. *E.g., T. W. Adorno,* et al., The Authoritarian Personality *(New York: Harper, 1950); and Milton Rokeach,* The Open and Closed Mind: Investigations into the Nature of Belief Systems and Personality Systems *(New York: Basic Books, 1960).*

Reprinted from William Graham Sumner, *Folkways* (Boston: Ginn & Company, 1906). Footnotes have been renumbered.

. . .

13. *The Concept of "Primitive Society"; We-group and Others-group.* The conception of "primitive society" which we ought to form is that of small groups scattered over a territory. The size of the groups is determined by the conditions of the struggle for existence. The internal organization of each group corresponds to its size. A group of groups may have some relation to each other (kin, neighborhood, alliance, connubium and commercium) which draws them together and differentiates them from others. Thus a differentiation arises between ourselves, the we-group, or in-group, and everybody else, or the others-groups, out-groups. The insiders in a we-group are in a relation of peace, order, law, government, and industry, to each other. Their relation to all outsiders, or others-groups, is one of war and plunder, except so far as agreements have modified it. If a group is exogamic, the women in it were born abroad somewhere. Other foreigners who might be found in it are adopted persons, guest friends, and slaves.

14. *Sentiments in the In-group and Towards the Out-group.* The relation of comradeship and peace in the we-group and that of hostility and war towards others-groups are correlative to each other. The exigencies of war with outsiders are what make peace inside, lest internal discord should weaken the we-group for war. These exigencies also make government and law in the in-group, in order to prevent quarrels and enforce discipline. Thus war and peace have reacted on each other and developed each other, one within the group, the other in the intergroup relation. The closer the neighbors, and the stronger they are, the intenser is the warfare, and then the intenser is the internal organization and discipline of each. Sentiments are produced to correspond. Loyalty to the group, sacrifice for it, hatred and contempt for outsiders, brotherhood within, warlikeness without,—all grow together, common products of the same situation. These relations and sentiments constitute a social philosophy. It is sanctified by connection with religion. Men of an others-group are outsiders with whose ancestors the ancestors of the we-group waged war. The ghosts of the latter will see with pleasure their descendants keep up the fight, and will help them. Virtue consists in killing, plundering, and enslaving outsiders.

15. *Ethnocentrism* is the technical name for this view of things in which one's own group is the center of everything, and all others are scaled and rated with reference to it. Folkways correspond to it to cover

both the inner and the outer relation. Each group nourishes its own pride and vanity, boasts itself superior, exalts its own divinities, and looks with contempt on outsiders. Each group thinks its own folkways the only right ones, and if it observes that other groups have other folkways, these excite its scorn. Opprobrious epithets are derived from these differences. "Pig-eater," "cow-eater," "uncircumcised," "jabberers," are epithets of contempt and abomination. The Tupis called the Portuguese by a derisive epithet descriptive of birds which have feathers around their feet, on account of trousers. For our present purpose the most important fact is that ethnocentrism leads a people to exaggerate and intensify everything in their own folkways which is peculiar and which differentiates them from others. It therefore strengthens the folkways.

16. *Illustrations of Ethnocentrism.* The Papuans on New Guinea are broken up into village units which are kept separate by hostility, cannibalism, head hunting, and divergences of language and religion. Each village is integrated by its own language, religion, and interests. A group of villages is sometimes united into a limited unity by connubium. A wife taken inside of this group unit has full status; one taken outside of it has not. The petty group units are peace groups within and are hostile to all outsiders. The Mbayas of South America believed that their deity had bidden them live by making war on others, taking their wives and property, and killing their men.

17. *When Caribs were asked whence they came, they answered, "We alone are people."* The meaning of the name Kiowa is "real or principal people." The Lapps call themselves "men," or "human beings." The Greenland Eskimo think that Europeans have been sent to Greenland to learn virtue and good manners from the Greenlanders. Their highest form of praise for a European is that he is, or soon will be, as good as a Greenlander. The Tunguses call themselves "men." As a rule it is found that nature peoples call themselves "men." Others are something else—perhaps not defined—but not real men. In myths the origin of their own tribe is that of the real human race. They do not account for the others. The Ainos derive their name from that of the first man, whom they worship as a god. Evidently the name of the god is derived from the tribe name. When the tribal name has another sense, it is always boastful or proud. The Ovambo name is a corruption of the name of the tribe for themselves, which means "the wealthy." Amongst the most remarkable people in the world for ethnocentrism

are the Seri of Lower California. They observe an attitude of suspicion and hostility to all outsiders, and strictly forbid marriage with outsiders.

18. The Jews divided all mankind into themselves and Gentiles. They were the "chosen people." The Greeks and Romans called all outsiders "barbarians." In Euripides' tragedy of *Iphigenia in Aulis* Iphigenia says that it is fitting that Greeks should rule over barbarians, but not contrariwise, because Greeks are free, and barbarians are slaves. The Arabs regarded themselves as the noblest nation and all others as more or less barbarous. In 1896, the Chinese minister of education and his counselors edited a manual in which this statement occurs: "How grand and glorious is the Empire of China, the middle kingdom! She is the largest and richest in the world. The grandest men in the world have all come from the middle empire." In all the literature of all the states equivalent statements occur, although they are not so naïvely expressed. In Russian books and newspapers the civilizing mission of Russia is talked about, just as, in the books and journals of France, Germany, and the United States, the civilizing mission of those countries is assumed and referred to as well understood. Each state now regards itself as the leader of civilization, the best, the freest, and the wisest, and all others as inferior. Within a few years our own man-on-the-curbstone has learned to class all foreigners of the Latin peoples as "dagos," and "dago" has become an epithet of contempt. These are all cases of ethnocentrism.

19. *Patriotism* is a sentiment which belongs to modern states. It stands in antithesis to the mediæval notion of catholicity. Patriotism is loyalty to the civic group to which one belongs by birth or other group bond. It is a sentiment of fellowship and coöperation in all the hopes, work, and suffering of the group. Mediæval catholicity would have made all Christians an in-group and would have set them in hostility to all Mohammedans and other non-Christians. It never could be realized. When the great modern states took form and assumed control of societal interests, group sentiment was produced in connection with those states. Men responded willingly to a demand for support and help from an institution which could and did serve interests. The state drew to itself the loyalty which had been given to men (lords), and it became the object of that group vanity and antagonism which had been ethnocentric. For the modern man patriotism has become one of the first of duties and one of the noblest of sentiments. It is what he owes to the state for what the state does for him, and the state is, for

the modern man, a cluster of civic institutions from which he draws security and conditions of welfare. The masses are always patriotic. For them the old ethnocentric jealousy, vanity, truculency, and ambition are the strongest elements in patriotism. Such sentiments are easily awakened in a crowd. They are sure to be popular. Wider knowledge always proves that they are not based on facts. That we are good and others are bad is never true. By history, literature, travel, and science men are made cosmopolitan. The selected classes of all states become associated; they intermarry. The differentiation by states loses importance. All states give the same security and conditions of welfare to all. The standards of civic institutions are the same, or tend to become such, and it is a matter of pride in each state to offer civic status and opportunities equal to the best. Every group of any kind whatsoever demands that each of its members shall help defend group interests. Every group stigmatizes any one who fails in zeal, labor, and sacrifices for group interests. Thus the sentiment of loyalty to the group, or the group head, which was so strong in the Middle Ages, is kept up, as far as possible, in regard to modern states and governments. The group force is also employed to enforce the obligations of devotion to group interests. It follows that judgments are precluded and criticism is silenced.

20. *Chauvinism.* That patriotism may degenerate into a vice is shown by the invention of a name for the vice: chauvinism. It is a name for boastful and truculent group self-assertion. It overrules personal judgment and character, and puts the whole group at the mercy of the clique which is ruling at the moment. It produces the dominance of watchwords and phrases which take the place of reason and conscience in determining conduct. The patriotic bias is a recognized perversion of thought and judgment against which our education should guard us.

6

Social Processes

II. Macroprocesses

27

WILLIAM F. OGBURN

On Cultural Lag

William Fielding Ogburn (1886–1959), unlike many of the American sociologists who were his contemporaries, had relatively little concern for methodology for its own sake or for what has often been called "grand theory." Ogburn's approach was a highly pragmatic one that centered around the question of social change.[1] *He saw cultural evolution as determined by four factors: invention, accumulation, diffusion, and adjustment. As Ogburn defined them, inventions were the result of combining existing cultural elements and materials to form new ones. Accumulation referred to the absorption of the invention into the cultural base of the society. Diffusion involved the spread or movement of the invention from one area to another, while adjustment referred to the processes whereby other elements in the culture "catch up" or come into some sort of congruity with the existence of the new invention. According to Ogburn, adjustments often are made after delays (frequently slow and relatively invisible). Ogburn called such delays* cultural lags.[2] *A typical pattern of cultural lag that might occur today would begin with the introduction of a technological advance. This would be followed by an economic reorganization, followed by changes in social institutions such as the family or government, and ultimately succeeded by ideological and philosophical changes in the value systems of the society.*

Reprinted from William Fielding Ogburn, *Social Change with Respect to Cultural and Original Nature* (New York: Dell, 1966 Delta Dell edition), pp. 200–213.

Bibliographical Notes

1. *Ogburn's major works include:* Social Change, With Respect to Culture and Original Nature (*1922, revision in 1950*); The Social Sciences and Their Interrelationships, *edited with A. A. Goldenweiser* (*1927*); Sociology, *with M. F. Nimkoff* (*1940, final revision in 1964*); *and* On Culture and Social Change: Selected Papers, *edited by O. D. Duncan and containing a full bibliography of Ogburn's work* (*1964*).

2. *For a negative critique of Ogburn's theory of social change, see: Pitirim A. Sorokin,* Contemporary Sociological Theories (*New York: Harper Torchbook, 1964*), *which was originally published in 1928, pp. 742–746 and up-dated in his* Sociological Theories of Today (*New York: Harper & Row, 1966*), *pp. 295–301.*

This rapidity of change in modern times raises the very important question of social adjustment. Problems of social adjustment are of two sorts. One concerns the adaptation of man to culture or perhaps preferably the adapting of culture to man. This subject is considered in Part V [of *Social Change with Respect to Cultural and Original Nature*]. The other problem is the question of adjustments, occasioned as a result of these rapid social changes, between the different parts of culture, which no doubt means ultimately the adaptation of culture to man. This second problem of adjustment between the different parts of culture is the immediate subject of our inquiry.

The thesis is that the various parts of modern culture are not changing at the same rate, some parts are changing much more rapidly than others; and that since there is a correlation and interdependence of parts, a rapid change in one part of our culture requires readjustments through other changes in the various correlated parts of culture. For instance, industry and education are correlated, hence a change in industry makes adjustments necessary through changes in the educational system. Industry and education are two variables, and if the change in industry occurs first and the adjustment through education follows, industry may be referred to as the independent variable and education as the dependent variable. Where one part of culture changes first, through some discovery or invention, and occasions changes in some part of culture dependent upon it, there frequently is a delay in the changes occasioned in the dependent part of culture. The extent of this lag will vary according to the nature of the cultural material, but may exist for a considerable number of years, during which time there may be said to be a maladjustment. It is desirable to reduce the period of maladjustment, to make the cultural adjustments as quickly as possible.

The foregoing account sets forth a problem that occurs when there is a rapid change in a culture of interdependent parts and when the rates of change in the parts are unequal. The discussion will be presented according to the following outlines. First the hypothesis will be presented, then examined and tested by a rather full consideration of the facts of a single instance, to be followed by several illustrations. Next the nature and cause of the phenomenon of cultural maladjustment in general will be analyzed. The extent of such cultural lags will be estimated, and finally the significance for society will be set forth.

A first simple statement of the hypothesis we wish to investigate now follows. A large part of our environment consists of the material conditions of life and a large part of our social heritage is our material culture. These material things consist of houses, factories, machines, raw materials, manufactured products, foodstuffs and other material objects. In using these material things we employ certain methods. Some of these methods are as simple as the technique of handling a tool. But a good many of the ways of using the material objects of culture involve rather larger usages and adjustments, such as customs, beliefs, philosophies, laws, governments. One important function of government, for instance, is the adjustment of the population to the material conditions of life, although there are other governmental functions. Sumner has called many of these processes of adjustments, mores. The cultural adjustments to material conditions, however, include a larger body of processes than the mores; certainly they include the folk ways and social institutions. These ways of adjustment may be called, for purposes of this particular analysis, the adaptive culture. The adaptive culture is therefore that portion of the non-material culture which is adjusted or adapted to the material conditions. Some parts of the non-material culture are thoroughly adaptive culture such as certain rules involved in handling technical appliances, and some parts are only indirectly or partially so, as for instance, religion. The family makes some adjustments to fit changed material conditions, while some of its functions remain constant. The family, therefore, under the terminology used here is a part of the non-material culture that is only partly adaptive. When the material conditions change, changes are occasioned in the adaptive culture. But these changes in the adaptive culture do not synchronize exactly with the change in the material culture. There is a lag which may last for varying lengths of time, sometimes indeed, for many years.

An illustration will serve to make the hypothesis more clearly understood. One class of material objects to which we adjust ourselves is the forests. The material conditions of forestry have changed a good deal in the United States during the past century. At one time the forests were quite plentiful for the needs of the small population. There was plenty of wood easily accessible for fuel, building and manufacture. The forests were sufficiently extensive to prevent in many large areas the washing of the soil, and the streams were clear. In fact, at one time the forests seemed to be too plentiful, from the point of view of the needs of the people. Food and agricultural products were at one time the first need of the people and the clearing of land of trees and stumps was a common undertaking of the community in the days of the early settlers. In some places, the quickest procedure was to kill and burn the trees and plant between the stumps. When the material conditions were like these, the method of adjustment to the forests was characterized by a policy which has been called exploitation. Exploitation in regard to the forests was indeed a part of the mores of the time, and describes a part of the adaptive culture in relation to forests.

As time went on, however, the population grew, manufacturing became highly developed, and the need for forests increased. But the forests were being destroyed. This was particularly true in the Appalachian, Great Lakes and Gulf regions. The policy of exploitation continued. Then rather suddenly it began to be realized in certain centres of thought that if the policy of cutting timber continued at the same rate and in the same manner the forests would in a short time be gone and very soon indeed they would be inadequate to supply the needs of the population. It was realized that the custom in regard to using the forests must be changed and a policy of conservation was advocated. The new policy of conservation means not only a restriction in the amount of cutting down of trees, but it means a more scientific method of cutting, and also reforestation. Forests may be cut in such a way, by selecting trees according to their size, age and location, as to yield a large quantity of timber and yet not diminish the forest area. Also by the proper distribution of cutting plots in a particular area, the cutting can be so timed that by the time the last plot is cut the young trees on the plot first cut will be grown. Some areas when cut leave a land which is well adapted to farming, whereas such section as mountainous regions when denuded of forests are poorly suited to agriculture. There of course are many other methods of conservation of forests. The science of forestry is, indeed, fairly highly developed in principle, though not in practice in the United States. A new adaptive culture, one of conservation, is therefore suited to the changed material conditions.

That the conservation of forests in the United States should have been begun earlier is quite generally admitted. We may say, therefore, that the old policy of exploitation has hung over longer than it should before the institution of the new policy. In other words, the material conditions in regard to our forests have changed but the old customs of the use of forests which once fitted the material conditions very well have hung over into a period of changed conditions. These old customs are not only satisfactorily adapted, but are really socially harmful. These customs of course have a utility, since they meet certain human needs; but methods of greater utility are needed. There seems to be a lag in the mores in regard to forestry after the material conditions have changed. Or translated into the general terms of the previous analysis, the material conditions have changed first; and there has been a lag in the adaptive culture, that is, that culture which is adapted to forests. The material conditions changed before the adaptive culture was changed to fit the new material conditions. This situation may be illustrated by the figure. Line 1 represents the material conditions, in

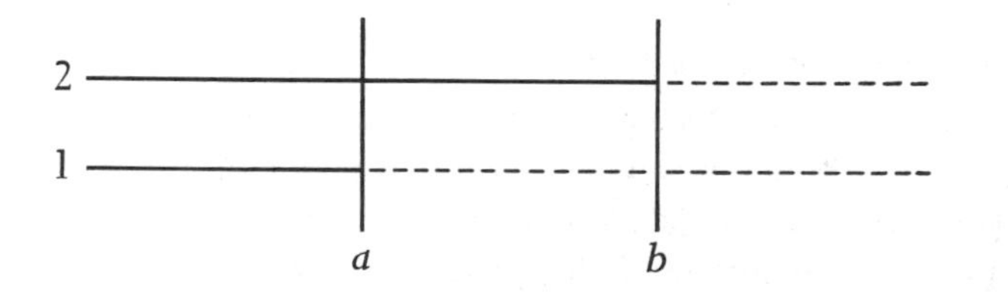

regard to forests in the United States. Line 2 represents the adaptive culture, the policy of using the forests. The continuous lines represent the plentiful forests, with the sparse population and the mores of exploitation, the dotted lines, the new conditions of forests which are small in relation to the population and the new policy of conservation. The space between *a* and *b* represents the period when the old adaptive culture or mores exists with the changed material conditions, and is a period of maladjustment.

It is difficult to locate exactly the points *a* and *b*. Consider first the location of point *b*, or the time of the change from the policy of exploitation to the policy of conservation. The policy of conservation of forests certainly did not begin prior to 1904, when the first National Conservation Congress met. It was during Roosevelt's administration that many active steps in the direction of conservation were taken. Large areas of national forest lands were withdrawn from public entry. Gifford Pinchot was very active in spreading the gospel of conservation, and the House of Governors called by President Roosevelt was in large measure concerned with programmes of conservation. About this time many books and articles in magazines and periodicals were written on the subject. The conservation movement can hardly be said to have started in any extensive manner before this time. It is true that, earlier, papers had been read on the subject before scientific societies and there had been some teaching of scientific forestry, but prior to this time the idea of forest conservation was little known and the movement was certainly not extensive. Nor had the government taken any significant steps in a genuine policy of conservation. Indeed it might be argued with some success that we have not yet adopted fully a policy of conservation. For a great many of the private holdings are still exploited in very much the same old way. Reforestation is still largely a matter of theory in the United States. It is true that the government has taken a number of steps to preserve the forests but the conservationists are far from being satisfied with the progress of the movement to date. Certainly we have not attained the high mark maintained in western Europe.

It is also difficult to locate point *a*, that is, to determine when we should have started the conservation movement. Some features of conservation probably should have been instituted perhaps early in the last century. Thus the allotment of permanent forest areas might very well have been done coincidently with the extension of our domain; and the destruction of forests on land little suited to agriculture might have been prevented as the population spread to these new regions. At the time of the Civil War the population had become quite large, and shortly afterward the era of railroad-building set in followed by a great development of industry, insuring large population and concentration. It was at this time that the wonderful forests of the Great Lakes region were cut down, and the cuttings in the Appalachian regions increased greatly. Some close observers saw at that time what development of population and industry would take place, but the relation of the forests to such a condition was not appreciated. If scientific forestry had been applied then, many of the unnecessarily wasted forests would still exist and now be furnishing lumber. There would not have been such a washing of soil and the danger of floods would have been less. While some methods of forest conservation might have been applied to advantage shortly after colonial days, the proper time for more extensive developments of conservation was probably in the era following the Civil War. The population was becoming large; the west was being settled; the Pacific coast had been reached; the territorial boundaries had been fixed; industries, railroads, factories, corporations, trusts were all growing with rapidity. The east was in greater need of conservation of forests than the Pacific Northwest or Alaska; nevertheless very probably for the whole country, though its stages of development were unequal, an extensive conservation movement should have been instituted about the middle of the last half of the nineteenth century. It would seem, therefore, that there has been a lag of at least a quarter of a century in changing our forestry policy.

The foregoing discussion of forestry illustrates the hypothesis which it is proposed to discuss. It is desirable to state more clearly and fully the points involved in the analysis. The first point concerns the degree of adjustment or correlation between the material conditions and the adaptive non-material culture. The degree of this adjustment may be only more or less perfect or satisfactory; but we do adjust ourselves to the material conditions through some form of culture; that is, we live, we get along, through this adjustment. The particular culture which is adjusted to the material conditions may be very complex, and, indeed, quite a number of widely different parts of culture may be adjusted to a fairly homogeneous material condition. Of a particular cultural form, such as the family or government, relationship to a particular material culture is only one of its purposes or functions. Not all functions of family organization, as, for instance, the affectional function, are primarily adaptive to material conditions.

Another point to observe is that the changes in the material culture precede changes in the adaptive culture. This statement is not in the form of a universal dictum. Conceivably, forms of adaptation might be worked out prior to a change in the material situation and the adaptation might be applied practically at the same time as the change in the material conditions. But such a situation presumes a very high degree of planning, prediction and control. The collection of data, it is thought, will show that at the present time there are a very large number of cases where the material conditions change and the changes in the adaptive culture follow later. There are certain general theoretical reasons why this is so; but it is not desirable to discuss these until later. For the present, the analysis will only concern those cases where changes in the adaptive culture do not precede changes in the material culture. Furthermore, it is not implied that changes may not occur in non-material culture while the material culture remains the same. Art or education, for instance, may undergo many changes with a constant material culture.

Still another point in the analysis is that the old, unchanged, adaptive culture is not adjusted to the new, changed, material conditions. It may be true that the old adaptive culture is never wholly unadjusted to the new conditions. There may be some degree of adjustment. But the thesis is that the unchanged adaptive culture was more harmoniously related to the old than to the new material conditions and that a new adaptive culture will be better suited to the new material conditions than was the old adaptive culture. Adjustment is therefore a relative term, and perhaps only in a few cases would there be a situation which might be called perfect adjustment or perfect lack of adjustment.

It is desirable, however, not to make the analysis too general until there has been a more careful consideration of particular instances. We now propose, therefore, to test the hypothesis by the facts in a definite case of social change. In attempting to verify the hypothesis in a particular case by measurement, the following series of steps will be followed. The old material conditions will be described, that part of the adaptive culture under consideration will be described, and the degree of adjustment between these two parts of culture shown. Then the changed material conditions and the changed adaptive culture will be defined and the degree of adaptation shown. It is necessary also to show that the unchanged adaptive culture is not as harmoniously adjusted to the new conditions as to the old and not as harmoniously adjusted to the new conditions as is a changed adaptive culture. Having made such a series of descriptions, the next step will be to measure the lag, which should be done by locating the point of change in the material culture and the point of change in the particular adaptive culture.

28

ROBERT MICHELS

On the Iron Law of Oligarchy

Robert Michels (1876–1936), who was born in Germany but possessed a highly cosmopolitan background (he studied in Germany, England and France), wrote several works that have been very influential in sociology. The most important of these by far is his remarkable volume Political Parties *(1911).*[1] *In this book Michels attempted to show that an organization ostensibly committed to the success of democratic processes would nonetheless inevitably develop a set of oligarchic tendencies that would seriously obstruct the realization of its democratic values. Michels argued that organizations move towards oligarchy through internal forces. This "iron law of oligarchy" has been of great interest to contemporary theorists. Today, it is generally acknowledged that Michels' iron law is not universal.*[2] *However, its applicability to a wide variety of existing organizations and their history has shown it to be quite descriptive of actual processes.*[3] *Contemporary scholars have concerned themselves with the need for modification of the doctrine and with the attempt to determine the conditions under which it retains validity.*[4]

Bibliographical Notes

1. Most of Michels' writings have not been translated into English. Other than his Political Parties, *the English-reading student should see* his First Lectures in Political Sociology, *translated by Alfred de Grazia (Minneapolis: University of Minnesota Press, 1949). A full bibliography of Michels' writings can be found in: Università Perugia, Facoltà*

Reprinted from Robert Michels, *Political Parties: A Sociological Study of the Oligarchical Tendencies of Modern Democracy* (New York: Hearst's International Library Co., 1915), pp. 10–11, 21–22, 365–367, 400–402, and 403. Footnotes have been abridged.

di Giurisprudenza, Studi in memoria di Roberto Michels, *Annali, Vol. 49* (1937), [*Padua: CEDAM*], 37–76.

2. *See, for example, S. M. Lipset, M. A. Trow, and J. S. Coleman,* Union Democracy: The Internal Politics of the International Typographical Union (*New York: Free Press, 1956*).

3 *See, for example, Paul M. Harrison,* Authority and Power in the Free Church Tradition: A Social Case Study of the American Baptist Convention (*Princeton, N. J.: Princeton University Press, 1959*).

4. *See, for example, Samuel J. Eldersveld,* Political Parties: A Behavioral Analysis (*Chicago: Rand-McNally, 1964*).

[In] modern party life aristocracy gladly presents itself in democratic guise, whilst the substance of democracy is permeated with aristocratic elements. On the one side we have aristocracy in a democratic form, and on the other democracy with an aristocratic content.

The democratic external form which characterizes the life of political parties may readily veil from superficial observers the tendency towards aristocracy, or rather towards oligarchy, which is inherent in all party organization. If we wish to obtain light upon this tendency, the best field of observation is offered by the intimate structure of the democratic parties, and, among these, of the socialist and revolutionary labor party. In the conservative parties, except during elections, the tendency to oligarchy manifests itself with that spontaneous vigor and clearness which corresponds with the essentially oligarchical character of these parties. But the parties which are subversive in their aims exhibit the like phenomena no less markedly. The study of the oligarchical manifestations in party life is most valuable and most decisive in its results when undertaken in relation to the revolutionary parties, for the reason that these parties, in respect of origin and of program, represent the negation of any such tendency, and have actually come into existence out of opposition thereto. Thus the appearance of oligarchical phenomena in the very bosom of the revolutionary parties is a conclusive proof of the existence of immanent oligarchical tendencies in every kind of human organization which strives for the attainment of definite ends.

. . .

Democracy is inconceivable without organization. A few words will suffice to demonstrate this proposition.

A class which unfurls in the face of society the banner of certain definite claims, and which aspires to the realization of a complex of ideal aims deriving from the economic functions which that class fulfils, needs an organization. Be the claims economic or be they political, organization appears the only means for the creation of a collective will. Organization, based as it is upon the principle of least effort, that is to say, upon the greatest possible economy of energy, is the weapon of the weak in their struggle with the strong.

The chances of success in any struggle will depend upon the degree to which this struggle is carried out upon a basis of solidarity between individuals whose interests are identical. In objecting, therefore, to the theories of the individualist anarchists that nothing could please the employers better than the dispersion and disaggregation of the forces of the workers, the socialists, the most fanatical of all the partisans of the idea of organization, enunciate an argument which harmonizes well with the results of scientific study of the nature of parties.

We live in a time in which the idea of cooperation has become so firmly established that even millionares perceive the necessity of common action. It is easy to understand, then, that organization has become a vital principle of the working class, for in default of it their success is *a priori* impossible. The refusal of the worker to participate in the collective life of his class cannot fail to entail disastrous consequences. In respect of culture and of economic, physical, and physiological conditions, the proletarian is the weakest element of our society. In fact, the isolated member of the working classes is defenseless in the hands of those who are economically stronger. It is only by combination to form a structural aggregate that the proletarians can acquire the faculty of political resistance and attain to a social dignity. The importance and the influence of the working class are directly proportional to its numerical strength. But for the representation of that numerical strength organization and coordination are indispensable. The principle of organization is an absolutely essential condition for the political struggle of the masses.

Yet this politically necessary principle of organization, while it overcomes that disorganization of forces which would be favorable to the adversary, brings other dangers in its train. We escape Scylla only to dash ourselves on Charybdis. Organization is, in fact, the source from which the conservative currents flow over the plain of democracy, occasioning there disastrous floods and rendering the plain unrecognizable.

. . .

. . . Is it impossible for a democratic party to practice a democratic policy, for a revolutionary party to pursue a revolutionary policy? Must we say that not *socialism* alone, but even a socialistic *policy*, is utopian? The present chapter will attempt a brief answer to this inquiry.

Within certain narrow limits, the Democratic Party, even when subjected to oligarchical control, can doubtless act upon the state in the democratic sense. The old political caste of society, and above all the "state" itself, are forced to undertake the revaluation of a considerable number of values—a revaluation both ideal and practical. The importance attributed to the masses increases, even when the leaders are demagogues. The legislature and the executive become accustomed to yield, not only to claims proceeding from above, but also to those proceeding from below. This may give rise, in practice, to great inconveniences, such as we recognize in the recent history of all the states under a parliamentary regime; in theory, however, this new order of things signifies an incalculable progress in respect of public rights, which thus come to conform better with the principles of social justice. This evolution will, however, be arrested from the moment when the governing classes succeed in attracting within the governmental orbit their enemies of the extreme left, in order to convert them into collaborators. Political organization leads to power. But power is always conservative. In any case, the influence exercised upon the governmental machine by an energetic opposition party is necessarily slow, is subject to frequent interruptions, and is always restricted by the nature of oligarchy.

. . .

. . . As the organization increases in size, the struggle for great principles becomes impossible. It may be noticed that in the democratic parties of today the great conflicts of view are fought out to an ever-diminishing extent in the field of ideas and with the weapons of pure theory, that they therefore degenerate more and more into personal struggles and invectives, to be settled finally upon considerations of a purely superficial character. The efforts made to cover internal dissensions with a pious veil are the inevitable outcome of organization based upon bureaucratic principles, for, since the chief aim of such an organization is to enroll the greatest possible number of members, every struggle on behalf of ideas within the limits of the organization is necessarily regarded as an obstacle to the realization of its ends, an obstacle, therefore, which must be avoided in every possible way. This tendency is reinforced by the parliamentary character of the political party. "Party organization" signifies the aspiration for the greatest number of members. "Parliamentarism" signifies the aspiration for the greatest number of votes. The principal fields of party activity are electoral agitation and direct agitation to secure new members. What, in fact, is the modern political party? It is the methodical organization of the electoral masses. The Socialist Party, as a political aggregate endeavoring simultaneously to recruit members and to recruit votes, finds here its vital interests, for every decline in membership and every loss in voting strength diminishes its political prestige. Consequently great respect must be paid, not only to new members, but also to possible adherents, to those who in Germany are termed *mitläufer*, in Italy *simpatizzanti*, in Holland *geestverwanten*, and in England *sympathizers*. To avoid alarming these individuals, who are still outside the ideal worlds of socialism or democracy, the pursuit of a policy based on strict principle is shunned, while the consideration is ignored whether the numerical increase of the organization thus effected is not likely to be gained at the expense of its quality.

. . .

[We] are led to conclude that the principal cause of oligarchy in the democratic parties is to be found in the technical indispensability of leadership.

The process which has begun in consequence of the differentiation of functions in the party is completed by a complex of qualities which the leaders acquire through their detachment from the mass. At the outset, leaders arise SPONTANEOUSLY; their functions are ACCESSORY and GRATUITOUS. Soon, however, they become PROFESSIONAL leaders, and in this second stage of development they are STABLE and IRREMOVABLE.

It follows that the explanation of the oligarchical phenomenon which thus results is partly PSYCHOLOGICAL; oligarchy derives, that is to say, from the psychical transformations which the leading personalities in the parties undergo in the course of their lives. But also, and still more, oligarchy depends upon what we may term the PSYCHOLOGY OF ORGANIZATION ITSELF, that is to say, upon the tactical and technical necessities which result from the consolidation of every disciplined political aggregate. Reduced to its most concise expression, the fundamental sociological law of political parties (the term "political" being here used in its most comprehensive significance) may be formulated in the following terms: "It is organization which gives birth to the dominion of the elected over the electors, of the mandataries over the mandators, of the delegates over the delegators. Who says organization, says oligarchy."

Every party organization represents an oligarchical power grounded upon a democratic basis. We find everywhere electors and elected. Also we find everywhere that the power of the elected leaders over the electing masses is almost unlimited. The oligarchical structure of the building suffocates the basic democratic principle. That which IS oppresses THAT WHICH OUGHT TO BE. For the masses, this essential difference between the reality and the ideal remains a mystery. Socialists often cherish a sincere belief that a new *élite* of politicians will keep faith better than did the old. The notion of the representation of popular interests, a notion to which the great majority of democrats, and in especial the working-class masses of the German-speaking lands, cleave with so much tenacity and confidence, is an illusion engendered by a false illumination, is an effect of mirage. In one of the most delightful pages of his analysis of modern Don Quixotism, Alphonse Daudet shows us how the "brav' commandant" Bravida, who has never quitted Tarascon, gradually comes to persuade himself, influenced by the burning southern sun, that he has been to Shanghai and has had all kinds of heroic adventures.[1] Similarly the modern proletariat, enduringly influenced by glib-tongued persons intellectually superior to the mass, ends by believing that by flocking to the poll and entrusting its social and economic cause to a delegate, its direct participation in power will be assured.

The formation of oligarchies within the various forms of democracy is the outcome of organic necessity, and consequently affects every organization, be it socialist or even anarchist. Haller long ago noted that in every form of social life relationships of dominion and of dependence are created by Nature herself.[2] The supremacy of the leaders in the democratic and revolutionary parties has to be taken into account in every historic situation present and to come, even though only a few and exceptional minds will be fully conscious of its existence. The mass will never rule except *in abstracto*. Consequently the question we have to discuss is not whether ideal democracy is realizable, but rather to what point and in what degree democracy is desirable, possible, and realizable at a given moment.

. . .

The obejctive immaturity of the mass is not a mere transitory phenomenon which will disappear with the progress of democratization *au lendemain du socialisme*. On the contrary, it derives from the very nature of the mass as mass, for this, even when organized, suffers from an incurable incompetence for the solution of the diverse problems which present themselves for solution—because the mass *per se* is amorphous, and therefore needs division of labor, specialization, and guidance. "The human species wants to be governed; it will be. I am ashamed of my kind," wrote Proudhon from his prison in 1850.[3] Man as individual is by nature predestined to be guided, and to be guided all the more in proportion as the functions of life undergo division and subdivision. To an enormously greater degree is guidance necessary for the social group.

NOTES

1. Alphonse Daudet, *Tartarin de Tarascon*, Marpon et Flammarion, Paris, 1887, p. 40.
2. Ludwig von Haller, *Restauration der Staatswissenschaften*, Winterthur, 1816, vol. 1, pp. 304 ct seq.
3. Charles Gide et Charles Rist, *Histoire des Doctrines économiques depuis les Physiocrates jusqu'à nos fours*, Larose et Tenin, Paris, 1909, p. 709.

29

VILFREDO PARETO

On the Circulation of Elites

The ideas of Vilfredo Pareto (*1848–1923*),[1] *the Italian economist and sociologist, have had great impact not only upon the thinking of numerous major contemporary sociologists,*[2] *but also on political ideology, especially that of Fascism.*[3] *Among his numerous contributions, few have been as influential as his conception of the* circulation of elites. *Arguing that "history is a graveyard of aristocracies," Pareto posited a cyclical theory of social change in which leadership always rotates between two elites composed of men of two different psychological orientations. A member of one elite is the* speculator (*or "fox"*), *a member of the other the* rentier (*or "lion"*). *The former has the characteristics of cunning, shrewdness, and instincts of combination; the latter has characteristics of boldness, resolute character, and instincts of aggregate persistence.*

Although Pareto was an extreme empiricist, stressing the methods of physical science, his highly influential conceptualization of elites was, as N. S. Timasheff has noted, "largely 'intuitive' and out of keeping with his own scientific admonitions." [4] *However, validation of the universal character of Pareto's generalization and the broader question of the importance of elites in and for society continue to be central issues in sociology.*[5]

Bibliographical Notes

1. *Pareto's principal sociological work, his four volume* Trattato di sociologia generale *was first published in 1916 and translated into*

Reprinted from Vilfredo Pareto, *The Mind and Society*, ed. Arthur Livingston, trans. Andrew Bongiorno (New York: Harcourt, Brace & Co., 1935), Vols. III and IV, pp. 2026–2029 and pp. 2233–2236, with the permission of The Pareto Fund. Footnotes have been renumbered.

English in 1935 as Mind and Society *by Andrew Bongiorno and edited by Arthur Livingston. For an excellent summary and interpretation of Pareto's work, see: Vilfredo Pareto,* Sociological Writings, *selected and introduced by S. E. Finer and translated by Derick Mirfin (New York: Frederick Praeger, 1966). For critiques of Pareto's works, see: James H. Meisel (ed.),* Pareto and Mosca *(Englewood Cliffs, New Jersey: Prentice-Hall, 1965).*

2. *Primary among these would be George C. Homans and Talcott Parsons. Cf., George C. Homans and Charles P. Curtis, Jr.,* An Introduction to Pareto: His Sociology *(New York: Knopf, 1934); George C. Homans,* The Human Group *(New York: Harcourt, Brace Jovanovich, 1950); and Talcott Parsons,* The Structure of Social Action *(New York: McGraw-Hill, 1937).*

3. *For an excellent tracing of this influence and some of its historical misrepresentations, see: Joseph Lopreato and Robert C. Ness, "Vilfredo Pareto: Sociologist or Idealogist?"* Sociological Quarterly, 7 *(1966), 21–38.*

4. *N. S. Timasheff,* Sociological Theory: Its Nature and Growth, *third edition (New York: Random House, 1967), p. 166.*

5. *For example, see: Suzanne Keller,* Beyond the Ruling Class: Strategic Elites in Modern Society *(New York: Random House, 1963); T. B. Bottomore,* Elites and Society *(New York: Basic Books, 1964); James H. Meisel,* The Myth of the Ruling Class: Gaetona Mosca and the Elite *(Ann Arbor, Michigan: University of Michigan Press, 1962); C. Wright Mills,* The Power Elite *(New York: Oxford University Press, 1956); and Harold D. Laswell,* et al. The Comparative Study of Elites *(Stanford, California: Stanford University Press, 1952).*

2026. *Social élites and their circulation.*[1] Suppose we begin by giving a theoretical definition of the thing we are dealing with, making it as exact as possible, and then go on to see what practical considerations we can replace it with to get a first approximation. Let us for the moment completely disregard considerations as to the good or bad, useful or harmful, praiseworthy or reprehensible character of the various traits in individuals, and confine ourselves to degrees—to whether, in other words, the trait in a given case be slight, average, intense, or more exactly, to the index that may be assigned to each individual with reference to the degree, or intensity, in him of the trait in question.

2027. Let us assume that in every branch of human activity each individual is given an index which stands as a sign of his capacity, very much the way grades are given in the various subjects in examinations in school. The highest type of lawyer, for instance, will be given 10. The man who does not get a client will be given I—reserving zero for the man who is an out-and-out idiot. To the man who has made his millions—honestly or dishonestly as the case may be—we will give 10. To the man who has earned his thousands we will give 6; to such as just manage to keep out of the poor-house, I, keeping zero for those who get in. To the woman "in politics," such as the Aspasia of Pericles, the Maintenon of Louis XIV, the Pompadour of Louis XV, who has managed to infatuate a man of power and play a part in the man's career, we shall give some higher number, such as 8 or 9; to the strumpet who merely satisfies the senses of such a man and exerts no influence on public affairs, we shall give zero. To a clever rascal who knows how to fool people and still keep clear of the penitentiary, we shall give 8, 9, or 10, according to the number of geese he has plucked and the amount of money he has been able to get out of them. To the sneak-thief who snatches a piece of silver from a restaurant table and runs away into the arms of a policeman, we shall give I. To a poet like Carducci we shall give 8 or 9 according to our tastes; to a scribbler who puts people to rout with his sonnets we shall give zero. For chess-players we can get very precise indices, noting what matches, and how many, they have won. And so on for all the branches of human activity.

2028. We are speaking, remember, of an actual, not a potential, state. If at an English examination a pupil says: "I could know English very well if I chose to; I do not know any because I have never seen fit to learn," the examiner replies: "I am not interested in your alibi. The grade for what you know is zero." If, similarly, someone says: "So-and-so does not steal, not because he couldn't, but because he is a gentleman," we reply: "Very well, we admire him for his self-control, but his grade as a thief is zero."

2029. There are people who worship Napoleon Bonaparte as a god. There are people who hate him as the lowest of criminals. Which are right? We do not choose to solve that question in connexion with a quite different matter. Whether Napoleon was a good man or a bad man, he was certainly not an idiot, nor a man of little account, as millions of others are. He had exceptional qualities, and that is enough for us to give him a high ranking, though without prejudice of any sort to questions that might be raised as to the ethics of his qualities or their social utility.

. . .

2233. The facts just mentioned put us in the way of making a more general classification in which the preceding classification would be included and to which we shall have frequent occasion to refer in explaining social phenomena hereafter (§§ 2313f).[2] Suppose we put in one category, which we may call S, individuals whose incomes are essentially variable and depend upon the person's wide-awakeness in discovering sources of gain. In that group, generally speaking and disregarding exceptions, will be found those promoters of enterprise—those *entrepreneurs*—whom we were considering some pages back; and with them will be stockholders in industrial and commercial corporations (but not bondholders, who will more fittingly be placed in our group next following). Then will come owners of real estate in cities where building speculation is rife; and also landowners—on a similar condition that there be speculation in the lands about them; and then stock-exchange speculators and bankers who make money on governmental, industrial, and commercial loans. We might further add all persons depending upon such people—lawyers, engineers, politicians, working-people, clerks—and deriving advantage from their operations. In a word, we are putting together all persons who directly or indirectly speculate and in one way or another manage to increase their incomes by ingeniously taking advantage of circumstances.

2234. And let us put into another category, which we may call R, persons who have fixed or virtually fixed incomes not depending to any great extent on ingenious combinations that may be conceived by an active mind. In this category, roughly, will be found persons who have savings and have deposited them in savings-banks or invested them in life-annuities; then people living on incomes from government bonds, certificates of the funded debt, corporation bonds, or other securities with fixed interest-rates; then owners of real estate and lands in places where there is no speculation; then farmers, working-people, clerks, depending upon such persons and in no way depending upon speculators. In a word, we so group together here all persons who neither directly nor indirectly depend on speculation and who have incomes that are fixed, or virtually fixed, or at least are but slightly variable.[3]

2235. Just to be rid of the inconvenience of using mere letters of the alphabet, suppose we use the term "speculators" for members of category S and the French term *rentiers* for members of category R.[4] Now we can repeat of the two groups of persons more or less what we said above (§ 2231) of mere owners of savings and *entrepreneurs*, and we shall find analogous conflicts, economic and social, between them. In the speculator group Class I residues predominate, in the *rentier* group, Class II residues. That that should be the case is readily understandable. A person of pronounced capacity for economic combinations is not satisfied with a fixed income, often a very small one. He wants to earn more, and if he finds a favourable opportunity, he moves into the *S* category. The two groups perform functions of differing utility in society. The *S* group is primarily responsible for change, for economic and social progress. The *R* group, instead, is a powerful element in stability, and in many cases counteracts the dangers attending the adventurous capers of the *S*'s. A society in which *R*'s almost exclusively predominate remains stationary and, as it were, crystallized. A society in which *S*'s predominate lacks stability, lives in a state of shaky equilibrium that may be upset by a slight accident from within or from without.

Members of the *R* group must not be mistaken for "conservatives," nor members of the *S* group for "progressives," innovators, revolutionaries (§§ 226, 228–44). They may have points in common with such, but there is no identity. There are evolutions, revolutions, innovations, that the *R*'s support, especially movements tending to restore to the ruling classes certain residues of group-persistence that had been banished by the *S*'s. A revolution may be made against the *S*'s—a revolution of that type founded the Roman Empire, and such, to some extent, was the revolution known as the Protestant Reformation. Then too, for the very reason that sentiments of group-persistence are dominant in them, the *R*'s may be so blinded by sentiment as to act against their own interests. They readily allow themselves to be duped by anyone who takes them on the side of sentiment, and time and time again they have been the artisans of their own ruin (§ 1873). If the old feudal lords, who were endowed with *R* traits in a very conspicuous degree, had not allowed themselves to be swept off their feet by a sum of sentiments in which religious enthusiasm was only one element, they would have seen at once that the Crusades were to be their ruin. In the eighteenth century, had the French nobility living on income, and that part of the French *bourgeoisie* which was in the same situation, not succumbed to the lure of humanitarian sentiments, they would not have prepared the ground for the Revolution that was to be their undoing. Not a few among the victims of the guillotine had for long years been continually, patiently, artfully grinding the blade that was to cut off their heads. In our day those among the *R*'s who are known as "intellectuals" are following in the footprints of the French nobles of the eighteenth century and are working with all their might to encompass the ruin of their own class (§ 2254).

Nor are the categories *R* and *S* to be confused with groupings that might be made according to economic occupation (§§ 1726–27). There again we find points of contact, but not full coincidence. A retail merchant often belongs to the *R* group, and a wholesale merchant too, but the wholesaler will more likely belong to the *S* group. Sometimes one same enterprise may change in character. An individual of the *S* type founds an industry as a result of fortunate speculations. When it yields or seems to be yielding a good return, he changes it into a corporation, retires from business, and passes over into the *R* group. A large number of stockholders in the new concern are also *R*'s—the ones who bought stock when they thought they were buying a sure thing. If they are not mistaken, the business changes in character, moving over from the *S* type to the *R* type. But in many cases the best speculation the founder ever made was in changing his business to a corporation. It is soon in jeopardy, with the *R*'s standing in line to pay for the broken crockery. There is no better business in this world than the business of fleecing the lambs—of exploiting the inexperience, the ingenuousness, the passions, of the *R*'s. In our societies the fortunes of many many wealthy individuals have no other foundations.[5]

2236. The differing relative proportions in which *S* types and *R* types are combined in the governing class correspond to differing types of civilization; and such proportions are among the principal traits that have to be considered in social heterogeneity.[6] Going back, for instance, to the protectionist cycle examined above (§§ 2209 f.), we may say that in modern democratic countries industrial protection increases the proportion of *S*'s in the governing class. That increase in turn serves to intensify protection, and the process would go on indefinitely if counter-forces did not come into play to check it (§ 2221).

NOTES

1. Kolabinska, *La circulation des élites en France*, p. 5: "The outstanding idea in the term '*élite*' is 'superiority.' That is the only one I keep. I disregard secondary connotations of appreciation or as to the utility of such superiority. I am not interested here in what is desirable. I am making a simple study of what is. In a broad sense I mean by the *élite* in a society people who possess in marked degree qualities of intelligence, character, skill, capacity, of whatever kind. . . . On the other hand I

entirely avoid any sort of judgment on the merits and utility of such classes." [The phrase "circulation of *élites*" is well established in Continental literature. Pareto himself renders it in Italian as "circulation of the élite (selected, chosen, ruling, "better") classes." It is a cumbersome phrase and not very exact, and I see no reason for preferring it to the more natural and, in most connexions, the more exact, English phrase, class-circulation.—A. L.]

2. The classification in question was first suggested in my "*Rentiers et speculateurs*," in *Indépendance*, May 1, 1911.
3. Monographs along the lines of Le Play's would be of great use in determining the character of the persons belonging in our *S* group, and those belonging to our *R* group. Here is one such, contributed by Prezzolini: *La Francia e i francesi del secolo XX osservati da un italiano*. I know it as quoted by E. Cesari in the *Vita italiana*, Oct. 15, 1917, pp. 367–70. The person in question is a well-known member of the French parliament—we suppress the proper name: for us here, he is not a person, but just a type. The figures given by Prezzolini are those publicly declared by the member himself, Monsieur X. X's fixed income yields a total of 17,500 francs, of which 15,000 are salary as a member of the parliament and 2,500 interest on his wife's dowry. Only the latter sum belongs in category R—the salary belongs rather in category S, because to get such a thing one must have the ability and the good fortune to be elected. X's expense-account shows a total of 64,200 francs, divided as follows: household expenses, 33,800; office expenses, 22,550; expenses for his election district (avowable expenses), 7,850. There ought, therefore, to be a deficit of 45,700 francs; but the deficit is not only covered but changes into a surplus in view of the following revenues: contributions to newspapers and other publications, 12,500 francs; honorarium as general agent of the *A.B.C.* Company, 21,000 francs; commissions on sales, 7,500. In this connexion, Prezzolini notes that X, reporting on the war budget, enters 100,000 francs for supplies delivered to himself, as general agent of the *A.B.C.* Company: that gives X his "sales commissions." Finally, because of the influence that he enjoys, our member, X, receives a stipend of 18,000 francs from a newspaper. In all, these revenues, which clearly belong in the category *S*, yield a total of 50,000 francs. Prezzolini adds that the member in question is not the only one, nor the least, of his species. He is just a better-known and an honester type.
4. It might be well to repeat that our use of such terms is not based on their ordinary senses, nor upon their etymologies. We are to use them strictly in the sense defined in §§2233–34, and the reader must refer to those definitions whenever he encounters them in the remainder of this volume. [I keep the term "speculator." English ordinarily analyzes the matter embraced under Pareto's term, especially in slang. Pareto's "speculator" is our "hustler," "man of pep," "wide-awake individual," "live-wire," and so on.—A. L.]
5. Many people conclude that such facts are enough to condemn our social organization, and hold it responsible for most of the pains from which we suffer. Others think that they can defend our present order only by denying the facts or minimizing their significance. Both are right from the ethical standpoint (§§2162, 2262), wrong from the standpoint of social utility experimentally considered (§2115). Obviously, if it be posited as an axiom that men *ought*, whatever happens, to observe certain rules, those who do not observe them necessarily stand condemned. Trying to put such a reasoning into logical form, one gets as its premise some proposition of the type mentioned in §§1886, 1896–97. If one goes on to say that the organization so condemned is in the main injurious to society, one must logically fall back on some premise that

confuses morality and utility (§§1495, 1903–98). On the other hand, if premises of those types are granted and one would, notwithstanding, still defend or approve the organization of our societies, there is nothing left but to deny the facts or say they are not significant. The experimental approach is altogether different. Anyone accepting it grants no axioms independent of experience, and therefore finds it necessary to discuss the premises of the reasonings mentioned. On so doing one soon perceives that it is a question of two phenomena that do indeed have points in common, but are in no sense identical (§2001), and that in every particular case experience has to be called in to decide whether one is dealing with a point of contact or a point of divergence. An instant's reflection is enough to see that if one accepts certain conclusions one adopts by that fact the premises to which they are indissolubly bound. But the power of sentiment and the influence of habitual manners of reasoning are such that people disregard the force of logic entirely and establish conclusions without reference to the premises or, at the very best, accept the premises as axioms not subject to discussion. Another effect of such power and such influence will be that in spite of the warnings we have given and over and over again repeated, there will always be someone to carry the import of the remarks that he is here reading on the *R*'s and *S*'s beyond the limits we have so strictly specified, interpreting all that we have been saying against one of those groups as implying that the influence of the group is, on the whole, harmful to society and the group itself "condemnable"; and all that we have been saying in its favour as a proof that the influence of the group is, in general, beneficial to society and the group itself worthy of praise. We have neither the means nor the least desire to prevent the fabrication of such interpretations. We are satisfied with recognizing them as one variety of our derivations (§1419, I-β).

6. As usual, one may raise the query: "If this social phenomenon is of such great moment, how comes it that people have not remarked it hitherto?" The answer, again as usual, is that people have indeed noticed it, but have proceeded to cover it over again with a cloak of derivations. The substratum underlying anti-Semitism is a movement against speculators. It is said that the Semite is more of a speculator than the "Aryan" and the Jew is therefore taken as representing the whole class. Consider the case of department-stores and bazaars in Europe. They are the targets, especially in Germany, of the anti-Semites. It is true that many such stores are owned by Jews, but plenty of others are owned by Christians, and in either event are equally harmful to the small retailer, whom the anti-Semites would protect—anti-Semite in this case meaning "anti-speculator" and nothing more. The same may be said of financial syndicates and other characteristic forms of speculations. Socialists pick their quarrel with "capitalists," and theoretically it is a good thing that for once the "capitalist" is not confused with the "speculator"; but practically, the mobs that follow Socialist leadership have never grasped head or tail of Marx's pretty theories as to "surplus value"; they are inspired solely by an instinctive impulse to take for themselves at least a part of the money that is going to "speculators." Theorists, too, when dealing with "capitalism" in history, confuse it, to some extent at least, with "speculator" rule. Finally, if anyone is inclined to go farther back in history, he may find ample traces of remarks and doctrines that reflect the conflict between speculators and the rest of the public. In the case of Athens the people in the Piraeus are at outs with the farmers, and Plato (*De legibus*, IV, 705) would place his republic far from the sea to keep it safe from the influence of speculators. In that he is a predecessor of the anti-Semites of our time.

Speculators may be found at work in all periods of history. Various the ways in which their influence manifests itself, various the names that are applied to it, various the derivations that it provokes; but the substance is ever the same.

30

MAX WEBER
On the Spirit of Capitalism

As we have already noted, Max Weber's influence upon contemporary American sociology has been ubiquitous. Undoubtedly, however, his greatest impact on intellectual history derives from his work dealing with the interrelationships of religious ideas and economic systems. In his book The Protestant Ethic and the Spirit of Capitalism, *Weber argues that Protestanism was a major and necessary condition for the development of capitalism. A great deal of controversy has been engendered by this thesis,*[1] *but it should be noted that Weber very carefully qualified his argument, especially in later writings.*[2] *Though Weber recognized the importance of the economic system, he tried to modify the Marxist approach by pointing out the importance of the interaction that exists between values and idea systems and the economic order. He did not argue, as some of his less careful critics have contended, that Protestantism* caused *capitalism, only that it was a determining factor. Even allowing for misinterpretations, however, Weber's thesis has become the subject of serious criticism,*[3] *and research is still needed to validate many of the points of controversy.*[4]

Bibliographical Notes

1. An excellent succinct overview of the controversy can be found in: Robert W. Green (ed.), Protestantism and Capitalism: The Weber Thesis and Its Critics *(Boston: D.C. Heath, 1959).*

For a list of works by and about Weber, see the introduction to his first statement in this book, pp. 16–17.

2. An excellent survey of his argument with its subsequent modifi-

Reprinted with the permission of Charles Scribner's Sons from *The Protestant Ethic and the Spirit of Capitalism* by Max Weber, translated by Talcott Parsons. Footnotes have been deleted.

cation is to be found in: Irving M. Zeitlin, Ideology and the Development of Sociological Theory *(Englewood Cliffs, N.J.: Prentice-Hall, 1968), pp. 122–155.*

3. E.g., *Kurt Samuelsson (trans. by E. Geoffrey French),* Religion and Economic Action *(New York: Basic Books, 1961).*

4. *A major recent addition to the on-going controversy is: Guy E. Swanson,* Religion and Regime: A Sociological Account of the Reformation *(Ann Arbor, Mich.: University of Michigan Press, 1967).*

In the title of this study is used the somewhat pretentious phrase, the *spirit* of capitalism. What is to be understood by it? The attempt to give anything like a definition of it brings out certain difficulties which are in the very nature of this type of investigation.

If any object can be found to which this term can be applied with any understandable meaning, it can only be an historical individual, i.e. a complex of elements associated in historical reality which we unite into a conceptual whole from the standpoint of their cultural significance.

Such an historical concept, however, since it refers in its content to a phenomenon significant for its unique individuality, cannot be defined according to the formula *genus proximum, differentia specifica,* but it must be gradually put together out of the individual parts which are taken from historical reality to make it up. Thus the final and definitive concept cannot stand at the beginning of the investigation, but must come at the end. We must, in other words, work out in the course of the discussion, as its most important result, the best conceptual formulation of what we here understand by the spirit of capitalism, that is the best from the point of view which interests us here. This point of view (the one of which we shall speak later) is, further, by no means the only possible one from which the historical phenomena we are investigating can be analysed. Other standpoints would, for this as for every historical phenomenon, yield other characteristics as the essential ones. The result is that it is by no means necessary to understand by the spirit of capitalism only what it will come to mean to *us* for the purposes of our analysis. This is a necessary result of the nature of historical concepts which attempt for their methodological purposes not to grasp historical reality in abstract general formulæ, but in concrete genetic sets of relations which are inevitably of a specifically unique and individual character.

Thus, if we try to determine the object, the analysis and historical explanation of which we are attempting, it cannot be in the form of a conceptual definition, but at least in the beginning only a provisional description of what is here meant by the spirit of capitalism. Such a description is, however, indispensable in order clearly to understand the object of the investigation. For this purpose we turn to a document of that spirit which contains what we are looking for in almost classical purity, and at the same time has the advantage of being free from all direct relationship to religion, being thus, for our purposes, free of preconceptions.

"Remember, that *time* is money. He that can earn ten shillings a day by his labour, and goes abroad, or sits idle, one half of that day, though he spends but sixpence during his diversion or idleness, ought not to reckon *that* the only expense; he has really spent, or rather thrown away, five shillings besides.

"Remember, that *credit* is money. If a man lets his money lie in my hands after it is due, he gives me the interest, or so much as I can make of it during that time. This amounts to a considerable sum where a man has good and large credit, and makes good use of it.

"Remember, that money is of the prolific, generating nature. Money can beget money, and its offspring can beget more, and so on. Five shillings turned is six, turned again it is seven and threepence, and so on, till it becomes a hundred pounds. The more there is of it, the more it produces every turning, so that the profits rise quicker and quicker. He that kills a breeding-sow, destroys all her offspring to the thousandth generation. He that murders a crown, destroys all that it might have produced, even scores of pounds."

"Remember, this saying, *The good paymaster is lord of another man's purse*. He that is known to pay punctually and exactly to the time he promises, may at any time, and on any occasion, raise all the money his friends can spare. This is sometimes of great use. After industry and frugality, nothing contributes more to the raising of a young man in the world than punctuality and justice in all his dealings; therefore never keep borrowed money an hour beyond the time you promised, lest a disappointment shut up your friend's purse for ever.

"The most trifling actions that affect a man's credit are to be regarded. The sound of your hammer at five in the morning, or eight at night, heard by a creditor, makes him easy six months longer; but if he sees you at a billiard-table, or hears your voice at a tavern, when you should be at work, he sends for his money the next day; demands it, before he can receive it, in a lump.

"It shows, besides, that you are mindful of what you owe; it makes you appear a careful as well as an honest man, and that still increases your credit.

"Beware of thinking all your own that you possess, and of living accordingly. It is a mistake that many people who have credit fall into. To prevent this, keep an exact account for some time both of your expenses and your income. If you take the pains at first to mention particulars, it will have this good effect: you will discover how wonderfully small, trifling expenses mount up to large sums, and will discern what might have been, and may for the future be saved, without occasioning any great inconvenience."

"For six pounds a year you may have the use of one hundred pounds, provided you are a man of known prudence and honesty.

"He that spends a groat a day idly, spends idly above six pounds a year, which is the price for the use of one hundred pounds.

"He that wastes idly a groat's worth of his time per day, one day with another, wastes the privilege of using one hundred pounds each day.

"He that idly loses five shillings' worth of time, loses five shillings, and might as prudently throw five shillings into the sea.

"He that loses five shillings, not only loses that sum, but all the advantage that might be made by turning it in dealing, which by the time that a young man becomes old, will amount to a considerable sum of money."

It is Benjamin Franklin who preaches to us in these sentences, the same which Ferdinand Kürnberger satirizes in his clever and malicious *Picture of American Culture* as the supposed confession of faith of the Yankee. That it is the spirit of capitalism which here speaks in characteristic fashion, no one will doubt, however little we may wish to claim that everything which could be understood as pertaining to that spirit is contained in it. Let us pause a moment to consider this passage, the philosophy of which Kürnberger sums up in the words, "They make tallow out of cattle and money out of man". The peculiarity of this philosophy of avarice appears to be the ideal of the honest man of recognized credit, and above all the idea of a duty of the individual toward the increase of his capital, which is assumed as an end in itself.

Truly what is here preached is not simply a means of making one's way in the world, but a peculiar ethic. The infraction of its rules is treated not as foolishness but as forgetfulness of duty. That is the essence of the matter. It is not mere business astuteness, that sort of thing is common enough, it is an ethos. *This* is the quality which interests us.

When Jacob Fugger, in speaking to a business associate who had retired and who wanted to persuade him to do the same, since he had made enough money and should let others have a chance, rejected that as pusillanimity and answered that "he (Fugger) thought otherwise, he wanted to make money as long as he could," the spirit of his statement is evidently quite different from that of Franklin. What in the former case was an expression of commercial daring and a personal inclination morally neutral, in the latter takes on the character of an ethically coloured maxim for the conduct of life. The concept spirit of capitalism is here used in this specific sense, it is the spirit of modern capitalism. For that we are here dealing only with Western European and American capitalism is obvious from the way in which the problem was stated. Capitalism existed in China, India, Babylon, in the classic world, and in the Middle Ages. But in all these cases, as we shall see, this particular ethos was lacking.

Now, all Franklin's moral attitudes are coloured with utilitarianism. Honesty is useful, because it assures credit; so are punctuality, industry, frugality, and that is the reason they are virtues. A logical deduction from this would be that where, for instance, the appearance of honesty serves the same purpose, that would suffice, and an unnecessary surplus of this virtue would evidently appear to Franklin's eyes as unproductive waste. And as a matter of fact, the story in his autobiography of his conversion to those virtues, or the discussion of the value of a strict maintenance of the appearance of modesty, the assiduous belittlement of one's own deserts in order to gain general recognition later, confirms this impression. According to Franklin, those virtues, like all others, are only in so far virtues as they are actually useful to the individual, and the surrogate of mere appearance is always sufficient when it accomplishes the end in view. It is a conclusion which is inevitable for strict utilitarianism. The impression of many Germans that the virtues professed by Americanism are pure hypocrisy seems to have been confirmed by this striking case. But in fact the matter is not by any means so simple. Benjamin Franklin's own character, as it appears in the really unusual candidness of his autobiography, belies that suspicion. The circumstance that he ascribes his recognition of the utility of virtue to a divine revelation which was intended to lead him in the path of righteousness, shows that something more than mere garnishing for purely egocentric motives is involved.

In fact, the *summum bonum* of this ethic, the earning of more and more money, combined with the strict avoidance of all spontaneous enjoyment of life, is above all completely devoid of any eudæmonistic, not to say hedonistic, admixture. It is thought of so purely as an end in itself, that from the point of view of the happiness of, or utility to, the single individual, it appears entirely transcendental and absolutely irrational. Man is dominated by the making of money, by acquisition as the ultimate purpose of his life. Economic acquisition is no longer subordinated to man as the means for the satisfaction of his material needs. This reversal of what we should call the natural relationship, so irrational from a naïve point of view, is evidently as definitely a leading principle of capitalism as it is foreign to all peoples not under capitalistic influence. At the same time it expresses a type of feeling which is closely connected with certain religious ideas. If we thus ask, *why* should "money be made out of men", Benjamin Franklin himself, although he was a colourless deist, answers in his autobiography with a quotation from the Bible, which his strict Calvinistic father drummed into him again and again in his youth: "Seest thou a man diligent in his business? He shall stand before kings" (Prov. xxii. 29). The earning of money within the modern economic order is, so long as it is done legally, the result and the expression of virtue and proficiency in a calling; and this virtue and proficiency are, as it is now not difficult to see, the real Alpha and Omega of Franklin's ethic, as expressed in the passages we have quoted, as well as in all his works without exception.

And in truth this peculiar idea, so familiar to us to-day, but in reality so little a matter of course, of one's duty in a calling, is what is most characteristic of the social ethic of capitalistic culture, and is in a sense the fundamental basis of it. It is an obligation which the individual is supposed to feel and does feel towards the content of his professional activity, no matter in what it consists, in particular no matter whether it appears on the surface as a utilization of his personal powers, or only of his material possessions (as capital).

Of course, this conception has not appeared only under capitalistic conditions. On the contrary, we shall later trace its origins back to a time previous to the advent of capitalism. Still less, naturally, do we maintain that a conscious acceptance of these ethical maxims on the part of the individuals, entrepreneurs or labourers, in modern capitalistic enterprises, is a condition of the further existence of present-day capitalism. The capitalistic economy of the present day is an immense cosmos into which the individual is born, and which presents itself to him, at least as an individual, as an unalterable order of things in which he must live. It forces the individual, in so far as he is involved in the system of market relationships, to conform to capitalistic rules of action. The manufacturer who in the long run acts counter to these norms, will just as inevitably be eliminated from the economic scene as the worker who cannot or will not adapt himself to them will be thrown into the streets without a job.

Thus the capitalism of to-day, which has come to dominate economic life, educates and selects the economic subjects which it needs through a process of economic survival of the fittest. But here one can easily see the limits of the concept of selection as a means of historical explanation. In order that a manner of life so well adapted to the peculiarities of capitalism could be selected at all, i.e. should come to dominate others, it had to originate somewhere, and not in isolated individuals alone, but as a way of life common to whole groups of men. This origin is what really needs explanation. Concerning the doctrine of the more naïve historical materialism, that such ideas originate as a reflection or superstructure of economic situations, we shall speak more in detail below. At this point it will suffice for our purpose to call attention to the fact that without doubt, in the country of Benjamin Franklin's birth (Massachusetts), the spirit of capitalism (in the sense we have attached to it) was present before the capitalistic order. There were complaints of a peculiarly calculating sort of profit-seeking in New England, as distinguished from the other parts of America, as early as 1632. It is further undoubted that capitalism remained far less developed in some of the neighbouring colonies, the later Southern States of the United States of America, in spite of the fact that these latter were founded by large capitalists for business motives, while the New England colonies were founded by preachers and seminary graduates with the help of small bourgeois, craftsmen and yoemen, for religious reasons. In this case the causal relation is certainly the reverse of that suggested by the materialistic standpoint.

But the origin and history of such ideas is much more complex than the theorists of the superstructure suppose. The spirit of capitalism, in the sense in which we are using the term, had to fight its way to supremacy against a whole world of hostile forces. A state of mind such as that expressed in the passages we have quoted from Franklin, and which called forth the applause of a whole people, would both in ancient times and in the Middle Ages have been proscribed as the lowest sort of avarice and as an attitude entirely lacking in self-respect. It is, in fact, still regularly thus looked upon by all those social groups which are least involved in or adapted to modern capitalistic conditions. This is not wholly because the instinct of acquisition was in those times unknown or undeveloped, as has often been said. Nor because the *auri sacra fames*, the greed for gold, was then, or now, less powerful outside of bourgeois capitalism than within its peculiar sphere, as the illusions of modern romanticists are wont to believe. The difference between the capitalistic and precapitalistic spirits is not to be found at this point. The greed of the Chinese Mandarin, the old Roman aristocrat, or the modern peasant, can stand up to any comparison. And the *auri sacra fames* of a Neapolitan cab-driver or *barcaiuolo*, and certainly of Asiatic representatives of similar trades, as well as of the craftsmen of southern European or Asiatic countries, is, as anyone can find out for himself, very much more intense, and especially more unscrupulous than that of, say, an Englishman in similar circumstances.

The universal reign of absolute unscrupulousness in the pursuit of selfish interests by the making of money has been a specific characteristic of precisely those countries whose bourgeois-capitalistic development, measured according to Occidental standards, has remained backward. As every employer knows, the lack of *coscienziosità* of the labourers of such countries, for instance Italy as compared with Germany, has been, and to a certain extent still is, one of the principal obstacles to their capitalistic development. Capitalism cannot make use of the labour of those who practise the doctrine of undisciplined *liberum arbitrium*, any more than it can make use of the business man who seems absolutely unscrupulous in his dealings with others, as we can learn from Franklin. Hence the difference does not lie in the degree of development of any impulse to make money. The *auri sacra fames* is as old as the history of man. But we shall see that those who submitted to it without reserve as an uncontrolled impulse, such as the Dutch sea-captain who "would go through hell for gain, even though he scorched his sails", were by no means the representatives of that attitude of mind from which the specifically modern capitalistic spirit as a mass phenomenon is derived, and that is what matters. At all periods of history, wherever it was possible, there has been ruthless acquisition, bound to no ethical norms whatever. Like war and piracy, trade has often been unrestrained in its relations with foreigners and those outside the group. The double ethic has permitted here what was forbidden in dealings among brothers.

Capitalistic acquisition as an adventure has been at home in all types of economic society which have known trade with the use of money and which have offered it opportunities, through *commenda*, farming of taxes, State loans, financing of wars, ducal courts and office-holders. Likewise the inner attitude of the adventurer, which laughs at all ethical limitations, has been universal. Absolute and conscious ruthlessness in acquisition has often stood in the closest connection with the strictest conformity to tradition. Moreover, with the breakdown of tradition and the more or less complete extension of free economic enterprise, even to within the social group, the new thing has not generally been ethically justified and encouraged, but only tolerated as a fact. And this fact has been treated either as ethically indifferent or as reprehensible, but unfortunately unavoidable. This has not been the normal attitude of all ethical teachings, but, what is more important, also that expressed in the practical action of the average man of pre-capitalistic times, pre-capitalistic in the sense that the rational utilization of capital in a permanent enterprise and the rational capitalistic organization of labour had not yet become dominant forces in the determination of economic activity. Now just this attitude was one of the strongest inner obstacles which the adaptation of men to the conditions of an ordered bourgeois-capitalistic economy has encountered everywhere.

7

Social Control, Deviance, and Collective Behavior

31

E. A. ROSS

On Social Control

Edward Alsworth Ross (1866–1951) was one of the early pioneers of American sociology. His work was especially remarkable in that it spanned an unusually long period, from his Foundations of Sociology *(1897–1904), a collection of his essays, to* New-age Sociology *(1940), an introductory textbook.*[1] *His great work* Social Control *represented an attempt to deal with the question of social order in a manner that integrated the emphasis on external norms found in the writings of William Graham Sumner (in his* Folkways*) and the stress on internal processes within the person found in the writings of Charles Horton Cooley (in his* Human Nature and the Social Order*). Ross was also concerned with a specification of the conditions necessitating social control and with the interrelationship of social control with the problems of social change. In addition to his concern with the theoretic issues, Ross was deeply involved in an effort to reform American society in line with his Populist-Progressive views, and his writings contained many specific suggestions for attaining this goal.*[2]

Bibliographical Notes

1. *Ross's principal works in addition to* Foundations of Sociology *and* New-age Sociology *include:* Social Control: A Survey of the Foundations of Order *(1901);* Sin and Society: An Analysis of Latter-day Iniquity *(1907);* Social Psychology *(1908);* Changing America: Studies in Contemporary Society *(1909);* What Is America? *(1919);* The Principles of Sociology *(1920);* The Social Trend *(1922);* World Drift *(1928); and* Seventy Years of It: An Autobiography *(1936).*

Reprinted from Edward A. Ross, *Social Control* (New York: Macmillan, 1901), pp. 77–86 and 411–414.

Ross's principal works have been neatly edited for the modern reader in: Edgar F. Borgatta and Henry J. Meyer: Social Control and the Foundations of Sociology: Pioneer Contributions of Edward Alsworth Ross to the Study of Society *(Boston: Beacon Press, 1959). For general surveys of Ross's work, see: William L. Kolb, "The Sociological Theories of Edward Alsworth Ross," in Harry Elmer Barnes (ed.),* An Introduction to the History of Sociology *(Chicago: University of Chicago Press, 1948), pp. 819–832; and Joyce O. Hertzler, "Edward Alsworth Ross: Sociological Pioneer and Interpreter,"* American Sociological Review, 16 *(1951), 597–613.*

2. *Examples of more recent work on the concept of social control include: A. B. Hollingshead, "The Concept of Social Control,"* American Sociological Review, 6 *(1942), 217–224; Donald Roy, "Efficiency and 'the Fix': Informal Intergroup Relations in a Piecework Machine Shop,"* American Journal of Sociology, 60 *(1955), 255–266; and O. E. Klapp, "Heroes, Villains, and Fools, as Agents of Social Control,"* American Sociological Review, 19 *(1955), 56–63.*

Radiant points of Social Control

A control that we have any right to call *social* has behind it practically the whole weight of society. But still this control often wells up and spreads out from certain centres which we might term *the radiant points of social control.* Uniform as it is to the eye, the social substance when tested resolves itself into froth and liquid, into chaff and wheat, into protoplasm and nuclei. Our task now is to fix upon the nuclei that determine the principal lines social control may take. In plain terms, the question before us is, What is the ultimate seat of authority? Where resides the will that guides the social energies? Who hold the levers which set in motion the social checks or stimuli that hold a man back or push him on?

That frequently these checks and stimuli are managed by a rather small knot of persons should not for a moment lead the reader to confuse social control with class control. Often enough, indeed, a minority, in virtue of its superior strength, courage, craft, or organization, seizes the reins of power; but such domination always entails a rupture of social consciousness. While outwardly there is but one society, there are in reality two or more societies which happen to interpenetrate as to substance. Between leaders and led, there is a bond of good will and trust. Between drones and workers, parasites and hosts, come distrust and hate, and their clash of interests is liable to pass at any moment into the clash of arms. In history the relations of Venetians and Cypriotes, Normans and Sicilians, Franks and Gauls, betray the presence of class control.

Totally different from class control in origin is the power of a minority to direct social control. Each category of people in society has its own point of view, and consequently its own way of envisaging the problems of conduct. Now, one of these views can prevail only in case the others are withdrawn. If a class finds itself leading the march at the head of the social procession, it is only because the other classes have more confidence in it than they have in themselves. *Social power is concentrated or diffused in proportion as men do or do not feel themselves in need of guidance or protection.* When it is concentrated it lodges in that class of men in which the people feel the most confidence. The many transfer their allegiance from one class to another—from elders to priests, or from priests to savants—when their supreme need changes, or when they have lost confidence in the old guidance. When they begin to feel secure and able to cope with evils in their own strength and wisdom, the many resume self-direction and the monopoly of social power by the few ceases.

Such is the underlying law of the transformations and displacements of power. The immediate cause of the location of power is prestige. The class that has the most prestige will have the most power. The prestige of *numbers* gives ascendency to the crowd. The prestige of *age* gives it to the elders. The prestige of *prowess* gives it to the war chief, or to the military caste. The prestige of *sanctity* gives it to the priestly caste. The prestige of *inspiration* gives it to the prophet. The prestige of *place* gives it to the official class. The prestige of *money* gives it to the capitalists. The prestige of *ideas* gives it to the élite. The prestige of *learning* gives it to the mandarins. The absence of prestige and the faith of each man in himself gives weight to the individual and reduces social control to a minimum.

In some cases there exists an appropriate name for the régime. When the priest guides, we call it *clericalism*. When the fighting caste is deferred to, we call it *militarism*. When the initiative lies with the minions of the state, we call it *officialism*. The leadership of the moneyed men is *capitalism*. That of the men of ideas is *liberalism*. The reliance of men upon their own wisdom and strength is *individualism*.

These distinctions, I need hardly add, are far deeper than distinctions, like *aristocracy, monarchy, republic,* which relate merely to the form of government. For the location of social power expresses much more truly the inner constitution of society than does the location of political power. And so the shiftings of power within the state, far from having causes of their own, are apt to follow and answer to the shiftings of power within society. Yet since political power is palpable and lies near the surface of things, political science long ago ascertained its forms and laws; while social power, lying hidden in the dim depths, has hardly even yet drawn the attention of social science.

When picked men flock together in a settlement or mining camp, authority resides at first in the Crowd. The mass is the sole seat of social power, and the mass meeting, in which one man is as good as another, expresses the will of the community. When in the course of time neighbors learn to know and appraise one another, men of superior character, sagacity, or disinterestedness come to influence their fellows more than they are influenced by them. The seat of the common will, then, is no longer the crowd, but the Public. In this organization of minds every man counts for something, but one man does not always count for as much as another.

When, on the other hand, a group is formed by the natural increase of families, the first seat of authority is the Elders. The long years of dependence on the parent make it difficult even for grown sons to throw off the paternal yoke. This prestige of the father becomes the prestige of *age* when ancestor worship teaches men that the old stand nearest to the Unseen, and will themselves soon become spirits, able to ban or to bless.

Like the kinship bond, the ascendency of the elders is all but universal in the childhood of societies. But one place where the graybeard is always at a disadvantage is in the fight. So when, as with lusty barbarians, fighting becomes the chief business of life, the war leader quite outshines the council of elders. Prowess finally surpasses age in prestige, just as from the same cause the bond of comradeship becomes stronger than the tie of blood. Warriors of fine qualities and brilliant exploits get together the biggest bands for foray, and so are able to amass wealth, keep retainers, and get looked upon as "noble." In the days of permanent conquest these men of social power become the captains of the host, the heads of the state, and the sole possessors of political power.

It is clear, then, that the Military Caste does not get social weight just because it is able to bully the rest of the people. Terrify men and they cling to the skirts of those powerful to save. When violence is loose the hind creeps under the castle wall, the trembling burgher pours out his florins for protection, and the Soldier strikes the dominant note in social opinion. When peace makes broad her wings the fighting man, becoming less necessary, becomes less influential.

In proportion as men do not understand the play of natural forces, they are likely to connect their fate with the good will or the ill will of unseen beings. If now, in an ignorant age, among imaginative men who see pain, disease, and death lurking on every hand, there arises a class of men who claim to enjoy high consideration with these unseen beings, that class will acquire enormous social power. Whether or not they finger the machinery of the state, their curse will be dreaded, their commands obeyed, and their intercessions sought by all men. It is no wonder, then, that the Priesthood, which in the civilized Roman Empire was the minister of society, became its master when this organization of intelligent men had only benighted, fanciful barbarians to deal with. The fact that between the sixth and the thirteenth centuries about one-third of the soil of Europe passed by free offering into the hands of religious corporations, while the best talent of the age turned to the monastic life, tells what confidence men had in the supernatural powers of the sacred caste.

The layman is far less supple to the will of the priest if there lie to hand written directions and formulas for controlling or pleasing the Unseen. An open Sacred Book, therefore, has saved both the Jew and the Mohammedan from the excesses of priestly domination; and when Luther and the Reformers sought to break the sacerdotal spell, they gave men the Bible, and bade them look therein for the way of life.

After safety from foes and from the Unseen, man's next desire is for the security of his daily bread. For most men this depends upon the willingness of some one to buy their wares or their labor, i.e. upon patronage. The Wealthy, then, who, as luxurious idlers, spend money and make trade, or, as captains of industry and lords of enterprise, employ the labor and organize the prosperity of kingdoms, will never be without great social power. From the dependence of the working many upon the moneyed few flows a patronal authority which sends its tinge far into law, religion, morals, and policy. For when any class of men play the part of earthly Providence to the multitude, their views as to what ought to be praised or blamed, commanded or forbidden, cannot but affect the character of social control.

The State is, in theory at least, a channel and not a source of control. It is supposed to be a device by which social power is collected, transmitted, and applied *so as to do work*. But, as a matter of fact, the state, when it becomes paternal and develops on the administrative side, is able in a measure to guide the society it professes to obey. With its hierarchy of officials and its army of functionaries, the state gets a glamour of its own, and becomes an independent centre of social power. And here again we can see that such a concentration of influence is a measure of man's need and trust. For the prestige of officialdom is not wholly a matter of numbers and pay. The more the state helps the citizen when he cannot help himself, protecting him from disease, foes, criminals, rivals abroad and monopolists at home, the more he will look to it for guidance. While, conversely, the more he uses it merely as a convenient alternative to self-help or free association, the less will he accept its lead.

Another radiant point in society is the Mandarinate, or the body of scholarly or learned men who have in some formal way been tested, accredited, and labelled. Such are the mandarins of China, the pundits of India, the *Gelehrte* of Germany, the academicians and professors in France, the clergy of nonsacerdotal bodies like the Reformed churches, and the rabbis of the Jewish congregations. The mandarinate ought to include the wisest and best in society; but the false worth that attaches to purely conventional learning, and the sifting and promoting of the learned by tests that are artificial and futile, are likely to prevent it.

The Élite, or those distinguished by ideas and talent, are the natural leaders of society, inasmuch as their ascendency depends on nothing false or factitious. Usually they appear as a small knot of persons who, united by allegiance to some group of ideas, are able to persuade the majority without allowing themselves, in turn, to be infected by vulgar prejudices. The Greek Philosophers, the Stoics, the Fathers, the Schoolmen, the Humanists, the Reformers, the Pietists, the Encyclopedists, the Liberals, are examples of an active leaven able to leaven the whole lump.

Finally, there is the Genius, who, as founder of religion, prophet, reformer, or artist, is able to build up a vast personal authority and sway the multitude at pleasure. Society can dispense with the guidance of the Élite and the genius only when the way is straight and the path is clear. A people creeping gradually across a vast empty land, as we Americans have been doing this century, may safely belittle leadership and deify the spirit of self-reliance. But when population thickens, interests clash, and the difficult problems of mutual adjustment become pressing, it is foolish and dangerous not to follow the lead of superior men.

The impulses streaming out from each of the eight principal centres we have described do not, of course, meet a perfectly yielding mass. The power of the Few to take the role of social cerebrum depends entirely upon how far the Many capitulate to it. The radiation of control from the elders is limited by the reaction of the young men, that from the priests is limited by the reaction of the laity, that from the bureaucracy is limited by the reaction of the citizens, that from the élite is limited by the reaction of the vulgar. When the energy of the resistance comes to equal that of the impulses, the class ceases to be a controlling centre and loses itself in the social mass.

What keeps social commands from multiplying and choking up life, as the rank growth of swamp weed chokes up water-courses, is, of course, the resistance of the individual. Naturally a man prefers to do as he pleases, and not as society pleases to have him do. The more, then, that social power dwells in the mass of persons whose necks are galled by social requirement, the more the yoke of the law will be lightened. On the other hand, the more distinct those who apply social pressure from those who must bear it, the more likely is regulation to be laid on lavishly in obedience to some class ideal. Hence we arrive at the law that *the volume of social requirement will be greater when social power is concentrated than when it is diffused.*

When the laws, standards, and ideals a man is required to conform to, spring up among the plain people, they will be ahead of the community, but not very far ahead. But when they originate with the few, they may be very far in advance of the community and so hurrying it forward, or they may be far in the rear and hence holding it back. It is a well-known fact that we never find a legal or moral code pitched high above the natural inclination of a people without signs of minority domination. It is safe, then, to frame the law, *the greater the ascendency of the few, the more possible is it for social control to affect the course of the social movement.*

Social control takes the tinge of the source from which it springs. When the reverend seniors monopolize power, much will be made of filial respect and obedience, infanticide will be a small offence, while parricide will be punished with horrible torments. Let the priests get the upper hand, and chastity, celibacy, humility, unquestioning belief, and scrupulous observance will be the leading virtues. The ascendency of the military caste shifts the accent to obedience, loyalty, pugnacity, and sensitiveness to personal honor. When the moneyed man holds the baton, we hear much of industriousness, thrift, sobriety, probity, and civility. The mandarins and *literati* have no moral programme of their own, but they are sure to exalt reverence for order, precedent, and rank.

The élite, whatever ideal they champion, will be sure to commend the ordering of one's life according to ideas and principles, rather than according to precedent and tradition. For only by fostering the radical spirit can they hope to lead men into untrodden paths. We may, then, lay it down as a law that *the chararacter of social requirement changes with every shifting of social power.*

Classes differ in readiness to twist social control to their own advantage. Elders, élite, or genius have rarely abused their social power. But ecclesiasticism claims exemptions and privileges for the clergy, makes the word of the priest binding even when he is living in open sin, and grants for money indulgence to commit the most horrible crimes. When the fighting caste guides social opinion, it is permissible to mulct the husbandman and the merchant, and to condone the violence and sensuality of the men of the camp. Under the ascendency of the rich and leisured, property becomes more sacred than person, moral standards vary with pecuniary status, and it is felt that "God will think twice before He damns a person of quality." In general, *the more distinct, knit together, and self-conscious the influential minority, the more likely is social control to be colored with class selfishness.*

. . .

The System of Social Control

In respect to their fundamental character, it is possible to divide most of the supports of order into two groups. Such instruments of control as public opinion, suggestion, personal ideal, social religion, art, and social valuation draw much of their strength from the primal moral feelings. They take their shape from sentiment rather than utility. They control men in many things which have little to do with the welfare of society regarded as a corporation. They are aimed to realize not merely a social order but what one might term a *moral* order. These we may call *ethical.*

On the other hand, law, belief, ceremony, education, and illusion need not spring from ethical feelings at all. They are frequently the means deliberately chosen in order to reach certain ends. They are likely to come under the control of the organized few, and be used, whether for the corporate benefit or for class benefit, as the tools of policy. They may be termed *political,* using the word "political" in its original sense of "pertaining to policy."

Now, the prominence of the one group or the other in the regulative scheme depends upon the constitution of the society. The *political* instruments operating through prejudice or fear will be preferred:—

1. In proportion as the population elements to be held together are antipathetic and jarring.

2. In proportion to the subordination of the individual will and welfare by the scheme of control.

3. In proportion as the social constitution stereotypes differences of status.

4. In proportion as the differences in economic condition and opportunity it consecrates are great and cumulative.

5. In proportion as the parasitic relation is maintained between races, classes, or sexes.

In confirmation of these statements, we have but to recall that the chief influences which history recognizes as stiffening State, Church, Hierarchy, Tradition, are conquest, caste, slavery, serfdom, gross inequalities of wealth, military discipline, paternal regimentation, and race antipathies within the bosom of the group. The disappearance of any one of these conditions permits a mellowing and liberalizing of social control.

On the other hand the *ethical* instruments, being more mild, enlightening, and suasive, will be preferred:—

1. In proportion as the population is homogeneous in race.

2. In proportion as its culture is uniform and diffused.

3. In proportion as the social contacts between the elements in the population are many and amicable.

4. In proportion as the total burden of requirement laid upon the individual is light.

5. In proportion as the social constitution does not consecrate distinctions of status or the parasitic relation, but conforms to common elementary notions of justice.

In confirmation of these propositions, we have but to remember that the mild, democratic regime is now recognized as presupposing a homogeneous and enlightened population, free social intercourse, minimum interference with the individual, sanctity of the person, and equality before the law. When any of these conditions fail, the democratic forms soon become farcical.

Again, the instruments of control may be distinguished in respect to the functions that devolve upon them. There is a tendency to assign to each form of control that work for which it is best fitted. Law represses that undesirable conduct which is at once important and capable of clear definition. Central positive qualities—courage or veracity in man, chastity in woman—are taken in charge by the sense of honor or self-respect. The supernatural sanction is ordinarily reserved for those acts and abstinences requiring the utmost backing. Religion mounts guard over the ancient, unvarying fundamentals of group life, but takes little note of the temporary adjustments required from time to time. The taking of life or property, adultery, unfilial conduct, and false swearing encounter its full force; but not adulteration, stock gambling, or corporation frauds. In its code, as well as in its ritual and creed, religion betrays its archaic character.

In morals as well as in microscopes there is provided a major and a minor adjusting apparatus. In adaptability public opinion stands at one end of a series of which religion constitutes the other extreme. Connected with this there is a gradation in the nature of the sanction. Public opinion bans many things not unlawful, law may require much more than self-respect, and self-respect may be wounded by that which is not regarded as sinful. But the universality of the sanction widens as the scope of prohibition narrows. In the first case the offender encounters the public here and now, in the second the crystallized disapproval of society, in the third the opinion of generations of men who have conspired to frame a standard or ideal, and in the last case the frown of the Ruler of the Universe.

The champions of each detail of regulation strive, therefore, to get all these successive sanctions behind their pet commandments. The opponents of drinking, dancing, divorce, usury, horse racing, duelling, speculation, or prize-fighting strive to make these practices first blameworthy, then unlawful, then shameful, and finally sinful. But this massing of sanctions very naturally stirs up resistance. The attempt to get God against a new vice, such as liquor selling, always encounters fierce opposition from those who find themselves suddenly deprived of the odor of sanctity. New moral tests, like new party tests or new denominational tests, endanger ground already won, and so imperil the sanctions for the cardinal virtues. It is not well, therefore, to associate loss of honor with white lies or the Divine Displeasure with card playing. Sympathy, religious sentiment, self-respect, sense of duty, fear, regard for public opinion, enlightened self-interest,—each of these motives has its due place and task and no one motive should be overworked.

32

EDWIN H. SUTHERLAND

White-Collar Criminality

Edwin Hardin Sutherland (1883–1950) was probably the major single force in shaping the current direction of American criminology.[1] *The work of Sutherland and his students*[2] *represents the dominant orientation in criminology and has centered (attempts at modification and elaboration continue) largely upon his* theory of differential association *as an explanation for criminality. This theory essentially states that persons become criminals or delinquents through intimate association with others who hold social definitions favorable to the violation of laws. In its simplest sense, the theory maintains that association with criminals breeds criminality. Sutherland's work was largely a reaction against the then common multiple-factor theory of criminality (in which crime is considered to be the result of the addition of a variety of concrete circumstances). His theory of differential association has since been quite modified by his students and others.*[3]

In testing his theory, Sutherland tried to incorporate data from the crimes of businessmen and corporations, crimes he felt had not been adequately explained by any other theory. This concern with white-collar *criminality marked an important departure in criminology and represents an important focus of attention today.*[4]

Bibliographical Notes

1. *Sutherland's principal works include:* Principles of Criminology *(1924);* Twenty Thousand Homeless Men: A Study of Unemployed Men in the Chicago Shelters, *with Harvey J. Locke (1936);* The Professional Thief *(1937); and* White Collar Crime *(1949). His articles*

Reprinted from the *American Sociological Review,* 5 (1940), pp. 1–12 by permission of the American Sociological Association.

are available in: Albert K. Cohen, et al., *(eds.),* The Sutherland Papers *(Bloomington: Indiana University Press, 1956).*

2. *These include* D. R. *Cressey,* A. K. *Cohen, and* L. E. *Ohlin, all prominent figures in contemporary criminology.*

3. *See, for example, Donald* R. *Cressey,* Delinquency, Crime and Differential Association *(The Hague: Nijhoff, 1964); Daniel Glaser, "Differential Association and Criminological Prediction,"* Social Problems, 8 *(1960), 6–14; James F. Short, Jr., "Differential Association as a Hypothesis: Problems of Empirical Testing,"* Social Problems, 8 *(1960), 14–25; Henry D. McKay, "Differential Association and Crime Prevention: Problems of Utilization,"* Social Problems, 8 *(1960), 25–37; and Sheldon Glueck, "Theory and Fact in Criminology,"* British Journal of Delinquency, 7 *(1956), 92–109.*

4. *For a representative selection of work on white-collar criminality, see: Gilbert Geis (ed.),* White Collar Criminal: The Offender in Business and the Professions *(New York: Atherton, 1968).*

This paper[1] is concerned with crime in relation to business. The economists are well acquainted with business methods but not accustomed to consider them from the point of view of crime; many sociologists are well acquainted with crime but not accustomed to consider it as expressed in business. This paper is an attempt to integrate these two bodies of knowledge. More accurately stated, it is a comparison of crime in the upper or white-collar class, composed of respectable or at least respected business and professional men, and crime in the lower class, composed of persons of low socioeconomic status. This comparison is made for the purpose of developing the theories of criminal behavior, not for the purpose of muckraking or of reforming anything except criminology.

The criminal statistics show unequivocally that crime, *as popularly conceived and officially measured,* has a high incidence in the lower class and a low incidence in the upper class; less than two percent of the persons committed to prisons in a year belong to the upper class. These statistics refer to criminals handled by the police, the criminal and juvenile courts, and the prisons, and to such crimes as murder, assault, burglary, robbery, larceny, sex offenses, and drunkenness, but exclude traffic violations.

The criminologists have used the case histories and criminal statistics derived from these agencies of criminal justice as their principal data. From them, they have derived general theories of criminal behavior. These theories are that, since crime is concentrated in the lower class, it is caused by poverty or by personal and social characteristics believed to be associated statistically with poverty, including feeblemindedness, psychopathic deviations, slum neighborhoods, and "deteriorated" families. This statement, of course, does not do justice to the qualifications and variations in the conventional theories of criminal behavior, but it presents correctly their central tendency.

The thesis of this paper is that the conception and explanations of crime which have just been described are misleading and incorrect, that crime is in fact not closely correlated with poverty or with the psychopathic and sociopathic conditions associated with poverty, and that an adequate explanation of criminal behavior must proceed along quite different lines. The conventional explanations are invalid principally because they are derived from biased samples. The samples are biased in that they have not included vast areas of criminal behavior of persons not in the lower class. One of these neglected areas is the criminal behavior of business and professional men, which will be analyzed in this paper.

The "robber barons" of the last half of the nineteenth century were white-collar criminals, as practically everyone now agrees. Their attitudes are illustrated by these statements: Colonel Vanderbilt asked, "You don't suppose you can run a railroad in accordance with the statutes, do you?" A. B. Stickney, a railroad president, said to sixteen other railroad presidents in the home of J. P. Morgan in 1890, "I have the utmost respect for you gentlemen, individually, but as railroad presidents I wouldn't trust you with my watch out of my sight." Charles Francis Adams said, "The difficulty in railroad management . . . lies in the covetousness, want of good faith, and low moral tone of railway managers, in the complete absence of any high standard of commercial honesty."

The present-day white-collar criminals, who are more suave and deceptive than the "robber barons," are represented by Krueger, Stavisky, Whitney, Mitchell, Foshay, Insull, the Van Sweringens, Musica-Coster, Fall, Sinclair, and many other merchant princes and captains of finance and industry, and by a host of lesser followers. Their criminality has been demonstrated again and again in the investigations of land offices, railways, insurance, munitions, banking, public utilities, stock exchanges, the oil industry, real estate, reorganization committees, receiverships, bankruptcies, and politics. Individual cases of such criminality are reported frequently, and in many periods more important crime news may be found on the financial pages of newspapers than on the front pages. White-collar criminality is found in every occupation, as can be discovered readily in casual conversation with a representative of an occupation by asking him, "What crooked practices are found in your occupation?"

White-collar criminality in business is expressed most frequently in the form of misrepresentation in financial statements of corporations, manipulation in the stock exchange, commercial bribery, bribery of public officials directly or indirectly in order to secure favorable contracts and legislation, misrepresentation in advertising and salesmanship, embezzlement and misapplication of funds, short weights and measures and misgrading of commodities, tax frauds, misapplication of funds in receiverships and bankruptcies. These are what Al Capone called "the legitimate rackets." These and many others are found in abundance in the business world.

In the medical profession, which is here used as an example because it is probably less criminalistic than some other professions, are found illegal sale of alcohol and narcotics, abortion, illegal services to underworld criminals, fraudulent reports and testimony in accident cases, extreme cases of unnecessary treatment, fake specialists, restriction of competition, and fee-splitting. Fee-splitting is a violation of a specific law in many states and a violation of the conditions of admission to the practice of medicine in all. The physician who participates in fee-splitting tends to send his patients to the surgeon who will give him the largest fee rather than to the surgeon who will do the best work. It has been reported that two thirds of the surgeons in New York City split fees, and that more than one half of the physicians in a central western city who answered a questionnaire on this point favored fee-splitting.

These varied types of white-collar crimes in business and the professions consist principally of violation of delegated or implied trust, and many of them can be reduced to two categories: misrepresentation of asset values and duplicity in the manipulation of power. The first is approximately the same as fraud or swindling; the second is similar to the double-cross. The latter is illustrated by the corporation director who, acting on inside information, purchases land which the corporation will need and sells it at a fantastic profit to his corporation. The principle of this duplicity is that the offender holds two antagonistic positions, one of which is a position of trust, which is violated, generally by misapplication of funds, in the interest of the other position. A football coach, permitted to referee a game in which his own team was playing, would illustrate this antagonism of positions. Such situations cannot be completely avoided in a complicated business structure, but many concerns make a practice of assuming such antagonistic functions and regularly violating the trust thus delegated to them. When compelled by law to make a separation of their functions, they make a nominal separation and continue by subterfuge to maintain the two positions.

An accurate statistical comparison of the crimes of the two classes is not available. The most extensive evidence regarding the nature and prevalence of white-collar criminality is found in the reports of the larger investigations to which reference was made. Because of its scattered character, that evidence is assumed rather than summarized here. A few statements will be presented, as illustrations rather than as proof of the prevalence of this criminality.

The Federal Trade Commission in 1920 reported that commercial bribery was a prevalent and common practice in many industries. In certain chain stores, the net shortage in weights was sufficient to pay 3.4 percent on the investment in those commodities. Of the cans of ether sold to the Army in 1923–1925, 70 percent were rejected because of impurities. In Indiana, during the summer of 1934, 40 percent of the ice cream samples tested in a routine manner by the Division of Public Health were in violation of law. The Comptroller of the Currency in 1908 reported that violations of law were found in 75 percent of the banks examined in a three months' period. Lie detector tests of all employees in several Chicago banks, supported in almost all cases by confessions, showed that 20 percent of them had stolen bank property. A public accountant estimated, in the period prior to the Securities and Exchange Commission, that 80 percent of the financial statements of corporations were misleading. James M. Beck said, "Diogenes would have been hard put to it to find an honest man in the Wall Street which I knew as a corporation lawyer" (in 1916).

White-collar criminality in politics, which is generally recognized as fairly prevalent, has been used by some as a rough gauge by which to measure white-collar criminality in business. James A. Farley said, "The standards of conduct are as high among officeholders and politicians as they are in commercial life," and Cermak, while mayor of Chicago, said, "There is less graft in politics than in business." John Flynn wrote, "The average politician is the merest amateur in the gentle art of graft, compared with his brother in the field of business." And Walter Lippmann wrote, "Poor as they are, the standards of public life are so much more social than those of business that financiers who enter politics regard themselves as philanthropists."

These statements obviously do not give a precise measurement of the relative criminality of the white-collar class, but they are adequate evidence that crime is not so highly concentrated in the lower class as the usual statistics indicate. Also, these statements obviously do not mean that every business and professional man is a criminal, just as the usual theories do not mean that every man in the lower class is a criminal. On the other hand, the preceding statements refer in many cases to the leading corporations in America and are not restricted to the disreputable business and professional men who are called quacks, ambulance chasers, bucket-shop operators, dead-beats, and fly-by-night swindlers.[2]

The financial cost of white-collar crime is probably several times as great as the financial cost of all the crimes which are customarily regarded as the "crime problem." An officer of a chain grocery store in one year embezzled $600,000, which was six times as much as the annual losses from five hundred burglaries and robberies of the stores in that chain. Public enemies numbered one to six secured $130,000 by burglary and robbery in 1938, while the sum stolen by Krueger is estimated at $250,000,000, or nearly two thousand times as much. *The New York Times* in 1931 reported four cases of embezzlement in the United States with a loss of more than a million dollars each and a combined loss of nine million dollars. Although a million-dollar burglar or robber is practically unheard of, these million-dollar embezzlers are small-fry among white-collar criminals. The estimated loss to investors in one investment trust from 1929 to 1935 was $580,000,000, due primarily to the fact that 75 percent of the values in the portfolio were in securities of affiliated companies, although it advertised the importance of diversification in investments and its expert services in selecting safe securities. In Chicago, the claim was made six years ago that householders had lost $54,000,000 in two years during the administration of a city sealer who granted immunity from inspection to stores which provided Christmas baskets for his constituents.

The financial loss from white-collar crime, great as it is, is less important than the damage to social relations. White-collar crimes violate trust and therefore create distrust, which lowers social morale and produces social disorganization on a large scale. Other crimes produce relatively little effect on social institutions or social organization.

White-collar crime is real crime. It is not ordinarily called crime, and calling it by this name does not make it worse, just as refraining from calling it crime does not make it better than it otherwise would be. It is called crime here in order to bring it within the scope of criminology, which is justified because it is in violation of the criminal law. The crucial question in this analysis is the criterion of violation of the criminal law. Conviction in the criminal court, which is sometimes suggested as the criterion, is not adequate because a large proportion of those who commit crimes are not convicted in criminal courts. This criterion, therefore, needs to be supplemented. When it is supplemented, the criterion of the crimes of one class must be kept consistent in general terms with the criterion of the crimes of the other class. The definition should not be the spirit of the law for white-collar crimes and the letter of the law for other crimes, or in other respects be more liberal for one class than for the other. Since this discussion is concerned with the conventional theories of the criminologists, the criterion of white-collar crime must be justified in terms of the procedures of those criminologists in dealing with other crimes. The criterion of white-collar crimes, as here proposed, supplements convictions in the criminal courts in four respects, in each of which the extension is justified because the criminologists who present the conventional theories of criminal behavior make the same extension in principle.

First, other agencies than the criminal court must be included, for the criminal court is not the only agency which makes official decisions regarding violations of the criminal law. The juvenile court, dealing largely with offenses of the children of the poor, in many states is not under the criminal jurisdiction. The criminologists have made much use of case histories and statistics of juvenile delinquents in constructing their theories of criminal behavior. This justifies the inclusion of agencies other than the criminal court which deal with white-collar offenses. The most important of these agencies are the administrative boards, bureaus, or commissions, and much of their work, although certainly not all, consists of cases which are in violation of the criminal law. The Federal Trade Commission recently ordered several automobile companies to stop advertising their interest rate on installment purchases as 6 percent, since it was actually 11½ percent. Also it filed complaint against *Good Housekeeping*, one of the Hearst publications, charging that its seals led the public to believe that all products bearing those seals had been tested in their laboratories, which was contrary to fact. Each of these involves a charge of dishonesty, which might have been tried in a criminal court as fraud. A large proportion of the cases before these boards should be included in the data of the criminologists. Failure to do so is a principal reason for the bias in their samples and the errors in their generalizations.

Second, for both classes, behavior which would have a reasonable expectancy of conviction if tried in a criminal court or substitute agency should be defined as criminal. In this respect, convictability rather than actual conviction should be the criterion of criminality. The criminologists would not hesitate to accept as data a verified case history of a person who was a criminal but had never been convicted. Similarly, it is justifiable to include white-collar criminals who have not been convicted, provided reliable evidence is available. Evidence regarding such cases appears in many civil suits, such as stockholders' suits and patent-infringement suits. These cases might have been referred to the criminal court but they were referred to the civil court because the injured party was more interested in securing damages than in seeing punishment inflicted. This also happens in embezzlement cases, regarding which surety companies have much evidence. In a short consecutive series of embezzlements known to a surety company, 90 percent were not prosecuted because prosecution would interfere with restitution or salvage. The evidence in cases of embezzlement is generally conclusive, and would probably have been sufficient to justify conviction in all of the cases in this series.

Third, behavior should be defined as criminal if conviction is avoided merely because of pressure which is brought to bear on the court or substitute agency. Gangsters and racketeers have been relatively immune in many cities because of their pressure on prospective witnesses and public officials, and professional thieves, such as pickpockets and confidence men who do not use strong-arm methods, are even more frequently immune. The conventional criminologists do not hesitate to include the life histories of such criminals as data, because they understand the generic relation of the pressures to the failure to convict. Similarly, white-collar criminals are relatively immune because of the class bias of the courts and the power of their class to influence the implementation and administration of the law. This class bias affects not merely present-day courts but to a much greater degree affected the earlier courts which established the precedents and rules of procedure of the present-day courts. Consequently, it is justifiable to interpret the actual or potential failures of conviction in the light of known facts regarding the pressures brought to bear on the agencies which deal with offenders.

Fourth, persons who are accessory to a crime should be included among white-collar criminals as they are among other criminals. When the Federal Bureau of Investigation deals with a case of kidnapping, it is not content with catching the offenders who carried away the victim;

they may catch and the court may convict twenty-five other persons who assisted by secreting the victim, negotiating the ransom, or putting the ransom money into circulation. On the other hand, the prosecution of white-collar criminals frequently stops with one offender. Political graft almost always involves collusion between politicians and business men but prosecutions are generally limited to the politicians. Judge Manton was found guilty of accepting $664,000 in bribes, but the six or eight important commercial concerns that paid the bribes have not been prosecuted. Pendergast, the late boss of Kansas City, was convicted for failure to report as a part of his income $315,000 received in bribes from insurance companies but the insurance companies which paid the bribes have not been prosecuted. In an investigation of an embezzlement by the president of a bank, at least a dozen other violations of law which were related to this embezzlement and involved most of the other officers of the bank and the officers of the clearing house, were discovered but none of the others was prosecuted.

This analysis of the criterion of white-collar criminality results in the conclusion that a description of white-collar criminality in general terms will be also a description of the criminality of the lower class. The respects in which the crimes of the two classes differ are the incidentals rather than the essentials of criminality. They differ principally in the implementation of the criminal laws which apply to them. The crimes of the lower class are handled by policemen, prosecutors, and judges, with penal sanctions in the form of fines, imprisonment, and death. The crimes of the upper class either result in no official action at all, or result in suits for damages in civil courts, or are handled by inspectors, and by administrative boards or commissions, with penal sanctions in the form of warnings, orders to cease and desist, occasionally the loss of a license, and only in extreme cases by fines or prison sentences. Thus, the white-collar criminals are segregated administratively from other criminals, and largely as a consequence of this are not regarded as real criminals by themselves, the general public, or the criminologists.

This difference in the implementation of the criminal law is due principally to the difference in the social position of the two types of offenders. Judge Woodward, when imposing sentence upon the officials of the H. O. Stone and Company, bankrupt real estate firm in Chicago, who had been convicted in 1933 of the use of the mails to defraud, said to them, "You are men of affairs, of experience, of refinement and culture, of excellent reputation and standing in the business and social world." That statement might be used as a general characterization of white-collar criminals for they are oriented basically to legitimate and respectable careers. Because of their social status they have a loud voice in determining what goes into the statutes and how the criminal law as it affects themselves is implemented and administered. This may be illustrated from the Pure Food and Drug Law. Between 1879 and 1906, 140 pure food and drug bills were presented in Congress and all failed because of the importance of the persons who would be affected. It took a highly dramatic performance by Dr. Wiley in 1906 to induce Congress to enact the law. That law, however, did not create a new crime, just as the federal Lindbergh kidnapping law did not create a new crime; it merely provided a more efficient implementation of a principle which had been formulated previously in state laws. When an amendment to this law, which would bring within the scope of its agents fraudulent statements made over the radio or in the press, was presented to Congress, the publishers and advertisers organized support and sent a lobby to Washington which successfully fought the amendment principally under the slogans of "freedom of the press" and "dangers of bureaucracy." This proposed amendment, also, would not have created a new crime, for the state laws already prohibited fraudulent statements over the radio or in the press; it would have implemented the law so it could have been enforced. Finally, the Administration has not been able to enforce the law as it has desired because of the pressures by the offenders against the law, sometimes brought to bear through the head of the Department of Agriculture, sometimes through congressmen who threaten cuts in the appropriation, and sometimes by others. The statement of Daniel Drew, a pious old fraud, describes the criminal law with some accuracy, "Law is like a cobweb; it's made for flies and the smaller kinds of insects, so to speak, but lets the big bumblebees break through. When technicalities of the law stood in my way, I have always been able to brush them aside easy as anything."

The preceding analysis should be regarded neither as an assertion that all efforts to influence legislation and its administration are reprehensible nor as a particularistic interpretation of the criminal law. It means only that the upper class has greater influence in moulding the criminal law and its administration to its own interests than does the lower class. The privileged position of white-collar criminals before the law results to a slight extent from bribery and political pressures, principally from the respect in which they are held and without special effort on their part. The most powerful group in medieval society secured relative immunity by "benefit of clergy," and now our most powerful groups secure relative immunity by "benefit of business or profession."

In contrast with the power of the white-collar criminals is the weakness of their victims. Consumers, investors, and stockholders are unorganized, lack technical knowledge, and cannot protect themselves. Daniel Drew, after taking a large sum of money by sharp practice from Vanderbilt in the Erie deal, concluded that it was a mistake to take money from a powerful man on the same level as himself and declared that in the future he would confine his efforts to outsiders, scattered all over the country, who wouldn't be able to organize and fight back. White-collar criminality flourishes at points where powerful business and professional men come in contact with persons who are weak. In this respect, it is similar to stealing candy from a baby. Many of the crimes of the lower class, on the other hand, are committed against persons of wealth and power in the form of burglary and robbery. Because of this difference in the comparative power of the victims, the white-collar criminals enjoy relative immunity.

Embezzlement is an interesting exception to white-collar criminality in this respect. Embezzlement is usually theft from an employer by an employee, and the employee is less capable of manipulating social and legal forces in his own interest than is the employer. As might have been expected, the laws regarding embezzlement were formulated long before laws for the protection of investors and consumers.

The theory that criminal behavior in general is due either to poverty or to the psychopathic and sociopathic conditions associated with poverty can now be shown to be invalid for three reasons. First, the generalization is based on a biased sample which omits almost entirely the behavior of white-collar criminals. The criminologists have restricted their data, for reasons of convenience and ignorance rather than of principle, largely to cases dealt with in criminal courts and juvenile courts, and these agencies are used principally for criminals from the lower economic strata. Consequently, their data are grossly biased from the point of view of the economic status of criminals and their generalization that criminality is closely associated with poverty is not justified.

Second, the generalization that criminality is closely associated with poverty obviously does not apply to white-collar criminals. With a small number of exceptions, they are not in poverty, were not reared in slums or badly deteriorated families, and are not feebleminded or psychopathic. They were seldom problem children in their earlier years and did not appear in juvenile courts of child guidance clinics. The proposition, derived from the data used by the conventional criminologists, that "the criminal of today was the problem child of yesterday" is seldom true of white-collar criminals. The idea that the causes of criminality are to be found almost exclusively in childhood similarly is fallacious. Even if poverty is extended to include the economic stresses which afflict business in a period of depression, it is not closely correlated with white-collar criminality. Probably at no time within fifty years have white-collar crimes in the field of investments and of corporate management been so extensive as during the boom period of the twenties.

Third, the conventional theories do not even explain lower class criminality. The sociopathic and psychopathic factors which have been emphasized doubtless have something to do with crime causation, but these factors have not been related to a general process which is found both in white-collar criminality and lower class criminality and therefore they do not explain the criminality of either class. They may explain the manner or method of crime—why lower class criminals commit burglary or robbery rather than false pretenses.

In view of these defects in the conventional theories, an hypothesis that will explain both white-collar criminality and lower class criminality is needed. For reasons of economy, simplicity, and logic, the hypothesis should apply to both classes, for this will make possible the analysis of causal factors freed from the encumbrances of the administrative devices which have led criminologists astray. Shaw and McKay and others, working exclusively in the field of lower class crime, have found the conventional theories inadequate to account for variations within the data of lower class crime and from that point of view have been working toward an explanation of crime in terms of a more general social process. Such efforts will be greatly aided by the procedure which has been described.

The hypothesis which is here suggested as a substitute for the conventional theories is that white-collar criminality, just as other systematic criminality, is learned; that it is learned in direct or indirect association with those who already practice the behavior; and that those who learn this criminal behavior are segregated from frequent and intimate contacts with law-abiding behavior. Whether a person becomes a criminal or not is determined largely by the comparative frequency and intimacy of his contacts with the two types of behavior. This may be called the process of differential association. It is a genetic explanation both of white-collar criminality and lower class criminality. Those who become white-collar criminals generally start their careers in good neighborhoods and good homes, graduate from colleges with some idealism, and with little selection on their part, get into particular business situations in which criminality is practically a folkway and are inducted into that system of behavior just as into any other folkway. The lower class criminals generally start their careers in deteriorated neighborhoods and families, find delinquents at hand from whom they acquire the attitudes toward, and techniques of, crime through association with delinquents and in partial segregation from law-abiding people. The essentials of the process are the same for the two classes of criminals. This is not entirely a process of assimilation, for inventions are frequently made, perhaps more frequently in white-collar crime than in lower class crime. The inventive geniuses for the lower class criminals are generally professional criminals, while the inventive geniuses for many kinds of white-collar crime are generally lawyers.

A second general process is social disorganization in the community. Differential association culminates in crime because the community is not organized solidly against that behavior. The law is pressing in one direction, and other forces are pressing in the opposite direction. In business, the "rules of the game" conflict with the legal rules. A business man who wants to obey the law is driven by his competitors to adopt their methods. This is well illustrated by the persistence of commercial bribery in spite of the strenuous efforts of business organizations to eliminate it. Groups and individuals are individuated; they are more concerned with their specialized group or individual interests than with the larger welfare. Consequently, it is not possible for the community to present a solid front in opposition to crime. The Better Business Bureaus and Crime Commissions, composed of business and professional men, attack burglary, robbery, and cheap swindles, but overlook the crimes of their own members. The forces which impinge on the lower class are similarly in conflict. Social disorganization affects the two classes in similar ways.

I have presented a brief and general description of white-collar criminality on a framework of argument regarding theories of criminal behavior. That argument, stripped of the description, may be stated in the following propositions:

1. White-collar criminality is real criminality, being in all cases in violation of the criminal law.

2. White-collar criminality differs from lower class criminality principally in an implementation of the criminal law which segregates white-collar criminals administratively from other criminals.

3. The theories of the criminologists that crime is due to poverty or to psychopathic and sociopathic conditions statistically associated with

poverty are invalid because, first, they are derived from samples which are grossly biased with respect to socioeconomic status; second, they do not apply to the white-collar criminals; and third, they do not even explain the criminality of the lower class, since the factors are not related to a general process characteristic of all criminality.

4. A theory of criminal behavior which will explain both white-collar criminality and lower class criminality is needed.

5. An hypothesis of this nature is suggested in terms of differential association and social disorganization.

NOTES

1. Thirty-fourth Annual Presidential Address delivered at Philadelphia, Pa., Dec. 27, 1939 in joint meeting with the American Economic Society (its Fifty-second) at which President Jacob Viner spoke on the relations of economic theory to the formulation of public policy.
2. Perhaps it should be repeated that "white-collar" (upper) and "lower" classes merely designate persons of high and low socioeconomic status. Income and amount of money involved in the crime are not the sole criteria. Many persons of "low" socioeconomic status are "white-collar" criminals in the sense that they are well-dressed, well-educated, and have high incomes, but "white-collar" as used in this paper means "respected," "socially accepted and approved," "looked up to." Some people in this class may not be well-dressed or well-educated, nor have high incomes, although the "upper" usually exceed the "lower" classes in these respects as well as in social status.

33

EVERETT V. STONEQUIST

On the Marginal Man

Everett Verner Stonequist (1901–) developed a concept which made a deep imprint on social psychologists of the period, especially those concerned with the special problems of immigrants and those who were members of subcultures in our society. This was the concept of the marginal man, *the "stranger" who is largely freed from sources of social control through his mobility but who is vulnerable to internal uncertainties and external stigma.*[1] *The concept of the* marginal man *has been especially useful as an explanation of social deviance, but has recently undergone reappraisals and modifications.*[2]

Bibliographical Notes

1. The concept was first introduced into the literature by Robert E. *Park in his article "Human Migration and the Marginal Man,"* American Journal of Sociology, 33 *(1928), 881–893. However, this paper only laid the groundwork for the fuller development of the term by Park's student, Everett Stonequist. Stonequist first presented his elaboration in his article "The Problem of the Marginal Man,"* American Journal of Sociology, 41 *(1936), 1–12. This was followed by his book* The Marginal Man *(New York: Charles Scribner's Sons, 1937).*

2. Some of these include: M. M. *Goldberg, "A Qualification of the Marginal Man Theory,"* American Sociological Review, 6 *(1942), 52–58; J. S. Slotkin, "The Status of the Marginal Man,"* Sociology and Social Research, 28 *(1943), 47–53; Arnold W. Green, "A Re-examination of the Marginal Man Concept,"* Social Forces, 26 *(1947), 167–*

Reprinted from Everett V. Stonequist, *The Marginal Man: A Study in Personality and Culture Conflict* (New York: Charles Scribner's Sons, 1937), pp. 210–222, by permission of Everett V. Stonequist.

171; and Alan C. Kerckhoff, "Marginal Status and Marginal Personality," Social Forces, 34 (*1955*), *48–55.*

The Concept

The personality problem which forms the theme of this study has often been noted and discussed in its separate and concrete aspects. The anomalous position and mental tensions of the racial hybrid have attracted much attention. The character of the Jew has interested Jews as well as Gentiles. Immigrants, as also the children of immigrants, have naturally received much consideration from those who are concerned about assimilation. And the conflicts of the êthos of East and West have caused more than one Kipling to burst into poetry and prophecy.

Out of common-sense observation and everyday relations come identifying names and epithets. Even words of respectability acquire questionable connotations because they are tinctured with attitudes of prejudice and associated with lowliness of status. As a consequence the term "Eurasian" is changed to "Anglo-Indian"; the Negro prefers to be called "African" or "Coloured"; and sometimes the immigrant hesitates about referring to himself as such. In particular situations special terms have arisen which point directly to the dual or marginal character: "Europeanized African," "Anglicised Indian," "half-caste," "métis," "déraciné," "parvenu," "allrightnick," "denationalized," "*haolefied,*" "hyphenated citizen," etc. Occasionally a writer makes a comparison between two of them.

By bringing such scattered terms under one embracing concept—the marginal man—comparison and analysis are furthered. Elements common to all may be abstracted, and the major outlines of the situation and personality defined. The essential and the universal become separable from the accidental and unique; the deviations or sub-types more accurately understood in terms of the special conditions. Thus a scientific conception can be developed. Dewey's statement with reference to the rôle of scientific conceptions is pertinent: "Scientific conceptions are not a revelation of prior and independent reality. They are a system of hypotheses worked out under conditions of definite test, by means of which our intellectual and practical traffic with nature is rendered freer, more secure and more significant." [1]

The Biological Factor

The assumption of this study has been that the marginal personality is a function of social conditions. An appeal to facts seems to support this assumption. Thus the marginal type appears in every major race, among unmixed groups as well as among racial hybrids, and in almost every culture. The common factor is not biological but a certain social situation. The chief way in which physical race enters is as a mark of identification. This facilitates the focussing of race prejudice, reduces social contact, and so impedes the natural process of assimilation. The clearest, or most obvious, marginal types are often those who culturally belong to the dominant group but who racially are members of the subordinate group.

Even within a specific type of problem, such as that of the mixed bloods, the marginal personality varies with the nature of the situation. This fact, taken together with the general resemblance of the racial hybrid to the cultural hybrid, suggests if it does not fully establish that race mixture as such does not produce unstable genetic constitutions or disharmonic personalities. Fuller proof for this must await further research in genetics as well as detailed studies of mixed bloods in different social environments.

The question is sometimes asked whether the marginal man does not reflect individual variations in inherited temperament and sensitivity. Do not those who are sensitive by nature become the most sensitive marginal men? There is probably some truth in this assertion, but it can easily be over-emphasized. Interviews and the life histories of many cases show that sensitivity develops largely with the crisis phase. Furthermore, it fluctuates with the situation in which the individual is living; rising and declining in terms of his experience. Finally, the variations between different groups can hardly be accounted for in terms of individual predisposition. Other factors seem to be more important in the individual's traits—especially the degree to which he has psychologically identified himself with the dominant culture and then been repulsed.

The Marginal Culture Area

Social anthropologists have sometimes referred to distant and border cultures, such as those of primitive Australia and Patagonia, as "marginal cultures." [2] It is evident that such cultures have little in common with the subject of this study; indeed, if isolated, they tend toward cultural stability, if not stagnation, rather than culture conflict.

The concept of "marginal area" refers to a region where two cultures overlap, and where the occupying group combines the traits of both cultures. This, as Goldenweiser states, is a purely objective concept: "Psychologically, the marginal area is but a type of cultural area, for its cultural content is as much of a unit and has the same value to its human carriers as the content of a full-fledged culture area." [3] Such marginal areas may or may not involve culture conflict. When they do, we may also expect to find marginal men.

The expansion of Western civilization over the globe has brought about marginal areas of conflict and produced persons living within both cultures. Such culture conflict is particularly evident in the urban centers. These are the points of maximum cultural interpenetration. From such centers the new influences radiate out along the paths of communication and transportation.

The rural indigenous population, as well as foreign immigrants, stream into the cities, and are sorted into areas inhabited by their own kind. Thus the modern large city is a mosaic of minor culture units which shift their residence as the city grows and gradually lose their identities in the process of assimilation. These centers are the real melting-pots of culture. Consequently, the place of residence within the city becomes a significant index of cultural status.[4] Competition and mobility, however, are so active that the conception of the marginal area as employed by the anthropologist does not fully indicate the dynamic complexity of the cultural process.

Culture Content and Culture Conflict

The core of traits which characterize the marginal personality springs from the conflict of cultures, and not from the specific content of any culture. Each society has a distinctive culture which creates its own type of personality: English, Italian, Japanese, Hawaiian. For the purposes of this study, such nationality differences—like the differences arising from individual heredity and differential experience within a culture—are excluded from consideration. It is the conflict of groups possessing different cultures which is the determining influence in creating the marginal man, and the typical traits are social-psychological, rather than cultural, in nature.

Membership within a social group is more vital to the individual than sharing any particular culture; the first is a prerequisite to the second. Accordingly, when his social status is endangered, the psychological consequences are fundamental. It is because the marginal individual has an uncertain status in two or more groups that he becomes a distinct type of personality irrespective of the particular content of the cultures.

Culture conflict is simply a form of group conflict where the source of the conflict lies in the cultural difference. This difference is interpreted in moral terms. Two systems of *mores* are struggling, each commanding the loyalty of its members. Fundamentally, it is a struggle for existence: which group shall control the situation? Each group—particularly the one in control—seeks to protect itself by keeping the other in its place. This is a matter of maintaining social distance; when the position of the controlling group is threatened by the advance of the subordinate group it responds with fear and antipathy—*i.e.*, race prejudice.[5]

Race prejudice is a collective attitude directed to the other racial group as a whole. Individual members of the latter are treated in terms of the attitude toward the group—not in accordance with their own personality traits. The educated Negro is placed in the same class as the uneducated Negro; the assimilated Jew or Oriental is regarded like the unassimilated Jew or Oriental. A few members of the dominant group who know the assimilated individual intimately may treat him in terms of his individual traits. Thus culture conflict and differential assimilation are the basic factors in creating the marginal man.

The Marginal Man and the Social Theory of Personality

The scientific study of personality is still in its early stages. Approaches in terms of physiology, individual psychology, psychiatry and psychoanalysis, with all their schools and personal interpretations, have as yet reached no common standpoint. In this conflict of interpretations and methods, sociological students have insisted upon the necessity of viewing personality as shaped by, as well as shaping, a social process. One may go back to the psychologist William James and his analysis of the self, particularly the "social self." The individual, writes James, "has as many different social selves as there are distinct *groups* of persons about whose opinion he cares. He generally shows a different side of himself to each of these differnt groups." [6] With the sociologist Charles H. Cooley the analysis of the self proceeds even more realistically and subtly than with James. There is always a "social reference" involved in the self, but in a "very large and interesting class of cases" it takes the form of a "reflected or looking-glass self" which consists of "the imagination of our appearance to the other person; the imagination of his judgment of that appearance, and some sort of self-feeling, such as pride or mortification." [7]

The "social reference" of the self is the social group. Accordingly one may define personality as "the sum and organization of those traits which determine the rôle of the individual in the group." [8] The concept of rôle in the group provides a frame of reference within which various traits play their parts both as causes and consequences of the rôle. Thus intelligence may help to make an individual into a leader, and the rôle of leadership in turn produces certain personality traits, such as self-confidence. But, since the individual usually belongs to several groups in each of which he has a rôle, his personality has multiple facets. Thence arises the problem of harmonizing and integrating his various selves, so that a stable character and meaningful inner life can be achieved. To the degree that the individual lives in a society where change is rapid, and where different codes of conduct exist, his problem of achieving a harmonious personality and a stable character is correspondingly increased.

Here we must distinguish between social change which comes from the gradual introduction of new ideas from within and without a given society, and the type of social change which results from the sudden contact of two or more societies with different cultures. In the second the clash of codes and philosophies is profound. The effect upon the subordinate group which must do the major share of adjusting is particularly severe. For the individual, the contrast between his group rôles and imagined selves is often acute. This contrast is not merely a conflict of social groups within a culture system: it is a conflict between two culture systems each having its subordinate groups. As a result the individual may have to readjust his life along several points: the language in which he communicates, the religion he believes in, the moral code he follows, the manner in which he earns his living, the government to which he owes allegiance, as well as in the subtler aspects of personality. The duality of cultures produces a duality of personality—a divided self.

It is the fact of cultural duality which is the determining influence in the life of the marginal man. His is not a clash between inborn temperament and social expectation, between congenial personality tendency and the patterns of a given culture.[9] His is not a problem of adjusting a single looking-glass self, but two or more such selves. And his adjustment pattern seldom secures complete cultural guidance and support, for his problem arises out of the shifting social order itself.

Today the social order is founded upon nationalities and races, real or fictitious. The political state is a reality to which all other loyalties must give way in times of test. In the past, religious loyalty has often been the supreme loyalty. Conflicts of religious identification have torn human souls asunder—vividly portrayed and dissected as they are in William James's *Varieties of Religious Experience.* Religious conflict in the deeper sense is a conflict of the inner moral or spiritual life; with God and the self, the ideal and the actual, as the objects of attention. Such conflicts also have their social reference, though less consciously so than with the marginal man whose concern is primarily with the objective social situation. The latter's divided self is not like those religious "sick souls who must be twice-born in order to be happy," nor has it a temperamental basis.[10] The gradations of duality, therefore, are more nicely correlated with the social situation.

The Marginal Man and the Cultural Process[11]

Culture is not only accumulated and transmitted from generation to generation: it is also diffused from group to group. Each process affects the other. Today no sooner does a new idea or method appear in one place than it reappears in another—either through simultaneous invention or through copying and diffusion. Diffusion in turn stimulates further discovery. Modern forms of communication and transportation have become the highways of culture change.

In the present, as well as in the past, migration performs a vital part in culture change. Through it the "cake of custom" is sufficiently disturbed and broken to release individuals for creative thought. Relatively isolated social groups do not suddenly change their mode of life except in direct or indirect response to changes in the physical environment. But where they live in close contact with other peoples they are also subject to human competition and conflict, and must—if they are to survive or remain independent—make constant readjustments. Population intrusion therefore sets in motion a process of culture change which breaks down old cultural forms, releases individuals from their domination, and so gives rise to periods of creative activity and advance. This is the theory developed by Frederick J. Teggart, who also calls attention to its implications in the study of great men:

> . . . Now, while, historically, advancement has been dependent upon the collision of groups, the resultant response has taken place in the minds of individuals, and so we are led to see that all transitional eras are alike in being periods of individual mental awakening, and of the release or emancipation of individual initiative in thought and action. This applies equally whether we consider the past or the present, and, consequently, since the antecedents of advance are realized only in exceptional cases, we are forced to rely, for the verification we are now discussing, upon the testimony of exceptional individuals. That the historical process of individualization of thought is also the form through which advancement proceeds today would be best shown by an extended examination of the biographies of notable men, but for the present we may accept the evidence adduced by psychologists and other investigators who have already called attention to the facts.[12]

The recently published study of Arnold J. Toynbee[13] may be considered as a partial answer to the last suggestion of Teggart. In the third volume of this study he makes brief analyses of the lives of such men of genius as Saint Paul, Gautama the Buddha, David, Cæsar, Muhammed, Peter the Great, Lenin, Confucius, Kant, etc., to discover the "interaction between individuals in growing civilizations." This he finds to consist of a "movement of withdrawal-and-return" in which the individual undergoes an "inward psychic experience."

> In terms of his external relations with other individual human beings in the social life which is the common ground of his and their respective fields of action, we shall be describing the same movement if we call it a disengagement and temporary withdrawal of the creative personality from his social milieu, and his subsequent return to the same milieu transfigured: in a new capacity and with new powers. The disengagement and withdrawal make it possible for the personality to realize individual potentialities which might have remained in abeyance if the individuals in whom they were immanent had not been released for a moment from his social toils and trammels.[14]

This analysis has much in common with the analysis of the marginal man presented above.[15] Here the "crisis experience" is the event which throws the individual back upon himself and produces a "disengagement and temporary withdrawal." Those individuals who have the potentialities to reconstruct their personalities and "return" as creative agents not only adjust themselves but also contribute to the solution of the conflict of races and cultures. Thus the career of Saint Paul,[16] for example, was a creative response to the impact of Greek culture upon Syriac society.

But the creative rôle of the individual varies with the situation. Typically, race relations develop in terms of a cycle[17] or sequence of processes. At first the relations of two or more races or nationalities who are living in a common territory under a single political and economic system assume a predominantly symbiotic or economic character. With the advance of time and acquaintance more intimate social relations develop. These include the mixing of blood and the transfer of culture. Out of this process emerge the marginal men, whether as racial hybrids or cultural hybrids. If sufficient time elapses a new racial stock and a new culture arise out of this contact and interaction, and the particular cycle of race relations comes to an end.

The Europeanization of the globe forms the setting for the latest act in the contacts of peoples. It has involved a twofold diffusion of European blood and of European culture. This diffusion has transformed the world from a collection of isolated or slowly interacting races, political units, and distinctive cultures into a condition where dynamic interchange and mutual economic if not political and cultural interdepedence dominate each part. The first phase of this process has meant the extension of Western political and economic control—"imperialism"; a rapid mixture of races; the disorganization of non-Western cultures; and the gradual assimilation of European ideas. The second phase is now developing—a phase in which nationalist and racial movements are seeking to remove Western domination and to supplant it with reorganized, self-determined societies and governments. But, as the rise of Japan testifies, such movements succeed only to the degree that Western instruments of economic, political and military power can be employed.

The marginal man is the key-personality in the contacts of cultures. It is in his mind that the cultures come together, conflict, and eventually work out some kind of mutual adjustment and interpenetration. He is the crucible of cultural fusion. His life history recapitulates something of the processes described in the race-relations cycle: at first he is unaware of the cultural conflict going on; then through some crisis experience or series of experiences he becomes aware of it, and the external conflict finds an echo in his mind; and, finally, he tries and sometimes succeeds in making an adjustment to his situation.

Thus the practical efforts of the marginal person to solve his own problem lead him consciously or unconsciously to change the situation itself. His interest may shift from himself to the objective social conditions and launch him upon the career of nationalist, conciliator, interpreter, reformer or teacher. In these rôles he inevitably promotes acculturation, either upon a basis of larger political and cultural unity, or in terms of a modified political and cultural differentiation—a new state. Consequently, the life histories of marginal men offer the most significant material for the analysis of the cultural process as it springs from the contacts of social groups. And it is in the mind of the marginal man that the inner significance and the driving motives of such culture change are most luminously revealed.

NOTES

1. John Dewey, *The Quest for Certainty* (New York, 1929), p. 165. An effort has been made to keep the concept empirically valid, and not to construct an "ideal type" as in Max Weber's sociology. See Theodore Abel, *Systematic Sociology in Germany* (New York, 1929), Chap. IV.
2. Clark Wissler, "*Man and Culture*" (New York, 1923), pp. 38, 147.
3. A. Goldenweiser, "Cultural Anthropology" in H. E. Barnes (Editor), *History and Prospects of the Social Sciences* (New York, 1925), p. 245.
4. For a number of special studies of this type see R. E. Park and E. W. Burgess, *The City* (Chicago, 1925); E. W. Burgess, *The Urban Community* (Chicago, 1926); F. Thrasher, *The Gang* (Chicago, 1927); E. W. Mowrer, *Family Disorganization* (Chicago, 1927); L. Wirth, *The Ghetto* (Chicago, 1928); H. Zorbaugh, *The Gold Coast and the Slum* (Chicago, 1929); Robert Redfield, *Tepoztlan* (Chicago, 1930); and E. F. Frazier, *The Negro Family in Chicago* (Chicago, 1932).
5. Robert E. Park, "The Bases of Race Prejudice," *Annals of the American Academy of Political and Social Science*, November, 1928, pp. 11–20.
6. William James, *Psychology* (Briefer Course) (New York, 1920), Chap. XII, p. 179.
7. Charles H. Cooley, *Human Nature and the Social Order* (New York, 1922, revised edition), p. 184.
8. Robert E. Park and Ernest W. Burgess, *Introduction to the Science of Sociology* (Chicago, 1921), p. 70.
9. For an excellent statement of this problem see Ruth Benedict, *Patterns of Culture* (Boston, 1934), especially Chap. VIII.
10. William James, *The Varieties of Religious Experience* (New York, 1902), p. 167. James was skeptical of the inborn temperamental basis. See p. 169.
11. In this section I am particularly indebted to suggestions of Robert E. Park which have been formulated in his article entitled "Migration and the Marginal Man," *The American Journal of Sociology*, May, 1928. It is important, of course, to differentiate between culture change originating from the accumulation of individual inventions within a people, and culture change which springs from the collisions of peoples. Although these two processes interact, this section is concerned only with the second.
12. *Processes of History* (New Haven, 1918), pp. 155–56. See also his *Theory of History* (New Haven, 1925).
13. A *Study of History* (London, 1934). Three parts, in three volumes, have appeared to date. The whole plan of the study includes thirteen parts.
14. Vol. III, p. 248.
15. Especially Chaps. V–X.
16. See Toynbee, Vol. III, pp. 263–64.
17. This is the "race relations cycle" defined by Robert E. Park. See *The Survey* (May, 1926), p. 192.

34

ROBERT E. PARK AND ERNEST W. BURGESS

On Collective Behavior

Robert E. Park and Ernest W. Burgess[1] *wrote what certainly constituted a seminal statement on social processes within the largely unorganized collectivity of persons. Park, especially, was to continue his interest in collective behavior,*[2] *as they named this field, and he largely determined the dominant contemporary approach to this area.*[3]

Park and Burgess saw collective behavior not as a separate field for investigation but as another approach towards the study of social order. The crowd represented a basically normal social process rather than some sort of irrational erratic event. It represented an attempt to bring about change in a society when the existing institutions impeded adjustments in the social structure which could bring about new institutions. They stressed the idea that collective behavior was still the group in action and was the result of social interactions.

Bibliographical Notes

1. *For a listing of the major writings by and about Park and Burgess, see the introduction to their first piece in this volume,* *pp. 115–117.*

2. *For Park's work in this area, see: Ralph H. Turner (ed.),* Robert E. Park on Social Control and Collective Behavior *(Chicago University of Chicago Press, 1967).*

3. *The dominant approach to collective behavior is represented by the* emergent norm *conceptualization in which a normative structure is seen as developing out of the social interaction of the collectivity. Cf., Ralph H. Turner and Lewis M. Killian,* Collective Behavior *(En-*

glewood Cliffs, N.J.: Prentice-Hall, 1957). For an excellent review of the contemporary state of the field, see: Ralph H. Turner, "Collective Behavior," in E. L. Faris (ed.), Handbook of Modern Sociology *(Chicago: Rand McNally, 1964), pp. 382–425.*

---

1. *Collective Behavior Defined*

A collection of individuals is not always, and by the mere fact of its collectivity, a society. On the other hand, when people come together anywhere, in the most casual way, on the street corner or at a railway station, no matter how great the social distances between them, the mere fact that they are aware of one another's presence sets up a lively exchange of influences, and the behavior that ensues is both social and collective. It is social, at the very least, in the sense that the train of thought and action in each individual is influenced more or less by the action of every other. It is collective in so far as each individual acts under the influence of a mood or a state of mind in which each shares, and in accordance with conventions which all quite unconsciously accept, and which the presence of each enforces upon the others.

The amount of individual eccentricity or deviation from normal and accepted modes of behavior which a community will endure without comment and without protest will vary naturally enough with the character of the community. A cosmopolitan community like New York City can and does endure a great deal in the way of individual eccentricity that a smaller city like Boston would not tolerate. In any case, and this is the point of these observations, even in the most casual relations of life, people do not behave in the presence of others as if they were living alone like Robinson Crusoe, each on his individual island. The very fact of their consciousness of each other tends to maintain and enforce a great body of convention and usage which otherwise falls into abeyance and is forgotten. Collective behavior, then, is the behavior of individuals under the influence of an impulse that is common and collective, an impulse, in other words, that is the result of social interaction.

2. *Social Unrest and Collective Behavior*

The most elementary form of collective behavior seems to be what is ordinarily referred to as "social unrest." Unrest in the individual becomes social when it is, or seems to be, transmitted from one individual to another, but more particularly when it produces something akin to the milling process in the herd, so that the manifestations of discontent in A communicated to B, and from B reflected back to A, produce the circular reaction described in the preceding chapter.

The significance of social unrest is that it represents at once a breaking up of the established routine and a preparation for new collective action. Social unrest is not of course a new phenomenon; it is possibly true, however, that it is peculiarly characteristic, as has been said, of modern life. The contrast between the conditions of modern life and of primitive society suggests why this may be true.

The conception which we ought to form of primitive society, says Sumner, is that of small groups scattered over territory. The size of the group will be determined by the conditions of the struggle for existence and the internal organization of each group will correspond (1) to the size of the group, and (2) to the nature and intensity of the struggle with its neighbors.

> Thus war and peace have reacted on each other and developed each other, one within the group, the other in the intergroup relation. The closer the neighbors, and the stronger they are, the intenser is the warfare, and then the intenser is the internal organization and discipline of each. Sentiments are produced to correspond. Loyalty to the group, sacrifice for it, hatred and contempt for outsiders, brotherhood within, warlikeness without—all grow together, common products of the same situation. These relations and sentiments constitute a social philosophy. It is sanctified by connection with religion. Men of an others-group are outsiders with whose ancestors the ancestors of the we-group waged war. The ghosts of the latter will see with pleasure their descendants keep up the fight, and will help them. Virtue consists in killing, plundering, and enslaving outsiders.[1]

The isolation, territorial and cultural, under which alone it is possible to maintain an organization which corresponds to Sumner's description, has disappeared within comparatively recent times from all the more inhabitable portions of the earth. In place of it there has come, and with increasing rapidity is coming, into existence a society which includes within its limits the total population of the earth and is so intimately bound together that the speculation of a grain merchant in

Chicago may increase the price of bread in Bombay, while the act of an assassin in a provincial town in the Balkans has been sufficient to plunge the world into a war which changed the political map of three continents and cost the lives, in Europe alone, of 8,500,000 combatants.

The first effect of modern conditions of life has been to increase and vastly complicate the economic interdependence of strange and distant peoples, i.e., to destroy distances and make the world, as far as national relations are concerned, small and tight.

The second effect has been to break down family, local, and national ties, and emancipate the individual man.

> When the family ceases, as it does in the city, to be an economic unit, when parents and children have vocations that not only intercept the traditional relations of family life, but make them well nigh impossible, the family ceases to function as an organ of social control. When the different nationalities, with their different national cultures, have so far interpenetrated one another that each has permanent colonies within the territorial limits of the other, it is inevitable that the old solidarities, the common loyalties and the common hatreds that formerly bound men together in primitive kinship and local groups should be undermined.

A survey of the world today shows that vast changes are everywhere in progress. Not only in Europe but in Asia and in Africa new cultural contacts have undermined and broken down the old cultures. The effect has been to loosen all the social bonds and reduce society to its individual atoms. The energies thus freed have produced a world-wide ferment. Individuals released from old associations enter all the more readily into new ones. Out of this confusion new and strange political and religious movements arise, which represent the groping of men for a new social order.

3. *The Crowd and the Public*

Gustave Le Bon, who was the first writer to call attention to the significance of the crowd as a social phenomenon,[2] said that mass movements mark the end of an old régime and the beginning of a new.

"When the structure of a civilization is rotten, it is always the masses that bring about its downfall." [3] On the other hand, "all founders of religious or political creeds have established them solely because they were successful in inspiring crowds with those fanatical sentiments which have as result that men find their happiness in worship and obedience and are ready to lay down their lives for their idol." [4]

The crowd was, for Le Bon, not merely any group brought together by the accident of some chance excitement, but it was above all the emancipated masses whose bonds of loyalty to the old order had been broken by "the destruction of those religious, political, and social beliefs in which all the elements of our civilization are rooted." The crowd, in other words, typified for Le Bon the existing social order. Ours is an age of crowds, he said, an age in which men, massed and herded together in great cities without real convictions or fundamental faiths, are likely to be stampeded in any direction for any chance purpose under the influence of any passing excitement.

Le Bon did not attempt to distinguish between the crowd and the public. This distinction was first made by Tarde in a paper entitled "Le Public et la foule," published first in *La Revue de Paris* in 1898, and included with several others on the same general theme under the title *L'Opinion et la foule* which appeared in 1901. The public, according to Tarde, was a product of the printing press. The limits of the crowd are determined by the length to which a voice will carry or the distance that the eye can survey. But the public presupposes a higher stage of social development in which suggestions are transmitted in the form of ideas and there is "contagion without contact." [5]

The fundamental distinction between the crowd and the public, however, is not to be measured by numbers nor by means of communication, but by the form and effects of the interactions. In the public, interaction takes the form of discussion. Individuals tend to act upon one another critically; issues are raised and parties form. Opinions clash and thus modify and moderate one another.

The crowd does not discuss and hence it does not reflect. It simply "mills." Out of this milling process a collective impulse is formed which dominates all members of the crowd. Crowds, when they act, do so impulsively. The crowd, says Le Bon, "is the slave of its impulses."

"The varying impulses which crowds obey may be, according to their exciting causes, generous or cruel, heroic or cowardly, but they will always be so imperious that the interest of the individual, even the interest of self-preservation, will not dominate them." [6]

When the crowd acts it becomes a mob. What happens when two mobs meet? We have in the literature no definite record. The nearest approach to it are the occasional accounts we find in the stories of travelers of the contacts and conflicts of armies of primitive peoples.

These undisciplined hordes are, as compared with the armies of civilized peoples, little more than armed mobs. Captain S. L. Hinde in his story of the Belgian conquest of the Congo describes several such battles. From the descriptions of battles carried on almost wholly between savage and undisciplined troops it is evident that the morale of an army of savages is a precarious thing. A very large part of the warfare consists in alarms and excursions interspersed with wordy duels to keep up the courage on one side and cause a corresponding depression on the other.[7]

Gangs are conflict groups. Their organization is usually quite informal and is determined by the nature and imminence of the conflicts with other groups. When one crowd encounters another it either goes to pieces or it changes its character and becomes a conflict group. When negotiations and palavers take place as they eventually do between conflict groups, these two groups, together with the neutrals who have participated vicariously in the conflict, constitute a public. It is possible that the two opposing savage hordes which seek, by threats and boastings and beatings of drums, to play upon each other's fears and so destroy each other's morale, may be said to constitute a very primitive type of public.

Discussion, as might be expected, takes curious and interesting forms among primitive peoples. In a volume, *Iz Derevni: 12 Pisem* ("From the Country: 12 Letters"), A. N. Engelgardt describes the way in which the Slavic peasants reach their decisions in the village council.

> In the discussion of some questions by the *mir* [organization of neighbors] there are no speeches, no debates, no votes. They shout, they abuse one another—they seem on the point of coming to blows; apparently they riot in the most senseless manner. Some one preserves silence, and then suddenly puts in a word, one word, or an ejaculation, and by this word, this ejaculation, he turns the whole thing upside down. In the end, you look into it and find that an admirable decision has been formed and, what is most important, a unanimous decision . . . (In the division of land) the cries, the noise, the hubbub do not subside until everyone is satisfied and no doubter is left.[8]

4. *Crowds and Sects*

Reference has been made to the crowds that act, but crowds do not always act. Sometimes they merely dance or, at least, make expressive motions which relieve their feelings. "The purest and most typical expression of simple feeling," as Hirn remarks, "is that which consists of mere random movements." [9] When these motions assume, as they so easily do, the character of a fixed sequence in time, that is to say when they are rhythmical, they can be and inevitably are, as by a sort of inner compulsion, imitated by the onlookers. "As soon as the expression is fixed in rhythmical form its contagious power is incalculably increased." [10]

This explains at once the function and social importance of the dance among primitive people. It is the form in which they prepare for battle and celebrate their victories. It gives the form at once to their religious ritual and to their art. Under the influence of the memories and the emotions which these dances stimulate the primitive group achieves a sense of corporate unity, which makes corporate action possible outside of the fixed and sacred routine of ordinary daily life.

If it is true, as has been suggested, that art and religion had their origin in the choral dance, it is also true that in modern times religious sects and social movements have had their origin in crowd excitements and spontaneous mass movements. The very names which have been commonly applied to them—Quakers, Shakers, Convulsionaires, Holy Rollers—suggest not merely the derision with which they were at one time regarded, but indicate likewise their origin in ecstatic or expressive crowds, the crowds that *do not act*.

All great mass movements tend to display, to a greater or less extent, the characteristics that Le Bon attributes to crowds. Speaking of the convictions of crowds, Le Bon says:

> When these convictions are closely examined, whether at epochs marked by fervent religious faith, or by great political upheavals such as those of the last century, it is apparent that they always assume a peculiar form which I cannot better define than by giving it the name of a religious sentiment.[11]

Le Bon's definition of religion and religious sentiment will hardly find general acceptance but it indicates at any rate his conception of the extent to which individual personalities are involved in the excitements that accompany mass movements.

> A person is not religious solely when he worships a divinity, but when he puts all the resources of his mind, the complete submission of his will, and the whole-souled ardour of fanaticism at the service of a cause or an individual who becomes the goal and guide of his thoughts and actions.[12]

Just as the gang may be regarded as the perpetuation and permanent form of "the crowd that acts," so the sect, religious or political, may be regarded as a perpetuation and permanent form of the orgiastic (ecstatic) or expressive crowd.

"The sect," says Sighele, "is a crowd *triée*, selected, and permanent; the crowd is a transient sect, which does not select its members. The sect is the *chronic* form of the crowd; the crowd is the *acute* form of the sect." [13] It is Sighele's conception that the crowd is an elementary organism, from which the sect issues, like the chick from the egg, and that all other types of social groups "may, in this same manner, be deduced from this primitive social protoplasm." This is a simplification which the facts hardly justify. It is true that, implicit in the practices and the doctrines of a religious sect, there is the kernel of a new independent culture.

5. *Sects and Institutions*

A sect is a religious organization that is at war with the existing mores. It seeks to cultivate a state of mind and establish a code of morals different from that of the world about it and for this it claims divine authority. In order to accomplish this end it invariably seeks to set itself off in contrast with the rest of the world. The simplest and most effective way to achieve this is to adopt a peculiar form of dress and speech. This, however, invariably makes its members objects of scorn and derision, and eventually of persecution. It would probably do this even if there was no assumption of moral superiority to the rest of the world in this adoption of a peculiar manner and dress.

Persecution tends to dignify and sanctify all the external marks of the sect, and it becomes a cardinal principle of the sect to maintain them. Any neglect of them is regarded as disloyalty and is punished as heresy. Persecution may eventually, as was the case with the Puritans, the Quakers, the Mormons, compel the sect to seek refuge in some part of the world where it may practice its way of life in peace.

Once the sect has achieved territorial isolation and territorial solidarity, so that it is the dominant power within the region that it occupies, it is able to control the civil organization, establish schools and a press, and so put the impress of a peculiar culture upon all the civil and political institutions that it controls. In this case it tends to assume the form of a state, and become a nationality. Something approaching this was achieved by the Mormons in Utah. The most striking illustration of the evolution of a nationality from a sect is Ulster, which now has a position not quite that of a nation within the English empire.

This sketch suggests that the sect, like most other social institutions, originates under conditions that are typical for all institutions of the same species; then it develops in definite and predictable ways, in accordance with a form or entelechy that is predetermined by characteristic internal processes and mechanisms, and that has, in short, a nature and natural history which can be described and explained in sociological terms. Sects have their origin in social unrest to which they give a direction and expression in forms and practices that are largely determined by historical circumstances; movements which were at first inchoate impulses and aspirations gradually take form; policies are defined, doctrine and dogmas formulated; and eventually an administrative machinery and efficiencies are developed to carry into effect policies and purposes. The Salvation Army, of which we have a more adequate history than of most other religious movements, is an example.

A sect in its final form may be described, then, as a movement of social reform and regeneration that has become institutionalized. Eventually, when it has succeeded in accommodating itself to the other rival organizations, when it has become tolerant and is tolerated, it tends to assume the form of a denomination. Denominations tend and are perhaps destined to unite in the form of religious federations—a thing which is inconceivable of a sect.

What is true of the sect, we may assume, and must assume if social movements are to become subjects for sociological investigation, is true of other social institutions. Existing institutions represent social movements that survived the conflict of cultures and the struggle for existence.

Sects, and that is what characterizes and distinguishes them from secular institutions, at least, have had their origin in movements that aimed to reform the mores—movements that sought to renovate and renew the inner life of the community. They have wrought upon society from within outwardly. Revolutionary and reform movements, on the contrary, have been directed against the outward fabric and formal structure of society. Revolutionary movements in particular have assumed that if the existing structure could be destroyed it would then be possible to erect a new moral order upon the ruins of the old social structures.

A cursory survey of the history of revolutions suggests that the most radical and the most successful of them have been religious. Of this type of revolution Christianity is the most conspicuous example.

6. *Classification of the Materials*

The materials in this chapter have been arranged under the headings: (*a*) social contagion, (*b*) the crowd, and (*c*) types of mass movements. The order of materials follows, in a general way, the order of institutional evolution. Social unrest is first communicated, then takes form in crowd and mass movements, and finally crystallizes in institutions. The history of almost any single social movement—woman's suffrage, prohibition, protestantism—exhibits in a general way, if not in detail, this progressive change in character. There is at first a vague general discontent and distress. Then a violent, confused, and disorderly, but enthusiastic and popular movement arises. Finally the movement takes form; develops leadership, organization; formulates doctrines and dogmas. Eventually it is accepted, established, legalized. The movement dies, but the institution remains.

a) *Social contagion.*—The ease and the rapidity with which a cultural trait originating in one cultural group finds its way to other distant groups is familiar to students of folklore and ethnology. The manner in which fashions are initiated in some metropolitan community, and thence make their way, with more or less rapidity, to the provinces is an illustration of the same phenomenon in a different context.

> Fashion plays a much larger rôle in social life than most of us imagine. Fashion dominates our manners and dress but it influences also our sentiments and our modes of thought. Everything in literature, art or philosophy that was characteristic of the middle of the nineteenth century, the "mid-Victorian period," is now quite out of date and no one who is intelligent now-a-days practices the pruderies, defends the doctrines, nor shares the enthusiasms of that period. Philosophy, also, changes with the fashion and Sumner says that even mathematics and science do the same. Lecky in his history of Rationalism in Europe describes in great detail how the belief in witches, so characteristic of the Middle Ages, gradually disappeared with the period of enlightenment and progress.[14] But the enlightenment of the eighteenth century was itself a fashion and is now quite out of date. In the meantime a new popular and scientific interest is growing up in obscure mental phenomena which no man with scientific training would have paid any attention to a few years ago because he did not believe in such things. It was not good form to do so.

But the changes of fashion are so pervasive, so familiar, and, indeed, universal phenomena that we do not regard the changes which they bring, no matter how fantastic, as quite out of the usual and expected order. Gabriel Tarde, however, regards the "social contagion" represented in fashion (imitation) as the fundamental social phenomenon.[15]

The term social epidemic, which is, like fashion, a form of social contagion, has a different origin and a different connotation. J. F. C. Hecker, whose study of the Dancing Mania of the Middle Ages, published in 1832, was an incident of his investigation of the Black Death, was perhaps the first to give currency to the term.[16] Both the Black Death and the Dancing Mania assumed the form of epidemics and the latter, the Dancing Mania, was in his estimation the sequel of the former, the Black Death. It was perhaps this similarity in the manner in which they spread—the one by physical and the other by psychical infection—that led him to speak of the spread of a popular delusion in terms of a physical science. Furthermore, the hysteria was directly traceable, as he believed, to the prevailing conditions of the time, and this seemed to put the manifestations in the world of intelligible and controllable phenomena, where they could be investigated.

It is this notion, then, that unrest which manifests itself in social epidemics is an indication of pathological social conditions, and the further, the more general, conception that unrest does not become social and hence contagious except when there are contributing causes in the environment—it is this that gives its special significance to the term and the facts. Unrest in the social organism with the social ferment that it induces is like fever in the individual organism, a highly important diagnostic symptom.

b) *The crowd.*—Neither Le Bon nor any of the other writers upon the subject of mass psychology has succeeded in distinguishing clearly between the organized or "psychological" crowd, as Le Bon calls it, and other similar types of social groups. These distinctions, if they are to be made objectively, must be made on the basis of case studies. It is the purpose of the materials under the general heading of "The 'Animal' Crowd," not so much to furnish a definition, as to indicate the nature and sources of materials from which a definition can be formulated. It is apparent that the different animal groups behave in ways that are distinctive and characteristic, ways which are predetermined in the organism to an extent that is not true of human beings.

One other distinction may possibly be made between the so-called "animal" and the human crowd. The organized crowd is controlled by *a common purpose* and acts to achieve, no matter how vaguely it is defined, a common end. The herd, on the other hand, has apparently no common purpose. Every sheep in the flock, at least as the behavior of the flock is ordinarily interpreted, behaves like every other. Action in a stampede, for example, is collective but it is not concerted. It is very difficult to understand how there can be concerted action in the herd or the flock unless it is on an instinctive basis. The crowd, however, responds to collective representations. The crowd does not imitate or follow its leader as sheep do a bellwether. On the contrary, the crowd *carries out the suggestions of the leader,* and even though there be no division of labor each individual acts more or less in his own way to achieve a common end.

In the case of a panic or a stampede, however, where there is no common end, the crowd acts like a flock of sheep. But a stampede or a panic is not a crowd in Le Bon's sense. It is not a psychological unity, nor a "single being," subject to "the mental unity of crowds." [17] The panic is the crowd in dissolution. All effective methods of dispersing crowds involve some method of distracting attention, breaking up the tension, and dissolving the mob into its individual units.

c) *Types of mass movements.*—The most elementary form of mass movements is a mass migration. Such a mass movement displays, in fact, any of the characteristics of the "animal" crowd. It is the "human" herd. The migration of a people, either as individuals or in organized groups, may be compared to the swarming of the hive. Peoples migrate in search of better living conditions, or merely in search of new experience. It is usually the younger generation, the more restless, active, and adaptable, who go out from the security of the old home to seek their fortunes in the new. Once settled on the new land, however, immigrants inevitably remember and idealize the home they have left. Their first disposition is to reproduce as far as possible in the new world the institutions and the social order of the old. Just as the spider spins his web out of his own body, so the immigrant tends to spin out of his experience and traditions, a social organization which reproduces, as far as circumstances will permit, the organization and the life of the ancestral community. In this way the older culture is transplanted and renews itself, under somewhat altered circumstances, in the new home. That explains, in part, at any rate, the fact that migration tends to follow the isotherms, since all the more fundamental cultural devices and experience are likely to be accommodations to geographical and climatic conditions.

In contrast with migrations are movements which are sometimes referred to as crusades, partly because of the religious fervor and fanaticism with which they are usually conducted and partly because they are an appeal to the masses of the people for direct action and depend for their success upon their ability to appeal to some universal human interest or to common experiences and interests that are keenly comprehended by the common man.

The Woman's Christian Temperance Crusade, referred to in the materials, may be regarded, if we are permitted to compare great things with small, as an illustration of collective behavior not unlike the crusades of the eleventh and twelfth centuries.

Crusades are reformatory and religious. This was true at any rate of the early crusades, inspired by Peter the Hermit, whatever may have been the political purposes of the popes who encouraged them. It was the same motive that led the people of the Middle Ages to make pilgrimages which led them to join the crusades. At bottom it was an inner restlessness, that sought peace in great hardship and inspiring action, which moved the masses.

Somewhat the same widespread contagious restlessness is the source of most of our *revolutions*. It is not, however, hardships and actual distress that inspire revolutions but hopes and dreams, dreams which find expression in those myths and "vital lies," as Vernon Lee calls them,[18] which according to Sorel are the only means of moving the masses.

The distinction between crusades, like the Woman's Temperance Crusade, and revolutions, like the French Revolution, is that one is a radical attempt to correct a recognized evil and the other is a radical attempt to reform an existing social order.

NOTES

1. W. G. Sumner, *Folkways*. A study of the sociological importance of usages, manners, customs, mores, and morals, pp. 12–13. (Boston, 1906.)
2. Scipio Sighele, in a note to the French edition of his *Psychology of Sects*, claims that his volume, *La Folla delinquente*, of which the second edition was published at Turin in 1895, and his article "Physiologie du succès," in the *Revue des Revues*, October 1, 1894, were the first attempts to describe the crowd from the point of view of collective psychology. Le Bon published two articles, "Psychologie des foules" in the *Revue scientifique*, April 6 and 20, 1895. These were later gathered together in his volume *Psychologie des foules*, Paris, 1895. See Sighele *Psychologie des sectes*, pp. 25, 39.
3. Gustave Le Bon, *The Crowd*. A study of the popular mind, p. 19. (New York, 1900.)
4. *Ibid.*, p. 83.
5. *L'Opinion et la foule*, pp. 6–7. (Paris, 1901.)
6. *The Crowd*, p. 41.
7. Sidney L. Hinde, *The Fall of the Congo Arabs*, p. 147. (London, 1897.)

Describing a characteristic incident in one of the strange confused battles Hinde says: "Wordy war, which also raged, had even more effect than our rifles. Mahomedi and Sefu led the Arabs, who were jeering and taunting Lutete's people, saying that they were in a bad case, and had better desert the white man, who was ignorant of the fact that Mohara with all the forces of Nyange was camped in his rear. Lutete's people replied: 'Oh, we know all about Mohara; we ate him the day before yesterday.' " This news became all the more depressing when it turned out to be true. See also Hirn, *The Origins of Art*, p. 269, for an explanation of the rôle of threats and boastings in savage warfare.

8. Robert E. Park and Herbert A. Miller, *Old World Traits Transplanted*. Document 23, pp. 32–33. (New York, 1921).
9. Yrjö Hirn, *The Origins of Art*. A psychological and sociological inquiry, p. 87. (London, 1900.)
10. *Ibid*., p. 89.
11. Le Bon, *op. cit*., p. 82.
12. *Ibid*., p. 82.
13. Scipio Sighele, *Psychologie des sectes*, p. 46. (Paris, 1898.)
14. W. E. H. Lecky, *History of the Rise and Influence of the Spirit of Rationalism in Europe*. 2 vols. (Vol. I.) (New York, 1866.)
15. See Gabriel Tarde, *Laws of Imitation*.
16. J. F. C. Hecker, *Die Tanzwuth, eine Volkskrankheit im Mittelalter*. (Berlin, 1832.) See Introduction of *The Black Death and the Dancing Mania*. Translated from the German by B. G. Babington. Cassell's National Library. (New York, 1888).
17. Le Bon, *op. cit*., p. 26.
18. Vernon Lee [pseud.], *Vital Lies*. Studies of some varieties of recent obscurantism. (London, 1912.)

8

The Nature of Sociological Knowledge

35

GEORGE A. LUNDBERG

Can Science Save Us?

George Andrew Lundberg (1895–1966) was a major twentieth-century sociological exponent of the position that sociological knowledge must be pursued by using the same basic methods as the natural sciences.[1] *This neopositivism was a direct descendant of the positivism of Comte and the "social facts" orientation of Durkheim. Lundberg was an outspoken advocate of ethical neutrality as the appropriate posture for sociology and espoused numerous views that were unconventional for his time.*[2] *He strongly believed that sociology had an important potentiality for helping to solve the social problems that beset mankind. He insisted, however, that to be truly useful and legitimate (i.e., unbiased), a science must avoid being contaminated by moral evaluations and ethnocentric perspectives that would make any objective perspective upon the social world impossible.*[3]

Bibliographical Notes

1. *Lundberg's principal works include:* Trends in American Society, *edited with R. Bain and N. Anderson (1929);* Leisure: A Suburban Study, *with M. Komarovsky and M. A. McInerny (1934);* Foundations of Sociology *(1939);* Can Science Save Us? *(1947); and* Sociology *with C. C. Schrag and O. N. Larsen (1958, last revision 1963). His full bibliography can be found in: Otto N. Larsen, "Publications of George A. Lundberg,"* Sociologiske meddelelser, 10 *(1965), 6–18. For a short biographical overview, see: William R. Catton, Jr., "Lundberg, George," in the* International Encyclopedia of the Social Sciences, *Vol. 9 (New York: Macmillan and Free Press, 1968), pp. 492–494.*

Reprinted from George A. Lundberg, *Can Science Save Us?* (New York: David McKay, 1947), pp. 21–34. Reprinted by permission David McKay Company, Inc. Footnotes have been deleted.

2. *For a critical account of Lundberg's more unconventional views, see Frank E. Hartung, "The Sociology of Positivism: Protofascist Aspects,"* Science and Society, *8 (1944), 328–341.*

3. *A recent exposition that strongly follows Lundberg's general orientation is: William R. Catton, Jr.,* From Animistic to Naturalistic Sociology *(New York: McGraw-Hill Book Company, 1966).*

Although I think it is unquestionably true that the social sciences have made, during the present century, more actual progress than in all preceding history, it would be absurd to pretend that this progress is, as yet, reflected to any great extent in our management of social affairs. Scientific information of a more or less reliable character is more widely diffused than ever before, but the scientific mode of thought has obviously made very little headway. Practically no one approaches the major social problems of the day in a spirit of disinterested scientific study. The idea that these problems are to be solved, if at all, by the use of instruments of precision in hands that do not shake with fear, with anger, or even with love, does not seem to have occurred even to many people who pass for social scientists. They have joined the journalist and the soapbox crusader in the hue and cry of the mob. Their supposedly scholarly works bristle with assessments of praise and blame, personalities and verbal exorcisms which have no place whatever in the scientific universe of discourse. Not only do these angry men pass in the public eye as great social scientists of the day, but they not infrequently presume to patronize honest scientists who stay with their proper tasks of building as science and the instruments by means of which any difficult problems are to be solved.

But behind this fog, this dust storm of books about the inside of various political movements, the private life and morals of its leaders, and the treatises on democracy, substantial work is going on. Men are patiently accumulating data about human behavior in a form which in the fullness of time will permit a type of generalization which has never before been possible. Some are engaged in the undramatic but fundamental work, basic to all science, of classifying the multitudes of human groups and behavior patterns as a first step toward the formulation of generalizations regarding them. Still others are pioneering in the construction of actuarial and other tables from which may be predicted not only the prevalence of births, deaths, marriages, and divorces, but also the probable relative degrees of happiness in marriage, the probable success or failure of probation and parole, and many other equally "human" eventualities. A wealth of valuable information and generalizations have already been developed about the social characteristics and behavior of populations, such as the distribution of wealth, occupations, mobility, intelligence, and the various conditions with which these characteristics vary. Important instruments have been invented in recent years for measuring opinion, status, social participation, and many phenomena of communication and interpersonal relations.

Indeed, the invention and perfection of instruments for the more accurate and precise observation and recording of social phenomena must be regarded as among the most important developments in the social sciences. It is easy to point to the flaws in these instruments as it was easy to point to the flaws in the early microscopes and telescopes. But, without these beginnings and the patient centuries of undramatic labor, sciences like bacteriology could not have appeared at all.

Finally, there are those, and they may be the most important of all, who are experimenting with and inventing new systems of symbolic representation of phenomena. New adaptations of mathematics by which otherwise hopeless complexities can be comprehended are quite fundamental but do not lend themselves to popular display. The work of Liebnitz, Faraday, and Hertz was not the popular science of their day. Yet it is by virtue of their strange calculations with strange symbols that men today fly and broadcast their speech around the earth. This should be remembered by "writers" and others who complain that social scientists are adopting "jargon" and "esoteric" symbols which go beyond the vocabulary of the current "best-seller."

If I deal primarily with these more obscure and undramatic labors of social scientists, it is because I regard them as more important in the long run than the conspicuous contemporary achievements which are common knowledge. I do not overlook or underestimate these more obvious and demonstrable achievements. The transition in our time to more humane treatment of children, the poor, and the unfortunate, by more enlightened education, social work, and penology must in large measure be attributed to the expanding sciences of psychology and sociology. I know, of course, that whenever a war or a depression occurs journalists and preachers point to the impotence of economists and political scientists either to predict or prevent these disasters. The fact is that the course of events following World War I, down to and including the present, was predicted with great accuracy by large numbers of social scientists. That nothing was done about it is not the special responsibility of social scientists. "Doing something about it" is the common responsibility of all members of a community, including scientists, and epecially of those who specialize in mass education, mass leadership, and practical programs.

It is not my main purpose to review the past and present achievements of the social sciences. . . . I am here concerned primarily with the probable future of the social sciences. Even if I should admit that social scientists are today merely chipping flint in the Stone Age of their science, I do not see that we have any choice but to follow the rough road that other sciences have traveled. The attainment of comparable success may seem remote, and the labors involved may seem staggering. But is the prospect really unreasonably remote? Suppose that someone four hundred years ago had delivered an address on the future of the physical sciences and suppose that he had envisioned only a small fraction of their present achievements. What would have been the reaction of even a sophisticated audience to predictions of men flying and speaking across oceans, seeing undreamed-of worlds, both through microscopes and telescopes, and the almost incredible feats of modern engineering and surgery? Nothing I have suggested, I think, in the way of mature social science with comparable practical application seems as improbable as would the story of our prophetic physicist of four hundred or even one hundred years ago.

The time is passing when the solid achievements of social science and its future prospects can be dismissed with a far-away look, an ethereal smile, and the remark that unfortunately science neglects "*the* human factor." *The* human factor is apparently something as mysterious and inscrutable as the soul or other ectoplasmic manifestations. In any event, no one seems to be able to give any further light on the nature of *the* human factor. The assumption that there is any such single factor is itself gratuitous. What we do find on inquiry are a lot of human factors—all the loves, hates, jealousies, prejudices, fears, hopes, and aspirations of men. We know what we know about these factors through observation of human behavior and what more we need or want to know is to be learned in that way and in no other. There is nothing more mysterious about human factors than about other pehnomena which have not yet become the subject of serious scientific study. Of course, the trades and professions which have a vested interest in obscurantism, mysteriousness, and ignorance will oppose the advancement of science into this field as they have in other domains. But I suspect their efforts will not avail. Science has already so firm a hold on the imaginations of men that they will insist on invoking this powerful tool also in the explanation of the mysterious human factor. *The* human factor will then be found to be no factor at all, but merely a vague word designating a great variety of behavior which social scientists have hitherto been too lazy or ignorant to approach by the same methods that have clarified the factors in other phenomena of nature.

We have hitherto lacked boldness and an adequate vision of the true task of social science. Research in this field is today for the most part a quest for superficial remedies, for commercial guidance, and for historical and contemporary "human interest" stories. Everybody recognizes the importance of bookkeeping, census taking, studying the condition of the Negro population, and predicting the number of girdles that will be purchased in department stores a year from now. But there are types of research the immediate practical uses of which are not so obvious, yet which are essential to scientific development.

Shall we or shall we not assume that we can formulate laws of human behavior which are comparable to the laws of gravity, thermodynamics, and bacteriology? These latter laws do not of themselves create engineering wonders or cure disease. Nevertheless they constitute knowledge of a kind which is indispensable. The present argument is obviously handicapped in its most crucial respect, namely, its inability, in the space here available, to exhibit laws of social behavior comparable to the physical laws mentioned. Yet we have made considerable progress in this direction.

Finally, we come to what is regarded by many people, including scientists, as the most fundamental difference of all between the physical and the social sciences. "To understand and describe a system involving values," says Huxley, "is impossible without some judgment of values." "Values," he goes on to say, "are deliberately excluded from the purview of natural science."

It would be difficult to find a better example of confused thinking than that offered by current discussions of "values" and their supposed incompatibility with science. A principal cause of the confusion is a semantic error which is extremely common in the social sciences. In this case, it consists in converting the verb "valuating," meaning any discriminatory or selective behavior, into a noun called "values." We then go hunting for the *things* denoted by this noun. But there are no such things. There are only the valuating *activities* we started with. What was said above about motives applies with equal force to values.

They are clearly inferences from behavior. That is, we say a thing *has* value or *is* a value when people behave toward it so as to retain or increase their possession of it. It may be economic goods and services, political office, a mate, graduation, prestige, a clear conscience, or anything you please. Since valuations or values are empirically observable patterns of behavior, they may be studied as such, by the same general techniques we use to study other behavior.

As a matter of fact, everybody is more or less regularly engaged in such study of other people's values. It is quite essential to any kind of satisfactory living in any community. We try to find out as soon as possible what the values of our neighbors are. How do we find out? We observe their behavior, including their verbal behavior. We listen to what other people say about them, we notice what they spend their money for, how they vote, whether they go to church, and a hundred other things. On a more formal and scientific level, opinion polls on men and issues are taken to reflect the values of large groups. Economists, of course, have been studying for years certain kinds of evaluations of men through the medium of prices.

There appears to be no reason why values should not be studied as objectively as any other phenomena, for they are an inseparable part of behavior. The conditions under which certain values arise, i.e., the conditions under which certain kinds of valuating behavior take place, and the effects of "the existence of certain values" (as we say) in given situations are precisely what the social sciences must study and what they are studying. These values or valuating behaviors, like all other behavior, are to be observed, classified, interpreted, and generalized by the accepted techniques of scientific procedure.

Why, then, is the value problem considered unique and insurmountable in the social sciences?

The main reason seems to be that social scientists, like other people, often have strong feelings about religion, art, politics, and economics. That is, they have their likes and dislikes in these matters as they have in wine, women, and song. As a result of these preferences, both physical and social scientists frequently join other citizens to form pressure groups to advance the things they favor, including their own economic or professional advancement, Labor, Capital, Democracy, the True Church, or what not. To do so is the right of every citizen, and there is no canon of science or of civil law which requires scientists to abjure the rights which are enjoyed by all other members of a community.

The confusion about values seems to have arisen because both scientists and the public have frequently assumed that, when scientists engage in ordinary pressure-group activity, that activity somehow becomes science or scientific activity. This is a most mischievous fallacy. It is not surprising, perhaps, that the public should be confused on this point, because it may not always be clear when a scientist is expressing a scientific conclusion and when he is expressing a personal preference. But it is unpardonable for scientists themselves to be confused about what they know and say in their capacity as scientists and what they favor in religion, morals, and public policy. To pose as disinterested scientists announcing scientific conclusions when in fact they are merely expressing personal preferences is simple fraud, no matter how laudable or socially desirable may be the scientists' "motives" and objectives.

But is it possible for a person to play two or more distinct roles, such as scientist and citizen, without confusing the two? The answer is that it is being done every day. It is the most obvious commonplace that the actress who plays Juliet in the afternoon and Lady Macbeth at night does not allow her moral or other preference for one of these roles to influence her performance of the other. In any event, her competence is measured by her ability to play each role convincingly. During the same day she may also be expected to fulfill the roles of wife, mother, etc. Likewise, the chemist who vigorously campaigns against the use of certain gases in war obviously cannot allow that attitude to influence in the slightest degree the methods of producing or analyzing these gases. Science, as such, is non-moral. There is nothing in scientific work, as such, which dictates to what ends the products of science shall be used.

In short, it is not true that "to understand and describe a system involving values is impossible without some judgment of values." I can certainly report and understand the bald fact that a certain tribe kills its aged and eats them, without saying one word about the goodness or badness of that practice according to my own standards, or allowing these standards of mine to prevent me from giving an accurate report of the facts mentioned. The only value judgments which any properly trained scientist makes about his data are judgments regarding their relevance to his problem, the weight to be assigned to each aspect, and the general interpretation to be made of the observed events. These are problems which no scientist can escape, and they are not at all unique or insuperable in the social sciences.

Have scientists, then, no special function or obligation in determining the ends for which scientific knowledge is to be used? As scientists, *it is their business to determine reliably the immediate and remote costs and consequences of alternate possible courses of action*, and to make these known to the public. Scientists may then *in their capacity as citizens* join with others in advocating one alternative rather than another, as they prefer.

To the extent that their reputation and prestige is great, and to the extent that their tastes are shared by the masses of men, scientists will, of course, be influential in causing others to accept the goals the scientists recommend. In this sense, social science will doubtless become, as physical science already is, an important influence in determining the wants of men. That is, as a result of scientific knowledge, men will not want impossible or mutally exclusive things. They will not seek to increase foreign trade and at the same time establish more comprehensive and higher tariffs. They will not seek to reduce crime but at the same time maintain a crime-promoting penal system. They will not destroy the productive power of a nation and still expect it to be peaceful, prosperous, and democratic. They will not expect a world organization to be conjured into existence by semantically deranged "statesmen," before the necessary preceding integration of the constituent units has been achieved.

The development of the social sciences and the diffusion of scientific knowledge will doubtless greatly influence in the above ways the wants, wishes, and choices of men. But there is still an important difference between a statement of fact and the dictation of conduct. It is one thing for a physician to tell a patient: "Unless you undergo this operation, which will cost so much in time, money, and pain, you will probably die in one month." It is another matter to say: "Science, for which I am an accredited spokesman, says you shall undergo this operation." Any scientist who pretends that science authorizes him to make the latter statement is a fraud and a menace. Dictation of this type has not accompanied the rise of physical science and it need not result from the full maturity of the social sciences. This needs to be kept in mind especially in these days of much worry about brain trusts and whether, with the development of atomic fission, scientists must become a priestly class dictating all public policy.

The misunderstanding regarding the relation of scientists to practical affairs is so widespread and mischievous as to warrant further emphasis. The *application* of scientific knowledge obviously involves value judgments of some sort. This problem is equally present in the other sciences. After we know how to produce dynamite and what it will do, there remains the question: Shall we drop it from airplanes to destroy cathedrals and cities, or shall we use it to build roads through the mountains? After we know the effects of certain drugs and gases, the question still remains: Shall we use them to alleviate pain and prevent disease, or shall we use them to destroy helpless and harmless populations? There is certainly nothing in the well-developed sciences of chemistry or physics which answers these questions. Neither is it the business of the social sciences to answer (except *conditionally*, as we have seen) the question of what form of government we should have, what our treatment of other races should be, whether we should tolerate or persecute certain religious groups, whether and to what degree civil liberties should be maintained, and a multitude of other questions which agitate us. What, then, are social scientists for and what should they be able to do?

Broadly speaking, it is the business of social scientists to be able to predict with high probability the social weather, just as meteorologists predict sunshine and storm. More specifically, social scientists should be able to say what is likely to happen socially under stated conditions. A competent economist or political scientist should be able to devise, for example, a tax program for a given country which will yield with high probability a certain revenue and which will fall in whatever desired degrees upon each of the income groups of the area concerned. Social scientists should be able to state also what will be the effect of the application of this program upon income, investments, consumption, production, and the outcome of the next election. Having devised such a tax program and clearly specified what it will do, it is not the business of the social scientists any more than it is the business of any other citizens to secure the adoption or defeat of such a program. In the same way, competent sociologists, educators, or psychologists should be able to advise a parent as to the most convenient way of converting a son into an Al Capone or into an approved citizen, according to what is desired.

My point is that no science tells us *what to do* with the knowledge that constitutes the science. Science only provides a car and a chauffeur for us. It does not directly, as science, tell us where to drive. The car and the chauffeur will take us into the ditch, over the precipice, against a stone wall, or into the highlands of age-long human aspirations with equal efficiency. If we agree as to where we want to go and tell the driver our goal, he should be able to take us there by any one of a number of possible routes the costs and conditions of each of which the scientist should be able to explain to us. When these alternatives have been made clear, it is also a proper function of the scientist to devise the quickest and most reliable instrument for detecting the wishes of his passengers. But, except in his capacity as one of the passengers, the scientist who serves as navigator and chauffeur has no scientific privilege or duty to tell the rest of the passengers what they *should* want. There is nothing in either physical or social science which answers this question. Confusion on this point is, I think, the main reason for the common delusion that the social sciences, at least, must make value judgments of this kind.

But it does follow, as we have seen, that science, by virtue of its true function, as outlined above, may be of the utmost importance in helping people to decide intelligently what they want. We shall return to this subject in the concluding chapter. In the meantime, it may be noted that the broad general wants of people are perhaps everywhere highly uniform. They want, for example, a certain amount of physical and social security and some fun. It is disagreement over the means toward these ends, as represented by fantastic ideologies, that results in conflict and chaos. I have pointed out that, in proportion as a science is well developed, it can describe with accuracy *the consequences* of a variety of widely disparate programs of action. These consequences, if reliably predicted, are bound strongly to influence what people will want. But it remains a fact that science, in the sense of a predicter of consequences, is only *one* of the numerous influences that determine an individual's wants and his consequent behavior. Science and scientists are still the servants, not the masters, of mankind. Accordingly, those scientists who contend that they can scientifically determine not only the means but the ends of social policy should be exposed as scientific fakers as well as would-be dictators. Yet this is the very group which professes to be concerned about the democratic implications of the position I am here defending!

Finally, this view seems to some people to do away with what they call "the moral basis of society." Obviously, it does nothing of the sort. The question is not about the moral basis of society but about the social basis of morals. We merely advocate a scientific basis for morality. Presumably, all will agree that morals exist for man, not man for morals. Morals are those rules of conduct which man thinks have been to his advantage through the ages. Why should we then not all agree that we want the most authentic possible appraisal of that subject?

There appears, then, to be no reason why the methods of science cannot solve social problems. Neither should we expect more from social than from physical science. As *science*, both physical and social sciences have a common function, namely, to answer scientific questions. These answers will always be of an impersonal, conditional type: "*If* the temperature falls to 32°F., *then* water (H^2O) will freeze." "*If* a certain type of tax is adopted, *then* certain types of industrial activity will decrease." Neither of these statements carries any implications as to whether or how the knowledge should be used. Far from being a weakness, this characteristic of scientific knowledge is its greatest strength. The wants of men will change with changing conditions through the ages. The value of scientific knowledge lies precisely in this impersonal, neutral, general validity for whatever purposes man desires to use it.

For this reason, those scientists and others who try to identify science with some particular social program, sect, or party must be regarded as the most dangerous enemies of science. They are more dangerous than its avowed enemies, because the defenders of "democratic," "communist," "religious," or "moral" science pose as defenders of science and carry on their agitation in the name of lofty social sentiments. That this group is confused rather than malicious is evident from their proposal that scientists should take an oath not to engage in scientific activity which may be "destructive" or contrary to "toleration," "justice," etc. The absurdity of the proposal is readily apparent, if we consider any actual scientific work. No scientist can foresee all the uses to which his work may be put, and in any event it is a commonplace that the *same* drug may be used to cure or to kill people. It may be granted that preposterous proposals of this kind are a temporary hysterical phenomenon superinduced by such dramatic developments as the atomic bomb. It may be granted that the agitators are motivated by lofty social sentiments. Unfortunately, the same has been said for prominent proponents of the Inquisition.

The uses to which scientific or other knowledge is to be put have always been and will continue to be a legitimate concern of men. Science, as we have noted, can be valuable in helping men to decide that question. . . . Our warning here has been directed against attempts to corrupt scientific methods and results by allowing them to be influenced by the temporary, provincial, ethnocentric preferences of particular scientists or pressure groups.

36

ROBERT S. LYND

Knowledge for What?

Robert Staughton Lynd (1892–1970) is best known for his major ethnographic studies of a midwest town done in collaboration with his wife Helen M. Lynd (1896–).[1] *Following these well-known community studies of Middletown (actually Muncie, Indiana), Lynd turned his attention to the question of the uses of sociology and the issue of the possibility of the sort of value-free science of social action envisaged by Max Weber.*[2] *In recent years, Weber's position has come under considerable attack,*[3] *and the issues raised in Lynd's* Knowledge for What? *have become central ones. Those who attack the value-free position of Weber argue that too many scientists are hiding behind the neutrality of their discipline as a shield against engagement in the important social issues of our day.*[4] *They argue that (1) the sociologist is first a man, and all men are responsible for their actions; (2) the neutrality of sociology has made it the tool of vested interests in society which often pay for sociological research and thereby determine its direction; and (3) the sociologist has more knowledge about the state of the social world and therefore has more responsibility for leadership in determining the course of social change. Many of these critics of Weber's position also argue that his conception is based on a false model of social science patterned after the more objective physical sciences. They would argue that the kind of objective, external viewpoint of the physicist is not fully compatible with the emphasis on subjective understanding which they see as a major goal of sociology.*

The issue is by no means a simple one, and we can not resolve it here. However, it should be noted that the interaction of facts and values works both ways. Since most of our values involve goals to be

Reprinted from Robert S. Lynd, *Knowledge for What?* (Princeton, N.J.: Princeton University Press, 1939), pp. 180–201, by permission of Princeton University Press. Footnotes have been modified for completeness.

implemented in the empirical world, a science which gives us a mapping of that world will automatically have great relevance and constraining force upon those values. Knowledge of the empirical facts may tell us that some of our values can not be realized in the world. Thus, it may well be that the question of value-free facts might better be re-examined in terms of the limitations in our ever obtaining fact-free values.

Bibliographical Notes

1. Middletown: A Study in Contemporary American Culture (1929) *was followed by* Middletown in Transition: A Study in Cultural Conflicts (1937).

2. *Cf., Robert S. Lynd,* Knowledge for What? *(Princeton, N.J.: Princeton University Press, 1939).*

3. E.g., *Maurice Stein and Arthur Vidich (eds.),* Sociology on Trial *(Englewood Cliffs, N.J.: Prentice-Hall, 1963).*

4. E.g., *cf., Steven E. Deutsch and John Howard (eds.),* Where It's At: Radical Perspectives in Sociology *(New York: Harper & Row, 1969).*

The rôle of the learned man in earlier times may have been to stabilize custom and to conserve the past; but the social scientist, as his modern counterpart in today's world of rapid scientific discovery, is bound more closely to the moving front edge of man's experience. "Personality," as Santayana vividly phrases it, "is a knife-edge pressed against the future"; and, as instruments by which man works his way ahead in this atmosphere of accelerated change, the social sciences partake of this projective quality in human life. While human behavior exhibits large conformity to habit, one of its most signal features is also the thrusting insistence with which it uses the sticks and stones of culture to get ahead. Motivation, though conditioned by the past, is always contemporary and colored by the immediate situation.[1] Each individual is constantly going from a unique, concrete present to a unique, concrete new situation. This means that, granting all due weight to the institutionalized past as it conditions present behavior, the variables in the social scientist's equation must include not only the given set of structured institutions, but also *what the present human carriers of those institutions are groping to become.*

The social sciences are, therefore, engaged in analyzing a process of change which, at least in certain important respects, presents real options, and these options are of paramount significance. For social science to overlook this is largely to sterilize its functions. At the risk of seeming to overplay the amount of option that actually exists, one may say that the social scientist works constantly in terms of the kind of universe the natural scientist would face if the latter held the power to postpone or to prevent its possible collapse as a place tolerating human life.

The social sciences exhibit reluctance, however, to accept this full partnership with man in the adventure of living. They tend to mute their rôle as implementers of innovation. So one observes these grave young sciences hiding behind their precocious beards of "dispassionate research" and "scientific objectivity." They observe, record, and analyze, but they shun prediction. And, above all else, they avoid having any commerce with "values." Values, they say, may not be derived by science, and therefore science should have nothing to do with them. Social science prefers to urge that all the fruits of scholarly curiosity are important, that there is more than enough work to do in filling in the infinite odd bits of the jigsaw puzzle of the unknown, and that science has no criteria by which to allot priorities in importance. It prefers to say that for science the word "ought" ought never to be used, except in saying that it ought never to be used.

There would be no social sciences if there were not perplexities in living in culture that call for solution. And it is precisely the rôle of the social sciences to be troublesome, to disconcert the habitual arrangements by which we manage to live along and to demonstrate the possibility of change in more adequate directions. Their rôle, like that of the skilled surgeon, is to get us into immediate trouble in order to prevent our chronic present troubles from becoming even more dangerous. In a culture like ours, in which power is normally held by the few and used offensively and defensively to bolster their instant advantage within the *status quo*, the rôle of such a constructive troublemaker is scarcely inviting. But that is simply another way of stating the predicament of the social sciences in our type of culture.

Nature may be neutral. The sun and lightning descend upon the just and upon the unjust. But culture is not neutral, because culture is interested personalities in action. The social scientist's reason for urging the neutrality of science in such a world of bias is understandable, but it has unfortunate results that curtail heavily the capacity of social science to do precisely the thing that it is the responsibility of social science to do.

Nobody questions the indispensability of detachment in weighing and appaising one's data. But in other respects, as a matter of fact, current social science is neither as "neutral" nor as "pure" as it pretends to be. On the negative side, it avoids many issues that the going culture would view as either impertinent or troublesome, and it allows the powerful biases of the culture to set for it the statement of many of the problems on which it works. On the positive side, it works in a general spirit of modest meliorism, seeking to make small changes for the better in the various institutions to which it applies itself. Thus economists try to "increase welfare" by "bettering business conditions," making business more "efficient" and "profitable," "reducing the amplitude of the business cycle," "stabilizing prices," and "lessening labor trouble." Political scientists seek to "improve" public administration and international relations. Sociologists, likewise, try to "improve" social organization, urban conditions, the family, and so on. Such aims, here and elsewhere in the social sciences, apply not merely to the social scientist as technician but also affect the selection of problems for research.

"Pure scientific curiosity" is a term to which students of semantics should turn their attention. There is "idle" curiosity and "focused" curiosity, but in the world of science there is no such thing as "pure" curiosity. No economist collects the dates on the coins passed over the counter of a soda fountain, or the precise hours of mailing of letters received by different types of retail stores on Monday and on Saturday, and no sociologist interested in urban problems counts and compares the number of bricks in the buildings on a slum block and on a Park Avenue block. Why do we train scientists? To give them refined techniques of observation, analysis, and control, to be sure. But, even more important, the outstanding characteristic of a well trained scientist is his ability to distinguish "significant" from "insignificant" problems and data. Good scientific training sensitizes one to important problems; it deliberately sets up before the imagination of the scientist a screen which lets through one type of data and bars another—in short, it gives the scientist a selective point of view. Research without an actively selective point of view becomes the ditty bag of an idiot, filled with bits of pebbles, straws, feathers, and other random hoardings. If nobody goes about endlessly counting throughout a lifetime the number of particles of sand along infinite miles of seashore over all the coasts of the world, why is this? Because there is no point to it, no need to complete this particular aspect of the jigsaw puzzle of the unknown.

The confusion that exists between the social scientist's professions to eschew all questions of value and what he so patently does is a confusion in the point at which valuing is applied. Values may be and are properly and necessarily applied in the preliminary selection of "significant," "important" problems for research. They may be but should not be applied thereafter to bias one's analysis or the interpretation of the meanings inherent in one's data. It is a commonplace that the man who cannot train himself to curb his personal concern in a problem so that it does not bias his appraisal of his data has no business in scientific work. But this does not justify social science in its wholesale official rejection of values. Actually, values are always present in the initial selection of a problem. If they are not overt and announced, they are none the less latent and tacitly accepted.

"Those who boast," says Morris Cohen,[2] "that they are not, as social scientists, interested in what ought to be, generally assume (tacitly) that the hitherto prevailing order is the proper ideal of what ought to be. . . . A theory of social values like a theory of metaphysics is none the better because it is held tacitly and is not, therefore, critically examined. . . .

"Because it is thus impossible to eliminate human bias in matters in which we are vitally interested, some sociologists (for example, the Deutsche Gessellschaft für Soziologie) have banished from their programme all questions of value and have sought to restrict themselves to the theory of social happenings. This effort to look upon human actions with the same ethical neutrality with which we view geometric figures is admirable. But the questions of human value are inescapable, and those who banish them at the front door admit them unavowedly and therefore uncritically at the back door."

In the current social science world, but newly escaped from the era of over-easy theory-building into the world of patient empiricism and quantification, and overwhelmed by the number of things to describe and quantify in an era of rapid change, the prevailing tendency is heavily on the side of accepting institutional things and their associated values as given. The modern professor confines himself to professing facts, and radical criticism and generalization must wait "until all the data are gathered." If the social scientist does not content himself simply with describing and analyzing what *was* or what *is* in terms of last year's statistics, he is apt to confine himself to short "next step" ameliorative research. No one denies the utility of slum clearance, of predicting recidivism in crime, of relocating the geographical boundaries of administrative units within the Chicago metropolitan district, or of reducing the wastes in distribution. But the little values implicit in myriad such researches on the next step here, and here, and here in the institutional system are not discrete and complete in themselves. Each of these next steps is important only as part of a more inclusive, long-term value to which it is relevant. By refusing commerce with such more inclusive values, the social scientist does not escape them. What he does is, rather, to accept tacitly the inclusive value-judgment of the culture as to the rightness of the "American way" and the need for only minor remedial changes. Whether and at what points this optimistic value-judgment is warranted should be a subject of inquiry by science, rather than a thing taken for granted.

When the empirical analyst says, as in the statement of the National Bureau of Economic Research quoted earlier, that "We confine ourselves to stating the facts as we find them. With opinions about the promise or the danger to American life from the growth of trade unions we have no concern as an organization of investigators," he is staying his hand at the point at which the culture is most in need of his help. One cannot assume that the meanings of "facts" are always clear or unequivocal. Somebody is going to interpret what the situation means, because the character of man's dilemmas is such as to brook no stay. When the social scientist, after intensive study of a problem, avoids extrapolating his data into the realm of wide meaning, however tentatively stated, he invites others presumably more biassed than himself—e.g., the National Association of Manufactures, the American Federation of Labor, the advertising man, the American Legion, and so on—to thrust upon the culture their interpretations of the meaning of the situation.

The depression has stepped up like a loudspeaker the dissonances generated in the attempt to operate a complex culture by these casual values tossed up by special interests pretending to speak for the public interest. Never before in our culture has the contrast between the casual and customary *and* the intelligent and humanly valuable been thrown into such unmistakable contrast. Perhaps never before have we had such an urgent sense of the difference it can make to know what current tendencies mean, to know what to value and why, and how to materialize those values. The culture is proceeding to this unavoidable assignment after the blind, shambling fashion of cultures. At this point the social sciences, the instruments for appraisal and direction-finding, plead immunity from the responsibility to guide the culture. It is not the business of social science, they claim, "to care," "to value," "to say what ought to be done." To which the rejoinder should be: Either the social sciences know more than do the "hard-headed" businessman, the "practical" politician and administrator, and the other *de facto* leaders of the culture as to what the findings of research mean, as to the options the institutional system presents, as to what human personalities want, why they want them, and how desirable changes can be effected, *or* the vast current industry of social science is an empty façade.

The point is not that social science should go in for pretentious soothsaying. Man's guess into the future is fragile, even when implemented by science. But the stubborn fact remains that we sail inevitably into the future, the sea is full of dangerous reefs and shoals, and drifting is more dangerous than choosing the course that our best intelligence dictates. If, then, social science should take the wheel, what does it know by which it can steer?

It was stated above that it is essential in the training of the social scientist to help him to discover a point of view, a selective screen which lets through the "significant" and eliminates the "insignificant." Scientific judgment and imagination cannot be taught, but the young scientist can learn them, if anywhere, from a great teacher-scientist who knows how to fill his laboratory and classroom with his conception of the significant.[3] What social science evidently needs is to seek to make explicit its tacit criteria of the "significant."

The most general criterion in current use is "a new contribution to knowledge." This criterion receives support from the honorific status of "knowledge" in our traditions; also from the empiricist's faith that, if each worker adds his brick of data to the heap, the whole will automatically build itself into a useful structure. But this vague reference of social science to the quantity of knowledge leaves unanswered the question of what it is to which knowledge is relevant.

Another criterion of relevance is often stated in such terms as "economic welfare" and "social welfare." But, again one asks, "welfare" defined in what terms and with reference to what? In this connection the concrete incident with which Floyd Allport begins his *Institutional Behavior*[4] is illuminating:

"At a meeting of the faculty of a certain large university a proposal for a new administrative policy was being discussed. The debate was long and intense before a final vote of adoption was taken. As the professors filed out of the room an instructor continued the discussion with one of the older deans.

" 'Well,' observed the latter official, 'it may be a little hard on some people; but I feel sure that, in the long run, the new plan will be for the best interests of the institution.'

" 'Do you mean that it will be good for the students?' inquired the younger man.

" 'No,' the dean replied, 'I mean it will be for the good of the whole institution.'

" 'Oh, you mean that it will benefit the faculty as well as the students?'

" 'No,' said the dean, a little annoyed, 'I don't mean *that;* I mean it will be a good thing for the institution itself.'

" 'Perhaps you mean the trustees then—or the Chancellor?'

" 'No, I mean the institution, the *institution!* Young man, don't you know what an institution is?' "

Evidently such terms as "economic welfare" and "social welfare" leave us still, therefore, with our point of reference blurred; and they accordingly invite the lack of common focus and articulation of data which now cripples the funtioning of the social sciences.

Since it is human beings that build culture and make it go, the social scientist's criteria of the significant cannot stop short of those human beings' criteria of the significant. The values of human beings living together in the pursuit of their deeper and more persistent purposes constitute the frame of reference that identifies significancc for social science. But the situation is confused by the fact that the social scientist at work on any single culture confronts in the behavior of people two sets of emphases upon what is significant: those stereotyped emphases which human beings *enmeshed in that particular culture* exhibit as they live toward the goals sanctioned most prominently by *that culture's* traditions and the example of its conspicuous leaders; and a more general order of emphases, common to human beings everywhere as persons living with their fellows, around which the selected emphases of single cultures oscillate. These latter may be characterized as the deeper and more primitive cravings of personalities.

This is not to suggest that there is a "natural man" independent of culture; but simply that human beings, structured and functioning organically alike, subjected at birth and in early infancy to many broadly common types of experience, and growing up inevitably dependent on each other, develop a set of roughly similar underlying cravings. The point here is that, in addition to their more immediately biological life-processes and in addition to their culturally conditioned ways of behaving, human beings develop needs that are less directly referable to either of the above than to certain bald and unescapable *human experiences*. All of us are born helpless infants into a world too big for us, where there are hunger and humanly unmanageable things like the weather. In our helplessness we have no choice as regards dependence upon other human beings. From our first moments in life we experience deeply and imperatively the need of living in certain ways, for instance, intimately and securely with other persons. We begin at once to cry out for other persons to succor our needs, we are active when the tides of energy run full, and we lapse into latency and sleep when they run low. We undergo certain experiences that make us feel comfortable and happy, and others that frustrate us. As a result, we acquire from earliest infancy certain very broad cravings *as human beings* which, while not independent of culture, are common to the situation of living on the earth rather than precisely referable to the particular qualities of any single culture. Our culture enmeshes us from birth in its specificities. It may have a structure that actively furthers many of these cravings in its own balance of emphases; or it may have class or other structuring that operates to insure satisfaction to some persons or classes and largely to cramp satisfaction in others. But the growing personality tends to carry along these primitive cravings, echoing and re-echoing within him as he conforms to or resists the precepts of those about him in his culture. The behavior one sees in any single culture is a kind of contrapuntal adaptation between the historically conditioned special emphases of that culture and these less special and more persisting cravings of persons.

Social scientists are wont to stress the *culture's* (institutions') special emphases as defining for them the significant, and to assume that this comprises the whole of the significant. This results in the tacit assumption that the special emphases in a particular culture, e.g., our own extreme emphasis upon competitiveness, are "natural," "inevitable," "what people really want." The task of social science tends, then, to become defined as helping to do and to get these things. These emphases upon the significant within any *single* culture are a less sure guide for social science than generalizations derived more broadly from the behavior of persons in all cultures. No protestations of scientific objectivity and ethical neutrality can excuse the social scientist from coming down into the arena and accepting as his guiding values, *in selecting and defining his problems*, these deep, more widely based, cravings which living personalities seek to realize. The day has passed when ethics could be regarded as a comfortable thing apart, given at the hands of God as an inscrutable "moral law implanted in the hearts of men," a thing to which social science could hand over all its problems of values. The old, aloof ethics has evaporated, and ethics today is but a component of the cravings of persons going about the daily round of living with each other. And the science of human behavior in culture, as a science charged with appraising man's optional futures in the light of himself and of present favoring and limiting conditions, can no more escape dealing with man's deep values and the potential futures they suggest than it can avoid dealing with the expressions, overlayings, and distortions of man's cravings which appear in the institutions of a particular culture.

What, then, are these values and cravings of the human personality? Adequate answer to this question awaits further research by a wide group of specialists, ranging all the way from biochemistry to each of the social sciences, the arts, and the humanities. But life does not wait upon the perfect formulation. One must take one's awareness at each given moment and use it. The following suggestions as to the persistent cravings of human personalities are set down not because these cravings as here stated have been finally proved by science, but because human behavior keeps continually affirming and reaffirming them. We are sufficiently sure of them to warrant the question: What possible changes in our culture might the social scientist explore with an eye to testing and mapping out ways of placing culture more actively in support of these needs of human beings? The list here suggested is a more explicit elaboration of the processes of rhythm, motivation, and growth discussed earlier, with the addition of stress upon certain more definitely *social* experiences. The items are pitched on a level at which "cravings" and "values" are synonymous, adhering to the level of personality and avoiding, on the one hand, cravings for such things as food, shelter, and sex, in their purely biological aspects, and, on the other hand, such explicitly cultural values as a mink coat or a midwinter vacation in Florida.[5] The point to be stressed here is not detail and nomenclature, but the fact of the generality of such desires—call them what one will—in human beings. For *social* science they represent a datum, as well as criteria of cultural adequacy, of incontestable importance.

1. The human personality craves to live not too far from its own physical and emotional tempo and rhythm. While capable of large adjustment in these respects, the personality suffers strain when the institutional demands of the culture cut too coercively across this personally natural tempo and rhythm. One may not assume that the standards of performance worked out in a culture at any given time represent the best possible, or even a desirable, adjustment. In a culture like our own,

which employs such impersonal devices as machines, time- and motion-studies, and cost-accounting to determine the profitable (defined in terms of dollars) competitive rate of "efficiency," the resulting demands for speed, energy-sustention, concentration, and tolerance of monotony in office and factory may have only the inescapable minimum of relevance to the cravings of the workers.

As a part of this craving to maintain a tempo and rhythm natural to it, the personality craves periods of latency and private recoil during which time, space, and other persons can be taken on its own terms without coercion.[6]

2. The human personality craves the sense of growth, of realization of personal powers, and it suffers in an environment that denies growth or frustrates it erratically or for reasons other than the similar needs for growth in others.

The more precise definition of degrees of necessary deference to "similar needs for growth in others" is a major task for social science; and it needs to be worked out in different types of situations and with full recognition both of individual differences in capacity and of the inescapable necessity for leadership. Our culture defines this situation at present with such exaggerated tolerance that it equates indiscriminately the need for the free hand by the finance capitalist or employer with that of the laborer. Due regard for the rights of others to grow in their capacities and achievements obviously stops considerably short of tolerance of the rights of vested power agents, even in an allegedly "free country" like ours, to give or to withhold or to obstruct opportunity. Dollars have no conscience, and they may not properly be made the arbiters in such situations.

3. The human personality craves to do things involving the felt sense of fairly immediate meaning. This sense of immediate meaning may derive from the interest in doing an intrinsically interesting new thing, i.e., the exhilaration of "getting the hang of it"; from the fun of doing something that *is* fun; from the sense of personal power involved in exercising one's craftsmanship; or even from doing something possessing slight intrinsic meaning but with a heavy, reasonably sure instrumental relationship to something else that has great immediate meaning. But immediate meaning tends to be dissipated when the activity in hand is too distasteful; or when the line of instrumentalism from doing something with little or no intrinsic meaning to the something else that has immediate meaning is over-prolonged or too markedly unreliable.

In our culture this craving is put in jeopardy by the fact that so many of us work at highly specialized, semi-mechanized, and routine tasks which we undertake primarily on the basis of their sheer availability and income yield, rather than because they are peculiarly adapted to us; by the fact that so much of our work goes into the struggle "to make both ends meet"; and by the unreliability of many of the chains of instrumental actions leading to the future, as suggested in Chapter III. The present widespread confusion as regards the hitherto taken-for-granted virtue of "saving for the future" derives from the undermining of its immediate meaning by the "big money" era of the 1920's and the subsequent helpless evaporation of savings in the depression.[7]

4. The human personality craves physical and psychological security (peace of mind, ability to "count on" life's continuities, and so on) to the degree that will still leave with the individual control over the options as to when to venture (for the fun of it, for the values involved) into insecurity.

5. But the human personality is active and cherishes in varying degrees the right to exercise these optional insecurities. It craves novelty (the learning and doing of new things), provided this can be taken on the personality's own terms, i.e., "in its stride." It craves risk as exhilarating—when it *is* exhilarating. But risk is exhilarating only at the points of peak energy storage in the individual's rhythms of personal living; and when risk is continuous or forced upon one the personality is put under unwelcome strain which invites discomfort, demoralization, and regression. The human personality dislikes to "go it blind" into important risks, but prefers to have its options implemented by the fullest possible information as to the precise nature of the risk and as to the best chances of minimizing that risk.

Our current American reliance upon individual offense and defense, upon living as untied-in, competitive ants in urban ant-heaps, upon casualness and *laissez-faire*, and the widening gap between the knowledge of the trained sophisticate and that of the masses—all of these things tend to force the individual to try continually to stabilize life on the wavering edge of chronic and often quite unnecessary risk. The sheer fact of living ahead into new experience inevitably entails risks. But, when such necessary and desirable risk is complicated by a mass of avoidable hazards created by the crude structure of the culture, by over-dependence upon individual rationality, and by lack of popular diffusion of relevant knowledge, energy is inevitably diverted to these needless risks that should go into the exhilarating risks of creative living.

6. As a corollary of the preceding, the human personality craves the expression of its capacities through rivalry and competition, with result-

ing recognition of status—but, again, under the same circumstances as noted in 5 above: only when energy and interest are ready for it and the personality is "set to go" and to go on its own terms. The small boy's spontaneous exclamation, "I'll race you to that tree!" and the friendly rivalry of two farmers in completing the mowing of their fields are fresh and unforced expressions of this desire for spontaneous rivalry. But the human personality does not crave competition when the latter is continuous, enforced, or too threatening. It seems safe to say that most human personalities do not crave as pervasive and continuously threatening competition as they tend to be subjected to in our culture.[8]

7. But if rivalry and the status it yields provide some of the arpeggios of living, the more continuous melody is the craving of the personality for human mutuality, the sharing of purposes, feeling, and action with others. The personality craves to belong to others richly and confidently and to have them belong in turn to it. It craves the expression and the receipt of affection. It craves to be actively accepted and given secure status as a person, *for* the person that it is—as well as for the work it can do. Sympathy is normal to it. Conversely, it suffers when forced to live in physical or psychological isolation. While this desire for mutuality pervades all aspects of living, it is particularly marked in the relations between the two sexes. The personality craves more than physical coitus, although the psychological accompaniments of physical union considered desirable vary markedly in different cultures.

8. The human personality craves coherence in the direction and meaning of the behavior to which it entrusts itself in the same or different areas of its experience. Contradictions and unresolved conflicts within the rules it learns from the culture create tensions and hinder functional satisfaction. Here is the point at which such aspects of our culture as the dual allegiance to the contradictory values of aggressive dominance and of gentleness and mutuality, noted in Chapter III, throw us continually into tension.

9. But the human personality also craves a sense of freedom and diversity in living that gives expression to its many areas of spontaneity without sacrificing unduly its corresponding need for a basic integration of continuities. It craves a cultural setting that offers active encouragement to creative individuation in terms of the whole range of one's personal interests and uniquenesses. And, conversely, it dislikes monotony, routine, and coercion that cramp and flatten out the rhythms of living and force a canalization of energy expenditure that deadens spontaneity.

The preceding itemization of persistent cravings of the human personality might be condensed or expanded. Some of these cravings fall into contrasting pairs—security and risk, coherence and spontaneity, novelty and latency, rivalry and mutuality. Confronted with such contrasting tendencies, there is some disposition to dismiss the whole matter and to say that they cannot ever be reconciled. The important thing for the social scientist to note, however, is that these pairs do not represent contradictions any more than sleep is a contradiction of waking. They are but different phases in the rhythm of living. Obviously, no individual craves the independent maximization of each of these values, or of all of them at the same instant. That would involve an anarchy within the personality that would be intolerable. What each of us craves is a pattern of degrees and rhythms of satisfaction of these separate cravings that hangs together in terms of our diverse motivations and "feels right to me as a person living with all these other people." The task of the sciences of human behavior, therefore, is not to "reconcile" these different needs, but to discover the flexible cultural patterning in which their varied expressions in personality can find most adequate expression in the sequences of living.

Individuals differ in bodily endowment and, consequently, in the vigor of their cravings—a weakling may crave security more than his stronger fellows. They differ also in their cravings at different points in the longitudinal life-span from youth to old age. The urgency of craving is also well-nigh infinitely variable, according to the cumulated emphases of a given culture. Life tends to achieve some semblance of satisfaction of these cravings even in cultures where marked degrees of distortion or denial of certain cravings are accepted as normal. What tends to happen in every culture is that, according as certain of these elementary cravings are under strain, or, conversely, are so amply catered to that they are taken for granted, the pattern of the culture exhibits resulting degrees and kinds of compensatory emphases. The heavy institutionalization of our own culture around personal competitive predation and risk gives to the pattern compensatory exaggerations of the importance of property as the source of security and of sex as the source of affection and mutuality. The regimentations and deferred consummations which the culture enforces on individuals also thrust up compensating emphases upon securing the sense of immediate meaning through such stereotyped things as explosive bursts of recreation, asserting one's superiority, being one of the first to wear a new spring style, or moving to a more socially eloquent address. Where the deeper and more individuated forms of spontaneity are denied, personality will write into the culture other forms of self-assertion.

In view of the range of individual differences and of the notorious sluggishness of culture in adapting itself to the modulations of personality, men may not expect even the most flexible and well adapted culture to meet with perfect timing and adequacy all the cravings of personality. It is not likely that all the ambivalences we feel in living may be blamed upon the culture, or that even in our most optimistic moments we can envisage a culture capable of resolving all of these for us. Furthermore, the satisfaction which culture yields to the persons who live by it depends less upon the presence or absence of any universally absolute quantum of emphasis upon a given craving than upon the balance and relationship among available satisfactions of the entire group of interacting cravings; and upon the hospitality of the culture to subtlety of individual patterning.

The situation social science faces is, therefore, complex; but, were this not the case, there would be little need for social science. We need not be staggered by the fact that some occasions giving rise to strain and to such resulting behavior as over-aggressiveness will probably always remain close to the surface of living. Confronted by such facts, the responsibility of social science is to ask: To what extent and how do our present institutions actually encourage such socially disruptive behavior? And how may these aggravating factors be removed or altered? Even after institutions are changed so as to minimize occasions for such behavior, social science still confronts the problem of discovering how the residue of over-aggressiveness can be canalized off through socially harmless outlets, so that it will not be unconsciously and recklessly displaced onto other situations where it does not belong.

This chapter has suggested that human cravings are not only inescapably parts of the datum with which social science works, but that they dictate the direction of emphasis of social science as man's working tool for continually rebuilding his culture. So viewed, "institutions," "social change," "trends," "lags," "disequilibria," and all the other conceptualizations of social science become relevant primarily to the wants and purposes of human personalities seeking to live. The central assumption becomes that men want to do, to be, to feel certain identifiable things, such as those outlined in the above chapter, as they live along together; and the derivative assumption regarding the rôle of social science is that its task is to find out ever more clearly what these things are that human beings persist in wanting, and how these things can be built into culture. If man's cravings are ambivalent, if he is but sporadically rational and intelligent, the task of social science becomes the discovery of what forms of culturally-structured learned behavior can maximize opportunities for rational behavior where it appears to be essential for human well-being, and at the same time provide opportunity for expression of his deep emotional spontaneities where those, too, are important.

The problems and hypotheses for research in the chapter that follows derive from such considerations as the preceding. In confronting each problem, the question was asked, "But what do human beings *want?* How do they *crave* to live?" And the resulting hypotheses flow from our knowledge of each problem (how it came to be a problem, what it does to human beings, and so on), seen in relation to the above question. If social science is not to be forever stalemated in the face of the future, some point of reference must be established by which it can get beyond the present paralyzing question, "But how are *we* to determine what *ought* to be? That can be no concern of the scientist." Lacking an answer to that question, there is no firm basis for doing more than following the determinisms of the moment, with such minor remedial improvisations as science may devise. The present chapter has sought to recover the sense of direction within the human stuff of us all. If such a sense of direction is as yet only partially grasped in such statements of the cravings of human personality, it affords nevertheless a stout instrument with which social science can take up its work of appraising and re-shaping our culture. It enables us to ask: What ones of our current institutions, appraised from this point of view, effectively support men's needs—and how effectively—and what ones block them? And what changes in these institutions are indicated?

NOTES

1. Gordon Allport, *Personality: A Psychological Interpretation* (New York: Holt, 1937), p. 194.
2. *Reason and Nature* (New York: Harcourt, Brace, 1931), pp. 343, 349.
3. In these days, when social science is increasingly being drawn into the controversies that beset our culture, the statement is frequently heard within faculty groups that "It is not the duty of our universities to reform the world." No claim is made throughout the present book that an entire science, university, or department of a university should be

placed behind the effort to effect any given single change in the economic or political structure of our culture; still less that classroom lectures should use hypotheses as accepted fact and propagandize for them. Either of these procedures would be an intolerable affront to education and to science. It is a subterfuge, however, when the individual social scientist employs such a statement to avoid his personal responsibility as a scientist to set his analysis of data in the long view, to "make up his mind" in terms of long-run hypotheses, however tentatively held, and to teach and to carry on research in an atmosphere of constant endeavor to clarify and to test these hypotheses. Hypotheses are an indispensable part of good teaching and research. A good scientist has a point of view. He holds it subject to constant correction, but without a point of view he is no scientist, and as a teacher he becomes simply a walking equivalent of an encyclopedia or a colorless textbook. A prevalent protest by alert students in the social sciences is that the immediacies of facts and data tend to operate in the university classroom as a monopolizing concern shutting off the listener from the ripe wisdom of many a mature teacher. It is the boast of some able professors that they handle controversial subjects in the classroom in such skilful manner that the students are never able to know "what the professor himself really thinks about the problem." This amounts, in the judgment of the writer, to sabotaging the inner meaning of social science and of education. Of course, no university should have a staff all the members of which think alike on a given problem. But the blurring of explicit statement of sharp and divergent hypotheses within a faculty is almost as dangerous.

4. (Chapel Hill: University of North Carolina Press, 1933), p. 3.
5. The cravings of human beings here set down are similar to the "four wishes" —for security, new experience, recognition (status), and emotional response—originally set forth by W. I. Thomas in the Methodological Note to *The Polish Peasant in Europe and America,* and restated in the above somewhat altered form in Chapter I of his *The Unadjusted Girl.*

   While these cravings are on a level of generality that is believed to make them characteristic in some degree of persons in all cultures, they are not presented as instincts in the sense of McDougall's "acquisitiveness," "constructiveness," "curiosity," "flight," "pugnacity," "reproduction," "repulsion," "submission," "self-display," and "gregariousness." They are more modifiable than instincts and are results of common early experiences shared by all human beings, rather than being biological in origin, as instincts were supposed to be.
6. See Chapters V and VI of Plant's *Personality and the Culture Pattern* for a description of the "barriers" the urban personality in our culture tends to set up to ward off the pressures of too many other people pressing too closely upon it.
7. See *Middletown in Transition,* pp. 477–9.
8. See the discussion of the prevalence of anxiety in Karen Horney, *The Neurotic Personality of Our Time* (New York: Norton, 1937).

37

KARL MANNHEIM

On the Sociology of Knowledge

Karl Mannheim (1893–1947) was born and educated for the most part in Germany. He taught at the University of London from 1933 until his death. Before coming to England, his primary concern had been with the social foundations and limitations of knowledge. This concern with the effects of social structure upon belief systems is called the sociology of knowledge. *Mannheim asserted that the basic categories of thought were functions of one's social status, roles, and position in society.*[1] *Extending the basically Marxian notion of a correlation between values and economic position (the former acting as a "superstructure" rationalizing the needs of the latter), Mannheim believed this to be true of all intellectual works.*[2] *Though Mannheim failed to successfully resolve central problems of relativity which his view would pose for the development of science, especially a social science, his many insights and the central questions that he asked about the relation of social structure to belief systems pose critical problems in methodology, and recent years have seen a growing concern with these questions.*[3]

Bibliographical Notes

1. *Mannheim's principal writings available in English are:* Essays on Sociology and Social Psychology (*1922–1940*); Essays on the Sociology of Knowledge (*1923–1929*); Ideology and Utopia: An Introduction to the Sociology of Knowledge (*1929–1931*); Man and Society in an Age of Reconstruction: Studies in Modern Social Structure (*1935*); Diagnosis

---

Reprinted from Karl Mannheim, *Ideology and Utopia,* translated by Louis Wirth and Edward Shils (New York: Harcourt Brace Jovanovich, 1957 Harvest Book edition), pp. 292–306, by permission of the publisher, Harcourt Brace Jovanovich. Footnotes have been deleted.

of Our Time: Wartime Essays of a Sociologist (*1939–1943*); Freedom, Power, and Democratic Planning (*1950*); *and* Essays on the Sociology of Culture (*1956*).

2. For overviews of Mannheim's position, see: Edward Shils, "Mannheim, Karl," International Encyclopedia of Social Sciences, Vol. 9 (*New York: Macmillan and Free Press, 1968*), *pp. 557–562; Alvin Boskoff,* Theory in American Sociology (*New York: Thomas Y. Crowell, 1969*), *pp. 159–181; Irving M. Zeitlin,* Ideology and the Development of Sociological Theory (*Englewood Cliffs, N.J.: Prentice-Hall, 1968*), *pp. 281–319; and Robert K. Merton, "Karl Mannheim and the Sociology of Knowledge," in his* Social Theory and Social Structure (*Glencoe, Ill.: Free Press, 1957 edition*), *pp. 489–508.*

3. E.g., *Peter Berger and Thomas Luckmann,* The Social Construction of Reality (*New York: Doubleday Anchor, 1966*); *Werner Stark,* The Sociology of Knowledge (*London: Routledge and Kegan Paul, 1958*); *and Irving Louis Horowitz,* Philosophy, Science and the Sociology of Knowledge (*Springfield, Ill.: Charles C. Thomas, 1961*). *For an excellent brief contemporary statement, see: Robert K. Merton, "The Sociology of Knowledge," in his* Social Theory and Social Structure, op. cit., *pp. 456–488.*

Once we realize that although epistemology is the basis of all the empirical sciences, it can only derive its principles from the data supplied by them, and once we realize, further, the extent to which epistemology has hitherto been profoundly influenced by the ideal of the exact sciences, then it is clearly our duty to inquire how the problem will be affected when other sciences are taken into consideration. This suggests the following arguments:—

Revision of the Thesis that the Genesis of a Proposition Is under All Circumstances Irrelevant to Its Truth. The abrupt absolute dualism between "validity" and "existence"—between "meaning" and "existence"—between "essence" and "fact" is, as has often been pointed out, one of the axioms of the "idealistic" epistemology and noology prevailing to-day. It is regarded as impregnable and is the most immediate obstacle to the unbiased utilization of the findings of the sociology of knowledge.

Indeed, if the type of knowledge represented by the example $2 \times 2 = 4$ is subjected to examination, then the correctness of this thesis is fairly well demonstrated. It is true of this type of knowledge that its genesis does not enter into the results of thought. From this it is only a short step to construct a sphere of truth in itself in such a manner that it becomes completely independent of the knowing subject. Moreover, this theory of the separability of the truth-content of a statement from the conditions of its origin had great value in the struggle against psychologism, for only with the aid of this theory was it possible to separate the known from the act of knowing. The observation that the genesis of an idea must be kept separate from its meaning applies also in the domain of explanatory psychology. It is only because in this realm it could be demonstrated in certain cases that the psychological processes which produce meanings are irrelevant to their validity, that this statement was legitimately incorporated into the truths of noology and epistemology. Between, for instance, the laws of the mechanism of association and the judgment arrived at by this associative mechanism, there exists a gap, which makes it plausible that a genesis of that kind does not contribute anything to the evaluation of meaning. There are, however, types of genesis which are not void of meaning, the peculiarities of which have until now never been analysed. Thus, for example, the relationship between existential position and the corresponding point of view may be considered as a genetic one, but in a sense different from that used previously. In this case, too, the question of genesis is involved, since there can be no doubt that we are here dealing with the conditions of emergence and existence of an assertion. If we speak of the "position behind a point of view" we have in mind a complex of conditions of emergence and existence which determine the nature and development of an assertion. But we would be falsely characterizing the existential situation of the assertor if we failed to take into account its meaning for the validity of the assertion. A position in the social structure carries with it, as we have seen, the probability that he who occupies it will think in a certain way. It signifies existence oriented with reference to certain meanings (*Sinnausgerichtetes Sein*). Social position cannot be described in terms which are devoid of social meanings as, for example, by mere chronological designation. 1789 as a chronological date is wholly meaningless. As historical designation, however, this date refers to a set of meaningful social events which in themselves demarcate the range of a certain type of experiences, conflicts, attitudes, and thoughts. Historical-social position can only be adequately characterized by meaningful designations (as, for instance, by such designations as "liberal position," "proletarian conditions of existence," etc.). "Social existence" is thus an area of being, or a sphere of existence, of which orthodox ontology which recognizes only the absolute dualism between being devoid of meaning on the one hand and meaning on the other hand takes no account. A genesis of this sort could be characterized by calling it a "meaningful genesis" (*Sinngenesis*) as contrasted with a "factual-genesis" (*Faktizitätsgenesis*). If a model of this sort had been kept in mind in stating the relationship between being and meaning, the duality of being and validity would not have been assumed as absolute in epistemology and noology. Instead, there would have been a series of gradations between these two poles, in which such intermediate cases as "being invested with meaning" and "being oriented to meaning" would have found a place and been incorporated into the fundamental conception.

The next task of epistemology, in our opinion, is to overcome its partial nature by incorporating into itself the multiplicity of relationships between existence and validity (*Sein und Geltung*) as discovered by the sociology of knowledge, and to give attention to the types of knowledge operating in a region of being which is full of meaning and which affects the truth-value of the assertions. Thereby epistemology is not supplanted by the sociology of knowledge but a new kind of epistemology is called for which will reckon with the facts brought to light by the sociology of knowledge.

Further Consequences of the Sociology of Knowledge for Epistemology. Having seen that most of the axioms of the prevailing noology and epistemology have been taken over from the quantifiable natural sciences and are, so to speak, mere extensions of the tendencies singularly characteristic of this form of knowledge, it becomes clear that the noological problem must be reformulated with reference to the counter-model of more or less existentially determined varieties of knowledge. We intend now in a few words to state the new formulation of the problem which is deemed necessary once we have recognized the partial character of the older noology.

The Discovery of the Activistic Element in Knowledge. That in the "idealistic" conception of knowledge knowing is regarded mostly as a purely "theoretical" act in the sense of pure perception, has its origins, in addition to the above-mentioned orientation toward mathematical models, in the fact that in the background of this epistemology there lies the philosophical ideal of the "contemplative life." We cannot concern ourselves here with the history of this ideal or the manner in which the purely contemplative conception of knowledge first penetrated into epistemology. (This would require examination of the prehistory of scientific logic and of the development of the philosopher from the seer, from whom the former took over the ideal of the "mystic vision.") It suffices for us to point out that this great esteem for the contemplatively perceived is not the outcome of the "pure" observation of the act of thinking and knowing, but springs from a hierarchy of values based on a certain philosophy of life. The idealistic philosophy, which represents this tradition, insisted that knowledge was pure only when it was purely theoretical. Idealistic philosophy was not upset by the discovery that the type of knowledge represented by pure theory was only a small segment of human knowledge, that in addition there can be knowledge where men, while thinking, are also acting, and finally, that in certain fields knowledge arises only when and in so far as it itself is action, i.e. when action is permeated by the intention of the mind, in the sense that the concepts and the total apparatus of thought are dominated by and reflect this activist orientation. Not purpose *in addition* to perception but purpose *in* perception itself reveals the qualitative richness of the world in certain fields. Also the phenomenologically demonstrable fact that in these fields the activist genesis penetrates into the structure of the perspective and is not separable from it could not deter the older noology and epistemology either from overlooking this type of knowledge, which is integrated with action, or from seeing in it only an "impure" form of knowledge. (It is interesting to note that the connotations of the designation "impure knowledge" seems to point to a magical origin of the term.) The problem henceforth consists not in rejecting this type of knowledge from the very beginning, but in considering the manner in which the concept of knowing must be reformulated so that knowledge can be had even where purposeful action is involved. This reformulation of the noological problem is not intended to open the gates to propaganda and value-judgments in the sciences. On the contrary, when we speak of the fundamental intent of the mind (*intentio animi*) which is inherent in every form of knowledge and which affects the perspective, we refer to the irreducible residue of the purposeful element in knowledge which remains even when all conscious and explicit evaluations and biases have been eliminated. It is self-evident that science (in so far as it is free from evaluation) is not a propagandistic device and does not exist for the purpose of communicating evaluations, but rather for the determination of facts. What the sociology of knowledge seeks to reveal is merely that, after knowledge has been freed from the elements of propaganda and evaluation, it still contains an activist element which, for the most part, has not become explicit, and which cannot be eliminated, but which, at best, can and should be raised into the sphere of the controllable.

The Essentially Perspectivistic Element in Certain Types of Knowledge. The second point of which we must take cognizance is that in certain areas of historical-social knowledge it should be regarded as right and inevitable that a given finding should contain the traces of the position of the knower. The problem lies not in trying to hide these perspectives or in apologizing for them, but in inquiring into the question of how, granted these perspectives, knowledge and objectivity are still possible. It is not a source of error that in the visual picture of an object in space we can, in the nature of the case, get only a perspectivistic view. The problem is not how we might arrive at a non-perspectivistic picture but how, by juxtaposing the various points of view, each perspective may be recognized as such as thereby a new level of objectivity attained. Thus we come to the point where the false ideal of a detached, impersonal point of view must be replaced by the ideal of an essentially human point of view which is within the limits of a human perspective, constantly striving to enlarge itself.

The Problem of the Sphere of Truth as Such. In examining the philosophy of life, which furnishes the background for the idealistic epistemology and noology, it became clear that the ideal of a realm of truth as such (which, so to speak, pre-exists independently of the historical-psychological act of thought, and in which every concrete act of knowing merely participates) is the last offshoot of the dualistic world-view which, alongside of our world of concrete immediate events, created a second world by adding another dimension of being.

The positing of a sphere of truth which is valid in itself (an offshoot of the doctrine of ideas) is intended to do the same for the act of knowing as the notion of the beyond or the transcendental did for dualistic metaphysics in the realm of ontology, namely to postulate a sphere of perfection which does not bear the scars of its origins and, measured by which, all events and processes are shown to be finite and incomplete. Furthermore, just as in this extreme spiritualistic metaphysics the quality of "being human" was conceived as "merely being human"—which had been stripped of everything vital, corporeal, historical, or social—so an attempt was made to set forth a conception of knowledge in which these human elements would be submerged. It is necessary to raise the question time and again whether we can imagine the concept of knowing without taking account of the whole complex of traits by which man is characterized, and how, without these presuppositions we can even think of the concept of knowing, to say nothing of actually engaging in the act of knowing.

In the realm of ontology, in modern times, this dualistic view (which originated for the purpose of proving the inadequacy of "this" world) was, furthermore, gradually broken down in the course of empirical research. In noology and epistemology, however, it is still a force. But since here the basic presuppositions in the field of the theory of science are not quite so transparent, it was believed that this ideal of a superhuman, supertemporal sphere of validity was not a possible construction arising out of one's world-view, but an essential datum and prerequisite for the interpretation of the phenomenon of "thinking." Our discussion here is intended to show that from the point of view of the phenomenology of thought, there is no necessity to regard knowledge as though it were an intrusion from the sphere of actual happenings into a sphere of "truth in itself." Such a construction at best is of a heuristic value for such modes of thought as are represented by the example $2 \times 2 = 4$. Our reflections aim, on the contrary, to show that the problem of knowing becomes more intelligible if we hold strictly to the data presented by the real factual thinking that we carry on in this world (which is the only kind of thinking known to us, and which is independent of this ideal sphere) and if we accept the phenomenon of knowing as the act of a living being. In other words, the sociology of knowledge regards the cognitive act in connection with the models to which it aspires in its existential as well as its meaningful quality, not as insight into "eternal" truths, arising from a purely theoretical, contemplative urge, or as some sort of participation in these truths (as Scheler still thought), but as an instrument for dealing with life-situations at the disposal of a certain kind of vital being under certain conditions of life. All these three factors, the nature and structure of the process of dealing with life-situations, the subjects' own make-up (in his biological as well as historical-social aspects), and the peculiarity of the conditions of life, especially the place and position of the thinker —all these influence the results of thought. But they also condition the ideal of truth which this living being is able to construct from the products of thought.

The conception of knowledge as an intellectual act, which is only then complete when it no longer bears the traces of its human derivation, has, as we have already indicated, its greatest heuristic value in those realms where, as in the example $2 \times 2 = 4$, the above-mentioned characteristics can phenomenologically, with greater or less justification, be shown actually to exist. It is misleading, however, and tends to obscure fundamental phenomena in those broader realms of the knowable where, if the human historical element is overlooked, the results of thought are completely denatured.

Only the phenomenological evidence derived from the existing models of thought may be used as an argument for or against certain concepts involved in knowledge. Disguised motives, arising out of a certain outlook on the world, have no bearing on the matter. There is no reason for retaining in our noology the disdain for corporeal, sensual, temporal, dynamic, and social things characteristic of the type of human being presupposed in the "idealistic" philosophy. At the present moment there are confronting each other two types of knowledge which are of representative significance, and correspondingly there are two possibilities of noological and epistemological explanations of knowledge. For the moment it would be well to keep these two approaches separate and to make the differences between them stand out rather than to minimize them. Only in the process of trial and error will it become clear which of these bases of interpretation is the more sound and whether we get farther if, as has been done hitherto, we take the situationally detached type of knowledge as our point of departure and treat the situationally conditioned as secondary and unimportant or contrariwise, whether we regard the situationally detached type of knowledge as a marginal and special case of the situationally conditioned.

If we were to inquire into the possible directions of epistemology if it followed the last-mentioned model of thought and recognized the inherent "situational determination" of certain types of knowledge and made it the basis for its further reflections, we should be confronted with two possible alternatives. The scientist, in this case has the task, first of all, of making explicit the possibilities of the further implications of his problem and to point out all the eventualities that are likely to come into his range of vision. He should content himself with asserting only what, in his present stage of penetration into the problem, he can honestly determine. The function of the thinker is not to pronounce judgment at any cost when a new problem first arises, but rather, in full awareness of the fact that research is still under way, to state only that which has become definitely perceivable. There are two alternatives that he may follow once he has arrived at this stage.

The Two Directions in Epistemology. One of the two directions taken by epistemology emphasizes the prevalence of situational determination, maintaining that in the course of the progress of social knowledge this element is ineradicable, and that, therefore, even one's own point of view may always be expected to be peculiar to one's position. This would require revision of the theoretical basis of knowledge by setting up the thesis of the inherently relational structure of human knowledge (just as the essentially perspectivistic nature of visually perceived objects is admitted without question).

This solution does not imply renunciation of the postulate of objectivity and the possibility of arriving at decisions in factual disputes; nor does it involve an acceptance of illusionism according to which everything is in appearance and nothing can be decided. It does imply rather that this objectivity and this competence to arrive at decisions can be attained only through indirect means. It is not intended to assert that objects do not exist or that reliance upon observation is useless and futile but rather that the answers we get to the questions we put to the subject matter are, in certain cases, in the nature of things, possible only within the limits of the observer's perspective. The result even here is not relativism in the sense of one assertion being as good as another. Relationism, as we use it, states that every assertion can only be relationally formulated. It becomes relativism only when it is linked with the older static ideal of eternal, unperspectivistic truths independent of the subjective experience of the observer, and when it is judged by this alien ideal of absolute truth.

In the case of situationally conditioned thought, objectivity comes to mean something quite new and different: (*a*) There is first of all the fact that in so far as different observers are immersed in the same system, they will, on the basis of the identity of their conceptual and categorical apparatus and through the common universe of discourse thereby created, arrive at similar results, and be in a position to eradicate as an error everything that deviates fom this unanimity; (*b*) and recently there is a recognition of the fact that when observers have different perspectives, "objectivity" is attainable only in a more roundabout fashion. In such a case, what has been correctly but differently perceived by the two perspectives must be understood in the light of the differences in structure of these varied modes of perception. An effort must be made to find a formula for translating the results of one into those of the other and to discover a common denominator for these varying perspectivistic insights. Once such a common denominator has been found, it is possible to separate the necessary differences of the two views from the arbitrarily conceived and mistaken elements, which here too should be considered as errors.

The controversy concerning visually perceived objects (which, in the nature of the case, can be viewed only in perspective) is not settled by setting up a non-perspectivist view (which is impossible). It is settled rather by understanding, in the light of one's own positionally determined vision, why the object appeared differently to one in a different position. Likewise, in our field also, objectivity is brought about by the translation of one perspective into the terms of another. It is natural that here we must ask which of the various points of view is the best. And for this too there is a criterion. As in the case of visual perspective, where certain positions have the advantage of revealing the decisive features of the object, so here pre-eminence is given to that perspective which gives evidence of the greatest comprehensiveness and the greatest fruitfulness in dealing with empirical materials.

The theory of knowledge can also pursue a second course by emphasizing the following facts: The impetus to research in the sociology of knowledge may be so guided that it will not absolutize the concept of "situational determination"; rather, it may be directed in such a fashion that precisely by discovering the element of situational determination in the views at hand, a first step will be taken towards the solution of the problem of situational determination itself. As soon as I identify a view which sets itself up as absolute, as representing merely a given angle of vision, I neutralize its partial nature in a certain sense. Most of our earlier discussion of this problem moved quite spontaneously in the direction of the neutralization of situational determination by attempting to rise above it. The idea of the continuously broadening basis of knowledge, the idea of the continuous extension of the self and of the integration of various social vantage points into the process of knowledge—observations which are all based on empirical facts—and the idea of an all-embracing ontology which is to be sought for—all move in this direction. This tendency in intellectual and social history is closely connected with the processes of group contact and interpenetration. In its first stage, this tendency neutralizes the various conflicting points of view (i.e. deprives them of their absolute character); in its second stage, it creates out of this neutralization a more comprehensive and serviceable basis of vision. It is interesting to note that the construction of a broader base is bound up with a higher degree of abstractness and tends in an increasing degree to formalize the phenomena with which we are concerned. This formalizing tendency consists in relegating to a subordinate position the analysis of the concrete qualitative assertions which lead in a given direction, and substituting in place of the qualitative and configurative description of phenomena a purely functional view modelled after a purely mechanical pattern. This theory of increasing abstractness will be designated as the theory of the social genesis of abstraction. According to this sociological derivation of abstraction (which is clearly observable in the emergence of the sociological point of view itself), the trend towards a higher stage of abstraction is a correlate of the amalgamation of social groups. The corroboration of this contention is found in the fact that the capacity for abstraction among individuals and groups grows in the measure that they are parts of heterogeneous groups and organizations in more inclusive collective units, capable of absorbing local or otherwise particular groups. But this tendency towards abstraction on a higher level is still in accord with the theory of the situational determination of thought, for the reason that the subject that engages in this thinking is by no means an absolutely autonomous "mind in itself," but is rather a subject which is ever more inclusive, and which neutralizes the earlier particular and concrete points of view.

All the categories justifiably formulated by formal sociology are products of this neutralizing and formalizing operation. The logical conclusion of this approach is that, in the end, it sees only a formal mechanism in operation. Thus, to cite an illustration from formal sociology, domination is a category which can only be abstracted from the concrete positions of the persons involved (i.e. the dominator and the dominated), because it contents itself with emphasizing the structural interrelationship (the mechanism, so to speak) of the behaviour involved in the process of interaction. This it does by operating with concepts like sub- and super-ordination, force, obedience, subjectibility, etc. The qualitative content of domination in the concrete (which would immediately present "domination" in an historical setting) is not accessible through this formula, and could be adequately portrayed only if the dominated as well as the dominator were to tell what their experiences actually were in the situations in which they live. For not even the formal definitions that we discover float in thin air; they arise rather out of the concrete problems of a situation. At this point the notion arises, which of course needs detailed verification, that the problem of perspectivism concerns primarily the qualitative aspect of a phenomenon. Because, however, the content of social-intellectual phenomena is primarily meaningful and because meaning is perceived in acts of understanding and interpretation, we may say that the problem of perspectivism in the sociology of knowledge refers, first of all, to what is understandable in social phenomena. But in this we are by no means denoting a narrowly circumscribed realm. The most elementary facts in the social sphere surpass in complexity the purely formal relations, and they can only be understood in referring to qualitative contents and meanings. In short, the problem of interpretation is a fundamental one.

Even where formalization has gone farthest and where we are concerned with mere relations, so to speak, there is still a minimum of evidence of the investigator's general direction of interest which could not be entirely eliminated. For example, when Max Weber, in classifying types of conduct, distinguished between "purposeful-rational" and "traditional" conduct, he was still expressing the situation of a generation in which one group had discovered and given evaluative emphasis to the rationalistic tendencies in capitalism, while another, demonstrably impelled by political motives, discovered the significance of tradition and emphasized it as over against the former. The interest in the problem of a typology of conduct itself arises out of this particular social situation. And when we find that precisely these types of conduct were singled out and formalized in precisely this direction, we must seek the source of this tendency towards abstraction in the concrete social situation of the epoch which was preoccupied with the phenomenon of conduct as seen from this angle. If another age had attempted a formal systematization of the types of conduct, it would no doubt have arrived at quite another typology. In another historical situation, different abstractions would have been found and singled out from the total complex of events. In our judgment the sociology of knowledge, by virtue of its premises, does not need to deny the existence or possibility of formalized and abstract thought. It need show only that, in this respect, too, thought is not independent of "existence," for it is not a super-social, super-human subject which is expressing itself in "as such" categories in this typology. Rather the neutralizations of the qualitative differences in the varying points of view, arising in certain definite situations, result in a scheme of orientation which allows only certain formal and structural components of the phenomena to emerge into the foreground of experience and thought. In a rudimentary form this process is already observable in the rules of etiquette and social intercourse which arise spontaneously in the contact between different groups. There, too, the more fleeting the contacts the less concern there is with the qualitative understanding of the mutual relationship, which is formalized to such an extent that it becomes a "formal sociological category" indicating, so to speak, only the specific role of the relationship. The other party is regarded merely as an "ambassador," "stranger," or "train conductor." In social intercourse we react to the other only with reference to these characteristics. In other words, the formalization in such cases is itself an expression of certain social situations, and the direction which formalization takes (whether we pick out, as we do in the case of the "ambassador," his function as a political representative or whether, as we do in the case of the "stranger," single out his ethnic traits) is dependent on the social situation, which enters, even though in a diluted form, into the categories that we use. In a similar vein, the observation may be made that in jurisprudence formalized law takes the place of informal justice, which arises out of concrete issues and represents a qualitative judgment derived from the situation and expressing the sense of right of a community, whenever an exchange economy reaches the point where its very existence depends on knowing in advance what the law will be. Henceforth, it is less important to do full justice to each case in its absolute uniqueness than to be able more and more correctly to classify and subsume each case under pre-established formalized categories.

As already indicated, we are not yet in a position to-day to decide the question as to which of the two above-mentioned alternatives the nature of the empirical data will force a scientific theory of knowledge to follow. In either case, however, we will have to reckon with situational determination as an inherent factor in knowledge, as well as with the theory of relationism and the theory of the changing basis of thought. In either case we must reject the notion that there is a "sphere of truth in itself" as a disruptive and unjustifiable hypothesis. It is instructive to note that the natural sciences seem to be, in many respects, in a closely analogous situation, especially if we use as our basis for comparison the interpretation of their present plight that has been so skillfully presented by W. Westphal. According to this view, once it was discovered that our conventional standards for measurement, such as clocks, etc., and the everyday language associated with them are possible and usable only for this everyday, common-sense scheme of orientation, it began to be understood that in the quantum theory, for instance, where we are dealing with the measurement of electrons, it is impossible to speak of a result of measurement which can be formulated independently of the measuring instrument used. For in the latter case the measuring instrument is interpreted as an object which itself relevantly influences the position and velocity of the electrons to be measured. Thus the thesis arose that position and velocity measurements are expressible only in "indeterminate relations" (Heisenberg) which specify the degree of indeterminacy. Furthermore, the next step from this idea was the denial of the assertion, which was closely allied to the older method of thinking, that the electrons *in themselves* must in reality have well-defined paths, on the ground that such "as such" assertions belong to that type of completely contentless assertion which, to be sure, do communicate a sort of intuitively derived image, but which are completely devoid of content, since no consequences can be drawn from them. The same was held to apply to the assumption that bodies in motion must have an absolute velocity. But since according to Einstein's relativity this is, in principle, not determinable, this assumption in the light of modern theory belongs quite as much with these empty assertions as the thesis that in addition to our world there exists another world which is, in the nature of the case, inaccessible to our experience.

If we followed this trend of thought, which in its unformulated relationism is surprisingly similar to our own, then the setting-up of the logical postulate that a sphere of "truth in itself" exists and has validity seems as difficult to justify as all of the other empty existential dualisms just mentioned. Because, as long as we see only relational determinabilities in the whole realm of empirical knowledge, the formulation of an "as such" sphere has no consequences whatsoever for the process of knowing.